INHABITED SPACES

Anglo-Saxon Constructions of Place

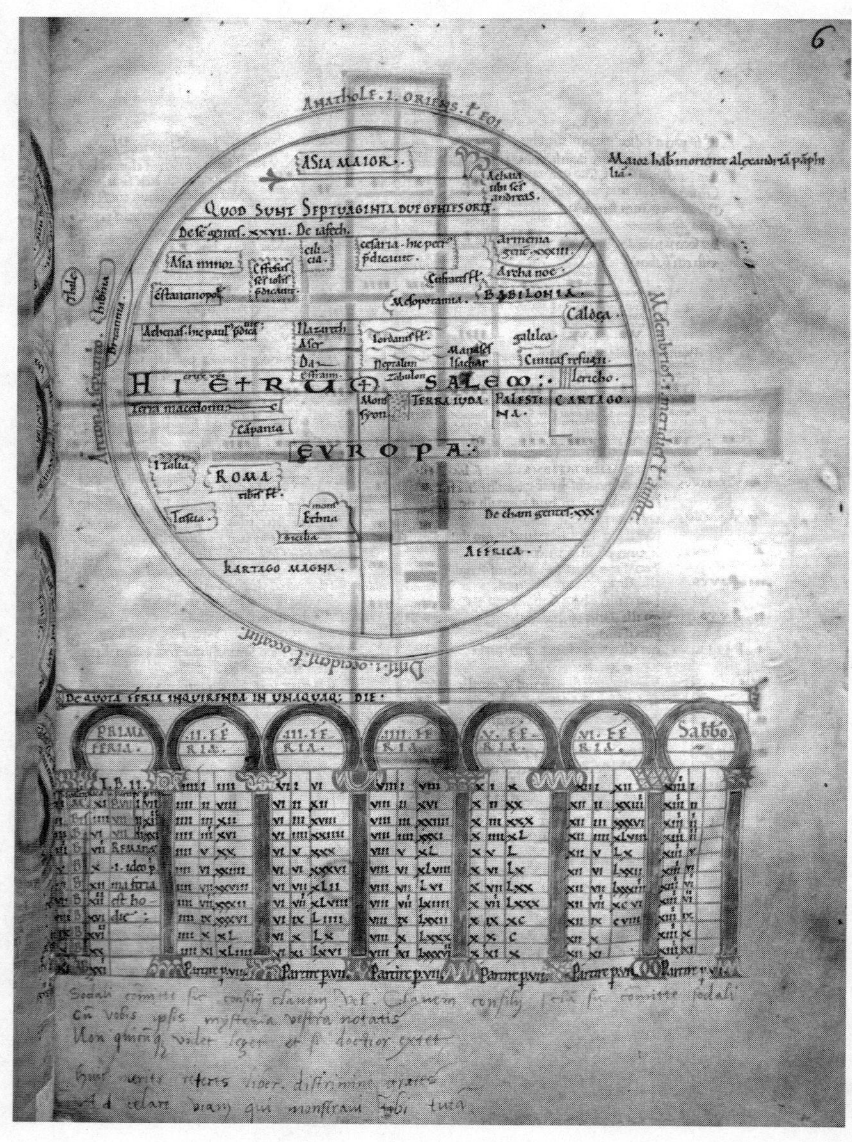

St John's MS. 17, fol. 6r. Reproduced by kind permission of the President and Fellows of St John's College, Oxford.

Inhabited Spaces

Anglo-Saxon Constructions of Place

NICOLE GUENTHER DISCENZA

UNIVERSITY OF TORONTO PRESS
Toronto Buffalo London

ISBN 978-1-4875-0065-8 (cloth)

Library and Archives Canada Cataloguing in Publication

Discenza, Nicole Guenther, 1969–, author
Inhabited spaces : Anglo-Saxon constructions of place / Nicole Guenther Discenza.

(Toronto Anglo-Saxon series ; 23)
Includes bibliographical references and index.
ISBN 978-1-4875-0065-8 (cloth)

1. Geographical perception – England – History – Medieval, 500–1500.
2. Sacred space – England – History – Medieval, 500–1500.   3. Space perception –
England – History – Medieval, 500–1500.   4. Human geography – England –
History – To 1500.   5. English literature – Old English, ca. 450–1100 – History
and criticism.   6. Latin literature, Medieval and modern – England – History
and criticism.   7. Geographical perception in literature.   8. Geography in
literature.   9. Space perception in literature.   10. England – Civilization –
To 1500.   I. Title.   II. Series: Toronto Anglo-Saxon series ; 23

GF551.D58 2017   304.2'309420902   C2016-903428-3

University of Toronto Press acknowledges the financial assistance to its
publishing program of the Canada Council for the Arts and the Ontario Arts
Council, an agency of the Government of Ontario.

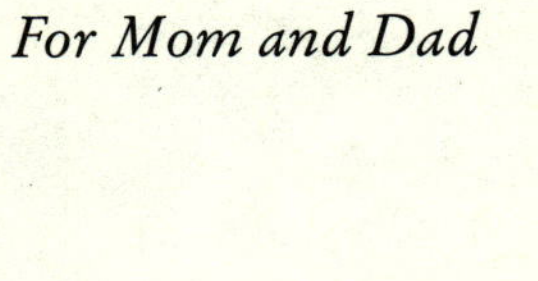

For Mom and Dad

Contents

Acknowledgments

Many people have helped to make this book a reality, and I am pleased to express my gratitude in print at last. My heartfelt thanks go to Katherine O'Brien O'Keeffe and Rebecca Stephenson for their help through many conversations, draft proposals, and draft chapters. Their suggestions and encouragement were invaluable. Laura Runge also gave me much useful feedback and support. Jack Niles's invitation to speak at Other Peoples' Thinking: Language and Mentality in England before the Conquest, Institute for Research in the Humanities, University of Wisconsin – Madison (17–18 April 2009) both enabled and forced me to pull together some of the strands of the study. I am grateful to the English Department draft group at the University of South Florida, and particularly to Tova Cooper and Michael Clune, who first organized it; and to the USF Medieval and Renaissance Colloquium, especially its organizers, Heather Meakin and Jay Zysk. I deeply appreciate the careful readings of my manuscript done by the anonymous readers for the University of Toronto Press, who helped me widen the book's appeal and strengthen the whole manuscript. Suzanne Rancourt at the Press has been helpful and encouraging since I introduced myself to her at a conference. I thank John St James for his careful copy-editing. I wish I had space enough and a memory sufficient to thank all the participants at conferences and the two groups at my university who pointed me down new roads, saved me from errors, and made me see more than I otherwise would have. I have thanked a few individuals in footnotes to particular places where I remember they helped, and I ask pardon of those whose assistance I have forgotten.

Institutional support has allowed this book to be completed and published. I thank the Humanities Institute at the University of South Florida for a grant in Summer, 2005, to work in the Bodleian Library at the University of Oxford, and the USF College of Arts and Sciences for a travel award in 2007 to present at the biennial meeting of the International Society of Anglo-Saxonists in London that year. A Lindsay Young Visiting Faculty Fellowship at the Marco Institute for Medieval and Renaissance Studies, University of Tennessee, Knoxville, in July 2014 helped me complete research on the book, particularly in their excellent John C. Hodges Library. The USF Library has been wonderful to me, especially Melanie Griffin, who helped with acquisitions and problems with resources; and the hardworking staff of Interlibrary Loan, who obtained articles and books for me from literally around the globe. Many thanks to Hunt Hawkins, the USF English Department, and the USF Publications Council for a subvention to make this book possible. Thanks to the British Library; the president and fellows of St John's College, the University of Oxford; the Bodleian Library; and Oxford Imaging Services for permissions and the image used in the cover and frontispiece. I also thank the Arizona Center for Medieval and Renaissance Studies press for permission to reuse material from my chapter "A Map of the Universe: Geography and Cosmology in the Program of Alfred the Great," which originally appeared in *Conversion and Colonization in Anglo-Saxon England*, ed. Catherine E. Karkov and Nicholas Howe, Essays in Anglo-Saxon Studies 1 (2006), 83–108; portions appear here heavily revised, primarily in the second and third chapter.

My deepest gratitude goes to family. My parents, Paul and Valerie Guenther, have always supported me in my love for the people and writings of the past. Dad, I'm sorry you did not get to see the final book. My husband, Joe, has talked through this project with me for over a decade. He asked many good questions and knows my subjects so well that he is frequently mistaken for a medievalist, despite being a mathematician in real life. My daughter Catherine has gone from preschool to high school in the time I worked on this study, and I am glad to share this space and place with her. All remaining errors are, of course, my own.

Abbreviations

ASCCE	*The Anglo-Saxon Chronicle: A Collaborative Edition*, ed. David Dumville and Simon Keynes
ASE	*Anglo-Saxon England*
ASPR	Anglo-Saxon Poetic Records
Bosworth-Toller	Joseph Bosworth, *An Anglo-Saxon Dictionary*; and T. Northcote Toller, *Supplement*
CCSL	Corpus Christianorum, Series Latina
Corpus	*The Dictionary of Old English Corpus on the World Wide Web*
CSASE	Cambridge Studies in Anglo-Saxon England
Dialogues	Wærferth, *Dialogues*
DMLBS	*Dictionary of Medieval Latin from British Sources*
DOE	*Dictionary of Old English: A to G* online
DNR	Bede, *De natura rerum*
Douay-Rheims	*The Challoner Revision of the Douay-Rheims Bible*
DTA	Ælfric, *De temporibus anni*
DTR	Bede, *De temporum ratione*
EETS	Early English Text Society
Ench	Byrhtferth, *Enchiridion*
Fontes	*Fontes Anglo-Saxonici*
Int Sig	Ælfric, *Interrogationes Sigeuulfi*
JEGP	*Journal of English and Germanic Philology*
Klaeber 4	*Klaeber's Beowulf and the Fight at Finnsburg*
Lewis and Short	Charlton T. Lewis and Charles Short, *A Latin Dictionary*
NM	*Neuphilologische Mitteilungen*
ns	new series

N&Q	*Notes and Queries*
OE	Old English
OED	*The Oxford English Dictionary*
os	original series
PBA	*Proceedings of the British Academy*
ss	supplementary series
TRHS	*Transactions of the Royal Historical Society*
Vulgate	*Biblia Sacra*

INHABITED SPACES

Introduction

As anyone who studies the past knows, it is all too easy to import modern modes of thought into earlier eras. We tend to assume, often unconsciously, that people think as we do. While we can never entirely leave ourselves behind, focused study can help us to identify our preconceptions and distinguish others', so that we recognize where they share our ideas and where they differ. Space and place are among the most basic concepts that any people have. We are always situated in and moving through space and place; we *live* them as much as we conceive them. We twenty-first-century people vary in some of our thinking, such as the area around our bodies we consider "personal space" and what distance we deem walkable. Still, many people throughout the world now share a number of assumptions about space and place.

The term "space" often conjures images of what lies beyond earth. Modern science tells us that space is vast, and the popular notion is that it is largely empty. Though more than 1900 exoplanets, or planets beyond our own solar system, have been identified as of June 2015, the distances between them are enormous.[1] The closest suspected exoplanet lies about 2.3 light years from earth: light that leaves that planet would take 2.3 years to reach earth.[2] Scientists do not agree that this space is empty; they posit dark matter to explain observable gravitational effects that cannot be

---

1 These planets are also known as extrasolar planets. See *The Extrasolar Planets Encyclopaedia* at http://exoplanet.eu/catalog/ for an up-to-date database.
2 Shannon Hall, "Nearby Brown Dwarf System May Harbor Closest Exoplanet to Earth," *Universe Today*, 16 January 2014, http://www.universetoday.com/108143/nearby-brown-dwarf-system-may-harbor-closest-exoplanet-to-earth/#ixzz3501oPT4D.

ascribed to visible matter. Yet it is called "dark matter" because it neither emits nor absorbs radiation at any observable level. Whether dark matter has already been detected or not is a topic of debate within the scientific community.[3] The terminology "dark matter" suggests another fundamental idea about space: it is dark, with occasional stars sending light over long distances. Planets do not produce their own light but can interfere with the stars'.

Most of us see a strong contrast between outer space and the space we ourselves inhabit. The bulk of the earth's land is divided into nation states, many of which have clear, undisputed borders. Some borders are determined by natural features such as rivers, seas, oceans, and mountains. Others are purely human creations. We are very much aware that these borders often bring together disparate ethnic and religious groups and may divide others, but most still accept this model of nation state even though particular cases offer uncertainty: where nations contest the exact location of a border, or where a state unites a majority with an oppressed minority, or where families are separated by policed borders. If anything, those disputed instances underscore the general acceptance of firm borders between countries even where no natural boundary exists.

In much of the twenty-first-century world, spatial boundaries seem ubiquitous: signs often alert us when we enter a country, state, or city. Often, borders require documents and bureaucratic approval to cross. We can easily find visual depictions of these borders on globes and maps, icons and bumper stickers. Many of us study geography in school and take quizzes about it on the Internet, testing not only our knowledge of the world but where we ought to live according to abstract conceptions of national character. If we do not know where a certain country or city is, or how far it is from us, a mobile phone can often provide the information as fast as we can query. Many of us feel knowledgeable about the world and connected to it; we use "www" to access the *World Wide* Web.

Of course, not everyone has access to the Internet, whether by circumstances or by choice. The experiences of place and space that I have just described will be familiar to most but not all readers. These generalizations also gloss over different ways of interpreting those phenomena. A popular saying declares, "The difference between America and England

---

3 See, for instance, "Possible evidence for dark matter particle presented at UCLA physics symposium," UCLA Newsroom, http://newsroom.ucla.edu/releases/possible-evidence-for-dark-matter-271600, 10 March 2014.

is that Americans think 100 years is a long time, while the English think 100 miles is a long way."[4] Even those of us globally connected by devices do not all process place and space in the same ways. Those who do not use the Internet have still different ways of thinking about location; non-Westerners, or those who have moved to the West only recently, have yet other modes of understanding.

Anglo-Saxons' experiences of space would vary widely as well. After the planning and building of *burgas* in the late ninth and early tenth century, the experience of entering towns that had recognizable bounds must have increased, and Offa's Dyke provided a visual and physical boundary separating England from Wales. Yet Anglo-Saxons would see far fewer boundary markers than a typical First World resident today. Many *burgas* or settlements would not have well-defined edges, nor were the bounds between Anglo-Saxon kingdoms early in the period, or English and Danish areas of influence later, clearly marked.[5] Early medieval England was not a modern nation state, and until the reign of Æthelstan, son of Edward the Elder, it was not even a single kingdom but a series of small kingdoms and then a West Saxon kingdom and a Danish area of control.[6] For much of the period, most Anglo-Saxons would not speak of an England (or *Englaland*, or *Ongelþeod*); they might speak of individual kingdoms such as Mercia or Northumbria or Wessex, or peoples such as Saxons or Angles. When they saw maps, the maps would be schematic, often dividing the world into three parts but not necessarily containing any further clear subdivisions.[7] Extant documents and objects show the world far more in words than in maps.

---

4 Various websites ascribe the quotation to writer Earle Hitchner, but none give a more exact citation. Other websites occasionally credit a different author or speaker.

5 For different senses of "burh," which included "city," "settlement," and "fortification," see especially chapter 5, below.

6 Bede's *Ecclesiastical History* (c. 731) describes seven separate kingdoms in England, and he did not detail the tribes that were not under the control of any of these kingdoms; *Bede's Ecclesiastical History of the English People*, ed. and trans. Bertram Colgrave and R.A.B. Mynors (Oxford: Clarendon Press, 1969). Edward the Elder (d. 924) and Æthelstan (d. 939) were the son and grandson of King Alfred of Wessex. Alfred extended the influence of Wessex into Mercia, helping to make Wessex the last of the old seven kingdoms to have its own king. Edward and Æthelstan then conquered areas that had been under Viking rule, uniting England into a single country which they successively ruled.

7 See chapters 1–2, esp. pp. 18 and 58–61, for more on Anglo-Saxon maps.

Within larger divisions of land, we have many finer distinctions, as did the Anglo-Saxons, but we do not always define them in the same way. Wasteland, by its very name, evokes land that is "not used or unfit for cultivation or building and allowed to run wild" (*OED*, "wasteland" 1b).[8] Such land can be opposed to fertile land, urban land, and water. Water and the land around it are now coveted for many purposes: economic, aesthetic, and sporting uses are among the most important. Often the explicit purpose of a vacation at the seaside, a cruise, or a fishing trip is "to get away from it all." Both wasteland and water thus seem opposite to cities, which are full of buildings and used intensively by people. Occasional Anglo-Saxons such as Guthlac sought to "get away from it all," but Guthlac got away from human society only to find a demonic society waiting in the wilderness for him. Waste and water were not empty but full of life, sometimes hostile life. Halls and cities were more human, but Anglo-Saxons recognized that such places would perish, and that life there was not as far from life in the waste as we might like to think.

These generalizations, like all generalizations, have exceptions and provisos. Still, in much of our daily lives, we accept these notions, and it is easy to project them back onto Anglo-Saxon daily lives. The purpose of this study is to help us recognize our own constructions of space and Anglo-Saxon constructions, particularly where they differ from ours. No one book can offer a complete guide to the many Anglo-Saxon constructions of space and place, but each of the chapters will offer its own ways of understanding how Anglo-Saxons made place.

First, the Anglo-Saxons, like any people, very much *made* place. The field of human geography emphasizes the constructed nature of space and place. "Space" is a broad notion; some, like Tim Cresswell, see it as abstract and without human meaning.[9] I use it more in the sense explained by Derek Gregory, where the term is still more capacious than "place" but not purely abstract or meaningless: it is defined by relationships among people, objects, and events, and is usually conceived as being in process,

---

8 1a is perhaps nearer what Anglo-Saxons would mean by their closest word: "Land in its natural, uncultivated state." My sense is that most people using the term now mean 1b rather than 1a.

9 Tim Cresswell, *Place: A Short Introduction*, Short Introductions to Geography (Malden, MA: Blackwell Publishing, 2004), 8. In his *Geographic Thought: A Critical Introduction* (Malden, MA: Wiley-Blackwell, 2013), Cresswell traces the roots of this idea of space to Aristotle (20).

with time as an important element.[10] Space does not simply exist but is created by people. At the same time, it is not strictly bounded; in Yi-Fu Tuan's formulation, "Place is security, space is freedom: we are attached to the one and long for the other."[11] Place too is a human creation, and it is more specific: a locale or location given human meaning. Place has boundaries and, like space, is always in process.[12] The Anglo-Saxons did not simply exist in ready-made spaces and places but constructed the places around them mentally and often materially. To make place is to make sense of the world around one and take ownership of it. The Anglo-Saxons constructed space as a proper place, in Michel de Certeau's terminology, in which the French *propre* means both "proper" (fitting, right) and "owned" or "belonging to."[13] Place becomes proper as Anglo-Saxons impose a mental order upon it, whether or not they have physically made it.

Yi-Fu Tuan speaks of the two poles of human space and place: the hearth, associated with home, safety, and intimacy; and the cosmos, associated with the world and heterogeneity: "Hearth, though nurturing, can be too confining; cosmos, though liberating, can be bewildering and

---

10 Derek Gregory, "Space," in *The Dictionary of Human Geography*, ed. Derek Gregory et al., 5th ed. (Malden, MA: Blackwell, 2009), 708. Gregory's major points on contemporary theories of space include "the integration of time and space," "the co-production of time and space," "the unruliness of time-space" and "the porousness of time-space" (709). For a similar emphasis on time, space, and process but a genre-based approach to Anglo-Saxon space, see Andrew Scheil, "Space and Place," in *A Handbook of Anglo-Saxon Studies*, ed. Jacqueline Stodnick and Renée R. Trilling (Malden, MA: Blackwell, 2012), 197–213.

11 *Space and Place: The Perspective of Experience* (Minneapolis: University of Minnesota Press, 1977), 3. See also Tuan's *Cosmos and Hearth: A Cosmopolite's Viewpoint* (Minneapolis: University of Minnesota Press, 1996), 1, for place as familiar but space as large and open.

12 George Henderson, "Place," in *The Dictionary of Human Geography*, 539–41. See also Cresswell, *Place*, 7–10, for place as space given human meaning; and Cresswell, *Geographic Thought*, 19–20, for the Greek roots of distinctions between space and place. The distinction most human geographers make and which I adopt here is almost the opposite of Michel de Certeau's, in which *"space is a practiced place"* and "place" "excludes the possibility of two things being in the same location," in *The Practice of Everyday Life*, trans. Steven Rendall (Berkeley: University of California Press, 1984), 117. See also Tuan's chapter "Space, Place, and the Child" in *Space and Place*, 19–33, about the development of the capacity to construct space and place.

13 For "proper" or "propre," see de Certeau, *Practice*, xix; for the role of the proper in space, see esp. 117–18. See also Tuan for the importance of naming in establishing proper place; *Space and Place*, 29–33.

threatening."[14] Tuan shows this dichotomy primarily in the modern world, in the United States and China, but he also locates it in ancient Greek thinkers and finds the opposition a common way of understanding human experience. He discusses ways of reconciling the two in a "cosmopolitan hearth" that values both difference and self-awareness.[15] Cosmos and hearth would be familiar to Anglo-Saxons as well, not always as opposites but in a tension that some authors tried to resolve as Tuan does.

To speak of the Anglo-Saxons as one people or of "England" in the Anglo-Saxon era already constructs a tendentious category. As noted above, much of the Anglo-Saxon era had no "England" as we know it now, but multiple kingdoms and, later, an English and a Danish sphere of influence. Two elements united the peoples of these polities until King Edward and his son King Æthelstan unified England politically: language and religion. The Anglo-Saxons spoke different dialects, but they shared a common language, and were at least nominally Christian by the age of Bede. While scholars often see Bede as the first to write about the English as a people, Stephen Harris argues that Bede generally uses the term *Angli* for Angles, a specific ethnicity that excludes the Saxons, Jutes, and others in England but names the Angles in England and those still on the Continent.[16] Sarah Foot's argument that Alfred and his program create England as *Angelcynn* must be modified in light of Sharon Rowley's recent study of the Old English *Bede*, which uses *Ongol*, *Ongolcynn*, and *Ongolþeod*.[17] Only at the very end of the ninth century do multiple authors and translators begin to construct England as a unity, and they still differ over the names of the people and place. This study focuses primarily on later texts, beginning with that late-ninth-century appearance of *Angelcynn* and *Ongolcynn* and *Ongolþeod* in texts, which showed a concept of the English people as one people who differ from and have relations with other

---

14 *Cosmos and Hearth*, 2. See also Gaston Bachelard, *The Poetics of Space*, trans. Maria Jolas, foreword by Étienne Gilson (Boston: Beacon Press, 1964), 38–73. For Bachelard, the house is an intimate, safe space, like Tuan's hearth.

15 See especially *Cosmos and Hearth*, 182–7.

16 *Race and Ethnicity in Anglo-Saxon Literature*, Studies in Medieval History and Culture (New York: Routledge, 2003).

17 Sarah Foot, "The Making of *Angelcynn*: English Identity before the Norman Conquest," *TRHS*, 6th ser., 6 (1996): 25–49; and Sharon M. Rowley, *The Old English Version of Bede's "Historia ecclesiastica,"* Anglo-Saxon Studies 16 (Woodbridge, UK: Boydell and Brewer, 2011).

peoples, mostly in other places.[18] I sometimes examine earlier texts as well. First, the works of Bede and occasionally Alcuin both reflect early Anglo-Saxon thinking and continue to affect it throughout the period. Second, Old English poems are notoriously difficult to date. Most of them reach us in forms written in manuscripts around the year 1000. Attempting to date the original composition of these poems would be a distraction from my main arguments. These manuscripts show that around the year 1000, people thought it valuable to write, or write down, or recopy these poems, which may or may not have existed earlier. Some treatments of space and place do seem to change during the period, but a number of concepts and attitudes remain fairly stable throughout the Anglo-Saxon era.

For Anglo-Saxons, outer space is vast, but not on the scale that we currently construct it. It is also not dark and empty but full of light and populated, as the first chapter will show. Bede and others believed that only earth's atmosphere blocks the light that suffuses the space beyond our air. In Latin and Old English texts, space has inhabitants: angels, demons, and occasionally dragons and holy men. God organizes the whole, and thus the universe reflects both divine power and a divine plan. There is some disagreement among Anglo-Saxons about exactly how that plan looks and works, but Anglo-Saxon authors write about space in ways that make it proper. Though they cannot shape outer space the way people can shape cities or halls, these writers can interpret space, to make sense of it for themselves and their audiences. Bede and Ælfric even hint that England's location gives them a special perspective on outer space.

The second and third chapters deal with England's place in a larger world. As a number of previous scholars have already noted, England appears marginal in early medieval maps: sometimes it can be found at the edges, and sometimes it cannot be found at all. Similarly, texts from outside England may touch on it only briefly or, more often, not mention it. Rome and Jerusalem are central to much early medieval thought. Anglo-Saxon England seems to have had relatively little interest in maps, though a few maps and a number of diagrams from the time survive. Verbal depictions

---

18 England was never purely Anglo-Saxon; there were always "other peoples" right at home. The Celts predated the Anglo-Saxons and continued to live in what would become England, although we do not have firm numbers or percentages. Danes and other Scandinavian people also settled in England before and after its unification as a kingdom. Anglo-Saxon writers were well aware of these non-Anglo-Saxon elements among them.

are at the heart of their geographical imagination, as Nicholas Howe has shown.[19] Asa Simon Mittman and Kathy Lavezzo have done important studies on England's relations with the rest of the world, focusing on difference and how the English construct themselves in opposition to others and the Other. Mittman writes of an opposition constructed between English humanity and monstrous Others.[20] Lavezzo argues that the very liminality of Britain was turned to advantage by the Anglo-Saxons to celebrate their special position.[21] Nicholas Howe also argued that the English saw themselves as uniquely positioned as part of the missionary work of the Church, themselves converted by visitors and then travelling from the margins back to the Continent to convert others in turn. My study will examine these relations in a somewhat different light: in terms of similarities and connections that sometimes make England seem more central than we might suppose from looking at maps or descriptions that place it on the edge of the world. England's importance, the second chapter demonstrates, derives in part from its links to the Mediterranean world and even beyond. Both prose and poetic texts, particularly historical narratives, make audiences more familiar with these distant places, thus notionally reducing the distances involved. England, in turn, becomes more connected to the centre, *closer* to the centre, as authors create place in ways that tie the English to Rome, the Holy Land, and even such exotic lands as Mermedonia and India. Early English accounts of other places show less interest in maps than in verbal depictions, and they are never static but full of history and interest in the customs of peoples and sometimes non-human inhabitants.

The third chapter comes closer to England, treating its ties with northern neighbours. No matter how central Rome or Jerusalem may be in maps and narratives, England is at the heart of Anglo-Saxon lived experience. Other places also distant from the Mediterranean can be brought closer by the same techniques that make Rome seem familiar and Jerusalem not that distant. England is rarely the starting point for texts dealing with the Mediterranean or beyond, but it can be for texts dealing with what we

---

19   Nicholas Howe, "Rome: Capital of Anglo-Saxon England," *Journal of Medieval and Early Modern Studies* 34 (2004): 147–72; and *Migration and Mythmaking in Anglo-Saxon England* (New Haven: Yale University Press, 1989).

20   Asa Simon Mittman, *Maps and Monsters in Medieval England* (New York: Routledge, 2006).

21   Kathy Lavezzo, *Angels on the Edge of the World: Geography, Literature, and English Community, 1000–1534* (Ithaca: Cornell University Press, 2006).

would now call northern Europe. Again, other peoples and places are related specifically to England, made more familiar by parallels drawn between Anglo-Saxons and Lapps, Danes, and Continental Germanic peoples. However, English texts sometimes renounce centrality, returning instead to a more cosmic perspective such as that seen in the first chapter, in which England is no greater or more central than Rome or Jerusalem, but no less so either.

The last two chapters turn to kinds of spaces rather than particular locations. Chapter 4 covers dangerously open spaces, examining two types in particular: wasteland and open water. Wasteland is not uninhabited; for Anglo-Saxons, land is never empty. *Guthlac A* and *Beowulf* pay particular attention to wastelands and whether they can be tamed, made useful to human beings; *Andreas* extends the notion of wasteland to cover land that human beings inhabit when they engage in the inhuman practice of cannibalism. Bodies of water are also dangerously improper places, as seen in *Beowulf*, *The Wanderer*, and *The Seafarer*. Both waste and water are *unheimlich*, "unhomely," simultaneously like home and not like home.[22] They have familiar elements, but the whole never becomes fully hospitable to people.

The last chapter looks at a very different kind of space: halls and cities, places constructed by people not only mentally but physically. Halls are probably the most familiar settings in Old English literature today thanks to the prominence of *Beowulf*. The hall is the hearth par excellence. Halls can be magnificent, but they are impermanent and always flawed because of their builders' and inhabitants' flaws. Anglo-Saxons did not themselves have what we would now call "cities," their settlements being much smaller, but they aspired to them. Sometimes, what we might call a village or a town, they call a city (*civitas, ceaster, burh*): London and York receive such appellations repeatedly. *Genesis* and *The Ruin* clearly show cities as at once desirable accomplishments and signs of human fallenness. Both halls and cities are great human achievements. Yet they are also places of sin, where the cosmos and hearth meet, bringing chaos to the order that fallen human beings attempt to impose. The only permanent cities and halls are heaven – and hell.

Ending with heaven will bring this study full circle, for it is with the heavens that we begin.

---

22 Sigmund Freud coined the term "unheimlich" for what is uncanny or, more literally, "unhomely" or "unfamiliar"; "The Uncanny," trans. Alix Strachey, in his *Collected Papers*, ed. Joan Riviere, vol. 4 (London: Hogarth, 1950), 368–407.

1 Earth's Place in the Cosmos

The Anglo-Saxons did not have a term for what we call "outer space," but some certainly had an interest in it. Their cosmology shaded into geography: the boundary between the two did not seem as sharp to Anglo-Saxons as it might to us. Texts such as Bede's *De natura rerum* (*Concerning the Nature of Things*) and computus manuscripts included both conditions on earth and observations of heavenly bodies, as this chapter will explore.[1] Learned Anglo-Saxons used classical sources to comprehend the relation of earth to the rest of the universe and supplemented those texts with their own observations and imagination. As Evelyn Edson writes, "The focus of much of medieval science had to do with model-building, constructing a cosmological picture which harmonized with Christian theology, authoritative texts inherited from antiquity, and practical observation."[2] Anglo-Saxon cosmologies did not always harmonize, however; some disparities appear among representations of the universe in word and in image.

Despite differences among them, Anglo-Saxon cosmologies consistently sought to create a coherent and readable understanding of the world and the universe. They took abstract *space* and made *places* within it.[3] Tim

---

1 Computus is the art of calculating the date of Easter and other moveable feasts. This
chapter focuses on the universe as the Anglo-Saxons could observe it. For the state
of the cosmos before the fall of man and how that fall diminished the light of celestial
bodies and made their orbits laboured, see Thomas J. Heffernan, "'The sun shall be
turned to darkness and the moon to blood': How Sin and Redemption Affect Heavenly
Space in an Old English Transfiguration Homily," in *Place, Space, and Landscape in
Medieval Narrative*, ed. Laura L. Howes, Tennessee Studies in Literature 43 (Knoxville:
University of Tennessee Press, 2007), 63–78, and his citations.

2 *Mapping Time and Space: How Medieval Mapmakers Viewed Their World*, British
Library Studies in Map History 1 (London: The British Library, 1997), 52–3.

3 For distinctions between space and place, see my Introduction, above.

Cresswell lists three elements necessary to places: "being located," "having a material visual form," and having "some relationship to humans and the human capacity to produce and consume meaning."[4] Anglo-Saxon writers and thinkers established the relative locations of different points and bodies in space, gave "material visual form" to the cosmos and its members, and subordinated the whole to God. As God's last and best creation, humanity had the task of understanding the universe. In early medieval England, learned authorities rendered space readable, giving what Michel de Certeau calls the "mastery of places through sight."[5]

Influenced by Latin and Christian sources, educated Anglo-Saxons constructed the universe around them in ways that reflected and reinforced their sense of the capaciousness of God's creative power and the marvellous order and symmetry of his plan. Whether they presented a fully spherical earth or (less often) a flattened world under the arc of the heavens, they conceived that space not as empty but full. The plenitude of creation throughout the cosmos reveals God's infinite capacities for light and life. Natalia Lozovsky has demonstrated how early medieval thinkers treated the world as a text; so too the Anglo-Saxons treated the cosmos as a work written by God – a scripture.[6] They used diagrams sometimes, particularly late in the Anglo-Saxon era, but most often they depicted space in words, human glosses upon a divine text.[7] They never simply *read* the text of the world or the universe. All readings are interpretations, and Anglo-Saxon interpretations of the cosmos created it as text.

Bede led the way with his *De natura rerum* (*On the Nature of Things*) and *De temporum ratione* (*On the Reckoning of Time*).[8] Both works were

---

4 Cresswell, *Place*, 7.

5 *Practice of Everyday Life*, 36.

6 *"The Earth Is Our Book": Geographical Knowledge in the Latin West ca. 400–1000* (Ann Arbor: University of Michigan Press, 2000), 112–13, 138.

7 See Nicholas Howe, *Writing the Map of Anglo-Saxon England: Essays in Cultural Geography* (New Haven: Yale University Press, 2008), esp. 1–7.

8 Bede's *De natura rerum* (*DNR*) is quoted from *Bedae Venerabilis Opera*, pars I: *Opera didascalica*, ed. Charles W. Jones, CCSL 123A (Turnhout: Brepols, 1975); all translations from this text are my own. Quotations from *De temporum ratione* (*DTR*) are from *Bedae Venerabilis Opera*, pars VI: *Opera Didascalica 2*, ed. Charles W. Jones, CCSL 123B (Turnhout: Brepols, 1977); translations from this text are from Faith Wallis, ed. and trans., *Bede: The Reckoning of Time*, Translated Texts for Historians 29 (Liverpool: Liverpool University Press, 1999), unless otherwise noted. I will not discuss Bede's first work on time, *De temporibus* (*On Times*), because the key teachings of the earlier work were subsumed into the later, along with many additional points and some refinements.

widely read and copied: Charles W. Jones found 134 whole or partial manuscripts of *De natura rerum* ranging from the eighth to the fifteenth centuries, and 245 of *De temporum ratione*, ranging from the eighth to the sixteenth centuries.[9] These works remained available throughout the Middle Ages in England and on the Continent, with other works complementing rather than replacing them.

During the Benedictine Reform, two authors rendered portions of Bede's work into Old English.[10] Ælfric of Eynsham, a Benedictine monk, scholar, and abbot, wrote *De temporibus anni* (*On the Times of the Year*) to introduce readers to fundamental concepts about the world and the cosmos.[11] Using little Latin and even less mathematics, the text renders the cosmos as a coherent, readable space. Its content and language suggest two possible audiences: new students, who would later study Bede's work in Latin; and students not preparing for the priesthood, which would require greater knowledge of computus. Byrhtferth of Ramsey, a monk active in the late tenth and early eleventh centuries, wrote an *Enchiridion* (*Handbook*) alternating English and Latin. The *Enchiridion* was meant to help pupils calculate the dates of Easter and related feasts while supplying them with many other facts from a variety of fields.[12] Though Byrhtferth's approach appears

---

9 For Jones's handlist for *DNR*, see *Bedae Venerabilis Opera*, pars I, CCSL 123A, 174–84; for *DTR*, see pars VI, CCSL 123B, 242–56. Many of the ideas Bede relates were drawn from Isidore's *De natura rerum* and *Etymologia*, Pliny's *Naturalis historia*, and other patristic and classical sources.

10 For the English Benedictine Reform, see Mechthild Gretsch, *The Intellectual Foundations of the English Benedictine Reform*, CSASE 25 (Cambridge: Cambridge University Press, 1999), and her extensive references. For Bede's influence on it, see Joyce Hill, *Bede and the Benedictine Reform*, Jarrow Lecture 1998 (Jarrow: St Paul's Parish Church Council, 1999).

11 *De temporibus anni* is now extant in four mostly complete and four partial manuscripts ranging from late tenth to (probably) the twelfth century. See *Ælfric's De temporibus anni*, ed. and trans. Martin Blake, Anglo-Saxon Texts 26 (Rochester, NY: Brewer, 2009); all translations from this text are his unless otherwise noted. Blake provides detailed descriptions of the manuscripts and discussion of their relationships on 9–35. Peter Clemoes dates the text to 992–1002 in *The Chronology of Ælfric's Works* (1959), repr. Old English Newsletter Subsidia 5 (Binghamton, NY: CEMERS, 1980).

12 The *Enchiridion* starts with each passage rendered in both languages but quickly begins to offer many in English only and some in Latin only. The *Enchiridion* seems designed to be read with a more technical computus such as one found (in a later copy) in St John's College MS 17, for which see below. For the problems of assessing Byrhtferth's intended and real audiences, see Peter S. Baker and Michael Lapidge, *Byrhtferth's Enchiridion*, EETS ss 15 (Oxford: Oxford University Press, 1995), cxv–cxxiv, where the manuscripts are discussed; and Rebecca Stephenson, *The Politics of Language: Byrhtferth, Aelfric, and the Multilingual Identity of the Benedictine Reform*, Toronto

more scattershot, the *Enchiridion* too transforms the world and the skies into a coherent, proper set of places whose relations can be understood by initiates. Both these works offer some of Bede's insights to broader audiences in ways that will be treated later in this chapter.

These three authors created and reinforced much of the astronomical and cosmological knowledge of the Anglo-Saxons. Other, anonymous texts, often in Latin computus manuscripts, echoed and even expanded some of the information and themes from these major works. Oxford, St John's College MS 17, an early twelfth-century manuscript from Thorney Abbey, Cambridgeshire, stands out for its wealth of information and diagrams; it contains extensive computus materials from England and France, two TO maps of the earth, and a few diagrams of the earth, the sun and moon, and the planets.[13] A wide range of other texts tender models of the cosmos. The

---

Anglo-Saxon Series (Toronto: University of Toronto Press, 2015). The *Enchiridion* is extant in one copy and two fragments, all from the eleventh century. Errors in copying and the displacement of one section show that the complete manuscript, Oxford, Bodleian Library, Ashmole 328, is a copy, not the original, and that its scribe did not fully understand the material; again, see Baker and Lapidge, cxv–cxxiv. Two other manuscripts contain short excerpts from the *Enchiridion*, but the excerpted passages do not relate to this study. All quotations from this text are from Baker and Lapidge, *Byrhtferth's Enchiridion*; all translations are theirs unless otherwise specified.

13 The most common kind of early medieval map was the TO map, so called for its circular outer edge and its division into three land masses (Europe, Asia, and Africa), as if a T trisected the O. For background on early medieval maps, see J.B. Harley and David Woodward, eds, *The History of Cartography*, vol. 1: *Cartography in Prehistoric, Ancient, and Medieval Europe and the Mediterranean* (Chicago: University of Chicago Press, 1987), now available online at http://www.press.uchicago.edu/books/HOC/ HOC_V1/Volume1.html. For a description of St John's College 17, short essays on related topics, and full views of the manuscript, see Faith Wallis, *The Calendar and the Cloister: Oxford, St John's College MS17* (2007). McGill University Library, Digital Collections Program, http://digital.library.mcgill.ca/ms-17. St John's College MS 17 is a *de luxe* manuscript and thus exceptional rather than representative of computus manuscripts, which tended to be working books with less color and illustration. Its TO map is fairly typical in form: see folio 6r, reproduced as the frontispiece of this volume and available in color at http://digital.library.mcgill.ca/ms-17/folio.php?p=6r. A second TO map appears on fol. 8r in the upper left hand corner at the centre of a larger diagram (http://digital.library.mcgill.ca/ms-17/folio.php?p=8r). The map portion shows a TO map at its most basic, marking only the three continents. For excellent studies of the Cotton map, the best-known Anglo-Saxon map, see Martin Foys, "The Virtual Reality of the Anglo-Saxon *Mappamundi*," *Literature Compass* 1 (2004): 1–17, and *Virtually Anglo-Saxon: Old Media, New Media, and Early Medieval Studies in the Late Age of Print* (Gainesville: University Press of Florida, 2007), esp. chapter 4, "The Virtual Reality of the Anglo-Saxon *Mappamundi*," 110–58. The Cotton map is larger and more complex than most maps in Anglo-Saxon manuscripts.

Old English *Boethius* (and its poetry *The Metres of Boethius*) and *Soliloquies* produce knowledge of the arrangement of the solar system and the stars.[14] Alcuin (c. 740–804), an Anglo-Saxon educated at York who became an influential part of Charlemagne's court, composed a Latin treatise in the late eighth century, *Interrogationes Sigeuulfi in Genesin* (*Questions of Sigewulf on Genesis*), to answer a priest's queries about Genesis. Ælfric abridged and translated Alcuin's text into English, making it available to a wider audience around the year 1000.[15] Even some Old English poems present glimpses of the construction of the heavens and the earth.

Together, these varied texts construct the universe as a set of proper places created by God and studied by those who would know Him better. As this chapter will show, most texts present the universe as a sphere demonstrating in physical form the perfection, unity, and coherence of God's conception. A few, however, hint at a different understanding of the shape of the earth or the cosmos. Regardless of the shape of the cosmos, a wide variety of sources agree upon its plenitude. The space beyond earth holds celestial bodies and light that the atmosphere simply prevents earth's inhabitants from seeing. Beings live at various levels, from inside our atmosphere all the way out to the seat of the Trinity at the edges of the universe. This knowledge points to God: truth can be read in the physical cosmos that reveals a realm beyond the physical. In their readings of space, Anglo-Saxons constructed a realm that embodied both poles Yi-Fu Tuan finds in tension in much human thinking about space, the ordered but limited hearth and the plentiful but chaotic cosmos.[16] Anglo-Saxon authors and sometimes illustrators present a cosmos that is at once ordered and copious.

---

14 See Alfred the Great, *The Old English Boethius: An Edition of the Old English Versions of Boethius's De consolatione philosophiae*, ed. Malcolm Godden and Susan Irvine with a chapter on the Metres by Mark Griffith and contributions by Rohini Jayatilaka, 2 vols. (Oxford: Oxford University Press, 2009); and *King Alfred's Version of St. Augustine's Soliloquies*, ed. Thomas A. Carnicelli (Cambridge, MA: Harvard University Press, 1969). Note that Godden and Irvine do not accept the traditional ascription to Alfred the Great. For the *Boethius*, the prose B-text is always cited unless the C-text diverges significantly. Both B- and C-text are printed in vol. 1.

15 "Ælfric's Version of *Alcuini interrogationes Sigeuulfi in Genesin*," ed. George Edwin MacLean, *Anglia* 7 (1884): 1–59. Peter Clemoes dates *Interrogationes* to 992–1002 in *Chronology*.

16 *Cosmos and Hearth*.

The Shape of the Universe

Generations have been brought up with what Jeffrey Burton Russell calls "the Flat Error," the idea that medieval people believed the earth flat.[17] His *Inventing the Flat Earth* demonstrates how and when this misconception of the past arose, and that it still pervades recent writings. Most educated Anglo-Saxons' own writings, however, show that they knew the earth was not flat. Just as we often refer to the earth as "round" rather than more precisely and accurately as "spherical," so too Anglo-Saxons used terms that could be ambiguous. *Sinewealt* could mean round or spherical; Bosworth-Toller defines "seonu-wealt": "I. *round, circular, cylindrical* ... II. *round, spherical, globular* ..."[18] Old English glossaries offer *sinewealt* to translate such Latin terms for "round" as *teres* or *teretus* and *rotundus*, but they also offer *sinewealtnes* for *globositas* (sphericity).[19] Anglo-Saxon astronomy and cosmology generally construct a spherical earth, though writers may call it simply "round," and it sits at the centre of a spherical universe.

Bede's *De natura rerum* refers to the "globo terrarum" ("globe of the earth," 6.7–8). He leaves no doubt about the earth's shape in his *De temporum ratione*:

> neque enim frustra et in scripturae diuinae et in communium literarum paginis orbis terrae uocatur. Est enim re uera orbis idem in medio totius mundi positus, non in latitudinis solum giro quasi instar scuti rotundus sed instar potius pilae undique uersum aequali rotunditate persimilis; neque autem in tantae mole magnitudinis, quamuis enormem montium ualliumque distantiam quantum in pila ludicra unum digitum tantum addere uel demere crediderim. (*DTR* 32.3–10)

("for not without reason is it called 'the orb of the world' on the pages of Holy Scripture and of ordinary literature. It is, in fact, a sphere set in the middle of the whole universe. It is not merely circular like a shield [or] spread out like a wheel, but resembles more a ball, being equally round in all directions, but not in a mass of equal magnitude – although I would believe that the

---

<ol start="17">
<li>Jeffrey Burton Russell, Inventing the Flat Earth: Columbus and Modern Historians, foreword by David Noble (New York: Praeger, 1991).</li>
<li>Bosworth-Toller, seonuwealt, 865. For usage, see the Corpus.</li>
<li>See the Corpus.</li>
</ol>

enormous distance of mountains and valleys neither adds to it nor diminishes it any more than a finger would a playing ball," trans. Wallis, *Reckoning*, 91)

Bede also cites Pliny in describing the earth as "pineae nucis" (*DTR* 34.75; "a pine cone," trans. Wallis, *Reckoning*, 99).[20] His description of the earth as a globe made slightly imperfect by irregular terrain also appears in chapter 46 of his *De natura rerum*, "Terram Globo Similem" ("Earth, Like a Globe," 46.1).[21] The fact that Bede feels the need to explain the earth's shape in detail, and repeatedly, suggests that when he wrote in the early eighth century, not everyone knew the earth to be spherical; TO maps indeed look like a shield or a wheel. Bede counters an excessively literal reading of these maps.[22]

This spherical earth inhabits the centre of the globe of the universe. Bede (*DNR* 5.1–12) and later Ælfric (*DTA* 372–4) describe the universe as spinning like a wheel on an axle, with the end-points of the axle formed by the pole stars.[23] The pole stars, and the earth at the centre, remain stationary while the rest of the cosmos spins about them. Byrhtferth also calls the zodiac a circle (*Enchiridion: circulus*, 1.1.24 and 26; and *circul*, 1.1.41) around the earth, and all his diagrams containing the zodiac are round.[24]

---

20 "pineae nucis" could also be translated "pine nut." Either translation works: both pine cones and pine nuts tend to be teardrop-shaped, but nearly spherical examples can be found of each. (Flat pine cones and flat pine nuts, on the other hand, are few and far between, unless one uses a heavy weight to compress one's specimens.)

21 Jones in his edition cites Pliny as the direct source for *DNR*, in brackets after the title of Chap. 46.

22 Faith Wallis notes that early Irish texts show confusion between round and spherical: see *Reckoning*, 92, n. 281; and Marina Smyth, *Understanding the Universe in Seventh-Century Ireland*, Studies in Celtic History 15 (Woodbridge, UK: Boydell, 1996), esp. 271–9. The Old English *Boethius* 18.18 refers to the earth as the boss on the shield of the heavens, an image that could suggest a flat or only slightly curved earth. While this metaphor could indicate confusion on the part of the translator, it is more likely just an oversimplification, given the work's otherwise sophisticated treatment of the heavens, as discussed below.

23 Jones identifies Bede as following here Isidore's *DNR* 12.2–6, with help from Isidore's *Etymologies* and Pliny and Augustine as well (*DNR*, notes to 5.1–12). See also Heinrich Henel's edition of *Aelfric's De temporibus anni*, EETS 213 (London: Oxford University Press, 1942), 69, for borrowings both from the Bedan passage and directly from Isidore, *DNR* 12.6.

24 Diagrams showing the zodiac as a circle appear in the *Enchiridion*; see Baker and Lapidge's figs. 1 and 13. A diagram in St John's College MS 17, fol. 35v, shows the sun making a circuit of earth, with captions explaining where the sun is at different hours, and that it is under the earth at night: http://digital.library.mcgill.ca/ms-17/folio.php?p=35v.

Ælfric and Byrhtferth paint verbal pictures of a mill-wheel (*DTA* 14–16, *Enchiridion* 2.1.252–8).

Bede's successors spend little or no time explaining the sphericity of the earth or cosmos; they assume or only briefly mention it. In the late ninth century, the Old English *Soliloquies* recapitulates the spherical model as old news and uses it to set up a later point: "on þam creft þu leornodest onn anum þoðere oðþe on æpple oððe on æge atefred það þu meahtest beo þære tefrunge ongytan þises roðores ymbehwirft and þara tungla færeld" ("In this art [geometry], you learned that you might understand the heaven's turnings and the progress of the stars as depicted on a ball or on an apple or on an eye," 60.16–18).[25] In *De temporibus anni*, Ælfric describes the world with the terms *sinewealt* and *sinewealtnys*; he presents earth's sphericity concisely by translating Bede (quoted above), "Seo eorðe stent on gelicnysse anre pinnhnyte" (*DTA* 256–7; "The earth stands in the likeness of a pine cone," trans. Blake, 87). Ælfric spends far less time on the concept than Bede does. Byrhtferth never even writes explicitly that the earth is spherical; his model of the universe and his diagrams simply assume that it is. The concept of the earth as a globe undergirds other ideas in these texts. Bede and Ælfric describe five climate zones on earth, a model that only

---

25 Gopa Roy argues that the usages in the *Soliloquies* apply to the universe and not the earth, and that Alfred and his contemporaries may have envisioned a disc-shaped earth in "The Anglo-Saxons and the Shape of the World," in *Essays on Anglo-Saxon and Related Themes in Memory of Lynne Grundy*, ed. Jane Roberts and Janet Nelson (London: King's College London, Centre for Late Antique and Medieval Studies, 2000), 455–81. The same terms and even the imagery of the wheel can be found in Ælfric, who knew that the earth was spherical, as Roy acknowledges. In the absence of more positive evidence that knowledge of the sphericity of the world was lost, I take these usages as being very much in accord with other Anglo-Saxon descriptions that alternate between describing the world as round (and therefore possibly flat) and as explicitly spherical.

   Some would date the *Soliloquies* later than the late ninth century as I have done here. The actual authorship of the translations associated with Alfred the Great, particularly the *Boethius* and the *Soliloquies*, has been called into question: Malcolm Godden argues that we have no evidence Alfred wrote anything in "Did King Alfred Write Anything?" *Medium Ævum* 76.1 (2007): 1–23. For responses, see Janet M. Bately, "Did King Alfred Actually Translate Anything? The Integrity of the Alfredian Canon Revisited," *Medium Ævum* 78 (2009): 189–215; and her "Alfred as Author and Translator," in *A Companion to Alfred the Great*, ed. Nicole Guenther Discenza and Paul E. Szarmach, Brill's Companions to the Christian Tradition 58 (Leiden: Brill, 2015), 113–42. Even scholars who accept a connection to Alfred admit that "Alfred" is a construction, perhaps the king with a team of advisers or perhaps simply a team operating under the king's patronage. My argument here is not affected by authorship or the difference between a late-ninth- and an early-tenth-century date.

makes sense with a spherical earth.[26] Ælfric's pithy discussion of the zones calls them "gyrdlas" (*DTA* 284) – girdles or belts. Prose writers after Bede do not reiterate in detail the shape of the earth and how it was known; they seem to take their audiences' acceptance of the model for granted.[27]

The shape of the world and the universe mattered to Anglo-Saxons because it helped reveal the nature of God and his plan for the universe. The sun's orbit was fixed, Bede tells us, "certa ratione constitutionis Dei" ("by the firm decree of God's law," trans. Wallis, *Reckoning*, 92). The combination of a spherical earth and the sun's orbit creates a cycle of rebirth ("renascens," *DTR* 32.15) for the sun, making seasons and their days and nights of varying lengths (*DTR* 32–5). The shape of the world also creates habitable and uninhabitable zones, Bede explains in chapter 34 of *De temporum ratione*. Ælfric, drawing largely on Bede's chapter 32, notes that the shape of the earth and the sun's orbit both occur "be Godes gesetnysse" (*DTA* 257; "by God's decree," trans. Blake, 87), and that shape prevents the day from being too long (*DTA* 259–61).[28] God established the geometry of the cosmos to serve earth and its inhabitants, giving them sufficient sunlight but not enough to harm them.

This sphericity also connotes perfection: when Ælfric first describes heaven, he associates the shape with completeness: "Eall heo is sinewealt 7 ansund" (*DTA* 17; "It is completely circular and entire," trans. Blake, 77), a sentence Byrhtferth repeats in his own work (*Enchiridion* 2.1.254–5). "Entire" may not do justice to *ansund*; *The Dictionary of Old English* defines *ansund* as "whole, sound, having integrity." This word is associated in many religious texts with integral, healthy, uncorrupted, or incorruptible bodies (*DOE*). God has given the earth and the cosmos a perfect shape, and study reveals that shape and its perfection to human minds.

---

26 Bede's description uses the two-dimensional metaphor of people around the fire and then tries to translate it into three dimensions, not without some difficulty for the reader; see *DTR* 34.78–90.

27 For the uninhabitable zones see also *The Old English Boethius*, 18.20–4. For a hot but habitable zone, see *Liber monstrorum* 1.9, where Ethiopians must live with great heat "quia sub tertio zonarum feruentissimo et torrido mundi circulo demorantur" ("because they dwell under the third, most seething and torrid circle of the world's zones," trans. Orchard, 263). Andy Orchard, *Pride and Prodigies: Studies in the Monsters of the Beowulf-Manuscript* (Cambridge: Brewer, 1995); he edits and translates *Liber monstrorum* at 254–317.

28 Henel, *Ælfric's De temporibus anni*, lists no sources for this sentence, 47. Mark Atherton, in "The Sources of Ælfric's *De temporibus anni* (Cameron C.B.1.9.4)," 1996, *Fontes*, lists Bede's *DNR* 5.2–5. Interestingly, the Bedan passage has no close equivalent for "ansund"; see below.

Yet poets and artists sometimes construct space in ways that compete with more scholarly texts. The prose model of a spherical earth exists side-by-side with one found occasionally in poetry or poetic codices that presents the earth as flat. The illustrations of Creation in Oxford, Bodleian Library, MS Junius 11 seem to show a flat world with edges and a semicircular firmament that curves over the top of it.[29] Catherine Karkov relates these illustrations to London, British Library, Royal I. E. VII; the Tiberius Psalter; and the Bury Psalter.[30] Karkov sees these illustrations as "diagrammatic" and adds, "The circles may also have been thought to convey something of the process of shaping, or becoming, as they are in marked contrast to the starkly rectilinear or architectural frames that characterize the rest of the first artist's illustrations."[31] The manuscript illustrations leave us uncertain whether the earth is envisioned as a flat disk or a sphere. Alessandra Molinari argues that the first poem in Junius 11, the Old English *Genesis*, presents a flat earth under the tabernacle of the heavens, based on the scriptural book of Genesis and its interpretations.[32] While it is difficult to be certain from the details given that the poet does indeed have a flat earth in mind, such a model may not only have been scripturally based but also have better matched the lived experience of many Anglo-Saxons. Though one may see a slight curve to the earth if one faces a very broad, open expanse on a clear day (as sailors may), in a practical way, much of the time the earth appears to be flat. Anglo-Saxons likely did most of their sailing close to coasts, not on the open seas, and many were land-bound. Nor should the competing constructions of spherical and flat earth be assumed to match a distinction between high and low culture. The authors of *Genesis* created a traditional Old English alliterative poem

---

29 The full manuscript can be viewed at http://image.ox.ac.uk/show?collection=bodleian &manuscript=msjunius11; these illustrations appear on pages 6–7. For another full-colour reproduction of the entire manuscript, this one with commentary and notes, see *A Digital Facsimile of Oxford, Bodleian Library, MS. Junius 11*, ed. Bernard J. Muir, software by Nick Kennedy, CD-ROM (Oxford: Bodleian Library, 2004).

30 Catherine E. Karkov, *Text and Picture in Anglo-Saxon England: Narrative Strategies in the Junius 11 Manuscript*, CSASE 31 (Cambridge: Cambridge University Press, 2001), 37–8. Pamela Z. Blum argues instead that these illustrations follow an ancient Eastern model of the universe evident in later Eastern Octateuch manuscripts; "The Cryptic Creation Cycle in Ms. Junius xi," *Gesta* 15.1/2 (1976): 217–19.

31 Karkov, *Text and Picture*, 37–8.

32 Alessandra Molinari, "Alcuni calchi dell'epos biblico anglosassone Genesis A," in *Il plurilinguismo in area germanica nel Medioevo. Atti del XXX convegno dell'Associazione Italiana di Filologia germanica, Bari, 4–6 giugno 2003*, ed. Lucia Sinisi, Palomar athenaeum 49 (Bari: Palomar, 2005), 129–90.

based primarily on the Latin Bible, and a portion of the extant poem was translated from an Old Saxon biblical poem. These poets may represent a different strand of learned culture, not necessarily a popular outlook.

The apparent coexistence of these two models of the shape of the earth and the cosmos around it implies a kind of "polythesis," as Pierre Bourdieu calls it, the ability of people to hold two contradictory mental maps.[33] *Genesis* and the illustrations that accompany it indicate that the scientific and theological model used by Bede and his successors was not the only way of thinking about the shape of the world and the cosmos available to Anglo-Saxons. The more classical model seems to dominate surviving texts, but whether it dominated Anglo-Saxon minds, we cannot determine at this remove.

The two models reveal different ways in which Anglo-Saxons construct-ed space as a readable text, enabling an overview not unlike the *"panoptic practice"* that de Certeau describes as one of the effects of "the establish-ment of a break between a place appropriated as one's own and its other."[34] Both models assert their users' ability to create proper place. Either a spherical universe or a partial sphere over an earth shaped more like a ta-bletop presents a legible space that can be represented in words or in il-lustrations and comprehended quickly, as *Genesis* and its illustrations reveal. Nor does the radical difference in shape affect other aspects of cos-mology; writers who present a spherical cosmos and those favouring a flatter one all represent the universe as plenitude.

Plenitude

Twenty-first-century people often conceive of space as an enormous region only infrequently interrupted by matter. The atmosphere thins as one moves away from earth until it gives way to a vast dark emptiness occasion-ally punctuated by bodies such as stars, planets, or asteroids, and speckled here and there with nebulas or debris.[35] As we do now, the Anglo-Saxons

---

33 Pierre Bourdieu, *Outline of a Theory of Practice*, trans. Richard Nice (Cambridge: Cambridge University Press, 1977), esp. 109–24. See also de Certeau, *Practice*, xi, for contradictory relations and practices embodied in the same individuals.

34 de Certeau, *Practice*, 36, his emphasis.

35 See, however, my introduction, pp. 3–4: scientists do not consider space empty because they examine phenomena not visible to the human eye that pervade space. The vast-ness of space compared with the visible objects within it becomes apparent from the measurements used by astronomers. An astronomical unit (AU) is the distance from the earth to the sun; a light-year, the distance light can travel in one year, is 63,240 AU;

distinguished between the area around earth, with its own atmosphere (*lyft*), and the space beyond that. In some ways, however, they constructed these regions very differently than we do. The Anglo-Saxons presented space as a fullness that human beings cannot directly perceive but merely strive to comprehend. The plenitude of the upper cosmos, the plenitude of a populated sky, and the plenitude of earth are all of a piece. While the Anglo-Saxons observed distinctions among layers, cosmology flowed neatly into geography, as seen in texts ranging from Bede's *De natura rerum* to vernacular poetry. Bede's treatise discusses the nature, singular, of both earth and the heavens. In poetic texts such as *Genesis* or *Christ and Satan*, what happens in the heavens has consequences on earth – and vice-versa.

The earth's atmosphere extends nearly but not all the way to the moon, Bede and Ælfric write. This atmosphere, like earth itself, is inhabited. The Old English *lyft* generally means the air or atmosphere; in translations it frequently renders the Latin *aer* (or, more rarely, *caelum* [heaven] or *firmamentum* [firmament]).[36] Bede writes, "Aer est omne quod inani simile uitalem hunc spiritum fundit, infra lunam, uolatus auium nubiumque, et tempestatum capax" ("The air is all that which, seemingly empty, extends this vital breath below the moon and [supports] the flight of birds and clouds, and the capacity for storms," *DNR* 25.2–3).[37] Ælfric breaks this sentence into parts in *DTA* (388–90, 391–2, 401–2), but otherwise renders it fairly faithfully.[38] The two writers emphasize the fullness of the

---

a parsec (the distance from earth at which stellar parallax is one second of arc) is 3.26 light years – or $3.08568025 \times 10^{16}$ kilometres. Popular culture frames the discourse differently but offers much the same picture, as in this oft-quoted passage from the fictional guidebook *The Hitchhiker's Guide to the Galaxy* in the novel of the same name: "'Space,' *it says*, 'is big. Really big. You just won't believe how vastly hugely mind-bogglingly big it is. I mean, you may think it's a long way down the road to the chemist, but that's just peanuts to space.'" Douglas Adams, *The Hitchhiker's Guide to the Galaxy* (New York: Pocket Books, 1979), 76.

36 *Lyft* renders *aer* nearly ninety times, *nubes* ("cloud") sixteen times, and *caelum* ("heaven") a mere eight (five of which are in Ælfric). Lewis and Short define the Latin *aer* thus: "*the air*, properly *the lower atmosphere* (in distinction from *aether*, the upper pure air)." The occasional Old English usage of *lyft* for cloud also parallels the Latin *aer*: "B. Also poet. For *a cloud, vapor, mist*" (Lewis and Short).

37 Bede draws here on Pliny, *Naturalis historia*, chap. 2; see notes by Jones, CCSL 123A, p. 216. Subsequent chapters give more detail about weather and how it forms in the air. While working with this text, I consulted *Bede: On the Nature of Things and on Times*, translated with introduction, notes, and commentary by Calvin B. Kendall and Faith Wallis (Liverpool: Liverpool University Press, 2010).

38 Henel's detailed notes in his edition, *Aelfric's De temporibus anni*, are still useful for sourcing some specific passages; see his page 73.

atmosphere: while Bede warns that it may seem empty ("inani simile"), Ælfric describes it as "lichamlic gesceaft swiðe þynne" (388, "a very thin material creation," my translation), never giving readers a chance to think of it as empty but emphasizing its physicality. Ælfric, like Bede, ensures that readers understand that *lyft* means not a void but a medium: "on ðam fleoð fugelas, swa swa fixas swymmað on wætere. Ne mihte heora nan fleon nære seo lyft ðe hi berð" (*DTA* 389–91; "in it birds fly, just as fish swim in water. None of them would be able to fly were it not for the air which supports them," trans. Blake, 93). Also, "Ne nan man ne nyten næfð nane orðunge buton ðurh ða lyfte" (*DTA* 391–2; "No man or beast would be able to breathe without air," trans. Blake, 93). Bede's admission of this space's seeming emptiness and the writers' efforts to counter that notion suggest that at least some Anglo-Saxons thought of space as empty, as many now do. Our learned authors advance a contrary idea: though the atmosphere is invisible and thin, it supports life.

Indeed, this atmosphere teems with life: birds, insects, demons, devils, holy men, and dragons live there. Bede and Ælfric's mentions of fowl in the air have already been quoted. Birds appear in close proximity to *lyft* in nineteen occurrences in thirteen different texts, both prose and poetry. Gnats also live there (Ælfric, *Hexameron* 459–65).[39] Moreover, of 273 occurrences of the simplex *lyft* in the *Old English Corpus*, twenty-six contain references to demons or devils.[40] The evil spirits that torment Guthlac in the poem of that name inhabit the *lyft* more than the land he comes to occupy; homilists also associate Simon Magus's ascent into the air in Acts of the Apostles with the demons that reside there.[41] These demons can be

---

39 *Exameron Anglice or The Old English Hexameron*, ed. S.J. Crawford, Bibliothek der angelsachsischen Prosa 10 (1921; repr. Darmstadt: Wissenschaftliche Buchgesellschaft, 1968). Ælfric's *Hexameron* is an adaptation of St Basil's work of the same name.

40 Over half of these are versions of Guthlac's story; for details, see the *Corpus*. In his introduction to *Christ and Satan: A Critical Edition* (Waterloo, ON: Wilfrid Laurier University Press, 1977), editor Robert Emmett Finnegan notes that Augustine, Gregory the Great, and Bede refer to devils being imprisoned in the air of the lower heavens (42–3). A similar idea appears in *Christ and Satan* 262–3: "sume on lyft scacan, / fleogan ofer foldan" ("some move in the air, / fly over the earth"). The poem *Guthlac A* and its demons are treated more in chapter 4 below.

41 See, for instance, Ælfric's *Catholic Homilies* 1.26 and *Ælfric's Lives of Saints* 32 ("Peter and Paul"). *Ælfric's Catholic Homilies: Introduction, Commentary and Glossary*, ed. Malcolm Godden, EETS ss 18 (Oxford: Oxford University Press, 2000); *Ælfric's Catholic Homilies: The First Series*, ed. Peter Clemoes, EETS ss 17 (Oxford: Oxford University Press, 1997); *Ælfric's Catholic Homilies: The Second Series, Text*, ed. Malcolm Godden, EETS ss 5 (Oxford: Oxford University Press, 1979); *Ælfric's Lives of Saints*,

found in Latin texts as well: after describing the air or atmosphere as the realm of breath, birds, clouds, and weather, Bede writes that aerial powers ("potestates *aereae*," *DNR* 25.4) wait there, suffering, until the final Judgment, sometimes appearing to men in shapes that reveal the punishments these demons merit (25.4–7).[42] These powers are surely the same as the "aerias ... turmas" ("aerial troops," 1327) who assail the hermit Balthere in Alcuin's poem on York.[43] In a homily on the parable of the seed, Ælfric equates the birds who eat the seed to devils because "Deoflu sind fugelas gecigede. for ðan ðe hi fleoð geond þas lyft ungesewenlice. swa swa fugelas. doð gesewenlice" ("Devils are called birds, because they fly around the air invisibly, just as birds do visibly," *Catholic Homilies* 2.6.70–2). Ælfric uses the visible birds of the air to make his audience aware of the invisible inhabitants and the threat they pose: in his "Admonitio ad filium spiritualem" ("Admonition to a Spiritual Son"), Ælfric warns, "ðin gewinn is æfre ongean ða awyrgedan gastas ðe geond ðas lyft fleoð to fordonne ða unwaran" ("your battle is ever against the accursed spirits who fly around the sky to destroy the unwary," section 2, p. 34).[44] Even dragons can be found there, albeit rarely; their seven associations with air appear in only three texts.[45] The air is full of life both visible and invisible, and the invisible can harm human beings.

---

ed. Walter W. Skeat, EETS os 76, 82, 94, 114 (London: Trübner, 1881–1900); and Wulfstan's homily 16 in *Wulfstan*, ed. Arthur Napier, Sammlung englischer Denkmäler 4 (Berlin: Weidmannsche, 1883), at 98.14–100.18.

42 See also Helen Foxhall Forbes, *Heaven and Earth in Anglo-Saxon England: Theology and Society in an Age of Faith* (Farnham, Surrey: Ashgate, 2013), esp. chap. 2, "Creator of All Things, Visible and Invisible," 63–127, on angels and fallen angels in Anglo-Saxon thought.

43 *Alcuin: The Bishops, Kings, and Saints of York*, ed. Peter Godman (Oxford: Clarendon Press, 1982).

44 *The Anglo-Saxon Version of the Hexameron of St. Basil, or, Be Godes Six Daga Weorcum, and the Anglo-Saxon Remains of St. Basil's Admonitio ad filium spiritualem*, ed. Henry W. Norman, 2nd ed. (London: John Russell Smith, 1849): https://books.google.com/books?id=lnAEAQAAIAAJ&dq=anglo-saxon%20version%20of%20the%20hexameron&pg=PA9#v=onepage&q=anglo-saxon%20version%20of%20the%20hexameron&f=false. See also Wulfstan's "Ammonitio amici," which matter-of-factly declares, "eall þis lyft ys full hellicra deofla, þa geondscriðað ealne middangeard; and forwel oft hig beswicað þeawfulle weras, þæt hig doð, þæt gode lað ys" ("All this air is full of devils from hell, who wander the whole earth; and very often they trick virtuous men, so that they do that which is hateful to good"), *Wulfstan*, ed. Napier, Homily 48, 250.2–4.

45 The dragon is connected with the air three times in *Beowulf*: 2315, 2832, and 3043 (see Klaeber 4). A dragon in the air also appears in the 793 entry in three versions of the *Anglo-Saxon Chronicle*, D, E, and F; see the ASCCE. Ælfric lists "wyrmas" along with gnats and fleas as residents of the air in *Hexameron* 459–65.

Balancing out these evils of the sky, Elijah and sometimes Enoch reside in the air as well and have for centuries. Ælfric, two anonymous homilists, and a glossator tell us specifically that one or both of the holy men were taken up from earth.[46] While others call it heaven, Ælfric specifies that they went "na to rodorlicere [heofenan]" ("not to the upper heaven," *Catholic Homilies* 1.21.198–9), but to the sky, the *lyft*, whence they will come again to battle the Antichrist. God has not abandoned the kingdom of the air solely to evil, but has placed two Old Testament prophets there until the end of time, and birds fly freely there now. Still, the realms above earth hold a tension for the Anglo-Saxons, filled with light and danger, with prophets and demons. They may even hold lesser souls, at least temporarily. In Alcuin's poem on York, Balthere hears a terrible clash one day:

Tunc anima ex superis cuiusdam nubibus eius
ante pedes cecidit nimio tremefacta timore,
quam mox turba minax ingenti horrore secuta est
cum variis miseram poenis torquere volentum.   (1337–40)

("Then a certain soul fell from the high clouds
before his feet, trembling in great fear,

---

46 See *Catholic Homilies* 1.21.196–201; 1.25.115–18 and 2.7.13–15 reiterate that these figures will return without specifically mentioning where they are. See also Ælfric's *Lives of Saints*, Book of Kings, vol. 1, 18.287–95. Ælfric mentions Enoch and Elijah numerous other times, sometimes separately, occasionally together. Two anonymous homilies also refer to their return from "heofonum" ("the heavens"; *Old English Corpus*). A Latin hymn and its Old English gloss similarly say "Hoc Eliam per aera / curru levavit igneo" "þæt [Eliam] geond lyftu / cræte up ahof on fyrenum" ("This [glory of fasting] lifted Elijah up through the air on a fiery chariot"); Inge B. Milfull, *The Hymns of the Anglo-Saxon Church: A Study and Edition of the "Durham Hymnal,"* CSASE 17 (Cambridge: Cambridge University Press, 1996), 58.7–8, her trans. A number of other sources refer to Enoch and Elijah being in a paradise whose location is unspecified (see the *Corpus*). Bede mentions them several times in his commentary on Genesis. He also writes in *Homeliarum euangelii libri ii* that Enoch and Elijah were taken from earth and lifted "in caelum ... aerium" ("into the airy heaven"); see *Library of Latin Texts* (Turnhout: Brepols, 2002–). For more on the location of Enoch and Elijah in various texts, see Ananya Jahanara Kabir, *Paradise, Death and Doomsday in Anglo-Saxon Literature*, CSASE 32 (Cambridge: Cambridge University Press, 2001), 37 and 175–82. Also on the tradition of Enoch and Elijah's ascents into a realm between earth and the upper heavens, see Carol Farr, *The Book of Kells: Its Function and Audiences* (London: British Library, 1997), 113–14. The idea began in the early Church and may have reached the Anglo-Saxons through Irish sources.

which at once a menacing crowd pursued most horribly
wanting to torture the miserable one with varied punishments.")

This soul's destination may not have been determined yet when it found Balthere; the demons lay claim to it to take it to hell, but Balthere's prayers result in angels coming to take it to heaven (1341–62). Thus, the upper atmosphere may contain saints or demons, dragons or birds, or even recently departed souls.[47] Some of Tuan's tension between cosmos and hearth emerges here: this area offers plenitude, even borderline chaos, more obviously than it offers order and safety.

The word *rodor* usually indicates the next layer, above the atmosphere, which Anglo-Saxons also made into a proper place. The word never translates the Latin *aer*, but twenty-eight times translates the Latin *aether* or *ether*, a higher portion of space.[48] The Latin *aether*, according to Lewis and Short, means *"the upper, pure, bright air, the ether"*; in literature, it is opposed to "the lower atmospheric air." *The Dictionary of Medieval Latin from British Sources* similarly offers "ether, fiery region above the air."[49] The Old English term also translates *firmamentum* twenty times and *Olimpho* (Olympus) six times (all in glosses).[50] Anglo-Saxon usage in other contexts bears out the distinction. The *rodor* extends all the way around the earth, at an equal distance everywhere, according to the *Boethius* (33.195–9).[51] The *rodor* holds stars and the sun; one or both terms are paired with *rodor* nearly fifty times in the Old English corpus. In the *Hexameron*, Ælfric's explanation of the six days of creation, *rodor* itself contains

---

47 The soul that Balthere encounters has been dead and suffering for thirty days; 1347–8. It is impossible to determine from the text whether Balthere's intervention truly decides the outcome between heaven and hell, or whether this is an early instance of purgatory and Balthere's prayers speed the soul to heaven. On purgatory for early Anglo-Saxons, see Foxhall Forbes, *Heaven and Earth*, esp. 201–38.

48 I found one occurrence in the *Boethius* and the rest in glosses.

49 *DMLBS*, vol. 1, 46.

50 The usage of *rodor* for *caelum* also appears twice in Ælfric's *De temporibus anni*, once in a passage in the Old English poem *Genesis* that seems to follow its scriptural source closely, once in the Paris Psalter, and once in the *Boethius*; see the *Corpus*.

51 Quotations and translations both come from Godden and Irvine, *The Old English Boethius*, unless otherwise specified. The *Metres of Boethius* positions fire between the layers: "ðæm fyre ðe fela geara / for lange betweox lyfte and rodere, / swæ him æt frymðe fæder getiode" (24.12–14; "the fire which for many years has continued for a long time between the air [*lyft*] and firmament [*rodor*], just as the father appointed it at the beginning," trans. Godden and Irvine, vol. 2, 168; my brackets). In other texts, the *lyft* seems simply to abut the *rodor*.

multiple levels of the heavens, the ancient concept of concentric spheres with fixed and freely moving bodies:

> Ne standað na ealle steorran   on ðam steapan rodere
> ac hi sume habbað   synderlicne gang
> beneoðan ðam rodere   mislice geendebyrde,
> *and* þa ðe on ðam rodere standað   tyrnað æfre abutan
> mid ðam bradan rodere   on ymbhwyrfte ðære eorðan,
> and heora nan ne fylð   of ðam fæstan rodere
> ða hwile ðe ðeos woruld   wunað swa gehal.   (*Hexameron* 229–35)

("Nor do all the stars remain in that high heaven, but some of them have their own circuit beneath the arrangement in the varied heaven, and those which remain in that heaven turn ever around the broad heaven in orbit around the earth, and none of them falls from the fixed heaven while this world remains whole as it is.")

Though the Anglo-Saxons did not often elaborate such a complex model of the heavens, at least in extant texts, Ælfric and others communicate a clear idea of layered space containing heavenly bodies in different orbits.

Heavenly bodies, however, are relatively infrequent even in Anglo-Saxon cosmology. What fills the vastness of space, according to Bede, is light, which "obiectio terrenae molis" (*DTR* 7.13; "the interposition of the earth's mass," trans. Wallis, 29) blocks us from seeing. Bede explains that the dark of night only extends to where the air meets the ether, and occasionally up to the moon, explaining lunar eclipses (7.17–22); beyond that, "circa fines telluris solis splendor undique diffusus, ea libere quae telluri procul absunt aspiciat; ideoque aetheris quae ultra lunam sunt spatia diurnae lucis plena semper efficiat, uel suo uidelicet uel siderum radiata fulgore" (7.22–5; "the sunlight, diffused everywhere around the confines of the Earth, shines without impediment on those [stars] which are at a great distance from the Earth. Therefore [the Sun] makes the tracts of ether which are beyond the Moon to be always full of daylight, either by his own brightness or by that which beams from the stars," trans. Wallis, 29; her brackets). He compares this to being some distance from a group of torches; one sees separate flames from far away, but when one is close, the whole area is full of light. Thus, if human beings could go beyond the atmosphere, we would see space everywhere full of light (7.25–33). Ælfric condenses the passage into two brief sentences: "Soðlice on ðam heofenlicum eðele nis nan niht gehæfd, ac ðær is singal leoht, buton ælcum ðeostrum" (*DTA* 94–6; "However, in the heavenly abode no night is ex-perienced; rather, there is perpetual light there without any darkness," trans. Blake, 81), and "Ðæt æmtige fæc bufon ðære lyfte is æfre scinende of ðam heofenlicum tunglum" (119–20; "The empty space above the air is always shining from the heavenly bodies," trans. Blake, 81).[52] The space is not *truly* empty ("æmtige") because the stars illuminate it constantly. Nor is it silent: "Micel sweg gæð of heora swiftum ryne · 7 of þam scinendan rodore · þeah þe we forþam mycclan fyrlene . hit gefredan ne magon" ("Great sound comes from [the planets'] swift course and from the shining heavens, although we cannot hear it because of the great distance"), Ælfric writes in *Interrogationes Sigewulfi* (142–4).[53] Heaven is not a dark, quiet void, as modern people think of it, but, as Faith Wallis remarks, "all bright-ness and order, with Earth as the one dark spot."[54] The darkness of night that earth experiences thus becomes the exception: if readers could only escape the mass of earth, we could see light everywhere, at all times. Heavenly light turns up in other contexts as well: Ælfric declares, "Nu synt we ute belocene fram ðam heofonlican leohte; 7 we ne magon on ðisum life þæs ecan leohtes brucan" ("Now we are locked out of the heav-enly light, and we cannot in this life enjoy the eternal light," *Catholic Homilies* 1.10.41–2). So too the whole earth is locked out of the heavenly light that exists everywhere outside the atmosphere.

Theology, astronomy, and metaphor support each other in a herme-neutic circle, each informing the other to create the understanding of an ordered, illuminated cosmos beyond what can be directly perceived with accuracy. Moreover, Bede's homely metaphor of people and torches makes the lesson immediate, memorable, and even somatic, not abstract and easily

---

52 Ælfric also describes the heavens thus in *Interrogationes Sigewulfi*, following Alcuin, his source: "Hwylces gecyndes is seo heofon? Fyres gecyndes 7 sine wealt 7 symle turniende seo tunglene heofon" ("Of what nature is heaven? Of a fiery nature and spherical and always turning is the starry heaven," 107–9). In *De falsis diis*, he says that Adam's sin actually dimmed the sun and moon: the sun used to be seven times brighter than it is now (59–60), and the moon as bright as the sun is now (60–1). They will shine again with their former brilliance after Judgment Day, and the moon will then stay whole instead of waxing and waning (62–5). Pope found no source for this passage; see *Homilies of Ælfric: A Supplementary Collection*, ed. John C. Pope, 2 vols., EETS 259–60 (London: Oxford University Press, 1968), 657–724.

53 Ælfric added this sentence to his source.

54 Wallis, *Reckoning*, commentary 277.

forgotten.[55] Here, the safety and orderliness of the hearth is projected onto the cosmos; the cosmos becomes simply a very large hearth, with a "perpetual light" that surely suggests the whole to be suffused with divinity. The space near earth may be full of both birds and demons, but the space beyond the atmosphere is a plenitude of radiance.

Heavenly Bodies

Because it offers glimpses of divine fullness and illumination, space invites further exploration. The Anglo-Saxons accepted the invitation that they had themselves written, and they enquired into celestial bodies, particularly the two that they used to calculate time: solar and lunar reckoning together determine the date of Easter.[56] Our writers' interest began with the calculation of dates, but extended well beyond. Bede gives fairly accurate figures for how long the moon takes to orbit the earth and how far it advances in the sky each night (*DTR*, chaps. 18–19); his methods and calculations remained influential in computus for centuries.

Yet Anglo-Saxons did not limit their interest to the computations needed to determine holy days. Indeed, Ælfric does not translate any of Bede's mathematical material; instead, he renders less technical portions on weather, the planets, and the stars. Byrhtferth and anonymous computus compilers all go well beyond calculations to a more organic notion of space. The Anglo-Saxons envision not a universe where men and women struggle to impose meaning on vast emptiness, but a cosmos already full of meaning for humanity to interpret. One must study the heavens to achieve a better, though always partial, understanding of the universe and thus of God. The cosmic knowledge that Anglo-Saxons created always sought to create further knowledge, a perpetual motion machine where one construction leads to another.

---

55 For the usefulness of metaphor, particularly metaphors based on the body and space, see George Lakoff and Mark Johnson, *Metaphors We Live By* (Chicago: University of Chicago Press, 1980); and Rafael E. Núñez, "Conceptual Metaphor and the Embodied Mind: What Makes Mathematics Possible?" in *Metaphor and Analogy in the Sciences*, ed. Fernand Hallyn, Origins: Studies in the Sources of Scientific Creativity 1 (London: Kluwer Academic, 2000), 125–45. The Anglo-Saxons, and particularly Bede (with his thought experiments and his use of fingers for calculation), would surely agree with Núñez on his argument for the embodiment of conceptualization.

56 For an overview of computus methods, calculations, and their history before Bede, see Wallis, *Reckoning*, Introduction, xviii–lxiii.

The ongoing study of the skies included examination of those bodies that filled the heavens. While their spherical shapes may be obvious from earth, the relative positions of the sun and moon in the sky can be deceptive. The sun had primary importance for the Anglo-Saxons, as a visible symbol of God and His power; the moon served to reflect the glory and might of God, but muted, as creation shows blurred and weakened images of God. Stars offer glimpses of divine splendour. Because these celestial objects carried not only scientific interest but theological import, Anglo-Saxon writers sought a proper understanding of their relationships.

The appearances of the sun and moon at times caused some perplexity. Bede explains at length in *De temporum ratione* why the moon, a closer and lesser object, sometimes appears to be above the sun. He presents a thought experiment based on lamps in a church (*DTR* 26.34–55): if one walks into a church lit by two lamps, one farther away than the other, the closer will seem higher, even if it is in fact lower.[57] So too the moon may appear higher than the sun at times, yet it is closer to the earth.[58] Ælfric also uses a domestic image to convey their orbits in his *De temporibus anni*: "Nu miht ðu understandan þæt læssan ymbgang hæfð se man þe gæð onbuton an hus, þonne se ðe ealle þa burh begæð. Swa eac se mona hæfð his ryne hraðor aurnen on ðam læssan ymbhwyrfte þonne seo sunne hæbbe on ðam maran" (*DTA* 170–3; "Now you can understand that the man who goes around a house has a shorter circuit than one who travels around the whole town. So also the moon has its own course, having run faster on its lesser circuit than the sun has on its greater one," trans. Blake, 83). Both authors seek to establish a correct understanding of the relative positions of sun and moon for their audiences.

These celestial objects matter because they bear visible witness to a God who can be perceived not directly, but through His creations. Psalm 88:38 states, "et thronus eius sicut sol in conspectu meo et sicut luna perfecta in aeternum et testis in caelo fidelis" ("And his throne as the sun before me: and as the moon perfect for ever, and a faithful witness in heaven," Douay-Rheims). Psalter glosses rendered the line in Old English: "& heahsetl

---

57 See also Wallis's excellent discussion of this thought experiment and her clear diagrams, *Reckoning*, 304–6.

58 Bede and some of his successors seem to have followed Pliny's account of the distances between celestial bodies: from the earth to the moon is 126,000 *stadii*, from the moon to the sun twice that, and from the sun to the zodiac three times that. Pliny, *Naturalis historia* 2.9.83; see Wallis, *Reckoning*, 77, n. 238. Lewis and Short give a *stadium* as a little under one eighth of an English mile.

his swa swa sunne on gesihðe minre & swa swa mona fulfremed on ec-
nysse & gewita on heofonum getrywe" ("and his high seat just as the sun
in my sight, and just as the moon perfect in eternity, and a true witness in
heaven," gloss to Psalm 88:38).[59]

Both nearby bodies were understood as spheres, again used by writers
such as Ælfric to connote perfection and completeness.[60] Aldhelm's *De
laude virginitatis* and its glosses, and glosses on other texts, refer to the
moon as a globe.[61] Bede notes, moreover, that the moon does not really
grow and shrink; it just reflects more or less light as it recedes from and
then approaches the sun (*De natura rerum* 20.2–4). Ælfric reuses Bede's
work here in his *De temporibus anni* (110–15). Bede and Ælfric use
Augustine's succinct formulation to explain the moon's light: "non ha-
bere lumen proprium, sed a sole illustrari" (*DTR* 25.15; "[the Moon] does
not have its own light, but is lit up by the Sun," trans. Wallis, *Reckoning*,
75; her brackets).[62] Each author clearly wanted readers to understand the
moon's completeness as a sphere of unchanging size and its operation in
reflecting the sun's light.

Bede shows some concern as well for establishing that the sun truly
does orbit the earth. He quotes Augustine:

Non tamen in aliam partem non est dies ubi praesentia solis est, nisi forte
poeticis figmentis cor inclinandum est, ut credamus solem mari se immergere
atque inde lotum ex alia parte mane surgere. Quamquam si ita esset, abyssus
ipsa praesentia solis illustraretur atque ibi esset dies, posset enim et aquas

---

59 The Old English Psalm glosses vary depending on manuscript; see the *Corpus* for
details, or, for Psalms 1–50, *Old English Glossed Psalters: Psalms 1–50*, ed. Phillip
Pulsiano, Toronto Old English Series 11 (Toronto: University of Toronto Press, 2001).
Translations of the Vulgate all come from the Douay-Rheims. This quotation comes
from Psalter K, but five other manuscripts have very similar glosses; for bibliographical
details and exact quotations from the other manuscripts, see the *Corpus*. All translations
of glosses are my own unless otherwise noted.

60 See above, p. 20.

61 See the *Corpus* for these glosses. The glossary known as the Corpus Glossary rattles off
a list of synonyms for "globus" – "Globus uolumen circulus luna et rota" ("Globe roll
circle moon and wheel," 7.105) – that both imply that the moon is a globe and blur the
distinction between circle and sphere.

62 Ælfric's translation is quite close: "Se mona næfð nan leoht buton of ðære sunnan
leoman" (*DTA* 106–7; "The moon has no light except from the sun's brightness,"
trans. Blake, 81).

illuminare quando ab eis non posset extingui. Sed hoc monstrosum est suspi-
cari. (*DTR* 5.32–8)

("Nonetheless, it does not happen that there is no day in that other region
where the Sun is present – unless perchance your heart favours poetic con-
ceits, so that you believe that the Sun sinks into the sea, and rises thence in
splendour from another quarter at dawn. Notwithstanding, were this so, the
abyss would be lit up by the very presence of the Sun, for it can illuminate
the waters, while it cannot be extinguished by them. But to suggest this, is
absurd," trans. Wallis, *Reckoning*, 20)

Bede follows Augustine's critical thinking about the poetic models available to late antique and early medieval thinkers. Ælfric too, following
Bede, notes that the sun goes as far below earth as it does above, and that
it lights the other side of the planet when not lighting ours (*DTA* 37–41).[63]
Both Bede and Ælfric explain that the darkness of night results from the
earth coming between observers and the sun (Bede, *DTR* 7.4–5, and
Ælfric, *DTA* 97–9). Again, the writers insist on the brightness of the heavens: earth and its shadow cause darkness, which is not the natural state of
the cosmos beyond the moon.

Exeter Book Riddle 29 runs at a tangent to Bede and Ælfric's understandings of the solar system. The Exeter Book Riddles are a series of
Old English alliterative poems that ask the reader to identify a creature
or object. Some are based on Latin poems, and all have ties to learned
and monastic traditions, but the Riddles also reflect more down-to-earth
tastes. Many of the answers are found in nature or in household items,
and a few are bawdy, with such solutions as "penis or onion" or "penis
or key."[64] Riddle 29 draws on common experience, that which "is eallum
cuð eorðbuendum" ("known to all earth-dwellers," 8), to describe celestial phenomena: a "lyftfæt leohtlic" ("light air-vessel," 3) appears with
plunder held between its horns (2), but another "wundorlicu wiht"

---

63 Henel locates the source in Bede's *DTR* 5; see his edition of *DTA*, 9.
64 See Riddle 25 for a riddle that could be solved "onion" or "penis," and 44 for "key"
    or "penis." I follow the ASPR 3's numbering here. Note that the ASPR does not
    include the possible sexual solutions in the notes. For an engaging piece on Riddle 25
    explaining possible solutions with good bibliography, see Megan Cavell, "Commen-
    tary for Riddle 25," in *The Riddle Ages*, 3 July 2014, https://theriddleages.wordpress.
    com/2014/07/03/commentary-for-riddle-25/; for 44, see Cavell, "Commentary for
    Riddle 44," 21 September 2015, https://theriddleages.wordpress.com/2015/09/21/
    commentary-for-riddle-44/.

("wonderful creature," 7) arrives to retake the plunder and drive the first away, to the west. Scholars generally agree that the first is the moon and the second the sun. The poem closes, however, "Nænig siþþan / wera gewiste þære wihte sið" ("No one knew the creature's journey afterwards," 13–14). This poem insists on the mystery of the spheres' courses, not knowledge of them. The poet may be playing with the audience and the tension between what readers know intellectually, that the moon and sun go around the earth, and what they know experientially: the moon and sun disappear in the west and reappear in the east, and their tracks in the sky shift over the course of the month and the year. Alternatively, Bede and Ælfric may be addressing a true ignorance that the poem shares: perhaps the poet does not expect his audience to know where heavenly bodies go, but Bede and Ælfric takes pains to educate their audiences.

While the course of the moon and sun were understood at least by some Anglo-Saxons, the size of the moon eluded them, though it had been more accurately known in classical times (with the exception of Pliny, Bede's major source).[65] Bede declares in *De natura rerum* that the moon is larger than the earth (19.2–3), and the Old English *Soliloquies* follows him (93.6–10).[66] In *De temporibus ratione*, however, Bede seems to have revised his views, for he quotes Pliny's *Historia naturalis* that the moon and the earth must be the same size for total solar eclipses to occur, but that the sun is larger than either (*DTR* 27.13–19). Ælfric refuses to commit himself, perhaps because he knew both passages from Bede and did not wish to pronounce on an astronomical point where his predecessor had been inconsistent (see *DTA* 124–5).

The moon's effects on the earth interested our writers more than the moon's measurement did. Tides are a great wonder for Bede: "Maxime autem prae omnibus admiranda tanta oceani cum lunae cursu societas" (*DTR* 29.2–3; "But more marvellous than anything else is the great fellowship that exists between the ocean and the course of the Moon," trans. Wallis, *Reckoning*, 82), a passage that Ælfric renders in Old English in *De temporibus anni* (350–3). Bede even attempts to explain the mechanism of tides: "Tamquam lunae quibusdam aspirationibus inuitus protrahatur, et

---

65 See Wallis, *Reckoning*, commentary to chap. 27, p. 306.
66 See Malcolm R. Godden, "The Sources of King Alfred's Old English Version of Augustine's *Soliloquies* (Cameron C.B.9.4)," 2001, *Fontes*; the translator could not derive this passage from Augustine's *Soliloquia*. Godden rates it only a possible source, along with Bede's *DTR* 26.23–4.

iterum eiusdem ui cessante in mensuram propriam refundatur" (*DTR* 29.9–11; "It is as if [the ocean] were dragged forwards against its will by certain exhalations of the moon, and when her power ceases, it is poured back again into his proper measure," trans. Wallis, *Reckoning*, 82–3).[67] In giving such an explanation, Bede goes beyond other computus texts, which generally note the connection between moon and tide without explanation. The relationships between the earth and other cosmic bodies rouse Bede's interest even where they have no effect on Easter dates. For Bede and later Ælfric, the effects show the harmony of the system God created: celestial bodies are balanced so that the moon influences earth in consistent and readable ways.

Bede not only generalizes, he details the workings of the tides, correcting Pliny and more recent cosmographers with personal observations. Though he followed Pliny's figure for the retardation of the moon in his *De natura rerum*, he corrects it in *De temporum ratione*, bringing it nearer modern measurements (see *DTR* 29.11–16).[68] Bede's correction demonstrates a critical attitude towards sources and a willingness to use observation to modify even established authorities. Later in the chapter Bede also notes that strong winds may increase or decrease the tides (29.53–8), and that "Scimus enim nos, qui diuersum Britannici Maris litus incolimus" (*DTR* 29.74–5, "we who live at various places along the coastline of the British Sea know," trans. Wallis, *Reckoning*, 85) that a rising tide at one place means a falling tide in another (74–101), contrary to Philippus Presbyter (29.72). The effects of the moon not only illustrate God's power but also have a real impact on people's lives in the island of Britain.

Here Bede claims a special knowledge of the cosmos based on geography: inhabitants of the British coast know the workings of the tides and therefore have particular insight into the workings of the moon. Bede's revisions to Pliny's figure for the moon's retardation between his *De natura rerum* and his treatment in *De temporum ratione* would only have been noted by those who read Bede's earlier work very closely. Bede could

---

67 Bede here quotes Ambrose's *Hexameron* 4.7.30 (136.3–5); see Wallis, *Reckoning*, 83, n. 255.

68 Faith Wallis notes that Pliny's time for the retardation of the moon is 47½ minutes per day; Bede corrects this time to 48 minutes in *DTR*, still not quite the correct 50 minutes, but a more accurate figure. In other words, the moon rises 50 minutes later each night than it did the previous night. See Wallis, *Reckoning*, commentary on chapter 29, 307–12, for details about Bede's sources and original work on tides, and particularly 309–10 for his corrections of Pliny and others on the time involved.

have made a silent change here, but he does not. Instead, he makes explicit claims for observation by inhabitants of the British Isles. He presents astronomy not as purely abstract or a matter of rote learning but as somatic and geographical, a study that rewards personal observation with one's own senses, and he offers the English as privileged observers in this case. The Anglo-Saxons have a special understanding of the cosmos. At the same time, knowledge of the cosmos is not an end in itself but a means to better understanding of God.

Ælfric follows Bede regarding the privileged position of the Anglo-Saxons. As Heinrich Henel notes, Ælfric makes virtually no personal additions as he translates the work of others for *De temporibus anni*, but he makes an exception for this comment: "On ðam ylcan earde norðeweardan beoð leohte nihta on sumera, swilce hit ealle niht dagige, swa swa we sylfe foroft gesawon" (*DTA* 270–1; "In the north of this country, the nights are light in summer, such that it remains light all night, as we ourselves have very often seen," trans. Blake, 89).[69] Martin Blake suggests that this sentence merely reflects one of Bede's statements and not personal experience, for we have no other evidence Ælfric spent time in the north.[70] The plural pronoun may reflect a sense of English identity, shared among different parts of the island, rather than a personal experience. Either way, the texts locate Anglo-Saxons in a special place, a favoured spot where the light that fills the cosmos, but which earth's atmosphere hides from most observers, can filter through a little more. Similarly, in St John's College MS 17, f. 35v, a diagram modified from a probable Mediterranean source reflects the longer summer-solstice day evident from the north of England.[71] God favours the Anglo-Saxons as readers and producers of cosmic knowledge by giving them an astronomically significant place in the world.

---

69 Henel, notes to *DTA*, xlv–xlvi.

70 See Blake's edition, note to 58 on 118: Ælfric's "wording here may be no more than a reflex of Bede's *ubi aestate lucidae noctes haud dubie testantur* ('where in summer the lightness of the nights can hardly be questioned': *DT* c. 7, 8–9), or *ubi aestate lucidae noctes haud dubie repromittunt, id quod cogit ratio credi* ('where the bright nights of summer confirm what reason compels us to believe' (tr. Wallis): *DTR* c. 31, 58–9)." Yet Blake also notes that Ælfric mentions the shortness of nights in his *Letter to the Monks of Eynsham* and again uses the first person plural. See also his introduction, section 2, "Ælfric's Life and Career," 4–7.

71 Wallis, *Calendar*, "6. Cosmographical Anthology: 1. Diagram of Solstices and Equinoxes," citing Barbara Obrist; http://digital.library.mcgill.ca/ms-17/folio.php?p=35v&showitem=35v_6Cosmography_1SolsticesEquinoxes.

Bede also links phases of the moon to the moisture of plant and animal bodies in *De temporum ratione*, chapter 28, "De Effectiua Lunae Potentia." He was by no means alone. *De temporum ratione* 28 draws upon a variety of classical and patristic sources; Bede relates the conventional wisdom of his day, wisdom that remained current for centuries. Ælfric incorporated some of this material into his *De temporibus anni* (347–54) and rendered part of Bede's chapter into Old English in one of his *Catholic Homilies* to distinguish allowable uses of moon lore from those that are not.[72] Some prescriptions in medical texts and advice in tables of fortunate days require that the moon be a particular age for treatment (especially bloodletting) or harvesting herbs. For instance, four of the treatments in the Old English *Herbarium* must be done during a waning moon, while one must be performed when the moon is in Capricorn.[73] Even today, some gardeners still follow the phases of the moon for planting and pruning.[74] Similarly, Bede's chapter 35, "De Quattuor Temporibus, Elementis, Humoribus" ("The Four Seasons, Elements, and Humors," trans. Wallis, *Reckoning*, 100) connects the theory of bodily humours to the seasons; this theory has not entirely died either.[75]

We may be tempted to praise Bede for his scientific approach to tides and then criticize him for pseudo-science in his recital of other lunar effects, but to do either would be anachronistic. Michel de Certeau remarks that modern treatments of myth and fable imagine that "primitive" people had some understanding of the world, but that the analysis "assumes that these forms

---

72 For Bede's use of Ambrose, Pliny, and other sources here, see Wallis's notes, *Reckoning*, 80–2. For Ælfric, see *Catholic Homily* 1.6.192–9.

73 Hubert Jan de Vriend, ed., *The Old English Herbarium and Medicina de quadrupedibus*, EETS os 286 (London: Oxford University Press, 1984), 8.1, 10.1, 61.1, 183.1, and 111.2, respectively. See also *Bald's Leechbook* 1, chap. 72, and 3, chap. 47, for detailed instructions on when bloodletting may and may not be done, depending on the moon and other factors: *Leechdoms, Wortcunning and Starcraft of Early England*, ed. T.O. Cockayne, Rolls Series 35, vol. 2 (London: Longman, Green, Longman, Roberts, and Green, 1865), available at https://books.google.com/books?id=iP9AAQAAMAAJ.

74 For just one example, see Caren Catterall, *Gardening by the Moon* (Guerneville, CA: Divine Inspiration Publications, 2000–14), http://www.gardeningbytheMoon.com/; a simple search on Google will turn up many more such web pages, and an Amazon.com search turns up a variety of books and calendars. Thanks to Ursula Lenker for alerting me to the ongoing practice of such lore.

75 A friend who is a respected and successful physician told me (without prompting) in 2000 or 2001 what humours dominated in me, my husband, his wife, and himself. He did not use the notions in treatment, but he found them interesting.

of speech do not understand what they say that is important" and highlights "lack of knowledge" on the part of the speakers.[76] Bede communicates his point clearly, even if we would not accept his evidence or his understanding of what has significance. His discussion of tides and his treatment of how the moon affects liquid in other bodies on earth both result from convictions that the moon has real effects on the earth, and that these connections are part of God's marvellous plan whose coherence they reflect.

Bede does not have a modern sense of experimental method. He does not test hypotheses so much as he relies on respected authorities, Christian and non-Christian alike. Bede writes that the moon affects selenite, the stone's shine increasing with a waxing moon and decreasing with a waning (*DTR* 28.32–6).[77] He later quotes Cyril of Alexandria to the effect that selenite can be used to determine the correct date of Easter (43.86–90). Yet Bede did not simply accept all moon lore uncritically, as already evidenced in his correction of Pliny's time for the retardation of the moon and tides. While Bede asserts the connection of the moon to various earthly phenomena involving moisture, he also uses his understanding of the moon's position in the heavens to critique and reject the idea that the moon predicts or affects weather:

Numquid credibile est lunae statum, qui fixus in aethere permanet, pro subiacentium mutatione flabrorum uel nubium posse aliorsum quam fuerat conuerti, et eam quasi futurae metu tempestatis aliquanto altius cornu quam naturae ordo poscebat attollere, maxime cum non omnibus in terris idem fluctuantium possit existere flatus aurarum? Lunae autem status idem eademque sit pro uariante solis digressu conuersio. (*DTR* 25.6–13)

("Is it really credible that the position of the Moon, which remains fixed in the ether, could be altered under the influence of a change in the winds or clouds which lie beneath it, and that it should lift up its horns any higher than nature dictates, as if it dreaded bad weather to come, particularly when such a blast of wayward wind would not occur everywhere on earth? The rotation of the Moon's position ought to be constant with respect to its varying degree of separation from the Sun," trans. Wallis, *Reckoning*, 74–5)

---

76 *Practice*, 160.

77 An Anglo-Saxon lapidary gives similar information; see "MS. Cotton Tiberius A III (MS. A)," in *English Mediaeval Lapidaries*, ed. Joan Evans and Mary S. Serjeantson, EETS os 190 (London: Oxford University Press, 1960), 14.

Instead, he argues in the rest of the chapter, the appearance of the moon relates to the sun's position and thus the season, which is what truly affects the weather. The fact that he found it necessary to rebut the idea indicates that it had some currency in his time. For Bede, understanding the moon's true effects and distinguishing them from false ones mattered because celestial objects revealed portions of the divine plan. The orderly workings of the cosmos must be distinguished from superstitious misunderstandings – which themselves afford glimpses of other constructions of space. Sadly, we have no texts to give us fuller ideas of the interpretations of the cosmos in which the moon responds to or predicts weather on earth; only Bede's rebuttal survives. Clearly, even Anglo-Saxons with differing beliefs found the moon and its appearance important for understanding the workings of their own lives and the world around them.

Given their curiosity about the moon and the sun, Anglo-Saxons' interest in eclipses comes as no surprise. Each major version of the *Anglo-Saxon Chronicle* records between six and ten eclipses. Bede treats lunar and solar eclipses at length in his *De temporum ratione*, chapter 27, "De Magnitudine vel Defectu Solis et Lunae" ("On the Size, or Eclipse, of the Sun and Moon," trans. Wallis, *Reckoning*, 78). With Pliny as his major source, Bede details the workings of solar and lunar eclipses. He quotes Pliny's words about the virtue of such studies: "Haec ratio mortales animos subducit in caelum ac uelut inde contemplantibus trium maximarum rerum naturae partium magnitudinem detegit" (27.11–13; "This theory draws mortal minds into the heavens, and discloses to their contemplation from this height, as it were, the magnitude of the dimensions of the three largest things in nature," trans. Wallis, *Reckoning*, 79).[78] Ælfric gives far less detail, but he briefly discusses solar eclipses in *De temporibus anni*, at 120–5.[79] In his *Catholic Homily* 1.40, "Dominica II in adventum Domini" ("Second Sunday in Advent"), Ælfric preaches about signs in the heavens and declares specifically that eclipses are natural phenomena, not portents:

Mid cwealme. 7 mid hungre we sind gelome geswencte. ac we nateshwon gyta swutele tacna on sunnan 7 on monan 7 on steorran ne gesawon; We rædað on

---

78 According to Jones in his edition of *DTR*, Bede quotes here from Pliny, *Naturalis historia* 2.10.47–50, and the passage parallels Augustine's Epistle 55, 7.

79 Byrhtferth does not say anything about either kind of eclipse. He had access to Bede's *De temporum ratione* and Ælfric's *De temporibus anni*, and he may have considered the subject thoroughly covered by the others.

tungelcræfte þ[æ]t seo sunne bið hwiltidum þurh ðæs monelican trendles un-
derscyte aþeostrod: 7 eac se fulla mona færlice fagettað þonne he þæs sunlican
leohtes bedæled bið þurh ðære eorðan sceadewunge. (525.37–42)

("We are often oppressed with pestilence and hunger, but we never yet saw
clear signs from the sun and the moon and the stars. We read in astronomy
that the sun is sometimes darkened through the intervention of the sphere of
the moon [between sun and earth]; and also the full moon suddenly changes
colour when it is deprived of the sun's light through the earth's shadow.")

Ælfric's words suggest that while he thinks his audience reads too much
into the phenomena, he expects them to understand a brief, almost allusive
explanation of how solar and lunar eclipses occur. The excerpt suggests
once again that not only learned writers but also the unlettered took an
interest in the sun and moon. Like Bede, Ælfric seeks to distinguish true
understandings of natural phenomena from misunderstandings. Between
them, the two Anglo-Saxon authors teach both advanced pupils and less
educated lay audiences about eclipses.

Objects that lay beyond that moon also revealed divine order. Though
diagrams such as Byrhtferth's depiction of the sun and moon (*Enchiridion*,
figure 21, MS A168) sometimes represent them as equidistant from the
earth for convenience's sake, at least by the tenth century, learned Anglo-
Saxons were well aware that celestial objects each had their own orbit,
moving westward across the sky, as evidenced by Ælfric, *DTA* 172–3 and
Interrogationes Sigeuulfi (115–19). Oxford, St John's College MS 17,
fol. 82v depicts the distances from earth to the moon, then to the sun, then
to the Zodiac graphically. These distances, according to the manuscript,
form a simple mathematical ratio: the moon's distance is one length, the
sun then twice that far from the moon, and the zodiac three times the distance.[80] The sun in this diagram has the largest circle and, lest any doubt of

---

80 http://digital.library.mcgill.ca/ms-17/folio.php?p=82v. The diagram reads (bottom to
    top): "usque ad lunam cxxvi stadiorum" ("to the moon is 126 *stadia*"), "A luna usque
    ad solem duplicatum, id e[st] cclii" ("from the moon to the sun twice the distance, that
    is 252 [*stadia*]"), and "A sole us[que] ad .xii. signa triplicatu[m]. id [est] ccclxxviiii"
    ("From the sun to the twelve signs thrice the distance, that is 379 [*stadia*]") – the scribe
    appears to have become too enthused in making his minims and added an extra one
    to the 378 he should have written.

its significance remain, where the earth is simply labelled "[t]erra," the moon "luna," and the zodiac ".xii. signa" ("twelve signs"), the large circle for the sun is inscribed, "Sol om[n]i[bus] signis maior est" ("The sun is largest of all the signs"). These authors and illustrators establish the proper places for each celestial object using simple mathematical ratios to reflect the elegance of the divine plan.

Latin and Old English each have sufficient vocabulary to discuss phenomena involving the earth, the sun, and the moon with little confusion. When discussion turns to planets, however, a complication arises. Latin can differentiate *stellae* (stars) from *planetes* (planets), though the distinction is not always maintained; in his *De natura rerum*, Bede refers to the planets, sun, and moon as "septem sidera ... quae uocantur errantia" (12.2–3; "seven stars ... which are called wandering"). In Old English, however, *tungol* means "a heavenly body" (Bosworth-Toller 1020): the term includes both planets and stars, and it can even be used for the sun or moon. *Steorra* can also refer to planets, both alone and in forms such as *morgensteorra* (morning star) and *æfensteorra* (evening star). This ambiguous terminology could restrict the ability to think about the solar system scientifically. If one considers Venus and Saturn to be in the same class of objects as stars, one may have trouble understanding that planets do not have the same source of light as stars.[81]

Sometimes Anglo-Saxons availed themselves of Latin terminology to distinguish planets from stars. Byrhtferth refers in his *Enchiridion* to "Þa steorran þe man hæt planete on Lyden" (2.3.198; "The stars called *planete* in Latin," trans. Baker and Lapidge 119).[82] Ælfric distinguishes in his homily "De falsis diis" ("Concerning false gods") between *steorra* in general and "þa syfan tunglan, sunnan and monan, and þa oðre fif, þe farað æfre ongean þone roder to eastdæle werd" ("the seven *tunglan*, sun and moon, and the other five, which go ever against the sky to the east," 183–5). He borrows the distinction directly from Bede, *De natura rerum* 12.2–4. To differentiate effectively in a context more focused on teaching science, however, he must fall back on Latin. He writes of the sun, moon, and five

---

81 To be fair, twenty-first-century people still refer to Venus as the Morning Star or the Evening Star, and many of us have a hard time distinguishing planets from stars as we look at the night sky.

82 Byrhtferth did not always maintain this distinction, however; see *Enchiridion* 1.1.41–4, where he calls the planets "steorran." For other references to Saturn as *steorra*, see the *Metres of Boethius* 24.17–25, and the prose *Boethius* 36.48 and 39.60–1.

known planets, "Þa seofon sind gehatene septem planete" (*DTA* 362; "The seven are called *septem planete*," trans. Blake, 93).

Despite the difficulties presented by vocabulary (and a complete lack of telescopes), learned Anglo-Saxons valued some knowledge of the planets. In both *De natura rerum* (chaps. 12–13) and *De temporum ratione* (8.30–57), Bede makes the effort to teach the planets in a memorable way, associating them with facts that will help readers recall them. He notes the connection to pagan gods. He reminds readers that days of the week are named after them. Finally, he relates the qualities with which they were associated, drawing upon Isidore's *De natura rerum* (3.4).[83] He then goes on to relate the reasoning behind these attributes and the length of each planet's orbit.[84] In his *De natura rerum*, Bede even tells how many days of the year the planets are invisible because they are too close to the sun (13.11–16). Ælfric foregoes some of the other information, but he translates Bede's data on orbits from *De natura rerum* in his *Interrogationes Sigeuulfi*, although some errors have crept in (121–35).[85] Byrhtferth too offers an account of orbits (*Enchiridion* 2.3.204–13); Baker and Lapidge trace his numbers to a *rota* (circular diagram) often found with Isidore's *De natura rerum*, chapter 23.[86] Such a rota, with the same figures except for Mars, is found in Oxford, St John's College MS 17, f. 37v.[87] After giving the orbits, Byrhtferth relates the planets to the days of the week (2.3.213–20) and tells what qualities the ancients ascribed to them (2.3.220–3), as Bede does, though Bede is not Byrhtferth's primary source for the

---

83 See Wallis, *Reckoning*, 33, n. 69.

84 In *DTR*, Bede relates the information about planets in the eighth chapter, titled "De hebdomada" ("On the week"), but he goes far beyond what is necessary to understand different practices for naming days of the week.

85 See Baker and Lapidge, Commentary, 310–12, for details about source relations in this passage, which Byrhtferth also uses.

86 Byrhtferth offers the same orbits for Saturn and Jupiter, thirty and twelve years respectively (which are fairly close to the actual durations of 29.46 and 11.86 years, Baker and Lapidge note), but he gives fifteen years for Mars (in reality, 687 days), nine for Venus (225 days), and twenty for Mercury (eighty-eight days); see Baker and Lapidge, Commentary, 310–12.

87 http://digital.library.mcgill.ca/ms-17/folio.php?p=37v. Baker and Lapidge supply "fiftyne" to match St John's College MS 17's figure, but their textual notes reveal the *Enchiridion* manuscript's actual figure of "twelf" (apparatus to 2.3.207). For more on the diagram and figures in related manuscripts, see Wallis, "6. Cosmographical Anthology: 7. Isidore of Seville on the Planets: Text and Diagram," *The Calendar and the Cloister*, http://digital.library.mcgill.ca/ms-17/folio.php?p=37v&showitem=37v_6 Cosmography_7IsidorePlanets.

wording here. These authors all teach the movements of the planets, covering both Latin and in English among them.

These figures for orbits, accurate or not, do not help Anglo-Saxons calculate the dates of holy days. The other information might seem to serve even less purpose: Bede and Byrhtferth tell what the ancients associated with each planet only to dismiss the associations as ignorant. Yet it is easier to recall that Saturn's period is thirty years when one thinks not of abstract numbers, but of Saturn as a cold old man (Bede, *DTR* 8.39 and 47–50), or at least the father of another supposed god (Byrhtferth, *Enchiridion* 2.3.228). Similarly, one can more easily recall that Mars has a shorter period when one thinks of Mars as a quick person (*scyndles*, *Enchiridion* 2.3.227) or "fervent" ("feruens," *DTR* 8.45; "ardore," burning, *DTR* 8.47). These writers relate the orbits as something worth knowing. Some cosmographical anthologies such as Oxford, St John's College MS 17, go even further, giving charts of planetary evagation derived from Pliny – that is, how far to the north and south (from earth's perspective) the planets move as they orbit, with the motions expressed as musical ratios.[88] While this lore may lack practical application, writers again use it to construct an orderly, comprehensible cosmos whose complexity gives glimpses of the divine plan.

Alfredian translations frequently change or omit details, so the preservation of mentions of Saturn in the *Boethius* and *Metres of Boethius* indicates that knowledge of the planets has value.[89]

---

88 As Wallis notes, "in terms of time, each planet's course is plotted independently, for the periods of their journeys through the zodiac cannot be reconciled"; the information has not been synthesized, merely passed on. "6. Cosmographical Anthology: 9 Planetary Evagations Diagram," http://digital.library.mcgill.ca/ms-17/folio.php?p=38r&showitem =38r_6Cosmography_9PlanetaryEvagations. She also lists as including such diagrams the Peterborough computus (London, British Library, Cotton Tiberius C.I fols. 2–17+ Harley 3667); the Winchcombe computus (London, British Library, Cotton Tiberius E.IV); Glasgow, University Library, Hunter 85 (T.4.2); Cambridge, St John's College I.15 (221); London, British Library, Cotton Vitellius A.XII; and Cambridge, Trinity College R.15.32 (945).

89 Mark Griffith argues persuasively that the *Metres* are not by the same translator as the prose: see especially "Authorship and Date: The Metres" and its notes in Godden and Irvine, *Boethius*, vol. 1, 146–51. For Alfredian adaptations of source texts, see my book *The King's English: Strategies of Translation in the Old English Boethius* (Binghamton: State University of New York Press, 2005) and relevant chapters and bibliography in *A Companion to Alfred the Great*, ed. Discenza and Szarmach.

Gif þu mihtest þe fligon ofer þam rodore, þonne mihtest þu gesion þa wolcnu under þe, and mihtest þe fliogan ofer þam fyre þe is betwux þam rodore and þære lyfte, and mihtest þe feran mid þære sunnan betwyx þam tunglum, and þonon weorþan on þam rodore, and siððan to þam cealdan stiorran þe we hatað Saturnes steorra. Se is eallisig; se wandrað ofer oðrum steorrum ufor þonne ænig oðer tungol. (*Boethius* 36.44–50)

("If you can fly above the firmament, then you can see the clouds underneath you, and can fly above the fire that is between the firmament and the air, and can travel with the sun among the stars, and from there come to the firmament, and after to the cold star which we call Saturn's star. That is all icy; it wanders above the other stars higher than any other star," trans. Godden and Irvine, vol. 2, 67–8)[90]

The versifier turns this passage into an even longer poem (C Metre 24). These passages go beyond the obvious source text (*De consolatione philosophiae* 4 Metre 1.1–12) to include scientific information that may derive from Bede's *De natura rerum* (13.2–3) or another scientific text.[91] The ideas have an analogue or a source in commentary on the *De consolatione*.[92] The *Metres of Boethius* preserve the image of Saturn as "se cealda/ eallisig tungl" (24.22–3; "the cold, all-icy star," trans. Godden and Irvine, vol. 2, 168), the most distant wandering star (24.17–24). A little later in the prose, Wisdom mentions Saturn's thirty-year period (*Boethius* 39.60–1).[93]

Information about the planets serves little practical purpose, yet Bede, Ælfric, Byrhtferth, and anonymous compilers such as those responsible for

---

90 Godden and Irvine translate both "tungol" and "steorra" as "star," and indeed the Old English author seems to be using the terms interchangeably here.

91 Boethius, *De consolatione philosophiae, Opuscula theologica*, ed. Claudio Moreschini, 2nd ed. (Munich: K.G. Saur, 2005). See my *Fontes* entries, "Sources of King Alfred's Old English Version of Boethius's *De consolatione* (Cameron C.B.9.3)," 2001: the *De consolatione* is a definite source here, Bede's *DNR* a possible source, and the so-called Remigian commentary at least an analogue. Godden and Irvine too offer Bede's *DNR* as a parallel and note wide variation in the commentary tradition on the line concerning Saturn; see their commentary in vol. 2 of the *Boethius*, 426–7.

92 On the commentary tradition, see Rosalind Love, "Latin Commentaries on Boethius's *Consolation of Philosophy*," in *A Companion to Alfred the Great*, ed. Discenza and Szarmach, 82–110, and her references.

93 See my *Fontes* entries on the *Boethius* for Bede, *DNR* 13.3 as a possible source. Godden and Irvine note in their commentary, "The thirty-year orbit of Saturn is a commonplace of astronomy; it is mentioned in a gloss to 1m2 … Cf. too Bede DNR, c. XIII.2–3" (vol. 2, 459).

St John's College MS. 17 all produce and transmit this knowledge in their scientific texts, and even the Old English *Boethius* sprinkles a little planetary lore among its philosophy. At the same time, however, Anglo-Saxons show little interest in more detailed explorations of planetary orbits. Bede and Byrhtferth offer no explanations or diagrams of epicycles or circumsolar orbits for any of the planets.[94] Anglo-Saxons sought knowledge of the heavens not as pure science, but in order to know their Creator and their own world better. Understanding the sun and moon and their motions helped them keep track of time and explain phenomena they experienced in everyday life. Perhaps more importantly, their readings of the sky connected them to a divine cycle of salvific time in which the two major celestial bodies help remind us of the Saviour's sacrifice: sun and moon must be observed to calculate correctly the dates of Good Friday, when Jesus was crucified; and Easter Sunday, when he arose from the dead.

The immediate sources of the heavenly lights they saw, however, seem to have perplexed the Anglo-Saxons. At times, they hold contradictory ideas about stellar radiance. Sometimes they clearly indicate that stars, like planets, reflect the light of the sun. Bede writes of "Stellae lumen a sole mutuantes" ("The stars, sharing light from the sun," *DNR* 11.2). He elaborates at greater length in *De temporum ratione* (6.32–50, qtg John 1:9). Similarly, the Alfredian *Boethius* describes how God gives all true goods as the sun lights all stars (OE *Boethius* 34.103–7).[95]

This understanding of stellar illumination is intertwined with Anglo-Saxons' theological understanding of the universe and related metaphors. In *De temporum ratione*, Bede writes,

---

94 Epicycles are small extra circles added to the main orbit of a planet around the earth; some ancient and Carolingian astronomers included them in their descriptions of planetary orbits so that the described orbits would match the observed positions of the planets. Most did not realize that the orbits did not match the observations because the planets do not orbit the earth but the sun. Some ancient and Carolingian astronomers, however, plotted circumsolar orbits for some planets – orbits around the sun rather than the earth. See Bruce Eastwood and Gerd Graßhoff, *Planetary Diagrams for Roman Astronomy in Medieval Europe, CA. 800–1500*, Transactions of the American Philosophical Society vol. 94, pt. 3 (Philadelphia: American Philosophical Society, 2004), esp. 82–90 and 92–4.

95 The Old English imagery of sun and stars in this passage comes not from Boethius's Latin text, which has no image here, but possibly from the passage in Bede given above (*DNR* 11.2), or from Bede's own source, Isidore (*DNR* 22); see Godden and Irvine, Commentary, vol. 2, 391.

luna autem et stellae, quae non proprio, ut dicunt, sed aduentitio et a sole mu-
tuato lumine fulgent, ipsum ecclesiae corpus et quosque uiritim sanctos insinu-
ant, qui, illuminari non illuminare ualentes, caelestis gratiae munus accipere
sciunt, dare nesciunt. Atque in celebratione maximae solemnitatis Christus ecclesiae debuit anteponi, quae non nisi per illum luceret. (*DTR* 6.40–6)

("while the Moon and stars, which shine, not with their own light (as they
say), but with an adventitious light borrowed from the Sun, suggest the body
of the Church as a whole, and each individual saint. These, capable of being
illumined but not of illuminating, know how to accept the gift of heavenly
grace but not how to give it. And in the celebration of the supreme solemnity,
it was necessary that Christ precede the Church, which cannot shine save
through Him," trans. Wallis, *Reckoning*, 25–6)

Bede continues in this vein for some time, developing connections between Christ and the sun and explaining how the Church takes its being
only from Christ (6.46–58).

Ælfric's cosmology reveals similar theological implications. His explanation that stars take their light from the sun alone (*DTA* 58–63) is clearly
enmeshed in the allegorical meaning he gives: "Seo sunne getacnað urne
Hælend Crist se ðe is rihtwisnysse sunne … Næfð ure nan nan leoht æni-
gre godnysse buton of Cristes gife, se ðe is soðre rihtwisnysse sunne gehaten" (*DTA* 63–4, 74–5; "The sun signifies our saviour Christ who is the
sun of righteousness … None of us has the light of any goodness except
through the grace of Christ, who is rightly called the sun of righteousness," trans. Blake, 79). Ælfric's association of the sun with God is even
stronger elsewhere: his *Catholic Homilies* 1.20 explains how the sun represents the Trinity: "Seo sunne ðe ofer us scinð is lichamlic gesceaft. 7 hæfð
swa ðeah ðreo agennyssa on hire; An is seo lichamlice edwist. þ[æ]t is ðære
sunnan trendel; Oðer is se leoma oððe beorhtnys. æfre of ðære sunnan seo
ðe onliht ealne middangeard; þridde is seo hætu" ("The sun which shines
over us is a material creation, and yet it has three properties in it: One is its
physical substance, that is the circle of the sun; the second is its light or
brightness, which always lights this whole earth from the sun; third is its
heat," 1.20.100–3).[96] This passage on the sun directly follows an explanation of the Trinity and its immanence and leads into further comparison
between sun and Trinity. In his rendering of Alcuin's *Interrogationes*

---

96 My translations for "agennyssa" and "edwist" rely on the *DOE*.

Sigeuulfi, Ælfric argues that it is fitting that light is God's first creation, because God Himself is light (156–62).[97]

Yet before the passage of *De natura rerum* in which Bede tells of the sun lending stars their light, he describes where the elements reside: "Igne, quo sidera lucent" ("Fire, by which stars shine," 3.3–4), suggesting that stars have their own individual fires and do not merely reflect the sun's light. In the *Boethius*, "Loca nu be þære sunnan and eac be oðrum tunglum þonne sweartan wolcnu him beforan gað; ne mahon hi þonne heora leoht sellan" (6.1–3; "Look now at the sun and also at other stars when dark clouds pass in front of them; they cannot then give their light," trans. Godden and Irvine, vol. 2, 9) seems to imply that the stars are other suns, each with their own light – particularly when compared with Boethius's Latin, "sidera lumen" ("light of the stars," *De consolatione philosophiae* 1 Metre 7.4), which at best hints that the stars *have* light but never compares them to the sun.[98] Bede's *De temporum ratione* tells us "ideoque aetheris quae ultra lunam sunt spatia diurnae lucis plena semper efficiat, uel suo uidelicet uel siderum radiata fulgore" (7.23–5; "Therefore [the Sun] makes the tracts of ether which are beyond the moon to be always full of daylight, either by his own brightness or by that which beams from the stars," Wallis, *Reckoning*, 29; her brackets).[99]

Anglo-Saxon writers cannot seem to decide whether stars are lit by their own fires or simply reflect light from our sun. In a mental model of the cosmos where the sun represents God, stars cannot unproblematically generate their own light, any more than creations could live without God. Anglo-Saxon understandings of how stars produce light here differ greatly from our own because they grow out of and reinforce theology. Yet at other times, sometimes even in the same texts, Anglo-Saxons accurately describe stars as producing their own light. In the last quotation, Bede seems to leave the question open to the audience: does the "or" mean that any given region of space could be lit by either the sun or the stars, or that Bede himself is uncertain whether it is the sun or the stars lighting space?

---

97 Here he follows and elaborates on Alcuin's work. See MacLean's edition of the *Interrogationes*, 156–62, and Alcuin's source passage, printed opposite.

98 A Latin hymn and its Old English glosses also refer to the sun as a star; see Milfull, *The Hymns of the Anglo-Saxon Church*, 21.5–8.

99 Wallis writes in a note to this passage, "Note that Bede retracts his previous statement that the stars shine only with borrowed light; this is not in any of the sources listed above" (29, n. 54).

Sometimes the similarities between Anglo-Saxon conceptions of space and our own hide startling differences, including this uncertainty about light from the stars. The two possibilities may have posed less of a problem for Anglo-Saxons than we might think. Again, Bourdieu's notion of "'poly-thesis,' the 'confusion of spheres,'" reminds us that the same person or people may invoke two or more contradictory models of the world.[100]

Nicholas Howe's description of Anglo-Saxon thinking about geography as a "vocabulary" rather than a "palimpsest" usefully reminds us that ideas coexist but may be used in different places, rather than one simply overwriting another.[101] Much of the time, those who hold such apparent mental contradictions do not notice them because they do not put both or all schemes into practice simultaneously; different models appear side by side, and therefore appear contradictory, only in our analysis. In ordinary life and in teaching, sometimes one explanation may be invoked, some-times another. Astronomy was not merely abstract but interwoven with daily life, for religious and practical reasons. Accordingly, our writers ap-proached the topic with religious and practical assumptions and methods, using knowledge culled from the Bible and patristic sources, on the one hand, and observations by themselves and their predecessors, on the other. When a model of the divine is at stake, the idea of the sun as the central source of all light dominates. When more pedestrian or secular concerns appear, the idea of the sun and stars as separate fires can come to the fore.

While Anglo-Saxons seem of two minds about the source of starlight, the importance of stars is not at issue. Their interest and knowledge ex-tended to specific stars. Learned Anglo-Saxons knew the zodiac. Bede, Ælfric, and Byrhtferth all introduce the term and explain that the zodiac is a band of stars around the earth, divided into twelve signs; Bede and Byrhtferth name the signs of the zodiac and their times of year.[102] As noted before, several Anglo-Saxon writers mention the heavens turning like a wheel, or at least on an axis.[103] Ælfric, like Alfred, describes both (axis at *DTA* 371–4, wheel at 14–16); the *Boethius* may have influenced his imagery

---

100 Bourdieu, *Outline*, 110. See also de Certeau, *Practice*, esp. xi.
101 *Writing the Map*, 78.
102 See Bede, *DNR*, chaps. 16–17, and *DTR* 6.85–110 and chaps. 16–17; Ælfric, *DTA* 108–10, 142–3, and 287–9; and Byrhtferth, *Enchiridion* 1.1.24–8 and 41–6, 2.3.35–53 and figs. 1, 13, and 16.
103 See pp. 18–19, above.

here.[104] Moreover, Bede and Ælfric note that different stars are visible in the southern hemisphere than in the northern (*DTR*, chap. 34; *DTA* 368–72). Of these authors, only Bede refers to the Milky Way ("Lacteus Circulus"; see *DNR* 18.2–4 and *DTR* 34.37–9). At least a few individual constellations and stars were known to the Anglo-Saxons as well.[105] The Anglo-Saxons also copied classical catalogues of stars, including Cicero's *Aratea*, which appeared in several early English manuscripts.[106]

The Anglo-Saxons show less interest in celestial measurements than their Carolingian contemporaries. On the Continent, manuscripts produced shortly after Ælfric and Byrhtferth's time contained texts (and related diagrams) by Calcidius and Martianus Capella that described eccentric solar orbits, solar epicycles, and even planets with circumsolar orbits; these appear to have come to England only later.[107] While the scientific value of this knowledge may seem clear to us, it neither helped medieval people calculate religious dates nor illustrated theological principles. Indeed, some of these ideas could undermine analogies between God and the visible cosmos. Anglo-Saxon writers neglected these scientific models in favour of ones that better sustained their understanding of the plenitude and order of creation.

Though Anglo-Saxon writers displayed interest in the stars and their religious implications, they were well aware that religious interpretations of astronomy could take a radical turn. Ælfric addresses the question,

---

104 Atherton, "The Sources of Ælfric's *De temporibus anni*," notes for the axis image Isidore, *DNR* 12.47–50, and Bede, *DNR* 5.8–13, both as certain sources; Bede, *DNR* 5.2–5 is listed as a certain source for the wheel. However, Ælfric's debts to Alfred are well known; *Fontes* shows Ælfric borrowing fourteen times from the *Boethius* and once from the *Pastoral Care* (with borrowings ranging from certain to possible). Alfredian uses of Bede and Isidore may have suggested their use here to Ælfric.

105 Stars and constellations named in multiple Anglo-Saxon texts include Ursa Major, called the *wæn* or *Carles wæn* in some texts and *Ursa* or Arcton in others; Boötes; the Pleiades; Sirius; and Orion (see the *Corpus* and Bede's Latin works for details). Bede also names the Hyades and Arcturus.

106 The *Aratea* travelled with Abbo's tractates on the planets in British Library Harley 2506 and appeared with cosmographical anthologies in Baltimore, Walters Art Gallery 73 and British Library, Cotton Tiberius B.V pt.1 (fols. 2–73 and 77–88) + Cotton Nero D.II fols. 238–41. Cambridge, Trinity College R.15.32 places the *Aratea* after Abbo's version of Helperic's computus. See Wallis, "Related Manuscripts," *The Calendar and the Cloister*, http://digital.library.mcgill.ca/ms-17/apparatus. php?page=related_manuscripts.

107 See Eastwood and Graßhoff, *Planetary Diagrams*.

apparently a live one in his time, of whether the sun, stars, and moon offer signs of a coming apocalypse. He begins *Catholic Homilies* 1.40 with a quotation from Luke 21.25: "Erunt signa in sole et luna et stellis. et reliqua" ("There shall be signs in the sun and moon and stars, and the rest [of the verse]," 40.3). He then argues that the signs seen thus far are natural phenomena such as eclipses, not the true extinguishing of the sun, moon, and stars that will be seen in the end times (40.32–54, with reference to Matthew 24.29–30).[108] His descriptions of solar and lunar eclipses resemble his own accounts in *De temporibus anni* (120–4); in each of his two texts, he draws on Bede's explanations (from *DNR* 22.2–4 or *DTR* 27.20–2).[109] Ælfric does not deny that celestial signs of the apocalypse may occur in the future; instead, he specifies them (40.46–54) and notes how they will differ from ordinary astronomical phenomena. Like Bede, he subjects claims about the environment to critical thinking, using Scripture as a basis for his critique.

Shooting stars and comets provoke similar interest. Bede explains, "Quamuis uideamus igniculos ex aethere lapsos portari uentis, uagique lumen sideris imitari, trucibus cito coorientibus uentis" (*DNR* 11.6–8; "However, we see little fires gliding, carried on winds from the ether, and they resemble the light of a wandering star, with wild winds arising suddenly"). Later he writes, "Cometae sunt stellae flammis crinitae" (*DNR* 24.2; "Comets are long-haired stars with flames"), using a classical formulation to name comets.[110] Ælfric avoids the traditional formula in favour of a little more explanation:

Comete sind gehatene þa steorran ðe færlice 7 ungewunelice æteowiað 7 sind geleomode swa þæt him gæð of se leoma swilce oðer sunbeam. Hi ne beoð na lange hwile gesewene, ac swa oft swa hi æteowiað hi gebicniað sum ðing niwes toweard þære leode ðe hi ofer scinað. (*DTA* 378–82)

("'Comets' is the name given to those stars which unexpectedly and strangely appear, and are so radiant that light comes off them like a second sunlight. They are not seen for long, but whenever they appear they signify something new towards the land over which they shine," trans. Blake, 93)

---

108 Godden, *Catholic Homilies*, Commentary to lines 37–51, pp. 336–7.
109 Godden, ibid., notes the passage in *DNR* (though not the one in *DTR*, which shares some of the same wording).
110 See Lewis and Short, *crinis*, definition II.

To modern minds, Ælfric's description seems a mix of science and superstition of the sort that he rejects in *Catholic Homily* 1.40. To Ælfric, however, science and superstition are not opposed categories, but the results of correct and incorrect readings of the same phenomena. God controls both nature and its signification; truths can be read in the natural world. When one reads correctly, one obtains *scientia*, "knowledge"; when one reads incorrectly, one has merely superstition, a set of beliefs informed by the pagan past or a misunderstanding of Christian tradition. Ælfric defines comets, giving them a Latin name and an English description to clarify, and then he speaks of their significance for human beings. He concludes that their courses are not for the unlearned to know (382–3) and moves on to a different topic. Even as he acknowledges that the comets have a "leohtbæran ryne" (383; "luminous course," trans. Blake 93) that, he implies, the learned could know, they do not behave independently of God. Their longer, more obscure courses may make them more appropriate divine heralds than the more predictable planets and familiar constellations. The *Anglo-Saxon Chronicle* implicitly takes a similar perspective, noting the appearances of comets in connection with other events in the same years, but offering no explanation of the workings of comets or of God.[111] The *Chronicle* ignores most other heavenly phenomena, only recording eclipses and not planetary or stellar motions. That the *Chronicle*, a series of year-by-year annals focused on kings, nobles, and church leaders in England, has any interest whatsoever in celestial events shows the importance of the heavens to many Anglo-Saxons. It fell to other writers to explain the movements of stars, planets, and comets in more detail; Bede, Ælfric, and Byrhtferth took up that work.

The Outer Reaches

The stars do not mark the farthest reaches of the cosmos for Anglo-Saxons, however. Beyond the starry heaven one can see, some accounts detail two more layers: the waters above the heavens, and the spiritual heaven. Bede explains that the higher or spiritual heaven contains angelic powers, spiritual beings who only put on corporeal bodies if they descend to our level,

---

111 References to comets appear in these annals (see the ASCCE): 677 (F)/678 (A, B, C, E); 729 (A, B, C, D, E, F); 891 (A)/892 (B, C, D); 905 (B and C, in the Mercian Register, D), 975 (A, B, C, D, E, F), 995 (C, D, E, F), 1066 (A, C, D); 1097 (E). The Old English *Bede* also contains a reference to a comet, 298.28–300.2.

then cast them off again as they rise (*DNR* 7.1–6). "Hoc Deus aquis glacialibus temperauit ne inferiora succenderet elementa. Dehinc inferius caelum non uniformi sed multiplici motu solidauit, nuncupans illud firmamentum propter sustentionem superiorum aquarum" ("This heaven God tempers with cold waters lest they incinerate the lower elements. From there the heaven below becomes solid not with uniform but variable motion; that is called the firmament because it holds up the higher waters," *DNR* 7.6–9). He writes that others, however, say these waters deluged the earth in the flood and serve to temper the fire of the stars (*DNR* 8.3–5).

Scriptural authority backs and probably suggested the model of waters above the heavens. God divides the waters in Genesis 1:7: "et fecit Deus firmamentum divisitque aquas quae erant sub firmamento ab his quae erant super firmamentum et factum est ita" ("And God made a firmament, and divided the waters that were under the firmament, from those that were above the firmament, and it was so," Douay-Rheims). Psalm 148:4–5 declares, "laudate eum caeli caelorum et aquae quae super caelos sunt / laudent nomen Domini" ("Praise him, ye heavens of heavens: and let all the waters that are above the heavens praise the name of the Lord," Douay-Rheims), a verse rendered in Old English, "Heriaþ hine heofonas heofona & wæteru þe ofer heofonas sind / Heriaþ naman drihtnes" ("Praise him, heavens of heavens, and let the waters which are over the heavens praise the name of the Lord").[112] St John's College MS 17, f. 39v, lists places in the universe in descending order:

> Sedes *sanctae* trinitatis et individue vnitatis ("Seat of the holy trinity and
>   singular unity")
> Caelum angelorum ("Heaven of the angels")
> Spatium aquarum ("Space of the waters")
> Firmamentv ("Firmament")[113]
> Olimpvs ("Olympus")
> Aether ("Ether")
> Aer ("Air")
> Terra ("Earth")
> Mare ("Sea")

---

112 See the *Old English Corpus* for this quotation and four other manuscripts that have very similar glosses on the same verses. Two extant Psalter canticles and one other gloss also contain variants.

113 *Sic*; the final 'm' of "firmamentum" has been omitted or replaced by a stylized dash.

Abyssys ("Abyss")
Infernus superior ("Higher hell")
Infernus inferior ("Lower hell")
Puteus inferni ("Pit of hell")[114]

Bede gives a similar list of the heavens but omits the waters above the heavens and inserts fire between Olympus and the firmament: "'Scinditur auricolor coeli septemplicis aether,' quorum haec sunt nomina, aer, aether, olympus, spatium igneum, firmamentum, coelum angelorum, et coelum Trinitatis" ("'The golden ether is divided into a sevenfold heaven,' of which these are the names: air, ether, Olympus, the region of fire, the firmament, the heaven of the angels, and the heaven of the Trinity").[115] The list in the St John's College manuscript descends while Bede's ascends, but the ordering of the heavens is fairly similar in each.

The model of higher and lower places is not confined to Latin sources. It appears in the vernacular in the Old English *Martyrology* for 19 March, the second day of creation:

On ðæm dæge God gescop ðone rodor betweoh heofone ond eorðan, ond betweoh ðæm twam sæum, ðæm uplican ond þæm niðerlican. Se uplica sæ is to þæm geseted þæt he celeð ðære tungla hæto, ðy læs heo to swiðe bærne þas nyþerlican gesceafte … (*Martyrology* 19 Mar)[116]

("On that day God made the firmament between heaven and earth and between the two seas, the upper and the lower. The upper sea is established so that it will cool the heat of the stars, lest it too greatly burn the lower creation …")

The Old English poem *Genesis* may allude to these waters in 150–3, and *Christ and Satan* in 5–6.[117] In the Vulgate, the Book of Daniel contains a

---

114 See *The Calendar and the Cloister*; http://digital.library.mcgill.ca/ms-17/folio.php?p=39v. I have expanded abbreviations and rendered hooked e as 'ae' in the quotation for ease of typography and reading.

115 Bede, *Expositio in primum librum Mosis, qui dicitur Hebraice Beresith, Graece autem Genesis*, PL 91 col. 192B–C.

116 *The Old English Martyrology: Edition, Translation, and Commentary*, ed. Christine Rauer, Anglo-Saxon Texts 10 (Cambridge: Brewer, 2013); translations here are my own.

117 For *Genesis*, see ASPR 1 and Krapp's notes, ASPR 1, 162; for *Christ and Satan*, see ASPR 1 and Finnegan's note in his own critical edition on page 91. Both editors refer to Genesis 1:7 as the source.

praise song from the youths in the fiery furnace that includes: "benedicite aquae omnes quae super caelos sunt Domino laudate et superexaltate eum in saecula" (3:60; "O all ye waters that are above the heavens, bless the Lord; praise and exalt him above all for ever," Douay-Rheims); the poems *Daniel* and *Azarias* render these lines into Old English.[118]

Conclusions

That spiritual heaven, the one above the waters where the Trinity and celestial powers reside, exceeds the scope of this study, which will now turn earthwards again.[119] We have seen that Anglo-Saxons created understandings of space as both order and plenitude. In most surviving texts, the earth lies at the centre of a spherical and divinely regulated universe, though Junius 11's illustrations, and perhaps even the poem *Genesis* itself, seem to present a flat earth in a spherical or semispherical cosmos. The nested sphere of earth inside the orbits of sun, moon, and planets; the more distant sphere of the zodiac; the waters above the firmament; and, finally, the celestial sphere all signify perfection and cycles of life and rebirth for Bede, Ælfric, and others. The earth's atmosphere (*aer* or *lyft*) provides a vital matrix for life, particularly birds but also demons, dragons – and Elijah and Enoch, awaiting the end of time. The space beyond our atmosphere contains celestial bodies and a light that earth's dense atmosphere prevents us from seeing.

That elusive light sparks further investigation among Anglo-Saxon writers, who studied the size, shape, and orbits of the sun and moon. Though they displayed less interest in the planets and stars than their Continental counterparts, the Anglo-Saxons established and handed down lore about these heavenly objects as well. In some of their models, the sun, like God, was the one true source of light, with all other apparent sources being mere

---

118 These poems seem to borrow from each other at times. Their handlings of this verse, at *Daniel* 364–6 and *Azarias* 73–6, differ, but they both render the simple *aquae* ("waters") as "hluttor wæter" ("clear water"). For *Daniel*, see ASPR 1; for *Azarias*, ASPR 3.

119 For a look primarily at earthly and interim paradises with some glances towards heaven, see Kabir, *Paradise, Death and Doomsday*. Foxhall Forbes gives some treatment of heaven in *Heaven and Earth*, esp. 313–23.

reflections. This view competed with the idea that stars have fire and light of their own. Either way, the sun was privileged and the solar system understood to be a rational, mathematical structure demonstrative of divine order. Study of the heavens, then, led to greater understanding of God. Bede and Ælfric even offer personal observations of particular astronomical matters, especially those involving the sun, moon, and tides, from the privileged site of England, whose northern location allows special insight that more southern peoples cannot experience directly.

Human sight cannot penetrate the farthest reaches of the cosmos. Beyond the stars, cold waters act as a kind of heat sink, preventing stellar heat from overpowering creation; here, Anglo-Saxon writers depend on Scripture as a foundation for their knowledge, because the evidence of their own eyes proves inadequate. Even farther lies the sphere in which the Trinity and angels reside. Though their eyes cannot have seen this place, our writers display complete confidence in its existence.

When what we would call outer space turns out to be full of light and even life, we should not be surprised that the earth itself teems with life of many kinds. The following chapters will explore how Anglo-Saxons constructed different types of spaces here on earth, how they characterized those spaces, and who inhabited them.

2 England, the Mediterranean, and Beyond

In early medieval world maps, Britain occupies a small space near the edge of the known world. In early world history, it plays little role. Many Anglo-Saxons would probably be unaware of their place in the world; as Margaret Bridges writes, "Of course the Anglo-Saxons were no closer to experiencing cosmic liminality than the Antipodeans were ever able to experience what it was like to be suspended upside down."[1] Yet texts could make that liminality clear to them. Nicholas Howe argues, "[Bede's] sense of living on a distant and isolated island came from having read Roman geographers, especially Pliny the Elder in his *Natural History*, who told him that he lived on a distant and isolated island."[2] Readers of Bede (and Gildas) would in turn be told that they were at the edge of the world.[3] Translations from Latin brought books rooted in the classical and late antique world to more people. Religious texts often dealt with events in the life of Christ, the apostles, or early Christian saints, transporting them to the Middle East and Rome. Most surviving Anglo-Saxon narrative poetry also takes place far from England. The audiences of these varied texts would find England relegated to the margins if it appeared at all. Whether they thought of themselves as Mercians, West Saxons, or even Anglo-Saxons, readers and hearers might see very little of themselves in these

---

1 Margaret Bridges, "Of Myths and Maps: The Anglo-Saxon Cosmographer's Europe," in *Writing & Culture*, ed. Balz Engler, Swiss Papers in English Language and Literature 6 (Tübingen: G. Narr, 1992), 72.

2 Nicholas Howe, "Rome: Capital of Anglo-Saxon England," *Journal of Medieval and Early Modern Studies* 34 (2004): 150.

3 Gildas emphasizes not only Britain's isolation but its coldness as a result, though he describes Christ as bringing light and warmth to the island; see Howe, "Rome," 151–2.

texts. Perhaps most Anglo-Saxons did not experience "cosmic liminality," but for some there must have been a dizzying moment of realizing that they *were* on the edge of the world known to classical and late antique authorities still revered and read in their own times. Bringing readers of *englisc* into dialogue with a broader Latin culture paradoxically risked making readers and hearers feel insignificant.

Such distancing would be in tension with the lived experience of the readers, for whom the centre might be where they lived, or perhaps where their king currently resided. Yi-Fu Tuan explains, "Human groups nearly everywhere tend to regard their own homeland as the centre of the world."[4] Anglo-Saxons would have heard about Rome and the pope, and the more educated among them certainly knew something of that great city's political and religious history; some had actually visited there or knew those who had.[5] Yet their world was around them, and to most, Rome must have seemed far off and marginal, Jerusalem distant and exotic. As Pierre Bourdieu writes,

> Because the dispositions durably inculcated by objective conditions ... engender aspirations and practices objectively compatible with those objective requirements, the most improbable practices are excluded, either totally without examination, as *unthinkable*, or at the cost of the *double negation* which inclines agents to make a virtue of necessity, that is, to refuse what is anyway refused and to love the inevitable.[6]

Bourdieu calls "that which is taken for granted" doxa: what everyone accepts without question.[7] Yet doxa for Anglo-Saxons was not reflected in most works written in Latin, while what might have otherwise been unthinkable to Anglo-Saxons had already been written in Latin – a world without their home. English works that used Latin sources also called doxa into question. What happened when "dispositions durably inculcated" by experience of the Anglo-Saxon world collided with the expectations of other worlds?

---

4 Tuan, *Space and Place*, 149.

5 See Howe, "Rome." For early English visitors and the impact that the city of Rome had on them and the people to whom they returned in England, see Éamonn Ó Carragáin, *The City of Rome and the World of Bede*, Jarrow Lecture 1994 (Jarrow: St Paul's Church, 1994).

6 Bourdieu, *Outline*, 77, his emphasis.

7 For doxa, see Bourdieu, *Outline*, 168.

Anglo-Saxons made room in their mental worlds for distant places and particularly for their inhabitants. Their interests lay in peoples and cultures far more than in location and topography. They sought to understand faraway places in terms of their residents and histories, and to transform abstract spaces into coherent places that had both elements alien to Anglo-Saxons and features familiar to them. They developed "imaginative geographies": "Representations of other places – of peoples and landscapes, cultures and 'natures' – that articulate the desires, fantasies and fears of their authors and the grids of power between them and their 'Others,'" in the words of Derek Gregory.[8] Those "grids of power" proved complex for the Anglo-Saxons, who envisioned a range of relations with different places inside and outside their own island.

This chapter will treat the construction of places known from Latin culture in English texts. First, it will show how texts could indeed make England appear insignificant. Then it will explore four strategies that translators and adaptors used to treat names of foreign peoples and places: omission, familiarization through repetition and connection, historical glossing, and emphasis on inhabitants. Old English texts brought their audiences closer to Rome and Jerusalem than we might expect, but they also brought them to places far beyond the Mediterranean that hosted fantastic inhabitants. From England to Rome to India, the Anglo-Saxons constructed place as a series of spaces made comprehensible through their connections to better-known places and to historical events. These places were never empty, but always inhabited.[9]

England at the Margins (or off the Edge)

The marginality of England is immediately evident on world maps. Early medieval maps were not navigation aids; instead, they were statements on theology, history, or some combination thereof.[10] The East was frequently at the top, and Jerusalem often represented "the civilized center of the

---

8 Derek Gregory, "Imaginative Geography," in *Dictionary of Human Geography*, ed. Gregory et al., 369–70.

9 Texts that circulated in early medieval England sometimes referred to uninhabitable zones of the earth, and so such spaces existed for the early English: see above, chapter 1, pp. 19–20. Yet little is said about them aside from the fact of their existence; Anglo-Saxons never make them into place.

10 Anna-Dorothee von den Brincken, "Europa in der Kartographie des Mittelalters," *Archiv für Kulturgeschichte* 55 (1973): 289–304.

Earth" according to David Woodward, although the convention of putting Jerusalem at the actual centre of the map was not fully established until the early twelfth century or later.[11] Maps and written descriptions tended to privilege eastern regions, "while the western and northern regions come last and least."[12] Jerusalem was usually one of the two most prominent cities on a map, the other being Rome.[13] Even maps that showed general outlines and named only a few specific places often named Rome and marked it as a walled city. Rome in the Anglo-Saxon era was both a religious centre and a city on a scale that dwarfed any settlement in England. Anglo-Saxons knew it for its empire but more for its religious importance as the heart of the Church and the seat of the pope.[14]

By contrast, the British Isles, when maps represent them at all, almost invariably appear as small shapes at or near the edge of the map.[15] Many *mappae* present Europe as a solid block, one of three sections in the orb of the world, and omit the British Isles entirely.[16] Many more wall maps

---

11 David Woodward, "Medieval *Mappaemundi*," in *The History of Cartography*, vol. 1: *Cartography in Prehistoric, Ancient, and Medieval Europe and the Mediterranean*, ed. J.B. Harley and David Woodward (Chicago: University of Chicago Press, 1987), 332; for centering on Jerusalem, see 340. The full volume is now available online at http://www.press.uchicago.edu/books/HOC/HOC_V1/Volume1.html. For the centring of maps around Jerusalem, see von den Brincken, "Europa," 294.

12 Bridges, "Of Myths and Maps," 71.

13 See Woodward, "Medieval *Mappaemundi*," 340, for maps centred on Jerusalem, Rome, or Mount Sinai. Although the Hereford Map is post-Anglo-Saxon, dating to about 1300, it is an excellent example of an early English map centred on Jerusalem and giving visual prominence to Jerusalem and Rome. The map is now available online at http://www.themappamundi.co.uk/, and Rome and Jerusalem are among the sites given special attention on the webpage. See also Scott Westrem, *The Hereford Map: A Transcription and Translation of the Legends with Commentary*, Terrarum Orbis 1 (Turnhout: Brepols, 2001), esp. section 6 and section 10 in the colour plates.

14 See the next chapter for Rome as empire and particularly as fallen empire.

15 See, for instance, Vat. lat. 6018, fols. 63v–64r, reproduced in Evelyn Edson's *Mapping Time and Space: How Medieval Mapmakers Viewed Their World*, British Library Studies in Map History 1 (London: The British Library, 1997), at 63. This rather odd map puts west at the top, and labels two islands as if they were seas: "mare mortun" ("sea of the dead") and "oceanus occiduus" ("western ocean." Edson, *Mapping*, 62). Other maps generally label those islands, if they name them at all, "Hibernia" and "Brittania." Many early maps travelled with manuscripts of Isidore of Seville. For instance, the map from Munich, Bayerische Staatsbibliothek, Clm 10058, f. 154v, dates to the eleventh century; see P.D.A. Harvey, *Medieval Maps* (Toronto: University of Toronto Press, 1991), 22.

16 See Woodward, "Medieval *Mappaemundi*," 297, 300–3, 343–7, and 350–5 for examples. See also chap. 1, note 13, on TO maps.

doubtless existed than are now extant, housed in palaces, churches, and monasteries.[17] Many Anglo-Saxons might thus have a visual awareness of England's place in the known world independent of texts. While no maps appear in extant copies of the texts treated in this chapter, some Anglo-Saxon writers and readers must have seen *mappae mundi*, which could only underscore a sense of Brittania as an island near the edge of the world.

At the same time, Nicholas Howe argues persuasively that the Anglo-Saxons constructed their world more in language than in maps.[18] Texts too often present England as marginal or entirely absent from the text's envisioned world. Jacqueline Stodnick observes that classical texts call the whole island "Brittania" and do not distinguish inhabitants or kingdoms; she writes, "Anglo-Saxon authors inherited a Latin geographical nomenclature 'without England' in many senses."[19] She finds that Bede shifts easily from referring to the whole island as "Brittania" to using the term only for the part inhabited by the *Angli*, as he calls them – and *Angli*, to further complicate matters, sometimes seem to indicate all the English and sometimes just Northumbrians.[20] Alfred the Great and his circle use the term *Angelcynn* for both the land and the people; *Engla lond* came into common usage only in the eleventh century. Sharon Rowley shows that the Old English *Bede*, a vernacular translation of Bede's Latin *Ecclesiastical History of the English People* done around the same time as the Alfredian translations or a little later, does not use the terminology of the Alfredian texts but instead several different names for the people in question, with a preference for *Ongelþeod*.[21] She argues that the term more likely meant a

---

17   See Woodward, "Medieval *Mappaemundi*," appendix 18.2 (359–68) for a list of major medieval *mappae mundi*, some of which are no longer extant. Others have doubtless been lost with no record.

18   See Howe, *Writing the Map of Anglo-Saxon England*.

19   Stodnick, "Writing Home: Place and Narrative in Anglo-Saxon England," PhD dissertation (University of Notre Dame 2002), 82.

20   Stodnick, "Writing Home," 82–96. Stephen Harris, by contrast, argues that when Bede writes "Angli," he means specifically Angles and not other Germanic peoples in England; see especially chapter 2, "The Election of the Angles," in his *Race and Ethnicity in Anglo-Saxon Literature*, Studies in Medieval History and Culture (New York: Routledge, 2003), 45–82. (Bede usually spells "Brittania" with two "t"s and one "n"; other classical and medieval sources often spell it "Britannia.")

21   For details about *gentes* names in the Old English *Bede*, see Sharon M. Rowley, *The Old English Version of Bede's "Historia ecclesiastica,"* Anglo-Saxon Studies 16 (Woodbridge, UK, and Rochester, NY: Boydell and Brewer, 2011), esp. 57–70. Rowley finds that the text "uses about twenty different translations for Bede's *gens Anglorum*,"

specific group of people rather than all the Anglo-Saxons as a unity. The translator only very rarely refers to England as a place. Thus, Old English translations of the late ninth and early to mid-tenth century were made for a people for whom translators were still developing a collective name, a people sidelined on maps and in histories and not always conceived as one people. Yet what we now call "the Anglo-Saxons" shared a language (albeit with multiple dialects), texts in that language, an island, and a set of relations to the rest of the world.

Scholars vary in how they treat the isolation of medieval England. Asa Simon Mittman argues in *Maps and Monsters in Medieval England* that the English felt themselves to be marginalized, even monstrous, and so sought Others more monstrous, thereby making themselves more central and normal:

> The medieval English were continually constructing monsters against which they might wage imagined struggles, behind which they might hide and through which they might define their very identity. Somewhere between God and the devil, angel and animal, the English struggled to maintain their distance from the natural world, but also from the supernatural and even unnatural world of strange, half-glimpsed beings they envisioned around themselves.[22]

Where Mittman emphasizes opposition and Othering, Kathy Lavezzo sees the English constructing England's marginality more positively:

> Built into that myth of a sublime English frontier was a related, imperial dream. If their otherworldliness made the English exceptional, their exceptionalism might also suggest how the English should be rightful masters of the earth itself. The exaltation of the English world margin, in other words, could authorize the expansion of England beyond its borders, into the world.[23]

---

most commonly *Ongolþeod* (fifty-four occurrences, including spelling variants; see 68). She finds the number of occurrences of the two most common people-names for the Anglo-Saxons "too small to foster any sense of community" (69). *Ongelcyn* is used "occasionally" to name the land but *Engla lond* only twice; *Breotone* is preferred, naming the island ninety-five times. She concludes that the island is conceived primarily as a group of peoples, not a unified people (69). Rowley also argues that the translation was independent of Alfred's programme.

22 *Maps and Monsters in Medieval England*, 208–9.
23 *Angels on the Edge of the World*, 21.

Lavezzo's study extends into the early modern era. Though Middle English texts that imagine Arthur as the ruler of a Continental empire show the idea in the later Middle Ages, Anglo-Saxons found value in their position in the known world without imagining a future English empire.[24]

While Mittman and Lavezzo interpret Anglo-Saxons' reactions to their own perceptions of marginality differently than I do, we all agree that their place on the edge of the known world did not go unremarked by Anglo-Saxons themselves. Mittman and Lavezzo provide useful explorations of aspects of Anglo-Saxon constructions of their own identity. I argue, however, that most texts did not primarily create Others to distinguish the English; rather, they forged connections between Anglo-Saxons and other peoples. This chapter will show how Anglo-Saxons encountered other places and peoples textually. Space was never empty and abstract but narrative and populated, even beyond earth, as the previous chapter demonstrated. The Anglo-Saxons came into contact with many different places: the more we learn from archaeology, the more we have to broaden our ideas of how far Anglo-Saxon connections stretched. Most Anglo-Saxons would never trade with someone from Rome or Jerusalem, let alone go to those places. Yet they would have heard of these cities and of far less famous places. The *Anglo-Saxon Chronicle* refers to trips to Rome, Francia, Scotland, visitors from Ireland, and invaders and later settlers from Scandinavia.

Recent archaeological work has tended to focus more on local and regional trade, but Anglo-Saxon England certainly imported wine, precious metals, oil, pottery, and stone from Francia (modern France and Germany), Scandinavia, and sometimes farther afield.[25] The most frequent exchanges took place with Francia and Rome. England exported salt and cloth to the

---

24 David A.E. Pelteret argues, however, that seeds of later English empire can be seen after the Norman Conquest in the founding of an Anglo-Saxon colony on the Black Sea and other adventures in the Mediterranean and beyond, "Eleventh-Century Anglo-Saxon Long-Haul Travelers: Jerusalem, Constantinople, and Beyond," in *The Maritime World of the Anglo-Saxons*, ed. Stacy S. Klein, William Schipper, and Shannon Lewis-Simpson, Medieval and Renaissance Texts and Studies 448, Essays in Anglo-Saxon Studies 5 (Tempe: Arizona Center for Medieval and Renaissance Studies, 2014), 128.

25 For imports and exports in Anglo-Saxon England from about 650–900, see John Naylor, *An Archaeology of Trade in Middle Saxon England*, BAR British Series 376 (Oxford: Archaeopress, 2004). Naylor focuses primarily on regional trade but intersperses mentions of trade with the Continent.

former, while contact with Rome was essential for the church and for kings of important regions and then, from Edward the Elder on, kings of a united England. Coins found in the south and west of England may be souvenirs of pilgrimages to Compostella, and a hoard of pennies from Æthelred II found in northern Spain also supports the idea of Anglo-Saxon pilgrimage to Spain.[26] Islamic coins brought to England in the Anglo-Saxon period suggest a broader Mediterranean context. Many of the silver dirhams have been found in areas controlled by Danes, and those finds drop off after Wessex took control of the Danelaw in the early tenth century, suggesting that many of the coins were brought by Scandinavians and not native Anglo-Saxons.[27] Some of those Scandinavians settled in England, bringing knowledge of the Islamic world, and certain finds indicate additional Anglo-Saxon links to Islam. A late-eighth-century imitation dinar struck under Offa imitates an Abbasid dinar dated to 773.[28] Much remains unknown about the dinar: how many were made, whether they were intended for use in England or abroad, and whether another imitation dinar that does not have the inscription "Offa rex" was also by Offa.[29] The existence of this and scattered other gold dinars and silver dirhams placed among earlier finds or in areas not controlled by Scandinavians suggest multiple ties to the Islamic world. Anglo-Saxon pilgrims even on occasion visited the Holy Land.[30] Katharine Scarfe Beckett writes that a number of trade goods, as common as pepper and as valuable as silk and blue dye, may have originated as far away as India and certainly came through Islamic lands.[31] Anglo-Saxon England had connections with much of the world known to the West in the Middle Ages; those connections were far stronger and denser with some areas than with others, but early England was not as "insular" as we may now sometimes think.

When classical and late antique history, contemporary world trade, and the Anglo-Saxon present met, writers and translators had to find strategies to deal with the great differences in perspective between the world views

---

26 Rory Naismith, "Islamic Coins from Early Medieval England," *Numismatic Chronicle* 165 (2005): 207–8.

27 Naismith, "Islamic Coins."

28 Ibid., 196–7.

29 Ibid.

30 See Katharine Scarfe Beckett, *Anglo-Saxon Perceptions of the Islamic World*, CSASE 33 (Cambridge: Cambridge University Press, 2003), esp. 44–54; Pelteret, "Eleventh-Century Anglo-Saxon Long-Haul Travelers," 75–129; and Naismith, "Islamic Coins," 208.

31 Scarfe Beckett, *Anglo-Saxon Perceptions*, esp. 60–8.

of the Roman empire or of the Bible and those of the authors themselves
and their readers. Thus, translations of Latin texts into Old English and
retellings of biblical stories are particularly valuable. The works of Alfred
and his circle – the Old English *Orosius*, *Dialogues*, *Pastoral Care*,
Boethius, *Soliloquies*, and Prose Psalms of the Paris Psalter – all invoke
non-English geography in ways that reward careful reading. The Old
English *Bede* engages with geography outside the British Isles as well as
within. Homilies, saints' lives, and Old English poems also take place in
the Mediterranean world, particularly the Holy Land and environs.
While we cannot always identify every place or people name with certainty, scholars have located the vast majority with some assurance, particularly in prose.[32] Across genres, Anglo-Saxon authors keep returning
to the Mediterranean.

Readers of Orosius's history would find no mention of England as such,
and even audiences of the Old English *Orosius* would feel their marginality strongly at times. This rendering of Paulus Orosius's late antique
Historiarum adversus paganos libri vii (*Seven Books of Histories against
the Pagans*) begins with a geography of the world outlining the three continents. Ireland forms the boundary of Europe (9.10 and 19.5), placing
Brittania just inside the bounds.[33] Brittania receives two brief mentions in
the geography derived from the Latin (12.19 and 18.26–7). Then the translator gives more details about each continent: the text lists hundreds of
place and people names, all from Orosius's point of view, sometimes expressed by "we" or "Orosius" within the text.[34] Europe's boundaries begin: "From þære ie Danais west oþ Rin þa ea, seo wilð of þæm beorge þe
mon Alpis hætt 7 irnð þonne norþryhte on þæs garsecges earm þe þæt
lond uton ymblið þe mon Bryttania hætt, 7 eft suþ oð Donua þa ea …"
("From the river Don west until the river Rhine, [Europe] runs from the
range called the Alps and runs then to the north and into the arm of the sea

---

32 For more details about my methodology and the difficulties of counting names,
    see notes 44 and 48 below.
33 *The Old English Orosius*, ed. Janet M. Bately, EETS ss 6 (London: Oxford University
    Press, 1980). Subsequent primary citations will be parenthetical, in the form (page
    number.line number). For the Latin text, see *Orose: Histoires (contre les Païens)*, ed.
    and trans. Marie-Pierre Arnaud-Lindet, 2nd ed., 3 vols. (Paris: Belles Lettres, 2003).
34 See Mary Kate Hurley, "Alfredian Temporalities: Time and Translation in the Old English
    Orosius," *JEGP* 112.4 (2013): 405–32, for the complex construction of a narrator called
    Orosius who makes statements that readers could sometimes recognize as ones the
    historical Orosius could never have made.

which lies around that land that one calls Brittania, and again south until the river Danube ..." 12.17–20).[35] Britain is literally nothing to write home about, receiving only a brief mention before the description returns to more central places such as Greece and Germania.

Even that brief mention is added by the translator, who has put in "Bryttania" where Paulus Orosius named "Galliam Belgicam" (Belgic Gaul, 1.2.52).[36] From the start, the Latin model proved inadequate for the Anglo-Saxon translator, so he modified his source. In many cases, only a reader with both texts at hand would realize the difference – and presumably most readers of the Old English would not possess or be able to read the Latin very well. Next, the *Orosius* launches into a series of particulars about Germania that do not derive from the Latin (12.24–13.28). As Janet Bately notes, it "seems to describe the area as it was known in the second half of the ninth century."[37] Britain later reappears in a few sentences that describe its dimensions, its relation to Ireland and Thule, and its weather (18.26–7, 19.11–20). Yet unlike the description of German lands, this later passage relies heavily upon the Latin and includes inaccurate information.[38] Britain's peoples are not listed, unlike in other parts of Europe, which receive more detail. Are the British Isles like Thule, too distant to be known? Or did the translator find it unnecessary to describe his people's own land to them? The first possibility suggests close adherence to the source text; the second does not require such closeness. Considering that the translator has already added Britain to the text once and cuts the main body of the text from seven books to six, I suggest that the translator was not being especially faithful to the source text but instead found the insertion of Brittania near the start of the passage on Europe sufficient. English readers of the Latin text would see very little of their homeland

---

35 Translations are my own, but I am indebted to Bately's excellent Glossaries for the *Orosius*. For changes to the geographical perspective in the Old English version, see Salvador Insa Sales, "The Treatment of Some Spanish Matters in the Old English *Orosius*," *SELIM* 9 (1999): 173–9; and especially Irmeli Valtonen's richly detailed *The North in the Old English Orosius: A Geographical Narrative in Context*, Mémoires de la Société Néophilologique de Helsinki 73 (Helsinki: Société Néophilologique, 2008).

36 *Orose*, ed. and trans. Arnaud-Lindet.

37 Bately, *Orosius*, notes to 12.23, 166–7, quotation at 166; see Valtonen's *North in the Old English Orosius*, 99–100 and 320–54, for more detail on the places named.

38 Bately adds, "In mitigation, it may be pointed out that [the OE *Orosius's*] inaccurate description of the position and size of Britain continued to be accepted well into the late Middle Ages"; *Orosius*, notes to 19.11–20, p. 206.

throughout the text. They would find their current homeland and Continental roots reflected in the geography largely because of changes made by the translator, but apart from a pair of inserted interviews, they would still find their island a small and unimportant part of the world.[39]

After the geographical introduction, the *Orosius* dives into history. Its attention, unsurprisingly, remains outside England, just as in the Latin source. Each chapter opens with a date "Ær ðæm ðe Romeburh getimbred wære" ("Before the city of Rome was built") followed by the number of years in book 1; in book 2, section 3, the formula becomes "Æfter þæm þe Romeburg getimbred wæs" ("After the city of Rome was built") and remains that way for the rest of the work. The founding of Rome provides the pivot from which all other events are dated. The Mediterranean and lands around it offer room for history to unfold in that time. Book 1 is largely biblical, involving mainly Assyria, Egypt, and Israel; book 2 concerns the founding and early days of Rome; book 3 still centres on Rome, but includes Laecedemon and Persia, and follows the adventures of Alexander the Great for a time; books 4 through 6 focus upon Rome, its wars, and its foreign affairs.[40] Britain receives few mentions: Julius Caesar's conquest gets ten lines in the Old English version (126.1–10), the later battles of Severus with the Picts and Scots merit almost four (142.11–14), reference to Constantius puts Brittania in the picture for a little over a page in the edition (147.3–8.9), and Britain elects Maximianus emperor in another two lines (153.28–9). Thus, Britain is mentioned in four passages totalling less than two pages in Bately's 156-page edition of the text. God has planned four empires, one in each direction. The last of these, Rome, is contemporary for Orosius; but, as Malcolm Godden writes, Anglo-Saxons thought that it too had fallen well before the ninth century.[41] There is no room for further empires, and Britain is of no interest to the first three and of only slight interest to the fourth.

Much of the *Orosius* reduces Britain to a speck. Virtually all places and events described lie outside the British Isles, and even within the islands, Ireland and Scotland receive as much attention as what will become England. The accounts of England in Old English and Latin concern not

---

39 For the insertion of the accounts of Ohthere and Wulfstan, which recentre the *Orosius* briefly in the North, see the next chapter.

40 The Old English condenses the seven books of the Latin *Historiarum* into six.

41 Malcolm R. Godden, "The Anglo-Saxons and the Goths: Rewriting the Sack of Rome," *ASE* 31 (2002): 47–68, esp. 64.

Anglo-Saxons, of whom Orosius himself did not know, but Scots, Irish, and Britons. England does not exist in world geography, and the Anglo-Saxons do not appear in this world history. The *Orosius*'s presentation of history as based on Paulus Orosius's Latin work must come into conflict with the doxa of its Anglo-Saxon audience's perceptions of history, their lived experience of a history that includes them.[42]

Nor is the *Orosius* the only text with a firm Mediterranean grounding to be translated by Alfred the Great and his circle. Wærferth's *Dialogues*, one of the earliest translations produced by Alfred's circle, renders a text written by Gregory the Great with the stated purpose of demonstrating that saints and miracles can still be found in Gregory's time – in Italy, where every anecdote takes place.[43] Anglo-Saxons looking to the text for reassurance that God still works among His people may have found a paradox in that those people among whom God worked all lived in a distant land in an earlier era. Even translations less obviously dependent upon place reminded Anglo-Saxons that they were not at the centre. Almost a hundred mentions of two dozen different places and peoples in or near the Holy Land fill the main text of the *Pastoral Care*, while England never appears.[44] The Old English *Boethius* contains a surprising degree of geographical and historical detail, with nearly thirty place and

---

42 The added accounts of Ohthere and Wulfstan briefly recentre geography on the North and allow English readers to find themselves in a text about great empires; their reports will be discussed in the next chapter.

43 The stories also must predate Gregory's death in 604, so they are removed from Anglo-Saxons chronologically as well as geographically. *Bischof Wærferths von Worcester.* On the continuing interest this text held for Anglo-Saxons, see David F. Johnson, "Divine Justice in Gregory the Great's *Dialogues*," in *Early Medieval Studies in Memory of Patrick Wormald*, ed. Stephen David Baxter et al., Studies in Early Medieval Britain (Farnham, Eng.: Ashgate, 2009), 115–28; and his "Alfredian Apocrypha," in *A Companion to Alfred the Great*, ed. Nicole Guenther Discenza and Paul E. Szarmach, Brill Companions to the Christian Tradition 58 (Leiden: Brill, 2015), 368–95.

44 Almost all frequency data come from the *Old English Corpus* or have been checked against it. The main exception is the *Boethius*, which I used as a case study. I read carefully through the prose-only and the prosimetrum versions myself, checking place and people names against those in the Latin source text. Some other Old English texts have been spot-checked against their sources. On the verse preface, see my "Alfred's Verse Preface to the *Pastoral Care* and the Chain of Authority," *Neophilologus* 85 (2001): 625–33, rpt. in *Classical and Medieval Literature Criticism*, vol. 79 (Detroit: Thomson Gale, 2006), 79–84. "English" is mentioned in only two places in the main text, and then as a language, not a people: Alfred uses the phrase "on Englisc" before he supplies a translation or synonym for another word or name at 139.15 and 367.5.

people-names occurring more than 50 times.[45] Its history is almost purely classical, from an account of the Golden Age (chapter 15) to many references to Roman emperors and a few to other Mediterranean powers. These late antique works generally leave no space for England.[46]

Like prose translations and many homilies, poetry often attends to distant places, and a number of Old English poems emphasize the Mediterranean as a centre of civilization. Most biblically based poems, unsurprisingly, are set in the Holy Land and environs.[47] Indeed, roughly half of the places or peoples named in poems ranging from *Andreas* to *Widsith* are located in the Middle East.[48] *Genesis* provides a good example. The poem starts in paradise, even naming its four rivers (ASPR 1, 222–34) before abandoning geographical specificity for generations, until Noah's ark makes landfall in Armenia (1423). A variety of names then transport readers to far distant locations, faithfully preserving many of the place and people names from the Old Testament. Over twenty different places are named more than seventy times in total, ranging from sites that must have seemed familiar, such as Egypt and Bethlehem, to those that may have

---

45 *The Old English Boethius*, ed. Godden and Irvine. For the sake of convenience, I cite the prose-only B-text unless otherwise specified; the prosimetrum C-text concurs except as noted. I use Godden and Irvine's translation unless otherwise noted, giving chapter and line number for the text (all in volume 1) and the volume and page number for the translation. People and place names occur 51 times in the B-text and 72 times in the C-text, whose Metres often repeat names.

46 Earlier editors such as Walter John Sedgefield have taken "bretene" (CM 20.99) as Britain, capitalizing the word accordingly, *King Alfred's Old English Version of Boethius De Consolatione Philosophiae* (Oxford: Clarendon Press, 1899). Godden and Irvine argue convincingly that "a reference to Britain would be singularly inappropriate in this context (a general account of natural growth in spring, in a hymn to God supposedly spoken by Boethius in prison in Italy), and it seems more likely that it is a form of the poetic adjective *bryten* 'broad, spacious,'" vol. 2, 235. Thanks to Paul E. Szarmach and Malcolm Godden for bringing this textual note to my attention.

47 *Genesis* (except for the parts set in heaven and hell) takes place in the Middle East, as do *Exodus*, *Judith*, the Psalms, *Daniel*, the three *Christ* poems, and *Christ and Satan*. Poems set in New Testament times or concerning early Christians such as *Andreas*, *The Fates of the Apostles*, *Juliana*, and even *Elene* also make the Mediterranean central, though some venture well away from that region – *Andreas* leaves Achaia for Mermedonia, *Elene* ranges from Germania to Rome to Jerusalem, and *Fates* disperses the apostles from Achaia to Ethiopia and India. "Middle East" is obviously a modern place term, but it is a useful shorthand for lands that appear in the Bible and near the centre of detailed TO maps in the early Middle Ages.

48 Over 500 of the more than 1000 people or place names I found are in the Middle East. I compiled a list of place names in poetry using the Anglo-Saxon Poetic Records with a few substitutions for the ASPR: For *Beowulf*, I used Klaeber 4. For the *Metres of*

seemed obscure, such as Pherezeus. The combination brings the distant space to life, inviting readers to connect the poem to other stories they already know (including from the life of Jesus) and then to feel that they have extended their geographical knowledge with places unknown outside of *Genesis*. England has no place in this wide-ranging poem, nor does it in any of the other poems based on Scripture, stories of the apostles after Christ's ascension (*Andreas*, *Fates of the Apostles*), or accounts of the achievements of early Christians (*Elene*). Even poems that are not strictly narrative sometimes refer to specific places in the Middle East: the *Metrical Psalms* frequently refer to Israel and its neighbours, *Seasons for Fasting* invokes Horeb and the Israelites, and *Widsith*'s list of people includes the Assyrians (*Exsyringum*, *Widsith* 82), Hebrews or Israelites (*Ebreum*, 83; *Israhelum*, 82), Medes (*Moidum*, 84), Persians (*Persum*, 85); and possibly the Elamites (*Eolum*, 87), Moabites (*Mofdingum*, 85), and Tyrians (*Eastþringum*, 86).[49] Places or peoples in the Middle East are named more than 500 times in poetry, as opposed to the seventy-five mentions of places or peoples in Britain.[50] Rome, the Holy Land, and North Africa dominate the landscape of narrative poetry.[51]

Boethius, I used *The Old English Boethius*, cited in full above. I added the D and E variants of the *Chronicle*'s "Death of Edgar" from the ASCCE. I found 1035 people and place names in poetry; the numbers remain somewhat approximate because some names cannot be identified with certainty. A small number could be names of peoples or simply descriptions, such as *Ælmyrcna* (*Andreas* 432) or *Guðmerce* (*Exodus* 59, ASPR 1), for which see below, pp. 158–9. A few cannot be located: Mermedonia might be in the Mediterranean, but it may not. *Widsith* lists nine different peoples who cannot be identified; see *Old English Minor Heroic Poems*, ed. Joyce Hill, Durham and St Andrews Medieval Texts 4 (Durham and Fife: Universities of Durham and St Andrews, 1983).

49 Editors are confident of the identifications of Israhelum as Israelites, Exsyringum as Assyrians, Moidum as Medes, and Persum as Persians; see Hill, *Minor Heroic Poems*. The Ebreum would seem clearly to be Hebrews, but why name them right after naming Israelites? From there, identification becomes increasingly uncertain. Hill tentatively identifies the Mofdingum as Moabites; the Amothingum could be the Ammonites, she writes, but they could also be Amorites, Amals, or Amðingas. The Eolum might be Elamites; the Idumingum, Idumeans or Edomites. I used ASPR 3 for the text of *Widsith* and ASPR 6 for *Seasons for Fasting*.

50 Places elsewhere in Europe (not counting Britain) receive nearly 400 mentions in poetry; these will be treated in the next chapter.

51 Africa appears eight times. Ethiopia or Ethiopeans appear thirteen additional times in Old English (*ethio-* or *sylh-*). Most mentions of Egypt and the Nile come in biblical narratives, particularly in *Genesis* and *Exodus*, so they are excluded here to be counted with the Middle East or Holy Land. Anglo-Saxons may, however, have thought of Egypt in connection with both Africa and the Holy Land.

Thus, prose and poetic texts frequently depicted Rome or the Holy Land as the centre of civilization. Actions that have consequences for the world as a whole originate in those places. England appears rarely in most of the texts mentioned in this section. The survivals of so many works set in distant places suggest that readers treasured these writings that enabled them to construct a wider picture of the world, allowing them to supplement their lived experience with virtual or textual experience. The Alfredian texts mentioned above were copied and show signs of use well after their time of translation.[52] The copying, recopying, and use of these texts indicate that Anglo-Saxons were not put off by a world that did not seem to reflect their own, but on the contrary were attracted to the distant places of classical and biblical history. The poems' importance to audiences is harder to know because the vast majority of Anglo-Saxon poetry, including biblical poems, survives only in one copy. Most extant poems were probably composed before 1000, but now exist only in copies made around the first millennium. How many readers any of these poems had, how many other copies might once have existed, whether these poems were performed aloud before or after being written, we cannot know. Though little evidence exists for how individual poems were experienced, the popularity of biblical themes and foreign places in multiple poems indicates that Anglo-Saxons had intellectual investments in foreign places, particularly biblical lands. Being able to read about these sites in their own language simultaneously reminded Anglo-Saxons how far they lived from the action and connected them to it in a special way. They did not have to be able to comprehend the languages of these distant places to know about them.

Anglo-Saxons reading or hearing a wide range of genres could find England relegated to the margins or completely missing from the mental world that texts created. Those who read Latin texts would have an additional, linguistic reminder of Rome's importance. England's place could have appeared insignificant in a world where great events in religion and history occurred mostly in the Middle East and Italy. Yet Anglo-Saxons translating and retelling these stories, and adding their own, found ways to connect their audiences with foreign places. The next chapter will show how such writers maintained England's importance in a variety of texts.

---

52 For manuscript information on each of the Alfredian texts used in their chapter, see the editions cited and the chapters on individual texts in *A Companion to Alfred the Great*, ed. Discenza and Szarmach.

The rest of this chapter will examine the ways in which they dealt with distant spaces in their texts and made their readers and hearers feel comfortable with places around the Mediterranean.

From England to the Mediterranean and Beyond

Anglo-Saxon writers frequently use four specific strategies to adapt texts of distant places for audiences in England. The most obvious strategy is that of omission: names of foreign peoples and places can be left out as texts are translated so that readers need not struggle with them. A second strategy is to repeat such names, following the source text or even adding references, so that these names become familiar to audiences. If twenty-first-century readers are not troubled by an inability to identify a distant people or country quickly on a map, Anglo-Saxons, with no Internet and far fewer graphic representations of the world, could surely feel comfortable with places whose names they had read but to which they could not point.[53] A third, related strategy is to connect names to history to assist readers' sense of recognition. A fourth strategy is to concentrate on who or what lives in a place. Recognition, by whichever strategy it comes, confers its own special pleasures: a sense of satisfaction and even "well-being" in the comfort felt with the art at hand.[54] Increasing recognition also enables a kind of appropriation: as Derek Gregory explains, "Imaginative geographies circulate in material forms (including novels, paintings, photographs …) which become sedimented over time to form an internally structured and, crucially, self-reinforcing *archive*."[55] Writers and readers together become maintainers of that archive, controlling knowledge where they could not control the place itself. Only the first strategy described here does not support the archive, and it is not one of the most used.

---

53 Googling for "geography quiz" turns up many quizzes that one can take online. Most of these not only supply one's individual score at the end but also compare it to that of other quiz takers. A quick perusal of such scores should demonstrate that even people interested enough to take geography quizzes voluntarily make frequent mistakes involving places that figure regularly in the news. We should not expect Anglo-Saxons to be better versed in geography than we are.

54 Pierre Bourdieu, *The Rules of Art: Genesis and Structure of the Literary Field*, trans. Susan Emanuel (Stanford, CA: Stanford University Press, 1996), 319–22.

55 Gregory, "Imaginative Geography," 371, his emphasis.

Omission

One strategy by which writers handle foreign places or peoples is omission. This strategy cannot work for all texts. Histories make little sense with places deleted: the *Orosius* and the Old English *Bede*, for instance, can only omit place names when they omit the events set in those places. Both texts do in fact engage in this strategy, but the geographical element seems secondary. The *Orosius* and *Bede* abridge their Latin source texts not to deal with problems of place but in the course of reshaping the narrative for other purposes.[56]

Omitting geographical names seems more logical for other texts. The *Boethius* delves into philosophical questions: why do good people suffer? What is true good? Do we truly possess free will? Next to these questions, problems of geography and history should seem insignificant. Readers learn from the Latin *De consolatione* that the narrator, Boethius, has been imprisoned in exile in Ravenna (1p4.17).[57] The translator, however, never tells his readers that the *Boethius*'s narrator is in Ravenna: the place name matters far less than the fact of imprisonment, which the Old English conveys as well as the Latin. Indeed, almost thirty names of places and peoples that appear in the Latin do not appear in the Old English. Some names might confuse readers or require explanations, thus distracting readers from the major points of a difficult text. Nineteen of these geographical names appear in passages that are not translated at all or are greatly shortened, such as Boethius's defence of himself in book 1, prose 4; virtually

---

56 For the treatment of the narratives in these Old English histories, see especially Janet Bately's "Treatment of the Sources" in the introduction to her edition, *The Old English Orosius*, xciii–c; Malcolm R. Godden, "The Old English *Orosius* and Its Sources," *Anglia* 129 (2011): 297–320; Rohini Jayatilaka, "The Sources of Orosius, *History against the Pagans* (Cameron C.B.9.2)," in *Fontes* (2001); and Rowley, *Old English Version*.

57 Moreover, a Latin *vita* tells some readers before they start the text, "apud Rauennam custodiae mancipatus est" ("he was taken into custody at Ravenna"). See Godden and Irvine, *Boethius*, vol. 2, 249, for this *vita*, which they have labeled Ia. This particular *vita* is extant now only in one eleventh-century manuscript, but they find it to be the one most closely matching the information in the openings of both the prose and the prosimentrum *Boethius*. Ravenna is also named in another *vita* (extant only later) that shares some details with this opening; see my paper "The Unauthorized Biographies of Anicius Manlius Severinus Boethius," *The Alfredian Boethius Project*, 9 Dec. 2003 (available at http://www.english.ox.ac.uk/boethius/Symposium2003.html). Godden and Irvine note that details were available elsewhere as well (*Boethius*, vol. 2, 249).

none of this chapter is rendered in the Old English, and all five place names are thus omitted. Several more are omitted from otherwise translated passages. For instance, when Boethius tells the story of Circe, he describes two of the animals into which Odysseus's men turn as "Marmaricus leo" ("African lion," 4m3.11) and "tigris … Indica" ("Indian tiger," 4m3.15). The Old English keeps the animal names but omits the place names; they become just "leon" ("lion," 38.31) and "þam deorcynne þe mon hat tigris" (38.34–5; "that kind of animal that is called 'tiger,'" trans. Godden and Irvine, vol. 2, 75). By omitting the names of peoples and places, the narrator can concentrate on crucial elements of an anecdote or argument without risking the confusion of unexplained proper nouns or the tedium of explicating minor points.

The example of the *Boethius* holds for other translated texts, including the *Orosius*, the Old English *Bede*, the *Dialogues*, and even the *Soliloquies*: translators generally only omit the names of distant peoples or places when they are omitting whole passages. They do not often keep narratives or illustrations stripped of their geographical details. We find similar practices in homilies treating specific saints and poems dealing with biblical and historical texts. Where place or people names are omitted, they tend to be less familiar ones. While omitting names of distant places might have helped Anglo-Saxons avoid a sense of marginalization in literature in their own language, authors and translators did not use that strategy as a major way of dealing with geography in their texts.

The strategy of omission seems most practical for some translators and adapters of Latin texts, but none of the ones I examined use it exclusively; all retain at least some people and place names. A second strategy, repetition of names in different contexts, with different modifiers, or in connection with different places, helps readers create a web of associations that brings a sense of familiarity, the "self-reinforcing archive" that Derek Gregory described.

Repetition and Connection

Familiarization through repetition and connection helps readers feel at ease with distant places or peoples. In some texts, authors connect faraway places with England or Britain; more often, connections are made between one distant place and another. Place names arise in many of the translations associated with Alfred and his court. These texts concern not so much geography as history (the *Orosius*), philosophy (*Boethius* and *Soliloquies*), theology and pastoral care (*Pastoral Care* and *Dialogues*), and

sacred scripture (the Prose Psalms). Wonder texts, particularly if taken as
a group, associate even exotic peoples and places with other peoples and
places to help readers fix them in a mental archive. Some religious narrative poems, such as *Daniel*, *Genesis*, and *Elene*, also retain geographical
items and endow them with meaning by repeating them and linking them
to other, sometimes more familiar place or people names. Anglo-Saxon
texts give special attention to Rome and Jerusalem as centres of learning
and religion.

The *Orosius*'s geographical introduction is unparalleled among Old
English texts. Some 438 lines in the standard edition of the Old English
contain over 500 occurrences of place or people names. More than two
hundred different places are named, from continents to cities, from the
ocean to rivers and straits, and over fifty different peoples. Many places
appear only once in this geographical introduction, and the number of
times a place is named by no means indicates its importance; Rome appears only once in the passage. Yet repetition of certain place names helps
readers to anchor lesser-known cognomens. Rome does not need repetition; it is among the most named cities in all of Old English literature.
The Mediterranean Sea appears more often in this introduction than any
other place does, starting eleven lines into the description (*Orosius* 8.21).
The Mediterranean (or *Wendelsæ*) becomes a convenient locus around
which Orosius and his translator could locate other places, both familiar
and unfamiliar. Even a reader who began reading the *Orosius* uncertain of
where and how big the Mediterranean is must acquire some sense of its
centrality and size by how many places appear in relation to it. One excerpt gives a sense of how the Old English geographical description uses
it to bind places together:

> … be westan Achie *and*lang þæs Wendelsæs is Dalmatia þæt land on norðheal-
> fe þæs sæs, 7 be norðan Dalmatia sindon Pulgare 7 Istria, 7 be suðan Istria
> is se Wendelsæ þe man hæt Atriaticum, 7 be westan þa beorgas þe man hæt
> Alpis, 7 be norðan þæt westen þæt is betux Carendan 7 [P]ulgarum.
>
> Þonne is Italia land westnorðlang 7 eastsuðlang, 7 hit belið Wendelsæ ymb
> eall utan buton westannorðan. Æt þæm ende hit belicgað ða beorgas þe man
> hæt Alpis: þa onginnað westane fram þæm Wendelsæ in [N]arbonense þære
> ðeode, 7 endiað eft east in Dalmatia þæm lande æt þæm sæ. (*Orosius* 18.13–23)

> ("by western Achaia along the Mediterranean is Dalmatia on the northern
> side of the sea, and to the north of Dalmatia are the Bulgarians and Istria, and
> to the south of Istria is [that part of] the Mediterranean called the Adriatic,

and to its west the mountains called Alps, and to the north is the wilderness
that is between Carentania and the Bulgarians.

"Next, Italy runs northwest to southeast, and the Mediterranean surrounds
it all except the northwest. At that end lie the mountains called the Alps: these
begin in the west from the Mediterranean into the region of Narbonensian
[Gaul], and they end again to the east in the land of Dalmatia at the sea.")

Here repetition of more familiar names helps the reader locate less familiar
ones. The Mediterranean and Italy provide a firm location for Anglo-
Saxon readers. Italy appears once in the *Metres of Boethius*, half a dozen
times in the work of Ælfric, and in scattered other prose works, while
specific places in Italy, most notably Rome, appear much more. By contrast, Achaia, Dalmatia, and Istria appear in English only in the *Orosius*;
readers may come to feel some acquaintance with them simply through
the connection here to the Mediterranean.[58] The geographical introduction employs this technique over and over, repeating some names in
relation to several different places to build webs of association among
neighbouring spaces.

This technique is a strategy, not a slavish following of the source text. As
Janet Bately makes clear in the introduction to her edition and throughout
the commentary, the author of the Old English *Orosius* "had no hesitation
in making radical but unacknowledged alterations to his primary source,
expanding freely but also cutting, rewriting some sections, but generally
retaining the order and arrangement of his original."[59] The passage just
quoted is a good example. The Old English version names Achaia, the
Mediterranean (four times), Dalmatia (three times), Bulgaria (or the
Bulgarians, twice), Istria (twice), the Adriatic, the Alps (twice), Carentia,
Italy, and Narbonensian Gaul. It thus names ten places a total of eighteen
times. The corresponding Latin passage names Achaia, the Myrtoan Sea,
the Sea of Crete, the Ionian Sea, Africa, the islands of Cephalonia and
Kassiopi, Corinth (twice), Macedonia (twice), Attica (twice), Athens,
Dalmatia, Dardania, Moesia, Istria, Liburnia and the Liburnian islands, and
finally the Adriatic. The Latin names eighteen different places a total of

---

58 *Pulgare* does not appear elsewhere in Old English, but *Bulgarisc* appears twice in the
   OE *Dialogues*, and the Adriatic similarly appears once in the *Dialogues*; see Wærferth,
   Bischof Wærferths von Worcester Übersetzung der Dialoge Gregors des Grossen, ed.
   H. Hecht (Leipzig, 1900–7; repr. Darmstadt: Wissenschaftliche Buchgesellschaft, 1965).
   Narbonne appears only once outside the *Orosius*, in *Chronicle E* alone.
59 Bately, "Introduction," *Orosius*, xciii.

twenty-one times in the corresponding passage. Only Achaia, Dalmatia, Istria, and the Adriatic – just four of the places named – occur in both texts at this point. The translator transforms the geography in the passage. Places clearly matter, or he would not spend space delineating and repeating them, but they are not the same places that matter to the Latin author, and they are often not described in the same way. The translator also repeats most of these names in the main text as he details historical events.

The repetition of place names in the *Orosius*'s geographical introduction is unusual for its quantity: a large number of names appear, and more than half of them appear more than once in these few pages. Yet the strategy is not unique to this passage or even this translator. In the B-text of the *Boethius*, twenty-eight different peoples or places are named, but twenty-one of those only once.[60] The Latin never refers explicitly to Greece, but the prose version introduces the Greeks four times to replace or explain less common geographical names, and the prosimetrum version refers to Greece or Greeks thirteen times. The Old English text refers twice to Mount Etna, Sicily, Africans, Scythians, and Troy; the mentions of Mount Etna locate it in Sicily, reinforcing their relationship. Gregory the Great's *Regula pastoralis* only invokes place names sparingly, but the Old English *Pastoral Care* keeps its thirteen mentions of Jerusalem. The Old English translation of Gregory the Great's *Dialogues* names Rome more than forty times. The Prose Psalms of the Paris Psalter go further. Assyria never appears explicitly in the Psalms, but the name appears in introductions to seven different Psalms (in five in the translator's likely source).[61] Babylon similarly never features in the Psalms themselves but appears in nine

---

60 The C-text contains slightly fewer names but more repetitions as a few are dropped in the Metres but more are reiterated. Twenty-six names of people or places appear: sixteen once, five twice (Etna, Africans, Alps, Scythia, and Sicily), one three times (Troy), one four times (Thrace), one six times (Goths), one ten times (Greeks), and one nineteen (Rome and Romans).

61 For the Psalms, I used *King Alfred's Old English Prose Translation of the First Fifty Psalms*, ed. Patrick P. O'Neill (Cambridge, MA: Medieval Academy of America, 2001), also available at http://www.medievalacademy.org/resource/resmgr/maa_books_online/ oneill_0104.htm. I found and counted place names using O'Neill's Glossary of Proper Names (346–7) and *The Dictionary of Old English Corpus* online. For a Latin text close to the translator's source for the introductions, I used *Liber Psalmorum: The West-Saxon Psalms, being the prose portion, or the "first fifty," of the so-called Paris Psalter, edited from the manuscript, with an introduction and an appendix*, ed. James Wilson Bright and Robert Lee Ramsay (Boston and London: D.C. Heath and Co., 1907).

introductions (here fully following the translator's source).[62] These Alfredian texts invoke the same places repeatedly to anchor themselves geographically; repetitions in varying contexts within the text help readers build webs of associations. Places become increasingly familiar as audiences progress through the texts.

The same process can be observed in many other texts, most notably with Rome and the Holy Land. The Holy Land will be treated below, but Rome holds a singular place in the Anglo-Saxon geographical imagination. Nicholas Howe contends that Anglo-Saxons felt they had a special relationship with Rome.[63] They were a people personally chosen for conversion by a pope who wanted to go on a mission to the Anglo-Saxons himself; when he could not, he sent others in his place.[64] Rome receives more than two dozen direct mentions in verse and over 1200 in prose, with another three dozen in glosses. Some occurrences arise in biblical contexts. Others refer to early saints, found particularly in Rome and the Holy Land. Still others appear in historical contexts: the Old English *Orosius* names Rome or Romans hundreds of times. Finally, references to learning might also lead authors to cite Rome – for instance, Ælfric refers to the Roman calendar in *Catholic Homilies* 1.6.132–3. Rome appears often in Anglo-Saxon literature, particularly in Latin literature and in English prose, and it is always a place of great significance.

Homilies are among the texts most interested in Rome. Ælfric names Rome a dozen times in his homily on Saint Gregory the Great, whose kin were prominent Romans (*Catholic Homilies* 2.9.13). Gregory built six monasteries in Sicily and returned to build a seventh in Rome itself (2.9.32–3), where he sees English boys for the first time and resolves to convert the English. Rome appears in many other homilies by Ælfric and by anonymous writers. Peter and Paul underwent trials at Rome, as did subsequent Christian martyrs. Some, such as Eugenia and Agnes, lived in Rome; others visited there or lived in the Roman empire. Ælfric names Rome over 130 times, primarily in his homilies and *Lives of Saints*. By

---

62 Other place names in the Psalms, such as Sion, follow the Latin Psalms.

63 Howe, "Rome."

64 Gregory's desire to come is told in some detail in Bede's *Historia ecclesiastica* and the OE *Bede* (book 2, chapter 1 in both), and Ælfric's Homily on St Gregory (*Catholic Homilies* 2.9.53–88). For Bede's Latin, see *Bede's Ecclesiastical History*, ed. and trans. Colgrave and Mynors. For the Old English version, see *The Old English Version of Bede's Ecclesiastical History of the English People*, ed. Thomas Miller, EETS 95, 96, 110, 111 (London: 1890–8; repr. Millwood, NY: Kraus Reprint, 1978).

contrast, he names England about fifty times total in all of his works. A wide variety of anonymous saints' lives and homilies, and the homilies of Wulfstan, also mention Rome roughly a hundred times; England or the English are specifically named fewer than thirty times in these works. The *Old English Martyrology* names Rome or Romans a hundred times and England or the English just sixteen (of which six occurrences are the Latin title *Historia Anglorum*, for Bede's *Historia ecclesiastica*). England does not need to be named, in a way, for the audiences of Anglo-Saxon homilies and saints' lives presumably need no reminders of where they live. Rome's prominence in homilies and the lives of saints is striking. Significant numbers of educated Anglo-Saxons must have encountered many mentions of Rome, and even less-educated churchgoers must have heard of it often.

Alfredian texts refer to Rome frequently as well. The Old English *Pastoral Care* begins with a verse preface identifying Gregory as "Rome papa" ("pope at Rome," 9.9) and "Romwara betest" ("best of Romans," 9.12), and the *Soliloquies* uses Rome as an image.[65] Boethius's Latin *De consolatione philosophiae* names Rome four times, but the Old English prose *Boethius* expands to mention Romans and Rome twenty-one times, and the prosimetrum does so twenty-four times. As we have seen, Rome is central to the *Orosius*'s world history. The Old English *Dialogues* name Rome more than forty times, usually as the site of miracles; the *Bede* names the city a hundred times.

A few poems also feature Rome prominently. *Elene* tells the story of the finding of the true cross by Constantine's mother Helena, or, in Old English, Elene. It begins with a battle at the Danube and moves briefly to Rome before it takes its heroine to the Holy Land.[66] While most of the action happens in Jerusalem, Constantine and Elene go to and from Rome, now their home. The soldiers whom Elene takes to Jerusalem are all Romans, exerting force over the holy city. The short poem *Seasons for Fasting* also makes three explicit references to Rome, and one each appears in *Fates of the Apostles*, *The Menologium*, and *The Creed*.

Nicholas Howe demonstrated a special relationship between England and Rome. He also argues that the Anglo-Saxons saw themselves as heirs

---

65 *King Alfred's West-Saxon Version of Gregory's Pastoral Care*, ed. Henry Sweet, EETS 45, 50 (London: N. Trübner and Co., 1871; repr. as 1 vol., Oxford: Oxford University Press, 1996). I used ASPR 6 for the verse preface.

66 See also Howe on the battle's transplantation from Rome to Germanic lands in his "Rome," 162–3. For *Elene*, see ASPR 2.

of Israel: a people chosen by God and led across the seas to a promised land where they would be his.[67] George Molyneaux contends that Old English texts, most notably the *Bede*, display an interest in the conversion of gentiles in general.[68] He argues that Anglo-Saxons did not see themselves as a new Israel, but that as dwellers on the margins of the world, they saw their conversion as necessary for the Second Coming, which could not happen until Christianity had spread to all peoples. Yet Molyneaux treats the Anglo-Saxon missions to the Continent fairly briefly and does not talk about other distant places that had yet to be converted. Bede himself was aware of Muslims, whom he called "Saracens," though he had little understanding of their religion.[69] According to Calvin B. Kendall, references to Saracens in Bede's later writings show some awareness of Arab armies in and around the Mediterranean. While Bede makes no explicit reference to their presence in Spain, for later Anglo-Saxons, Muslims must have presented a clear obstacle to the conversion of the world.[70] Ælfric too mentions "Saracens": though he follows his sources closely on the destruction of Jerusalem, he adds "Seo burh wearð syððan on oðre stowe getimbrod and mid þam sarasceniscum geset" ("That city was afterwards rebuilt in another place and occupied by the Saracens," *Catholic Homilies* 1.28.58–9).[71] Kendall concludes,

This was not, to reiterate, a picture of Christianity versus Islam, of which he knew nothing, but rather of the true faith in a shrinking area of Europe menaced by an ill-defined, fierce, hostile, mighty force both in the East and in the West – a force characterised by unbelief, idolatry, and heresy, but nevertheless, mysteriously, a recipient of God's promise of greatness.[72]

---

67 *Migration and Mythmaking in Anglo-Saxon England* (New Haven: Yale University Press, 1989).

68 George Molyneaux, "The *Old English Bede*: English Ideology or Christian Instruction?" *English Historical Review* 124 (2009): 1289–1323.

69 Calvin B. Kendall, "Bede and Islam," in *Bede and the Future*, ed. Peter Darby and Faith Wallis, Studies in Medieval Britain and Ireland (Farnham, Surrey: Ashgate, 2014), 93–114; see also Scarfe Beckett, *Anglo-Saxon Perceptions*, esp. 123–38.

70 Kendall, "Bede and Islam," esp. 104–14.

71 For Ælfric's sources and his use of them here, see Malcolm Godden's Commentary in *Ælfric's Catholic Homilies: Introduction, Commentary and Glossary*, EETS ss 18 (Oxford: Oxford University Press, 2000), 231–3.

72 Kendall, "Bede and Islam," at 114.

The Anglo-Saxons and even their Continental cousins did not represent the last frontier for Christianity. The peoples who appear in wonder texts (treated later in this chapter) might also have posed a problem for Anglo-Saxons waiting for the conversion of the world to be completed. Howe offers a useful framework in which to understand Anglo-Saxons' conceptions of themselves and their relations with God, Rome, and the Holy Land.

For the Holy Land held great importance to Anglo-Saxon readers. Israel (*Israhel-* or *Israel-*) is named nearly a hundred times in Old English verse, almost 600 times in prose, and hundreds more in glosses. Jerusalem (*Hierusalem, Ierusalem, Gerusalem, Hierusolimae, Solimæ*) must have come to hold some familiarity for Anglo-Saxons: although many could not point to it or map it, they could say that it was the land of the Hebrews or the Jews and in fact did so frequently. The city is named more than thirty times in the poetic corpus alone; all places and peoples in Britain together are named only seventy-five times in extant poetry. In addition, Jerusalem appears over 300 times in Old English prose and well over 400 times in glosses (almost all on Scripture). Bethlehem (*Bethlem, Bethleem*) appears nine times in poetry, forty-three times in prose, and twenty-five in glosses. Other specific locations in or near the Holy Land also produce striking numbers: the Anglo-Saxons wrote about the Middle East a great deal in Old English, and even more in Latin texts such as pilgrimage accounts, Adomnán's *De locis sanctis* and Bede's version of it, and commentaries on the Bible.

Latin works would have restricted audiences, but vernacular homilies helped to familiarize wider Anglo-Saxon audiences with scriptural geography. Jesus was born in Bethlehem, named about forty times in Old English homilies and saints' lives, and he lived much of his life and died in Jerusalem. Ælfric names Jerusalem nearly a hundred times in his homilies, saints' lives, and occasionally letters.[73] Homilies by others name it another seventy times, and the *Martyrology* a further sixteen. The Jewish people are named even more often: Ælfric refers to *Iudei, Iudeiscan*, and other variants almost 400 times. Other homilists prefer *Judea, Judea folc*, or *Judeas*, which appear in the work of Wulfstan and others about 150 times. The River Jordan appears over a hundred times, the Red Sea receives almost forty mentions, and so on; biblical places occur frequently in homilies.

---

73 Most notably, *Catholic Homilies* 1.28 focuses on the siege and destruction of Jerusalem.

Other prose texts repeat and connect places in the Holy Land as well. The Prose Psalms of the Paris Psalter refer to seventeen different places and races in the Holy Land, mentioned over eighty times and appearing to centre God and Judeo-Christian history in the Holy Land. Many of these references are in the introductions to the Psalms: David's kingdom is mentioned in the introduction to Psalm 7, and his flight from Saul (and thus Israel) into the wilderness in the introductions to 10, 35, and 38. Direct references to Assyria and the Babylonian captivity appear in seventeen introductions, and other introductions feature historical figures, people, tribes, and places. The Prose Psalms themselves name "Israele" or "Israhela" eight times; God's holy mountain or Mount Sion thirteen times; and Mount Libanus, Cades, Tarsus and Cilicia, Hermon, the River Jordan, and Tyre. The Psalms would seem to fix God and pre-Christian history firmly in the Holy Land, just as many maps and other descriptions (by Adomnán and Bede, among others) centre there, on the Promised Land of the Old Testament and the place of Christ's life, death, and resurrection in the New.[74]

Wonder texts in Anglo-Saxon England also make use of repetition and connection. The Latin *Letter of Alexander to Aristotle* names 57 people or places, but only 13 unique ones; most names are repeated. The Latin *Wonders of the East* names 48, only 27 unique. The Old English versions of the *Letter* and *Wonders* produce very similar counts. *Liber monstrorum* (in Latin only) has the most names: 174, 76 unique. Of the 106 different people and places named in the wonder texts as a group, just over half, 54, have no other appearances in Old English texts. Readers of individual wonder texts, and particularly those who read more than one wonder text, will encounter the same names repeatedly. Even if those names sound very foreign at first, by the time a reader of the *Beowulf* manuscript, for instance, finished *The Wonders of the East* and *The Letter of Alexander to Aristotle*, contained in the same manuscript, he or she would have encountered Babylon nine times, Bactriacen twice, the Brixontes four times, and so on. An enthusiast of wonder texts who read the Latin texts in their different manuscripts would find an even richer network of place and people names.

---

74 Adomnán wrote his *De locis sanctis* based on the account of Bishop Arculf, who gave an oral description and some maps of churches in Jerusalem. Bede later adapted *De locis sanctis*, keeping it in Latin.

Even those simply dipping their toes in the waters of wonder texts would not be completely at sea with the names, if they were acquainted with other works of history or natural science. Only 25 of the 106 different names in the wonder texts appear neither in other Old English texts nor in Latin texts; 81 of the names can be located elsewhere in at least one language. Some 52, or nearly half, can be found in other Old English texts, and 49 of those same names also appear in Latin texts (with an additional 14 appearing in a third type of text, Old English glossaries). Readers of wonder texts would forge mental links with other peoples and places, reinforcing connections that could also be made or bolstered elsewhere.

Prose works are not alone in making places familiar by repeating names, associating one place with another, and making Rome familiar to Anglo-Saxon audiences. Narrative poems often do the same. The poem *Daniel* helps reinforce its audience's sense of place by twice invoking the plains of Sennar as the poem draws to a close (ASPR 1, 601, 726), though the Vulgate account names the place only once, and not in the part of the story where the poet names it (Daniel 1:2). The reference may remind readers of *Genesis*, which names the place four times (1655, 1668, 1701, 1963), and whose one extant copy shares a manuscript with *Daniel*. As readers and hearers become more familiar with the stories from the Bible, so too do they come to feel some sense of acquaintance with their settings. Thus, Anglo-Saxon poets and audiences construct a sense of places most would never visit. Distances and directions are often not specified; the Anglo-Saxons did not have the same kind of mental maps we do. Instead, people and place names gain recognition through reuse and context.

Jerusalem plays a role in poetry as well. In *Daniel*, it receives relatively little description, for what matters is its role in salvation. *Daniel* begins with a memory of Jerusalem as a place given to the Israelites by God himself, a happy and rich place:

Gefrægn ic Hebreos   eadge lifgean
in Hierusalem,   goldhord dælan,
cyningdom habban,   swa him gecynde wæs,
siððan þurh metodes mægen   on Moyses hand
wearð wig gifen,   wigena mænieo,
and hie of Egyptum   ut aforon,
mægene micle.   (*Dan* 1–7)

("I learned that the Hebrews lived happily in Jerusalem, shared a gold-hoard, had a kingdom, as was rightful for them, since through the power of the

Creator, war and a band of warriors were given into the hand of Moses, and they went out from Egypt, a great force.")

Christ A, *B*, and *C* only mention a handful of places, but Jerusalem figures among them as a central place in the life of Jesus (ASPR 3). Many of the psalms name Jerusalem, making it the central place in a text that was much studied and copied in Latin and in Old English translation (both poetry and prose).

Jerusalem stands unique among human places for its past and future, even if that future is in some ways metaphorical: Jerusalem's significance is often not for what it was at the time of the Anglo-Saxons, but as the place where Christ walked and as the heavenly Jerusalem. The latter has no geographical location but becomes God's city and the home of the blessed. Ælfric tells us, "Þeos hierusalem hæfde getacnunge ðære heofonlican hierusalem. on ðære is fulfremed sibb. to ðære we sind geladode. and we ðider cumað untwylice gif we hit on andweardan life geearniað" ("This Jerusalem had the signification of the heavenly Jerusalem, in which is the perfect peace to which we are invited, and we certainly come there if we earn it in this present life," *Catholic Homilies* 2.4.236–9).

Elene divides its main action between the two distant places most important to Anglo-Saxons: Rome and Jerusalem. Rome was the site of the papacy and the origins of the mission that Bede credited with Christianizing the Anglo-Saxons. Jerusalem represented both the past and the future of Christians. The poem connects Rome and Jerusalem and conveys a sense of the great distance between them by taking Elene via "Creca land" ("Greek lands," 250, 262, and 998). Anglo-Saxon ship voyages would often stay within sight of a coast, as Elene's ship makes its way along the northern coast of the Mediterranean instead of across the great sea. The detail of how navigators reached their destination makes the journey more real to readers, even if they could not explain the exact locations of Rome, Greece, and Jerusalem. The body of the poem centres primarily on the Holy Land, moving from Germanic lands to Rome to Jerusalem and Calvary. Yet like prose translations, this poetic reimagining brings English readers closer to distant places. Sites are not left unspecified but are named, some repeatedly: the Danube (37, 136), Bethlehem (391), Calvary (672, 676, 1010, 1097), Jerusalem (273, 1055), and Nazareth (912). Reference is even made to the Trojan war (645–6). More than a dozen different places and tribes are named in *Elene* a total of forty-six times in a poem that runs only 1321 lines. Some peoples and places are more remote than others, but all are connected to Rome or Jerusalem by the narrative. The Franks,

Huns, *Hugas*, and *Hreða* are Germanic peoples with whom some Anglo-Saxons might have contact or feel some kinship. Jerusalem, Nazareth, and Bethlehem provide the backdrop for Jesus's life.[75] Troy, by contrast, must have seemed very distant indeed, in time and space. The persistent naming of peoples, cities, and other places demonstrates interest in the world outside England, a world with significance even for the margin-dwellers.[76] It also draws less familiar places (such as Troy) into webs centred around more familiar ones.

Anglo-Saxon interest in the Mediterranean seems clearly motivated: the centres of much political, religious, and cultural power were located there. The Church held its seat at Rome. The Bible narrated events in the Holy Land, Greece, and Rome. Learning came from these areas, as Alfred the Great's preface to the *Pastoral Care* relates; when Alfred looks for precedent for his translation program,

Ða gemunde ic hu sio æ wæs ærest on Ebr[e]isc geðiode funden, & eft, ða hie Creacas geliornodon, ða wendon hie hie on hiora agen geðiode ealle, & eac ealle oðre bec. & eft Lædenware swæ same, siððan hie hie geliornodon, hie hie wendon eall[a] ðurh wise wealhstodas on hiora agen geðiode. Ond eac ealla oðræ Cristnæ ðioda sumne dæl hiora on hiora agen geðiode wendon. (*PC* 5.25–7.5)

("Then I recalled how the law was first established in Hebrew, and again, when the Greeks learned it, then they translated it all into their own language, and also all other books. And again the Romans did the same: once they had learned them, they translated them all through wise translators into their own language. And also all other Christian peoples translated some part of them into their own language.")

---

75 Bethlehem becomes so familiar that at least one poet adds it, and Rome, to gloss a Latin text with no place names: the poetic *Creed* (ASPR 6) glosses the Latin "[Credo] Et in Iesum Christum filium eius unicum, dominum nostrum" ("[I believe] also in Jesus Christ [God's] only son, our lord") with sixteen lines, including a mention of angels announcing Christ's birth at Bethlehem (23–4). "Passus sub Pontio Pilato" ("suffered under Pontius Pilate") receives eight poetic lines, one of which mentions Pilate's power "under Romwarum" ("under the Romans," 26).

76 Not all poems show the same level of interest. *Christ* only names five places and one people, for a total of only 11 mentions in 1664 lines, a much lower density of place naming than seen in *Elene* or *The Fates of the Apostles*.

This passage makes noteworthy distinctions. While "all other Christian peoples" earn some mention, they remain unnamed and only translated "some part" of learning into their own tongues. Specificity, and thus emphasis, go to Hebrew as a language, and then to the Greeks and then the Romans as readers, translators, and transmitters of culture. These cradles of culture receive particular attention not only from Alfred but from many Anglo-Saxons, as shown above. Greece played little political role in later Anglo-Saxon times; Anglo-Saxon texts show a continuing respect for it as a place of culture and learning, but more for Rome.

Rome and Israel became so familiar to writers and audiences that they sometimes appear without historical justification or a need for citation. To give just one illustration: Ælfric's *Catholic Homily* 1.20 takes the Trinity as its theme. When Ælfric mentions the crucifixion, he names the Jews three times (235, 243, 254), though his mention of Christ's death is only in lines 235–56 of the homily; most of the homily deals with no particular people or place but elucidates the nature of the Trinity through a series of propositions and images. He uses the image of the sun's three parts – its physical shape, its light, and its heat – to explain how something can be three and yet one.[77] His explanation of how the sun's light reaches Earth paints a clear (if scientifically incorrect) picture: "Swa hraðe swa heo upaspringð on ærne mergien. heo scinð on hierusalem and on romebyrig 7 on ðisum earde; 7 on eallum eardum ætgædere" ("As soon as the sun rises in the early morning, it shines on Jerusalem and on Rome and on this land, and on all lands together," *Catholic Homilies* 1.20.179–81). Jews, Jerusalem, and Rome are touchstones for his audience, exemplary people and places that simultaneously feel distant and familiar.

Thus, writers reiterate and contextualize place and people names to offer Anglo-Saxon readers a measure of familiarity with places most will never see. This strategy appears in Ælfric's choice to explain his point with Jerusalem and Rome, places with historic and religious significance, rather than places closer to home. Rome, Jerusalem, and other well-known sites in the Mediterranean world give works a geographical grounding and connect audiences to a wider world from their places in the local church. They act as reference points for less familiar names so that writers can introduce such places, from Bulgaria to the plains of Sennar.

---

77 For more on this passage, see the previous chapter, p. 46.

History

Another strategy by which authors create meaningful places out of foreign spaces around the Mediterranean is to provide historical explanations of place or people names, often in combination with repetition and connection. Indeed, as Irmeli Valtonen has written, in the early Middle Ages, "geography did not exist as an independent subject ... [but] provided a setting for historical events and ethnographic descriptions, and it could shape perceptions of distant peoples and places and consequently manipulate the narrating society's self-perception."[78] As writers tell what happened in an area, readers gain a sense of that place even if they cannot point to it or describe the terrain. This strategy too crosses forms and genres. It works not only in overtly historical texts such as the *Orosius* but also in the philosophical *Boethius*, homilies and saints' lives, and Old English poetry.

The *Orosius*, with its wealth of foreign place and people names, expands Anglo-Saxon access to a broader world. Paradoxically, even as the *Orosius* might threaten the English with the vertigo of looking down from the edge of the world towards the centre, it strengthens English ties to that centre. In learning the names and the histories of these places and peoples, readers acquired cultural capital that connected them with the rest of the world.[79] No longer could only speakers of Latin learn God's plan for the world, which Orosius aims to describe; English speakers could learn it in their own tongue.

Throughout the Old English text, the translator develops Orosius's theme of four great empires, giving readers a historical framework in which to put these unfamiliar places:

> An wæs Babylonicum, þær Ninus ricsade. Þæt oðer wæs Creca, þær Alexander ricsade. Þridda wæs Affricanum, þæ[r] Ptolome ricsedon. Se feorða is Romane, þe giet ricsiende sindon. Þas feower heafodricu sindon on feower endum þyses middangeardes mid unasecgendlicre Godes tacnunge. (36.12–16)

---

78 *The North in the Old English Orosius*, 147.

79 For cultural capital, see Bourdieu, *Outline*, 183–8; and his *Practical Reason: On the Theory of Action* (Stanford: Stanford University Press, 1998), 20–4. See also John Guillory, *Cultural Capital: The Problem of Literary Canon Formation* (Chicago: University of Chicago Press, 1993), which addresses in more depth issues of cultural capital in institutions of higher learning. I argue for the transmission of cultural capital in Alfredian translation in my book *The King's English*.

("The first [empire] was the Babylonian, where Ninus ruled. The second was Greek, where Alexander ruled. The third was African, where Ptolemy ruled. The fourth is Roman, which is yet ruling. These four empires are in the four ends of this earth through the dispensation of the ineffable God.")

The rest of the *Orosius* describes the rise and fall of these empires and the men who ruled them. The reader comes to know these places through the events that transpired there. They have an ordering in chronology as well as space. The geographical introduction is only an introduction, and the body of the *Orosius* fleshes out, at length, the histories of the places only quickly sketched at the outset.

Roughly contemporary, the *Boethius* also uses history to connect readers with places. The translator retains people and place names with relatively well-known histories, especially the ones closely connected with Rome (as seen above). The translator obviously felt comfortable omitting or changing names of people or places: of forty-six different people or place names that appear in the Latin, the translator kept only nine. Another seven were rendered by other terms, such as the broader *Creca* ("Greeks," 7.107) for *Lydorum* ("Lydians," book 2, prose 2.11) or the generic *bleowum* ("blue," B 15.11; omitted in C) for the Latin *Tyrio* ("Tyrian," 2m5.9), describing a dye. Words for Romans are kept twice (2p7.8 and .9; 18.56 and .63), and Etna twice as well (2m5.25 and 2p6.1; 15.19 and 16.14). The Old English text insists on place more than the Latin *De consolatione* does. Readers are transported to Rome, the setting of many of the *Boethius*'s anecdotes, illustrations, and images. The translator's failure to mention Ravenna allows readers to think that the narrator is imprisoned in Rome itself; he periodically reminds audiences that that the main character is a Roman and his earthly concerns lie with Rome.[80] Two additional settings for the text come

---

80 The less connection a people or place name has with Rome, the more likely the translator is to omit it. Only two of Boethius's own uses of words for Romans are omitted ("Romana" at 1p4.26 and "Romani" at 2p7.9). Places in Italy may be dropped when the passages that contain them are omitted (such as Rome, Campania, and Ravenna, all lost when Boethius's defence of himself in 1p4 is omitted). More remote places tend more to be deleted. The first metre of book 5 is not translated, with its opening references to "Rupis Achaemeniae scopulis" ("the rocky Persian banks," 5m1.1) and "Tigris et Euphrates" (5m1.3). Tagus, Hermus, and Indus (3m10.7–9) disappear from the Old English. Two words for Carthaginians, *Poeni* (3m2.7) and *Marmaricus* (4m3.11), are omitted. Thrace and India are named in the Old English text but not every time they appear in Latin; they are dropped in the translations of 1m3.7 and 4m3.15.

from religious history: the translator adds to the source text the story of the Tower of Babel, complete with references to Sennar, Deira, and Babylon (35.131–2). All these place names except Deira appear elsewhere in the extant Old English corpus. The translator may have expected some familiarity with them, may have been attempting to make audiences more familiar with them, or (most likely) a combination: introducing audiences to new place names through more familiar ones and historical lessons.

The translator sometimes glosses less common place names in the *Boethius* to help the audience make sense of them, usually by connecting them to past events. For instance, Philosophy offers two references to figures who experienced reversals of fortune: "Busiridem accepimus necare hospites solitum ab Hercule hospite fuisse mactatum. Regulus plures Poenorum bello captos in uincla coniecerat, sed mox ipse uictorum catenis manus praebuit" ("We hear that Busirides, accustomed to killing his guests, was killed by a guest, Hercules. Regulus threw many Carthaginian captives into chains in the war, but soon he himself offered his hands to the chains of his conquerors," 2p6.10–11). The names are no doubt sufficient to Boethius's target audience, but these stories would be far less familiar to Anglo-Saxons. The Old English offers a much longer passage explaining that Busirides lived in Egypt (16.71–2) and tried to kill Hercules in the Nile (16.76–7), but instead, Hercules drowned him there (16.77–9). Regulus fought against Africans (16.80) and took Africans captive (16.81–2); in choosing "Africans," the translator uses a broader, more common term than "Carthaginians" so that readers can understand. He transforms these mentions from oblique allusions to grounded history.

Homilies and saints' lives by their very nature tend to connect places to events in the lives of significant people: Christ, the apostles, or later saints. Jerusalem appears over 300 times in prose, including nearly a hundred in the homilies and *Lives of Saints* of Ælfric alone. Egypt is named well over 400 times in prose, including almost fifty mentions in Ælfric's homilies and *Lives of Saints* and nearly thirty in anonymous homilies and lives. These places are often connected to each other and to other places, as noted above, and they are named in homilies because significant things happened there. Ælfric does not drop Egypt into homilies to show off his learning but to increase his people's biblical literacy. For Mary and Joseph's flight with the baby Jesus, Egypt is the destination (*Catholic Homilies* 1.5.34–9), but it is the point of departure for Moses leading his people to the promised land (*Catholic Homilies* 1.12, appendix A 2–4; 1.22.5; 2.13.243–4; 2.15.8–33), and it is the one refuge in a time of great famine in Genesis (*Catholic Homilies* 2.12). Over the course of his homilies, Ælfric's audience build a sense of the history of Egypt.

Poems most obviously connect places with history when they recount historical narratives. Longer biblical poems are particularly rich in place and people names. *Genesis* tells the early story of the world from Creation through Abraham's averted sacrifice of Isaac. *Genesis A* names thirty-one different places or peoples, unsurprisingly returning most often to those that have stories connected with them: the Hebrews, a people who will find their place later, are named nine times; Abraham's travels in and out of Egypt lead to the land or its people being named ten times. Though Sodom and Gomorrah occupy a relatively small part of the text, from Lot's settlement there to the destruction of the two cities, Gomorrah becomes one of the most named places with seven explicit mentions, and Sodom surpasses all other place and people names in the text with an extraordinary nineteen. The poem does not convey a strong sense of where these places are. When Egypt is first named in the poem, Abraham is leaving it to go to Canaan (1768), but the relative locations of the two are unclear. We get slightly more information about Sodom and Gomorrah. Their location merits a half-line: they are "be Iordane," by the Jordan (*Genesis* 1921). The stories of these places are far more important than their locations. Audiences need not know exactly where Sodom and Gomorrah lie in relation to Canaan or Jerusalem or England; instead, they remember the sins and complete destruction of the cities.

Overwhelmingly, the histories of places are more important to Anglo-Saxons than their locations in fixed relation to other defined places. References to specific distances are not very common in Old English literature; the entire *Corpus* only uses the word "mile" 160 times, and most of those uses are restricted to a few texts – the *Orosius*, the *Bede*, and the *Anglo-Saxon Chronicle* chief among them. As we have seen, even in its geographical introduction, the *Orosius* establishes many spaces not by measurements but by connection to other lands. The body of the *Orosius* connects each of its places to historical events. Such connections are unsurprising in a history, but they appear also in works as different as the *Boethius* and *Genesis*. Historical details help Anglo-Saxons construct a mental archive of places and peoples, a store of meaningful information about distant lands and folk that turn space into inhabited place.

Habitation

In the fourth strategy, writers describe who or what lives in a faraway space, with special interest in humans and human-animal hybrids. Again, readers connect with place not as an abstract location or a point on a map, but through what and particularly whom they might see there. People names appear more frequently in Old English than place names.[81] Writers concentrate on the identity of a people more than the physical characteristics of the place they inhabit. As shown above, interest in inhabitants sometimes takes the form of relating histories. Translations from Latin, homilies, and religious poems display interest in place almost solely in terms of what happens in a place, and they name peoples to tell what the peoples did or experienced. As they tell episodes in history or narrate events in the life of Christ or a saint, these texts unsurprisingly describe people inhabiting the setting.

Some texts, however, take a less historical approach to regions and their inhabitants. Outside of Europe and beyond the Mediterranean, wonder texts described what lay past places such as Rome and Jerusalem that, while distant, still seemed knowable from a range of texts. Asa Mittman reads maps and wonder texts and texts of monsters, arguing that the English emphasized these frightening others to make themselves seem less marginal. Maps and literary works offered ways of containing the dangers of the Other, even though monstrosity could be found at home. He concludes: "For the Anglo-Saxons – a marginal, hybrid society – and the medieval English cultures that followed them, maps and monsters were able to fill the most vital of roles. Together, they declared their creators to be peripheral yet normal people, and therefore worthy of salvation despite their damnable location."[82]

---

81 Distinguishing people names from place names can be difficult because they often have identical forms, as is true of Modern English; when I say that something is "English," do I mean "from England" or "from the English people"? Similarly, "Israel" or "Israhel" can describe a people or a land, depending on whether it is paired with "folc" or other words for people, or "land" or other words for place. When the name itself is not paired with one of these terms, context does not always clarify. Moreover, even a term that appears to be unambiguously a place name may retain a sense of the people. "England" in Old English usually has traces of a people name: *Englaland* is the same as *Engla land*, "land of the Angles." *Angelcyn* is sometimes used as a place name, but the normal meaning is "the Angle people." For more on these usages, see Stodnick, "Writing Home," especially her first chapter. Examination of the *Corpus* does appear to show a shift between naming the people, usually a plural, and naming the place, often a singular; later works are more likely to name place than people. Compare Ælfric's work with the Alfredian translations, or later entries in the *Anglo-Saxon Chronicle* with earlier. However, the distinction is rarely clear-cut. Even Latin texts may be problematic: the Latin texts of *The Letter of Alexander to Aristotle* and *Liber monstrorum* sometimes give "India" a plural form, "Indorum," which may refer to the place or the people. For *The Letter*, see the appendices to Andy Orchard, *Pride and Prodigies: Studies in the Monsters of the Beowulf-Manuscript* (Cambridge: Brewer, 1995).
82 Mittman, *Maps and Monsters*, 209.

While Mittman rightly finds monstrosity both at a distance and in England itself, he overstates English distance. Anglo-Saxons consistently represent their connections to Rome and Jerusalem, as seen above – with such links, their home was hardly a "damnable" place. Repetition and the connection of places to historical events helped Anglo-Saxons construct not only their own but also distant spaces as coherent places, and accounts of the inhabitants did the same for places with little or no known history.

Anglo-Saxons represented themselves again and again not as outcasts or as distant from salvation but as part of a broader Christian community, as this study has shown. Occasionally, writers and translators gave the early English windows on an even wider world outside of Christianity. Anglo-Saxons found not only distance and danger in faraway peoples but also elements of commonality: monsters fascinate and frighten because they are uncanny, containing elements of both the familiar and the unfamiliar at once.[83] The mental archive of Anglo-Saxons proves capacious enough for peoples with whom they feel close connections and for those who are dangerously different. The best-known texts of distant wonders that circulated in Anglo-Saxon England are *The Wonders of the East* (in Latin and Old English); *The Letter of Alexander to Aristotle* (also in both languages); and the *Liber monstrorum* (in Latin only).[84] These texts all present distant places and take some care to name them. Each offers dozens of people and place names, most outside Europe. Eleven people or place names recur in at least three of the texts; four appear in all five.[85]

Wonders of the East, extant in two Latin copies and two Old English, contains animals, but significantly most of those animals are put into a human context.[86] Red chickens are not remarkable for being red but for burning the entire body of anyone who touches one (§3). *Wonders* next

---

83 See Freud, "The Uncanny."

84 For these three texts, I use the editions and translations in the appendices to Orchard, *Pride and Prodigies*. Where I quote Orchard's translation of the OE *Wonders*, the Latin and Old English match closely enough for the translation to stand in for both. Where any of the Latin, Old English, or Orchard's Modern English diverge, I note differences.

85 Almost every place named in the Latin *Wonders* or *Letter of Alexander* appears in the Old English version of the text and vice versa. Those appearing in all five texts (Latin and OE *Wonders*, Latin and OE *Letter*, and Latin *Liber monstrorum*) are Ethiopia, India, Macedonia, and Persia, and names for their inhabitants.

86 Jacques Le Goff argues that marvels in the medieval West oppose humanism: "Marvels feature a world of animals, minerals, and plants"; "The Marvelous in the Medieval West," in *The Medieval Imagination*, trans. Arthur Goldhammer (Chicago: University of Chicago Press, 1988), 32. That may be true of some wonder texts, but those circulating in Anglo-Saxon England do not fit his model.

describes beasts that have no name (except "bestiae," "beasts," or "wildor," "wild animals," §4); they would be remarkable enough for their eight feet, eyes of gorgons ("gorgoneos") or valkyries ("wælkyrian"), and two heads, but in the Old English, again the section ends by declaring that if anyone touches them, they set their bodies on fire.[87] The Latin uses "quis," "anyone," for the one doing the touching; the Old English specifies a human being, "hwylc mann." Not all the creatures described are depicted interacting with people, but most are. Even those not described in terms of human interaction are located in relation to human spaces. Donkeys with horns like those of oxen can be found "in dextera parte a Babilonia" ("to the right of Babylon," §6; the Old English specifies "suð," "south," rather than "right"). Similarly, the hybrid dogs, or Conopoenas, are not shown interacting with people, but they are described as living south of Egypt – and specifically near cities of great wealth (§7). The exceptions are the Lertices, in §14, who are located in relation to a river, Brixontes, and not to a human city or people; and the Gryphon (§34) and Phoenix (35), who live on Mount Adamans. A number of the wonders are people who differ in some respect from the norm. Jacques Le Goff writes of marvellous hybrids: "In the Christian system marvels were scandalous because they transformed human beings, created 'in God's image,' into animals."[88] Yet the writer and translator seem less than scandalized. Most of these beings are still "homines" or "men[n] ("men," §8, 11–13, 15, 18, 20–2, 25, 28, 30, 32, 36) or, in two cases, "mulieres" or "wif" ("women," §26 and 27).[89] No matter how strange these people may seem, the author and translator choose to call them people.

Two groups are called "Homodubii" (§8 and 17; "'doubtful ones,'" trans. Orchard 189 and 195), a name that suggests that they are simultaneously human and not. The first group are six feet tall, with beards to their knees and hair to their heels; they are called "homines" and "menn" before they are dubbed "Homodubii." The second group look human to the navel, but the rest of the body is like that a donkey, with avian legs and a soft

---

87   Orchard translates "they set their bodies aflame"; *Pride and Prodigies*, 187. The Old English has singular "mann" for the toucher, plural "hy" and "onælað" for the beasts being touched and setting themselves on fire, and a plural "hiera lichoman" for the bodies burning, so the beasts might immolate themselves and those touching them. The Latin verb is "inarmant," "they arm themselves" – a different kind of defence.

88   "The Marvelous in the Medieval West," 41.

89   The Old English §20, 30, and 32 use the word "moncynn" or "man(n)kynn" rather than "men(n)."

voice (§17). By applying the term to two different groups of people, the texts indicate that the name is a failure of classification rather than a classification itself. Yet both have recognizably human characteristics that excite wonder.

Wonders of the East thus demonstrates the range of beings to be found on the earth. Many of its wonders are described as human or humanoid, even if at least two are on the margins between human and beast. Descriptions also take for granted certain human features and only mention explicitly those that vary from most human beings'. We can identify the assumptions by recognizing what merits description. Two faces, of course, get our attention immediately (§11), as do large mouths (§12), tusks (§27), a lack of heads (resulting in faces on chests, §15), and eyes that emit light (§22). One people have "large heads and ears like fans" (§21; Orchard 197). Great height deserves mention (§8, 11, 13, 15, 21, 27). Colour can be a distinguishing feature: some people are extraordinarily white (§11, 21, 27), or black (§12, 13, 32, 36), or multicoloured (§12). Unusual hair also registers: the first Homodubii "have beards to their knees, and hair to their heels" (§8; Orchard 189), the people who are fifteen feet tall have black hair (§11), women with long beards live in Babylon (§26), and the women with tusks wear hair to their heels and have tails like oxen (§27). Wondrous races are also conspicuous for their eating habits. The first Homodubii eat raw fish (§8), a people past the Brixontes eat other people (§13), and another people eat raw meat (§28). Hybrid forms stand out. Both kinds of Homodubii are like but not like humans. The Donestre are described in Latin and Old English as "diviners" to the navel and human below; it is not clear what it means to look like a diviner or soothsayer or how that differs from human, but the sense of hybridity comes through despite, or perhaps because of, the ambiguities of the text (§20).[90]

As Asa Mittman writes, hybrid monsters "are both the Other and the Self, both 'Them' and 'Us.'"[91] The most obvious hybrids are not the only hybrids. All the humanoid wonders are by definition as "wonders" hybrid: human and something else, or human less something. Whenever the texts do not tell us otherwise, we assume that the beings described have two arms and two legs, possess feet and hands, walk upright, and are no

---

90 "diuini" in the Latin (Orchard's edition, his MS G; T has "diuine" and B "diuinum"); "frihteras" in the Old English ("frifteras" in MS V). Mittman discusses hybridity in several places in *Maps and Monsters*.

91 Mittman, *Maps and Monsters*, 46.

taller than six feet. They have hair that does not go to the heels, beards only if they are men (and not to the knees), mouth and eyes in the normal places (and not producing light or sprouting tusks), and a skin colour that is not black, white, or red. Only a few eating habits are related, and those unsurprisingly suggest that Anglo-Saxons did not eat people and preferred their meat and fish cooked. Each of these wondrous peoples stands out in some ways, but *none* stands out in *every* way. They all have much in common with the authors, translators, and readers of the *Wonders*. Little negative comment is made about most of them. The exception that illuminates the rest is §27. The texts tell of women that

> have boar's tusks and hair down to their heels and ox-tails on their loins. Those women are thirteen feet tall and their bodies are of the whiteness of marble. And they have camel's feet and boar's teeth. Because of their uncleanness they were killed by Alexander the Great of Macedon. He killed them because he could not capture them alive, because they have offensive and disgusting bodies. (§27; Orchard 201)

These women differ from their readers in many respects: their mouths, the length of their hair, the presence of tails, their height, the colour of their bodies, and their feet. When the texts say that Alexander killed them, readers can recall that no other people has been described as so repulsive that they needed to be killed; indeed, almost no negative adjectives are attached to the other descriptions at all.[92] Apparently, these women are too uncanny: too much like humans for their nudity to be acceptable, too much like animals to be decent humans. Their gender may make their trespass unforgiveable, but another group of women are said to have long beards and to hunt. This latter group seems transgressive too, but no negative adjectives are attached to their descriptions, and no one kills them in the texts. Only the one group of women is found unworthy enough to die, apparently for

---

92 In the Latin, the language that defines the women as abberant is "sunt publicato corpore et inhonesto" ("their bodies were made public/prostituted and unseemly"); in Old English, "hi syndon æwisce on lichoman 7 unweorðe": more literally, "they were foul and worthless in their bodies." I have quoted Orchard's translation of the Old English above, which is also reasonably close to the Latin. *Publico* in Latin can mean "to make public property," sense I; II.1 "to make known"; or it can mean "to ... prostitute," sense II.2: see Lewis and Short, *publico*. Thanks to Damian Fleming, Heide Estes, Larry Swain, Jonathan Herold, and Dominic Mark Holtz for help with this passage.

sexual transgressions. Other differences are merely wonders, inspiring awe or admiration but not disgust and violence.

Places hold interest in *The Wonders of the East* primarily for the people living in them, secondarily for other creatures, and much less for landscape or climate. Even when other creatures bring interest to a place, those beasts are usually described in terms of their interactions with humans. *The Letter of Alexander to Aristotle* takes the same interests a step further: the wonders there hold interest specifically for how Alexander and his people interact with them, be they human, fauna, or flora.[93] Jennifer Neville writes of Alexander's dealings with the wonders, "Although Alexander always triumphs over the natural world, he needs an army to do it, and many individuals lose their lives in the process."[94] The author presents wonders not simply for admiration but in terms of their often frightening power against human beings. Of these three texts, all available in Anglo-Saxon England in multiple copies, only *Liber monstrorum* shows significant engagement with non-human wonders outside of interactions with humans. The *Liber* explicitly begins with "quae leuiore discretu ab humano genere distant" (Prologue; "those things which differ by a rather trifling amount from humankind," trans. Orchard 257) and moves to those that differ more from humanity. The term "homines" (or "genus humanum" or "mulieres") is favoured until I.31, when "monstrum" begins to be used much more.[95] Books 2 and 3 feature less human "belua" ("beasts"). Perhaps as a result, *Liber monstrorum* has no (extant) Old English translation: its surviving copies suggest popularity in early medieval Europe, but this text does not seem to have enticed Anglo-Saxon translators.

Though not generally classed as a wonder text, the poem *The Phoenix* shares some qualities found in those works: it transports audiences to distant places and introduces them to a remarkable inhabitant. *The Phoenix* gives a greater portion of its lines to description of places than any other

---

93 *The Letter of Alexander to Aristotle* contrasts with the *Orosius*, which relates Alexander's triumphs in these far-off lands matter-of-factly; places that in a text like *Wonders of the East* or *Alexander's Letter to Aristotle* would be filled with wondrous peoples and animals are here simply the settings for battles in *Orosius*, and it is Alexander's relatively conventional victories that excite admiration. A rare exception occurs at 68.24–7, with an extraordinarily cold river.

94 *Representations of the Natural World in Old English Poetry* (Cambridge: Cambridge University Press, 1999), 34.

95 The term "monstrum" appears from the beginning in some manuscripts, describing Hygelac in I.2; Y has "homines" instead of "monstra" here.

poem in English. Its first eighty-four lines establish the homeland of the phoenix, a kind of terrestrial paradise.[96] It "afyrred is / þurh meotudes meaht manfremmendum" ("is removed by the power of God from evil-doers," 5–6), possibly with paranomasia on "manfremmendum": the first part of the compound is "man," which can mean "harm, evil" or "human being." Humans seem the most likely to be evil-doers or harm-dealers. The site is far away, in the east, and we receive no further location (1–2). It is also a plain ("wong," 7, 13, 19, and 149, plus compounds in "-wong"). It has no steep hills or mountains and no valleys or gorges (21–6). It is wooded and has perfect climate; seven lines list the kinds of weather that do not afflict the place (14b–18, 60–2a). The poet insists on its verdancy, using the word "grene" three times before giving a glimpse of the phoenix (13, 36, 78) and once after (154). Through its height, twelve cubits higher than any other mountain on earth (28–32), this island escaped the Flood (41–9). Nothing harmful lives there (50–9), and it is well watered (62–8). The place is not called "neorxnawong" ("paradise," 397) until the second part of the poem, where the allegory of the first part is explained, but readers surely do not need the word to recognize the paradisiacal nature of the place. The poet paints the perfect landscape.

The Phoenix's lengthy description of the island is extraordinary. As Catherine Clarke points out, the corresponding passage in the Latin source text, Lactantius's *Carmen de ave phoenice*, runs only thirty lines.[97] The Old English poem is longer, more than doubling Lactantius's 170 lines to 380 (before adding nearly 300 more to explicate the allegory), but if the Old English poet kept the same proportions as Lactantius throughout, the passage would still be only 67 lines, not 84. Moreover, the poet chose to translate this particular Latin poem. He even borrowed from other Latin poems in his expansion.[98] He uses the Latin *locus amoenus* ("pleasant spot") topos with English elements: emphasis on a field (*wong*) and the fact that it is an island.[99]

---

96 Ananya Jahanara Kabir interprets the home of the phoenix as the interim paradise (where Enoch and Elijah are), but notes that it is described as a terrestrial one; *Paradise, Death and Doomsday in Anglo-Saxon Literature*, CSASE 32 (Cambridge: Cambridge University Press, 2001), 164–5. For *The Phoenix*, see ASPR 3.

97 Catherine A.M. Clarke, *Literary Landscapes and the Idea of England, 700–1400* (Woodbridge, UK: Brewer, 2006), 42.

98 See E.K.C. Gorst, "Latin Sources of the Old English *Phoenix*," *N&Q* ns 53 (2006): 136–42.

99 Again, see Clarke, *Literary Landscapes*, 43–4.

The poet's interest is not primarily in place, however; the first description builds up to the introduction of the phoenix itself. Each detail illuminates the nature of the phoenix. The place is always fruitful and watered well, as Christ's grace is a never-ending font. It holds nothing harmful, as Christ has nothing but good for us. It was not covered by water in the Flood because it was free from the taint of human sin. This place is too perfect to be sullied by death; the phoenix alone lives there, but when it is fully grown, the phoenix will leave. He waits "þusende ... wintra" ("a thousand winters," 151–2), a traditional way of counting time that contrasts with the lack of seasonal change in paradise that the poet has already described. He departs for "side rice / middangeardes, þær no men bugað / eard ond eþel" ("a wide land / on earth, where no men inhabit / the land and country," 156–8). He takes leadership of other birds, who flock to him (158–60); the place they live for a time is described only as "westen," "a wasteland" (161). Once the poem has set the scene, lengthy descriptions become unnecessary, and the poet can dispose of the setting in a line or two while turning his attention, and the audience's, to the remarkable inhabitant. This second site receives almost no description.

The third site appears in a little more detail, though nowhere near as much as the first. When the phoenix and accompanying birds leave, "hy gesecað Syrwara lond" ("they seek the land of the Syrians," 166). The third place is also called "weste stowe," a "waste" or "deserted" place (169), but that does not mean it is barren. Instead, this third place has the perfect tree: God has granted it to be

>   ... ealra beama
> on eorðwege uplædendra
> beorhtast geblowen; ne mæg him bitres with
> scyldum sceððan, ac gescylded a
> wunað ungewyrded, þended woruld stondeð.   (177–81)

> ("... of all trees
> on earth growing upwards
> the brightest blossoming; nor may anything
> harm it with guilt, but it dwells always protected,
> unharmed as long as the world lasts.")

While we receive no more description of the land around the tree, we know that the attending birds gather "wyrta wynsume ond wudubleda" ("lovely plants and leaves from trees," 194), which the phoenix itself brings to the tree (199–200). Then "hus getimbreð" ("it builds a house," 202), which is or has a "solere" ("solarium," 204). Ultimately, the nest catches fire from the heat of the sun, the phoenix burns to death, and then the phoenix is born anew to return to the homeland first described and begin the cycle again. By the time the phoenix is immolated, however, the poet has led us away from consideration of it as a bird and towards considering its dwelling as a place humans could inhabit: a house, a sunroom.

The Phoenix displays great interest in setting as it frames the title being. This example may seem to differ from most in this study because the poem is allegorical, but that did not mean that it was not real. Scholars have long known that medieval people could accept things as simultaneously real and allegorical, because God had the power to infuse real objects and events with allegorical significance; this method of reading is most evident in glosses and commentaries on the Bible, but could be applied more broadly. The fact that the island is unreachable by people does not mean that it cannot exist, any more than that Enoch and Elijah cannot be waiting above the earth for the end times because people cannot now reach them.[100] Though it cannot be seen on its island, the phoenix's death is located in relation to human lands ("Syrwara lond," 166), and on its return from death to its island, it allows itself to be seen by people, who flock to see it in wonder (322–35). In this text, place is intimately connected with the wondrous nature of its inhabitant.

The Phoenix is unique in extant Old English literature. Old English narratives more commonly portray place in relation to human inhabitants. In addition to recounting events from the first book of the Bible, *Genesis* paints portraits of the inhabitants of different regions. Here some landscapes serve as comparisons and contrasts to the people who live there. *Genesis* presents Egypt as a place of wondrous buildings. Abraham sees there "hornsele hwite and hea byrig / beorhte blican" ("white horn-halls and a high city shining bright," *Genesis* 1821–2). That is *all* the description the poet provides of Egypt; twice as many lines are immediately thereafter spent on Sarah's beauty and how it may tempt the Egyptians to kill Abraham so they may have Sarah. Despite the exotic setting of Egypt, the *hornsele* might remind readers of the *hornsalu* of Riddle 3.8 (ASPR 3), the

---

100 See the previous chapter for Enoch and Elijah.

horngestreon of *The Ruin* 25 (ASPR 3), or the *horngeap* hall of *Beowulf* 82, also described as "hornreced" (704). Egypt may seem distant, and its white buildings unusual, but the horn-hall gives audiences a structure to which they can relate. The residents of the shining buildings admire Sarah's beauty until their ruler takes her for himself (1847–57); their aesthetics exceed their grasp, and an angry God ensures that Abraham and Sarah leave the luxury of Egypt to return to a more honest "wonge" or plain (1882).

When Abraham offers Lot a choice of land because he fears the two of them cannot share what they have without tension, Lot chooses the land

be Iordane,   grene eorðan.
Seo wæs wætrum weaht   and wæstmum þeaht,
lagostreamum leoht,   and gelic godes
neorxnawange,   oðþæt nergend god
for wera synnum   wylme gesealde
Sodoman and Gomorran,   sweartan lige.   (*Genesis* 1920–6)

("by the Jordan, green earth. It was refreshed by waters and covered with fruit, watered by streams, and like God's paradise, until God the Saviour gave Sodom and Gomorrah to fire, dark flames, for men's sins.")

His choice of the easier land seems only to cause him problems. First, Lot is abducted in the battle of the four kings, requiring Abraham to raise an army and rescue him (1960–2172). Then Lot returns to Sodom and disaster. While Lot seems hapless, the Sodomites actively contrast with the goodness of their land: "Þær folcstede fægre wæron, / men arlease, metode laðe" ("There were fair folk-places, / men without honour, hostile to the Creator," *Genesis* 1933–4); again, "folk-places" is an Anglo-Saxon term. Lot simultaneously sees the sin and the beauty: "facen and fyrene, and hine fægre heold"("treachery and sin, and [yet he] held [the land] fair," 1940–1). As in *The Phoenix*, the land is of interest in how it reflects on its inhabitants; unlike *The Phoenix*, *Genesis* uses description of landscape and city primarily to demonstrate the ironic gap between the beauty of the places and the moral worth of those who live there. Abraham's land receives little attention: we need no such illustrations to show his character, nor has he been seduced by green land to ignore the qualities of the inhabitants.

Genesis is full of oppositions between wastelands and *burhs* (cities or fortifications), between the wide "eorðe" to be farmed and populated and the cities that keep springing up.[101] Concern in these texts centres on peoples more than on places. *Genesis* is unusual in referring to Egypt as a place more than to its people. *Exodus*, more typically, refers to Egyptian people more than to Egypt. *Elene* refers to "Iudea cyn" ("the Jewish people," 209, 836), or to "Iudeum" or "Iudeas" ("Jews," 216, 268, 278, 328, 977, 1202) four times as often as to "Hierusalem" ("Jerusalem," 273) and "Ierusalem" ("Jerusalem," 1055).[102] *Andreas* also refers repeatedly to the Jewish people (ASPR 2, "Iudeum," 13, 966, 1408; "Iudea," 166, 1325; "Iudea cynn" 560), but it never names Jerusalem, even when Andreas tells of going to the temple with Jesus.

These texts display an interest in peoples that gives meaning to their locations. Studying the inhabitants of a place still plays an important role in the discipline of geography; for Anglo-Saxons who had not yet identified geography as a separate subject, inhabitants could define a place. Omission of foreign places and peoples sometimes helped Anglo-Saxon translators fit a text to established doxa, but more often translators, homilists, and poets chose to use place and people names and construct them in ways their audiences could comprehend. Sometimes they linked more familiar place or people names to less familiar ones. Sometimes history gave a place an intellectual reality. Sometimes the inhabitants helped establish what a place was. Authors frequently combined the different techniques to construct coherent places for Anglo-Saxon audiences.

Conclusions

We may think that our satellite photos and non-Mercator maps give us an objective view of the world.[103] Exploring the geography of the Anglo-Saxons reminds us that space is always constructed and situated, in place and in time. They regarded it pragmatically, creating word-pictures of places populated and full of history. Geography conveys psychological

---

101 Cities will be examined in more detail in chapter 5.

102 "Creca lond" ("land of the Greeks") receives three mentions: 250, 262, and 998.

103 Mercator maps have long been familiar, but many people are now also familiar with the major criticism of them: while they preserve the relative shapes of continents, these projections distort their size, making Europe and North America much larger than they should be relative to Africa and South America. How best to represent a globe on a flat map has been a perennial problem for map-makers. For a good visual introduction to the issue, see Dave Goldberg, "What's the Best Map Projection?" *A User's Guide to the Universe*, 3 March 2011 http://usersguidetotheuniverse.com/index.php/2011/03/03/whats-the-best-map-projection/.

meaning more than a sense of physical reality. Rome might be distant, but its ties to England were durable and significant. Jerusalem would never be seen by the vast majority of Anglo-Saxons, yet it could become familiar to readers or hearers. Vivid details and evocative words brought Egypt and Sodom to life, highlighted their sterility, and contrasted them with the productive, verdant lands given to Abraham and his descendants. The Anglo-Saxons had great interest in a geography more qualitative than quantitative.

Anglo-Saxon texts reveal that distant places are filled with peoples and animals. Space is never empty, and once the inhabitants of a space become known, it can be constructed instead as place. Peoples can be named and described, producing knowledge and a sense of mastery – an archive. When people as distant and different from the centre as Homodubii can be known and found to have recognizably human elements, then differences between the peoples of England and those of Rome and the Holy Land seem small indeed. Anglo-Saxons need not live with a constant, vertiginous sense of their own marginality when others can be marginal and yet understandable. In a world bounded by India and Thule, Rome and Jerusalem seem close to England. Though the world out there looms large, the people and places can be imaginatively incorporated into Anglo-Saxon culture.

Naming distant peoples and places reminds Anglo-Saxons of their differences from those people and gives them a sense of power through knowledge about places and the people in them. At the same time, a few of these texts give England brief but significant mentions, and several other texts give far more importance to Anglo-Saxon lands. The following chapter will examine approaches to geography that recentre Anglo-Saxon experience within northern Europe and make England as relevant as any other place.

3 Recentring: The North and England's Place

The previous chapter explored how Anglo-Saxon texts dealt with England's marginality on the world stage, particularly in relation to the most distant places, those on the Mediterranean and beyond. While many English texts recognized that Britain lay near the end of the known world, they did not allow its physical location to keep the Anglo-Saxons sidelined. Omitting mention of other places might help avoid problems that audiences could face in a text centred elsewhere, but Anglo-Saxon authors and translators made only limited use of that strategy, at most following it for some passages but not entire works. Instead, texts gave Anglo-Saxon readers knowledge of remote places, asserting a certain kind of control: to know a space well enough to render it a coherent place, one must feel some connection to it. Writers made faraway places seem familiar by repeating their names and forging bonds between those places and other, often more familiar locations or peoples; by linking places with historical events; and by exploring the inhabitants of those places. All these strategies helped Anglo-Saxon translators, writers, readers, and auditors make places in their mental archives for Rome, the Middle East, northern Africa, and sometimes even more distant locales.

Not all texts present England as absent or marginalized. Anglo-Saxon lives centred around England and particular places in England, so it is not surprising that many places in Europe appear in English texts specifically as they relate to England, building on audiences' existing knowledge, expectations, and lived experience of the world. The previous chapter showed such a perspective at work in the Mediterranean and beyond. Another orientation takes England itself as its starting point and can be found everywhere from charters to chronicles to poetry. Some texts can use more than one perspective: Alfredian translations can connect to

Rome or the Holy Land, the Northmen or Weland, after prefaces that begin with England.

A third approach avoids or moves away from a specific, earthly geographical centre to remind audiences of the broader cosmic perspective seen in the first chapter. While texts may take any of these perspectives temporarily, and some shift from one to another, most Anglo-Saxon texts ultimately find a way to recentre themselves upon England, redirect readers to a more universal perspective, or both.[1] The Anglo-Saxons constructed a place for themselves in their own times.

Recentring: England

Some texts recentred themselves and readers directly on Brittania, England, the land of the Anglo-Saxons. Call it what you will – and in the period this study covers, the Anglo-Saxon did not yet call it any one thing consistently – England comes into focus, sometimes even in the very texts that marginalize it.[2] First and foremost, the act of translation into English itself validates the vernacular and puts the Anglo-Saxons into contact with world cultures as explored in the previous chapter.[3] A geographical recentring takes place as well, if only temporarily, combatting perceptions of England's insignificance to world history and geography that classical and late antique texts alone would have conveyed. Bede's *Ecclesiastical History* and its old English translation, the *Anglo-Saxon Chronicle*, and to a lesser extent Cynewulf make so much of the connection between Rome and England that Nicholas Howe titled one of his articles "Rome: Capital of Anglo-Saxon England."[4]

---

1 In *Angels on the Edge of the World*, Kathy Lavezzo argues that the English turn their own distance and "strangeness" into a form of authority and ultimately power, but her treatment covers the start of the early modern period, when English people could more easily imagine empire for themselves. I argue here and in chapter 2 for a different construction of authority and power based on knowledge and language use.

2 For terminology for England, see pp. 60–1 in the previous chapter.

3 For the politics of translation, see especially Kathleen Davis, "National Writing in the Ninth Century: A Reminder for Postcolonial Thinking about the Nation," *Journal of Medieval and Early Modern Studies* 28.3 (1998): 611–37; her "The Performance of Translation Theory in King Alfred's National Literary Program," in *Manuscript, Narrative, Lexicon: Essays on Literary and Cultural Transmission in Honor of Whitney F. Bolton*, ed. Robert Boenig and Kathleen Davis (Lewisburg, PA: Bucknell University Press, 2000), 149–70; and my book *The King's English*.

4 *Journal of Medieval and Early Modern Studies* 34 (2004): 147–72.

Bede makes it clear from the very first words of his *Historia* that his account has its centre in England through a preface that begins: "Gloriosissimo regi Ceoluulfo Beda famulus Christi et presbyter" (2; "To the most glorious King Ceolwulf, Bede, servant of Christ and priest," trans. Colgrave and Mynors, 3).[5] The work has been written for an English king with an English name. In his next sentence, Bede calls it "Historiam gentis Anglorum ecclesiasticam" ("Ecclesiastical history of the English people").[6] Later he writes: "Auctor ante omnes atque adiutor opusculi huius Albinus abba reuerentissismus ... qui in ecclesia Cantuariorum a beatae memoriae Theodoro archiepiscopo et Hadriano abbate ..." (2; "My principal authority and helper in this modest work has been the revered Abbot Albinus ... who was educated in the Kentish Church by Archbishop Theodore and Abbot Hadrian," trans. Colgrave and Mynors, 3). Bede's main source and support is an Englishman, albeit one educated by foreign missionaries. He then lists other informants: Nothhelm of London; Daniel, bishop of the West Saxons; monks from Lastingham (4) and Abbot Esi of that monastery; Bishop Cyneberht of Lindsey (6); "aliorum fidelium uirorum" (6; "other trustworthy men," trans. Colgrave and Mynors, 7); and the monks at Lindisfarne (6). He obtained records from Kent and some from Rome (4). Bede's informants all inhabit England, and even the documents from Rome were brought back by an Englishman (4). They may be from different peoples within England, but his preface encourages us to consider these potentially separate races as the subject of a single study. The Old English translation follows the Latin preface so closely that a reader who did not know of the Latin text could think that the Old English text

---

5 *Bede's Ecclesiastical History of the English People*, ed. and trans. Colgrave and Mynors, 2 and 3. I use their translations except as indicated.

6 I have not followed Colgrave and Minors here, for they render the title at this point *"History of the English Church and Nation"* (3), suggesting that the English nation is one of two objects of study where Bede clearly subordinates the "gentis Anglorum" to the "Historiam ecclesiasticam": he studies the history of the church of the English people, not the English people per se. Alternatively, "Anglorum" could be taken as "of the Angles" – not all the English, but a specific group descended from the Continental Angles. Bede's text focuses more on Anglian areas than on others, but it does include most of England at some points, so here I would take "Anglorum" as referring to all the people we call "Anglo-Saxons." Yet see Harris, *Race and Ethnicity*, esp. chap. 2, "The Election of the Angles," 45–82, for the argument that Bede's text focuses first and foremost on the Angles (*Angli*) with other *gentes* joining them in becoming Christian.

was itself the direct work of Bede.[7] Both the Latin and the English texts position themselves very much as works by Angles or Englishmen.

Clearly not one of the authors who marginalizes England, Bede begins with a description of Britain in the first line of his first chapter and situates it within Europe:

Brittania Oceani insula, cui quondam Albion nomen fuit, inter septentrionem et occidentem locata est, Germaniae Galliae Hispaniae, maximis Europae partibus, multo interuallo aduersa. (*Historia* 1.1)

("Britain, once called Albion, is an island of the ocean and lies to the northwest, being opposite Germany, Gaul, and Spain, which form the greater part of Europe, though at a considerable distance from them," Colgrave and Mynors, 15)

For Bede, living before a unified England, the geographical boundaries of the British Isles differ greatly from the area inhabited by the Anglians. He includes Britain, Ireland, and the Orkneys, though his story will never again touch on the Orkneys; after the geographical introduction, the Orkneys appear only in his chronological summary at the end (560, under 46 CE). The length, breadth, and coastline are given in miles. Bede's geography seems more classical or modern than early medieval: he focuses not just on the peoples and history of the places, but conditions of the land and waters and even measurements, which figure in very few Anglo-Saxon treatments of place. He may have taken the notion of beginning with geography from Gildas's *De excidio Brittaniae*, Orosius's *Libri VII*

---

7 See my "The Old English *Bede* and the Construction of Anglo-Saxon Authority," *ASE* 31 (2002): 69–80. The Old English version notably omits documentation, especially that from non-Anglo-Saxon writers, emphasizing the English nature of the text. See also Sharon M. Rowley, *The Old English Version of Bede's "Historia ecclesiastica,"* Anglo-Saxon Studies 16 (Rochester, NY: Boydell and Brewer, 2011). George Molyneaux rejects my argument in "The *Old English Bede*: English Ideology or Christian Instruction?," pointing out that documents involving English matters were also dropped. I maintain that the overall effect of dropping so many documents was to centre the *Bede* on England and English authority, for the omission of English documents is balanced by the fact that the text relies on a clearly English authority in giving his account in English; the omission of Roman documents simply diminishes the amount of authority from Rome in the text.

historiarum contra paganos, and the *Historia Francorum* by Gregory of Tours, all of which he quotes in his opening.[8]

Bede itemizes the animals that live in and around Britain, and the salt pits, waters, and minerals found there; he recalls its twenty-eight former cities (14–16). He also notes that because of its location in the North, Britain has longer days in summer and shorter in winter than Armenia, Macedonia, and Italy (16). After listing the five languages of the British Isles, beginning with English and ending with Latin, he relates a brief history of the non-English races before discussing Ireland's animals and people (16–20). The amount of detail Bede gives surpasses anything in his sources. This opening sets the tone for the entire work. Readers may find themselves periodically transported to Rome or even briefly to the Holy Land with excerpts from Arculf's travelogue dictated to Adomnán (506–13), but they always return to England.[9] Bede combines a classical approach to geography with a very non-classical interest.

For Bede's *Historia* concentrates on England, not the whole of the British Isles, despite the coverage of the Orkneys, Scotland, and Ireland in his introduction. He refers to Rome only as it pertains to England, occasionally through the broader history of Christianity but usually because of direct contact between the two places: the invasion by Caesar in 60 BCE and the subsequent conquest by Claudius, for instance. His most detailed accounts generally concern northern England, in the areas he knows best and where he finds informants. Stephen Harris argues that Bede begins with the Angles, or Anglians, as his focus. "As it develops, though, the compass of his collective identity philanthropically expands to include all the *gentes Christianorum* on the island."[10] Gregory's discovery of English boys and his puns on *Angli/angelici* (Angles/angelic), *Deiri/De ira* (Deira/ the wrath of God), and *Ælle/Alleluia* ([King] Ælle/alleluia) open book 2 in Bede's history and its Old English translation, connecting Rome to England and leading to the mission that converts the English. Bede's *Historia* keeps England central, even while it touches on events on the Continent that affect England and glances as far as Jerusalem. Bede's *Historia ecclesiastica* gave Anglo-Saxons a text that made for them a place, though one not simple or unified.[11]

---

8 See footnote 1, page 14, in the edition by Colgrave and Mynors.

9 The OE *Bede* does not include the chapter treating Arculf and his text.

10 Harris, *Race and Ethnicity*, 15.

11 See especially Harris's second chapter, "The Election of the Angles"; ibid., 45–82.

Though they receive less attention than the Anglians, other Germanic peoples now in England appear repeatedly in the *Historia*: the Mercians, Kentish people, and the East, West, and South Saxons. While Bede may have aimed primarily to provide a history of and for Anglians, dedicated to the Northumbrian King Ceolwulf (2), his text received a much wider audience. Deliberately or not, Bede's *Historia ecclesiastica gentis Anglorum* followed the *Historia Francorum* by Gregory of Tours in establishing the sense of a people unified by language. The work had resonance outside Northumbria (and even outside England), as amply demonstrated by its copying and preservation: R.A.B. Mynors lists over 160 manuscripts or fragments in the introduction to his edition with Bertram Colgrave.[12] One or more Mercians found the work worthy of translating into Old English in the late ninth or early tenth century.[13]

The Old English *Bede* concentrates even more on England than its Latin source, omitting the Pelagian controversy, some of the correspondence with Rome, and Adomnán's account of the Holy Land.[14] The text begins with Bede's preface, allowing audiences to think that Bede addresses them directly in Old English.[15] It then moves smoothly to the geographical introduction, rendering the first four lines of the Latin directly into Old English and thus giving the names of Britain and its length and width (24.29–26.1).[16] The Old English *Bede* condenses what follows but retains interest in what lives in and around the island: fish, sea mammals, and molluscs (26.1–20). It even keeps mentions of salt pits, hot springs, minerals, gems, and hours of sunlight (26.20–6). The main body of the text retains Bede's emphasis on English history. The translator and subsequent

---

12 *Bede's Ecclesiastical History*, xlii–lxxvi.

13 For more on the translator or translators, see Rowley, *Old English Version*.

14 See note 7 above on documentation in the *Bede*. Pelagius was a late antique writer said by several sources to be from Britain. His writings survive only in fragments; his arguments have been reconstructed from rebuttals by his opponents. In these accounts, Pelagius rejected the Christian doctrine of original sin, the idea that in Adam and Eve's first disobedience all humanity incurred guilt and a tendency towards sin. He taught that all people choose freely between good and evil and that one can live a good life and be saved without divine grace. In the *Historia ecclesiastica*, Bede treats this heresy as a major part of his first book and an evil that did great harm to the Britons. The Old English version removes the heresy, changing the characterization of the Britons as well as the thematic workings of book 1. For more details, see Rowley, *Old English Version*, esp. 77–83.

15 See my "Old English *Bede*."

16 For sources of the OE *Bede*, see J. Hart, "The Sources of The Old English Bede, History of the English Church and People (Cameron C.B.9.6)," *Fontes*.

scribes were not deterred by the primacy of Anglians in the text they adapted to their own dialect; Sharon Rowley argues that the translator had access to more complete information on Mercia and quietly altered the text to cover the Mercians' perspective as well.[17]

The *Anglo-Saxon Chronicle* follows Bede's lead. Manuscripts D, E, and F open with a geography taken directly from Bede's *Historia* that follows the Latin even more closely than the Old English *Bede*'s version of the passage does.[18] This preface in the *Chronicle* begins with the measurements of Britain, then a description of its inhabitants (though it confuses Armorica, which Bede cites as the origin of the Britons, with Armenia, which, Bede notes, shares a latitude with Macedonia and Italy). The *Chronicle* versions emphasize who settled where, showing attention to history and inhabitants in line with that shown in the previous chapter, but they omit descriptions of the waters, salt pits, minerals, and hours of sunlight. The *Chronicle* then tells the story of what we now call England from 60 BCE, when the Romans first attempted to conquer the island, until the various versions end in different years.[19] After 449, the *Chronicle* traces the rise of the Anglo-Saxon people culminating, in the first recension, in Alfred the Great.[20] In keeping with the opening, little description of landscapes or animals appears; attention goes to the people and the events in the many places named.

The *Chronicle* sometimes leaves England for Francia and Frisia, specifically in order to track the movement of the *Dena* (Danes) or *Northmen*

---

17 Rowley, *Old English Version*; see esp. chap. 5, "Who Read Æthelbert's Letter? Translation, Mediation and Authority in the *OEHE*," 98–113.

18 See Susan Irvine, "The Sources of the Anglo-Saxon Chronicle MS E (Cameron C.B.17.9)," *Fontes*. The other manuscripts have not been individually sourced, but Irvine's work can be generalized to passages shared by other versions.

19 A runs to 1093, B to 977, C to 1066, D to 1080, E all the way to 1154, and F to 1058. For the construction of England in the *Chronicle*, see especially Stodnick, "Writing Home"; Susan Irvine, "The Anglo-Saxon Chronicle," in *A Companion to Alfred the Great*, ed. Nicole Guenther Discenza and Paul E. Szarmach, Brill Companions to the Christian Tradition 58 (Leiden: Brill, 2015), 344–67; and their bibliographies.

20 For recensions of the *Chronicle*, see Janet M. Bately, "The Compilation of the *Anglo-Saxon Chronicle* 60 BC to AD 890: Vocabulary as Evidence," *PBA* 64 (1978): 93–129, repr. as the Sir Israel Gollancz Memorial Lecture, 1986, and in *British Academy Papers on Anglo-Saxon England*, selected and introduced by E.G. Stanley (Oxford: Oxford University Press, 1990), 261–97; and "The Compilation of the *Anglo-Saxon Chronicle* Once More," *Leeds Studies in Engl.* ns 16 (1985): 7–26, also in a separate volume entitled *Sources and Relations: Studies in Honour of J.E. Cross*, ed. Marie Collins, Jocelyn Price, and Andrew Hamer (Leeds: University of Leeds School of English, 1985).

– the Viking raiders who beset England starting in the late eighth century. Some annals retell their activities in Francia with nearly the same level of detail given to foreign armies in England (compare, for instance, 879, in England, to 881, in Francia). The connections between England and Francia become quite clear in subsequent annals: when the Scandinavian armies attack Francia, they usually leave England, giving Anglo-Saxons some time to rebuild and shore up defences. The details in some entries not only indicate likely Continental sources, but also suggest that audiences might recognize Continental place names:

> AN. .dccclxxxvii. Her for se here up þurh þa brycge æt Paris 7 þa up andlang Sigene oþ Mæterne oþ Cariei, 7 þa sæton þara 7 innan Ionan tu winter on þam twam stedum. (A, 887)[21]

> ("887. In this year the enemy went up through the bridge at Paris and then the length of the Seine to the Marne and then to Chézy, and then they stayed there and around the Yonne two winters in that place.")

When the enemy army returns to England, the *Chronicle* leaves the Continent again to relate events at home. Francia and Scandinavia have importance in the *Chronicle* solely as they relate to England.

Rome looms larger in the *Chronicle* than the rest of the Continent does. Nicholas Howe describes the *Chronicle* as one of the "two great Anglo-Saxon works of history ... rooted not simply in the events of Rome but more deeply in Rome's vision for interpreting the map of the world."[22] Though Howe describes "Rome's ability to determine events in England," particularly as evidenced by Gregory's letters to Augustine, the *Chronicle* depicts more of a mutual relationship.[23] Alfred's dispatch of messengers with alms to Rome demonstrates close, regular ties to this still-important city (A–E 887, 888, 889, 890) and suggests that England can make a difference to Rome as well, as does the ongoing presence of an English quarter (*scolu*) in Rome.[24] The Anglo-Saxons are not isolated, as Orosius's Latin *Historia* seemed to imply. Surely this representation of history fits Anglo-Saxon dispositions much more comfortably than classical histories did.

---

21 *MS A*, ed. Janet M. Bately, ASCCE 3 (Cambridge: Brewer, 1986).
22 Howe, "Rome," 149. Bede's *Historia* is the other.
23 Howe, "Rome," 154.
24 See the *Chronicle* in the ASCCE: 816 in A, and 885 (ADEF) or 886 (BC).

The audience of the Old English *Orosius* would have a very different experience than one reading Bede's *Historia*, the Old English *Bede*, or the *Anglo-Saxon Chronicle*. They would encounter reminders of their marginality throughout the text, but significantly, only after being greeted:

> Ure ieldran ealne þisne ymbhwyrft þises middangeardes, cwæþ Orosius, swa swa Oceanus utan ymbligeþ, þone [mon] garsæcg hateð, on þreo todældon 7 hie þa þrie dælas on þreo tonemdon: Asiam 7 Europem 7 Affricam, þeah þe sume men sæden þæt þær nære buton twegen dælas: Asia 7 þæ`t´oþer Europe. (*Orosius* 8.11–15)[25]

> ("Our ancestors divided all this circuit of the earth, as far as *Oceanus* (which men call the ocean) extends, said Orosius, into three, and they distinguished the three portions with three names: Asia and Europe and Africa, although some men said that there were only two parts: Asia and Europe.")

Readers thus inhabit a dual position: the word "Ure" includes them; these appear to be "*our* ancestors" at the outset. Then "cwæþ Orosius" intervenes, breaking the identification for a moment – not "our ancestors" but Orosius's ancestors.[26] Yet readers encounter not Latin but English. Accounts of voyages by men named Ohthere and Wulfstan interrupt the long classical geography with details about northern Europe recounted in English.[27] Fabienne Michelet notes that the failure to interpolate more English geography into the *Orosius*, especially when other elements of the geographical introduction are altered to conform to present knowledge, indicates that England is assumed to be the focal point around which the rest of the world turns.[28] Moreover, at least one manuscript counterbalanced the *Orosius*'s coverage of a world nearly excluding the English with a focus on the English: Cotton Tiberius B. i begins with the *Orosius* and ends with the *Anglo-Saxon Chronicle* C.[29] Anglo-Saxon history serves

---

25 All citations from the *Orosius* come from *The Old English Orosius*, ed. Bately.

26 Mary Kate Hurley reads this as less of a disruption than I do and more the creation of a virtual community of readers asked to read like fifth-century Romans while still being ninth-century Anglo-Saxons; see her "Alfredian Temporalities: Time and Translation in the Old English *Orosius*," *JEGP* 112.4 (2013): 405–32.

27 Ohthere and Wulfstan's voyages will be discussed more below.

28 *Creation, Migration, and Conquest: Imaginary Geography and Sense of Space in Old English Literature* (Oxford: Oxford University Press, 2006), 132–6.

29 For a full description of the manuscript, see *MS C*, ed. Katherine O'Brien O'Keeffe, ASCCE 5 (Cambridge: Brewer, 2001), xv–lvi; contents are listed on xxv–vi.

here as a continuation of the Old English *Orosius*. Now that the four empires have fallen, each in turn, this manuscript presents England as a place full of history and worthy of study along with Babylonia, the empires ruled by Alexander and Ptolemy, and the Roman empire.[30]

Language and references to the royal court also set the Old English translation of Gregory the Great's *Pastoral Care* into a specifically Anglo-Saxon frame, though the main text does not envision England at all. Alfred's prose and verse prefaces to the *Pastoral Care* centre on England, not Rome. While the prose preface shows a clear awareness of the higher status of Latin, Alfred insists on *Angelcynn*, a word he uses seven times in the preface (though it was then a new term, as Sarah Foot has demonstrated), and the *englisc* language, named six times in the preface and once in the verse preface.[31] Respect for Latin language and culture actually encourages respect for English language and culture, because Alfred positions the Anglo-Saxons as the heirs of ancient cultures, establishing a genealogy of authority in which Hebrew, Greek, and Latin culture culminate in Anglo-Saxon culture.[32] The prose preface invokes "Angelcynn" immediately (*PC* 3.3 and 3.4) and becomes even more specific shortly thereafter, dividing "behionan Humbre" ("on this side of the Humber," 3.14) from "begiondan Humbre" ("beyond the Humber," 3.16) and then further qualifying "besuðan Temese" ("south of the Thames," 3.18). The *Pastoral Care* itself might make England seem marginal, or even off the

---

30 For more on these four empires, see the previous chapters and below, pp. 126–7.

31 *Angelcynn* appears at 3.3, 3.4, 3.13, 5.10, 5.20, 7.10, and 7.16; *King Alfred's West-Saxon Version*, ed. Sweet. See Sarah Foot, "The Making of *Angelcynn*: English Identity before the Norman Conquest," *TRHS*, 6th ser., 6 (1996): 25–49. *Englisc* appears in the prose preface at 3.15 (twice), 7.13, 7.18, 7.19, and 7.24; and in the verse preface at 9.13 (ASPR 6). Alfred also invokes the English language twice in the body of the *Pastoral Care*.

32 Kathleen Davis comments upon Alfred's emphasis on following church tradition: Gregory is his source author, while Continental models such as Charlemagne worked very much in a church context as well ("Performance" 151–4). Davis argues in "National Writing," "Alfred never considers that the vernacular might be inappropriate or inferior, but suggests that Latin was retained only because 'woldon ðæt her ðy mara wisdom on londe wære ðy we ma geðeoda cuðon' [they would have it that the more languages we knew, the greater would be wisdom in this land] (5/24–5). According to this formulation, translation is necessary, but it is not an unfortunate compromise. Rather, the English vernacular stands as one among many legitimate languages" (615). Surely Alfred and his audience recognized the superior status of Latin; by not explicitly addressing or apologizing for the difference, however, Alfred avoids reinforcing it at the very moment he seeks to legitimate English.

map entirely, but readers come to it only after reading a prose preface that concentrates on England, not the Mediterranean. The invocation of Gregory alone might have been enough to make readers think of their connection with the saint known as the converter of the English.[33] England takes its place in this genealogy of learning as the heir of Greece and Rome.

The verse preface also constructs a *translatio studii*, or translation of learning, in the one reference that most directly invokes the Mediterranean world:

> Ðis ærendgewrit   Agustinus
> ofer sealtne sæ   suðan brohte
> iegbuendum,   swa hit ær fore
> adihtode   dryhtnes cempa,
> Rome papa.   Ryhtspell monig
> Gregorius   gleawmod gindwod
> ðurh sefan snyttro,   searoðonca hord.

("Augustine brought this document over the salt sea from the south to the island dwellers, as God's champion, the pope at Rome, composed it earlier. Clever-minded Gregory knew thoroughly many true discourses through the wisdom of his heart, his hoard of clever thoughts.")

Knowledge was transmitted by Augustine of Canterbury, who brought the book from Rome, at the command of the same pope who wrote the book in question. Readers hear how the very work they are reading travelled from Rome to their own land.[34]

The *Pastoral Care* brings *Angelcynn* notionally closer to Rome: the Anglo-Saxons become the direct heir of this glorious culture as embodied in the translated text. For, as Bourdieu argues, authorization "can only succeed if [it] … is guaranteed by the whole group or by a recognized institution."[35]

---

33 Colgrave and Mynors note in their edition when Bede tells of Gregory the Great and his role in the conversion of England: "This story which Bede says is traditional is found in a shorter and slightly different form in the Whitby *Life*. Both authors are probably quoting from different forms of the oral tradition" (footnote on 133). The audience might not even have needed familiarity with Bede's writings to know this anecdote.

34 For more about the construction of authority and *translatio studii* in the verse preface, see my "Alfred's Verse Preface."

35 Bourdieu, *Language and Symbolic Power*, ed. John B. Thomson and trans. Gino Raymond and Matthew Adamson (Cambridge, MA: Harvard University Press, 1991), 125.

The *Pastoral Care* itself remains predominantly focused within: on the ruler's disposition and how he leads those under him. Alfred certainly found these instructions as applicable to his people as to Gregory's Romans. The fact that later people found the text worthy to be copied indicates that his successors valued it as well.[36]

The *Dialogues* similarly have prefaces to set the text firmly in an English context, although they do not have the explicit *translatio studii* of these two prefaces to the *Pastoral Care*. Readers encountering the Old English translation of Gregory's *Dialogi* in Cambridge, Corpus Christi College 322, and Oxford, Bodleian Hatton 76, find this preface:

> Ic ÆLFRED geofendum Criste mid cynehades mærnysse geweorðod, habbe gearolice ongyten 7 þurh haligra boca gesægene oft gehyred, þætte us, þam þe God swa micle heanesse worldgeþingða forgifen hafað, is seo mæste ðearf, þæt we hwilon ure mod betwix þas eorþlican ymbhigdo geleoðigen 7 gebigen to ðam godcundan 7 þam gastlican rihte. 7 forþan ic sohte 7 wilnade to minum getreowum freondum, þæt hi me of Godes bocum be haligra manna þeawum 7 wundrum awriten þas æfterfylgendan lare, þæt ic þurh þa myne-gunge 7 lufe gescyrped on minum mode betwih þas eorðlican gedrefednesse hwilum gehicge þa heofonlican. (1.1–21)[37]

("I, Alfred, honoured with the renown of kingship by the gift of Christ, have eagerly perceived and often heard it said in holy books that for us, whom God has given so much greatness in worldly things, there is the greatest need that we sometimes loose the earthly cares from our mind and submit to divine and spiritual rule. And therefore I sought and wished of my true friends that they would write for me the following learning from God's books concerning the customs and miracles of holy men, so that I, roused through these admonitions and love, might sometimes consider the heavenly things amidst these earthly burdens.")

---

36 Four of the six extant manuscripts are later copies; for the manuscripts and later use, see David F. Johnson, "Alfredian Apocrypha," in *A Companion to Alfred the Great*, ed. Discenza and Szarmach, 368–95.

37 Italics indicate where Hecht has supplied letters abbreviated in the manuscript: *Bischof Wærferths von Worcester*. I have quoted from MS C: Cambridge, Corpus Christi College 322. In the Hatton manuscript, synonyms have been substituted for several words. For the revisions in Hatton, see David Yerkes, *Two Versions of Wærferth's Translation of Gregory's Dialogues: An Old English Thesaurus* (Toronto: University of Toronto Press, 1979).

The preface seems to offer the very personal reflection of an Englishman upon the book to come. None other than Alfred, king of the West Saxons (or, as he styled himself later in his reign, king of the Anglo-Saxons), welcomes readers to the book. This royal Anglo-Saxon reader finds personal relevance in tales of miracles worked in Gregory's Rome and environs and invites readers to do the same. Malcolm Godden has argued that the preface is not by Alfred, but regardless of whether the king truly wrote this preface or someone else wrote it in his voice, readers are greeted first by an Anglo-Saxon king and only then introduced to the translated voice of a Roman pope.[38]

Readers of the now-damaged British Library, Cotton Otho C.i, vol. 2, would encounter not Alfred's voice but the book's own. That copy has a verse preface that begins "Se ðe me rædan ðencð tyneð mid rihtum geðance" ("He who sets out to read me will close me with proper understanding").[39] This voice comes from the very object in front of the readers, grounding the text in an immediate, physical experience, as well as an intellectual and spiritual one. This verse preface also invokes the name of an English prelate: "Me awriten het Wulfsige bisceop" (line 12; "Bishop Wulfsige commanded me to be written," trans. Irvine and Godden, 405), the book declares, later asking readers for prayers with the words: "Bideþ þe se bisceop se þe ðas boc begeat, / þe þu on þinum handum nu hafast ond sceawast / þæt þu him to þeossum halgum helpe bidde" (16–18; "The bishop who procured this book, which you now have in your hands and gaze at, requests that you should pray these holy men … to help him," trans. Irvine and Godden, 405).[40] This invocation connects the English bishop physically with the reader; the latter is handling the work of the former,

---

38 Godden, "Wærferth and King Alfred: The Fate of the Old English *Dialogues*," in *Alfred the Wise: Studies in Honour of Janet Bately on the Occasion of Her Sixty-fifth Birthday*, ed. Jane Roberts and Janet L. Nelson with Malcolm Godden (Cambridge: Brewer, 1997), 35–51.

39 Text and translation from *The Old English Boethius with Verse Prologues and Epilogues Associated with King Alfred*, ed. and trans. Susan Irvine and Malcolm R. Godden, Dumbarton Oaks Medieval Library 19 (Cambridge, MA: Harvard University Press, 2012), 404–5.

40 The identity of the bishop here is problematic. The manuscript now reads "Wulfstan," but an erasure under the *–tan* originally read *–ige*: Wulfsige (see Godden, "Wærferth and King Alfred," 39). Malcolm Godden postulates that Wulfsige received an early copy, one that lacked "Alfred's" preface, and so composed his own before having it copied; a later copyist then replaced the name Wulfsige with the more current Wulfstan; see "Wærferth and King Alfred," 39–40.

creating a tactile connection before the reader ventures into the Mediterranean world of Gregory the Great. The two different prefaces suggest that the work may have originally appeared with no preface, but that at least two different writers, scribes, or readers desired to link a text about Italian saints firmly to their own English home. Though they did so in different ways, one effect remains the same: England's importance is foregrounded before one even begins reading the *Dialogues*.

Even such a difficult philosophical text as the *Boethius* forges links between England and Rome. The prose (B) text opens, "Ælfred kuning wæs wealhstod ðisse bec and hie of boclædene on Englisc wende swa hio nu is gedon" (Preface 1–2; "King Alfred was translator of this book, and turned it from Latin into English, as it is now done," trans. Godden and Irvine, vol. 2, 1). The proem reiterates the process a few lines later: despite the difficulties that the translator encountered, he "þas boc hæfde geleornode and of Lædene to Engliscum spelle gewende" (Preface 7–8; "had learnt this book and turned it from Latin into English prose," trans. Godden and Irvine, vol. 2, 1). The vernacular meets the language of authority. I have argued elsewhere that this preface did not originate with Alfred but was added later; the addition suggests that at least one reader felt a need to connect this late antique text explicitly to England, as readers of the translated *Dialogues* did when they added prefaces.[41]

Similarly, some homilies make connections between England and the Mediterranean world. As noted before, Ælfric names people and places in the Holy Land far more often than he names England. However, Ælfric also builds links between them. In a homily on the Trinity, Rome and Jerusalem are juxtaposed with "ðisum earde" ("this land," *Catholic Homilies* 1.20.181).[42] The story of Gregory's encounter with the English slave boys and his subsequent pun on "Angle" and "angel" appears not only in Bede's Latin *Ecclesiastical History* and its Old English translation (book 2, chapter 1 in both) but also in Ælfric's homily on Gregory (*Catholic Homilies* 2.9), as noted in the previous chapter. The distance from England to Rome is hardly uncrossable: in addition to the many stories of travels to and from Rome by officials (and occasionally penitents) related by Bede, the *Chronicle*, and other sources, in Ælfric's account of Swithun, we hear

---

41 "Alfred the Great and the Anonymous Prose Proem to the *Boethius*," *JEGP* 107 (2008): 57–76.

42 For the *Catholic Homilies*, see Ælfric's *Catholic Homilies: The First Series: Text*, ed. Clemoes; *Ælfric's Catholic Homilies: The Second Series: Text*, ed. Godden; and *Ælfric's Catholic Homilies: Introduction*, ed. Godden.

of a man who goes from England to Rome and then back again in search of healing.[43]

Old English biblical poems have settings quite distant and different from England, but some poems take place much closer to home. Poems set within England may name Britain, England, or the English, but more often they simply name specific places within England. Here writers need not attach place names to better-known places; where the *Orosius* often introduces a place in relation to the Mediterranean and biblical poems cite Jerusalem frequently, English writers name *Eligbyrig* (Ely, *Death of Alfred* 18) or Brunanburh (*The Battle of Brunanburh*) without needing to explain who lived there.

Seasons for Fasting weaves together Rome, Israel, and England, moving from the historical "ealddagum Israheala folc" ("the Israelites in the old days," *Seasons* 1, ASPR 6) and "Romwara" ("Romans," 50) to the contemporary "Brytena leodum" ("people of Britain," 56) who must now observe proper fasts. *The Menologium* outdoes *Seasons*, alternating references to events from the life of Christ, the apostles, and certain saints with their application to England. The poem opens with Christ's birth and baptism, then brings the reader or hearer back "on Brytene" ("in Britain," 14, ASPR 6) to celebrate. Mentions of St Matthew and St Gregory might bring the Holy Land and Rome to mind, but then the poet tells us that St Gregory is "breme in Brytene" ("honoured in Britain," 40). Further mentions of Mary, the apostles, and St Helena give way to a reminder of Augustine of Canterbury, who fulfilled Gregory's behest: "he on Brytene her / eaðmode him eorlas funde / to godes willan" ("he found here in Britain nobles obedient to him, according to God's will," 98–100). Augustine "Nu on Brytene rest / on Cantwarum cynestole neah, / mystre mærum" ("now lies in Britain among those in Kent, near the high seat, the famous minster," 104–6). The poem mentions Rome (123) when it reaches Peter and Paul, but then returns explicitly to "Brytene" to celebrate the feast of Bartholomew (155). "Engle and Seaxe," "Angles and Saxons," are named (185), and the poem closes,

> Nu ge findan magon
> haligra tiida   þe man healdan sceal,
> swa bebugeð gebod   geond Brytenricu[44]
> Sexna kyninges   on þas sylfan tiid.
>
> (228–31)

---

43 *Ælfric's Lives of Saints*, ed. and trans. Skeat, "Saint Swithun, Bishop," 1.21.193–201. I will examine this passage more closely below, pp. 134–5.

44 "brytenricu" is ambiguous. The *DOE* lists only two occurrences of the word "brytenrice": "1. spacious kingdom; 'destructive power' has also been proposed, if *bryten* is

("Now you may find the holy days which one must hold as far as the commandment of the Saxon king extends through the kingdoms of Britain in these times.")

Feast days and fast days connect Britain with Rome and Jerusalem; they enjoy simultaneous observances, uniting them in God.

Thus, while many works transport readers outside England, many others stay within England or move back and forth between England and foreign lands. In translations, homilies, and poetry, writers invoke the names of famous, distant places in connection with England itself. England seems less sidelined when writers emphasize its connections with these places, ones more central on maps and more prevalent than in most Latin texts. In these works by Anglo-Saxons, England's place in the world reflects and shapes the lived experiences of their audiences. Writers cannot constantly invoke England in texts from or set in foreign lands, however, so two other strategies help audiences make distant spaces relevant to their own lives in England.

Recentring: Northern Europe

Anglo-Saxons did not have a name for non-Mediterranean Europe, yet they treated it differently than they treated such places as the Holy Land, Rome, and Greece. What we might call northern Europe, including much of what is now France, Germany, and the Scandinavian countries, had inhabitants who differed in language, customs, and history from those of Italy, northern Africa, the Middle East, or Asia. Northern Europe was physically closer to England than the rest of the world was, and ethnic, trade, and cultural ties between parts of northern Europe and England were stronger than the ties between England and anywhere else except Rome. These spaces are between Yi-Fu Tuan's notional cosmos and hearth, combining elements of each: the variety of the cosmos with some of the safety and familiarity of the hearth.[45]

A world not centred on Rome and Jerusalem appears unexpectedly in the middle of *Orosius*'s traditional geography, which places Brittania at the very margins as discussed in the previous chapter. Two interviews inserted

---

related to brȳtan 'to destroy'" and "2. ? spacious kingdom ? kingdom of Britain."
Given that the poem unambiguously names "Bryten" at 14, 40, 98, 104, and 155,
the first element of "Brytenricu" seems likely to refer to Britain here.

45 *Cosmos and Hearth*.

into the extended world geography suddenly reorient the text with new voices and a new geographical centre. Replacing the usual "Orosius cwæð" ("Orosius said"), the text announces, "Ohthere sæde his hlaforde, Ælfrede cyninge …" ("Ohthere said to his lord, King Alfred …" 13.29), and a little later, "Wulfstan sæde …" ("Wulfstan said," 16.21). The voice explicitly changes. The interviews say nothing of England itself, but the shifted viewpoint makes that unnecessary: England becomes the centre to which these explorers come after they have gone to more marginal lands, and Alfred is "lord" to at least Ohthere and possibly Wulfstan.[46]

The first of the two interpolated interviews begins "Ohthere sæde his hlaforde, Ælfrede cyninge" ("Ohthere said to his lord, King Alfred," 13.29).[47] This opening positions audiences as auditors of the interview themselves. The first thing Ohthere tells Alfred is "þæt he ealra Norðmonna norþmest bude" ("that he lived farthest north of all Northmen," 13.29–30), and then, "He cwæð þæt nan man ne bude be norðan him" ("He said that no one lived to the north of him," 16.1–2). The interview's rhetoric makes Alfred's court central and Ohthere's home distant and exotic. Ohthere ventured even farther than his home, going on voyages of several days to see how far north the land went and whether anyone lived up there (14.5–26). He finds other peoples there, undermining his claim to live farthest to the North, yet the claim remains, suggesting that these peoples do not really count in the same way that Ohthere and his audience do; they are too strange or too marginal. He must work his way back south before he encounters the Lapps (divided into *Finnas* and *Cwenas*), Biarmians (*Beormas*), and Terfinnas.[48] Ohthere gives an unusually detailed account of

---

46 See Valtonen, *The North in the Old English Orosius*, esp. 476–8, where she argues that the accounts place England at the centre and other Germanic lands at the periphery. Whether Wulfstan addresses Alfred or someone else, and indeed whether his account was even a single oral account, a composite of multiple accounts, or a revision of a written account, has not been conclusively settled. For other recent work on these issues, see Anton Englert and Athena Trakadas, eds, *Wulfstan's Voyage: The Baltic Sea Region in the Early Viking Age as Seen from Shipboard*, Maritime Culture of the North 2 (Roskilde: Viking Ship Museum, 2009), especially Rudolf Simek, "Wulfstan's Account in the Context of Early Medieval Travel Literature" (37–42) and Przemysław Urbańczyk, "On the Reliability of Wulfstan's Report" (43–7).

47 The meaning of "his hlaforde" has been debated, but as Valtonen writes in *The North*, "*hlaford* … was an appropriate form of formal address" and does not indicate that Ohthere served Alfred himself directly, 286.

48 I rely on Bately's glossary of proper names in her edition of the *Orosius* for translations of proper nouns in that work. For more on Ohthere and his journeys, see also Janet

the conditions and measurements of "Norðmanna land" ("the land of the Northmen," 15.21), explaining that parts are rocky, parts are moors, and parts are cultivated. The cultivated land is sixty or more miles wide where the Finns dwell but tapers to thirty and then less, so that in some places the width would take a man two weeks to walk but in others only six days (15.21–38). The measurements stand out because they are rare in Old English, particularly in passages that are not translations from Latin.

Wulfstan too gives some sense of distance, not in miles but in the number of days it took him to sail from one place to the next. He travelled more east than north. Again, England plays no role in his travels, but they appear in the Old English text with the confidence that England does not need to be named. Unlike Ohthere, Wulfstan has no stated interlocutor, but his portion too begins "Wulfstan sæde" ("Wulfstan said," 16.21), positioning readers and hearers of the text again as if they were hearers of Wulfstan himself.

Both Ohthere and Wulfstan primarily describe the inhabitants of the regions they visited, showing the same kind of interest in places as the previous chapters discussed, less for physical boundaries than for who and what occupies a place. The peoples Ohthere describes rely heavily on the sea and hunt whales.[49] The Biarmians and Lapps speak almost the same language (14.29–30). The *Finnas* value reindeer highly, keeping tame ones to attract wild ones (15.9–11).[50] Their wealth lies in furs, feathers, ivory, and ropes made of whale or seal hides (15.14–20), but they cultivate some land (15.21–31). The *Cwenas* have small, light ships that they can use on their freshwater lakes or out at sea (15.33–38). Wulfstan memorably tells of the Ests, whose nobles drink mares' milk (17.3) and whose funeral customs include spreading out the deceased's goods so that the men can compete in a horse race, with the first to reach a given pile becoming its owner (17.6–26).

Bately and Anton Englert, eds, *Ohthere's Voyages: A Late 9th-Century Account of Voyages along the Coasts of Norway and Denmark and Its Cultural Context*, Maritime Culture of the North 1 (Roskilde: Viking Ship Museum, 2007).

49 For whale hunting and its rarity in Anglo-Saxon England, see the set of four essays in the section "From the Sea: Whales," in *The Maritime World of the Anglo-Saxons*, ed. Klein, Schipper, and Lewis-Simpson, 275–354. Whale hunting most likely seemed quite exotic at Alfred's court, in a time when whales were certainly known but probably not hunted.

50 *Finnas* and *Cwenas* have not been identified with certainty, so I keep Ohthere's names for them; for possible identifications, see Valtonen, *The North*, esp. 373–83 and 386–93, respectively.

The reports of Ohthere and Wulfstan combine anthropological and geographical interests in accounts explicitly directed towards English audiences. Those audiences of the *Orosius* would have to read the text from two points of view throughout. They would maintain their own perspective in England, which gives an important vantage point on neighbours to the north and east. Most events are distant, but the language is familiar. Yet readers must also hold a Mediterranean perspective for almost the entire text, one from which England is remote even as the language brings the English reader closer to the unfamiliar spaces.[51] The *Orosius* is unusual for combining a focus on the Mediterranean with an interest in northern Europe. The interpolated travellers' accounts provide some counterbalance to the text's attention to Africa and the Middle East. A few other texts produce such mixtures to varying degrees.

One of these is the *Boethius*, which has strong Mediterranean roots but produces a notable northern European reference. Where the Latin asks, "Vbi nunc fidelis ossa Fabricii manent" ("Where do the bones of faithful Fabricius lie now?" 2m7.15), the Old English asks, "[Hwær] sint nu þæs foremeran and þæs wisan goldsmiðes ban Welondes?" ("Where are the bones of the very famous and wise goldsmith Weland now?" 19.20–1, my translation). This change might seem obtrusive to modern readers comparing Latin texts to English translations. Yet Anglo-Saxon readers would not make such a comparison. To audiences for whom *Angelcynn* was always a central reference point in life, such glimpses of England or Germanic myth would probably have been less jarring than the steady stream of Latin cultural references. If glances had not been spared for the North, readers might have been more alienated by the foreignness of the translations.[52] The one moment in the *Boethius* that brings readers to the North specifically does so in relation to place even as it insists that the exact place is unknown. The allusion to Weland may paradoxically make readers feel more at home even as they do not know the location of his bones either.

---

51 See also Hurley, "Alfredian Temporalities," on the ways in which the text simultaneously reinforces and collapses distinctions between ninth-century English readers and fifth-century Romans.

52 Valtonen treats in depth the ways in which descriptions of the North in the Old English *Orosius* employ terms and features familiar to Anglo-Saxons to keep the audience engaged with peoples who could have seemed exotic or frighteningly foreign; see *The North*, especially chapter 4, "The North in the *Old English Orosius*," 259–479.
For the adaptation of Boethius's Latin *Consolation of Philosophy* for Anglo-Saxon audiences, see my *King's English*, esp. chap. 3, "The Making of an English Dialogue," 57–86.

Old English poetry connects audiences with the northern world more than prose. Nicholas Howe has already pointed out how Cynewulf transforms the story of the finding of the True Cross from a tale that moves between Rome and Jerusalem to one that begins with Constantine battling Huns and Goths at the Danube: "In *Elene*, history is made on the northern edge of empire."[53] Other poems have much denser northern European connections: *Deor* and *Widsith* place northern Europe in a context that includes the whole known world, while *Beowulf* creates a world that seems limited to northern Europe.

Deor and *Widsith* both beguile and frustrate modern scholars with their scaffolds of allusions, many of whose stories we do not know. In each, an English-speaking *scop* (bard) offers a catalogue, presumably of poems he could perform for a patron, yet these Old English poems never mention England or the English. Instead, they concentrate on Germanic and Scandinavian figures and tribes. *Widsith* names the Irish and the Scots (79). One might expect the English to follow this mention, but instead the poet turns to the *Lidwicingum* (80), a people in Brittany.[54] He has no need to list the Anglo-Saxons because they are the people to whom he delivers his litany, in their native language. Widsith ranges as far as China ("Sercingum" and "Seringum," 75) and visits the Israelites, Assyrians, Indians, Medes, Persians, and possibly Moabites, Ammonites, Elamites, and others (82–6).[55] The names from the Middle East diverge enough from most of the rest of the poem that some or all of lines 75 and 82–7 are generally thought to be a later interpolation.[56] Even if they are an interpolation, however, they have become part of the poem by the time a scribe copied it into the Exeter Book in the late tenth century. The only extant copy puts Israelites and Persians between Romans and Goths. *Widsith* contains over a hundred names of peoples; of these, over eighty are in the British Isles or Europe. Most of those are Germanic or Scandinavian. The Greeks and Romans appear (69, 76, and 78), but they are listed only briefly among the

---

53 "Rome," 163. For more on this poem and its treatment of the Mediterreanean world, see my previous chapter.

54 Joyce Hill's edition *Old English Minor Heroic Poems*, Durham and St Andrews Medieval Texts 4 (Durham and Fife: Universities of Durham and St Andrews, 1983), provides invaluable help with the names of individuals, tribes and peoples, and places. I follow her identifications unless otherwise noted; for further details, see her edition, especially the glossary of proper names. For the texts of *Deor* and *Widsith*, I follow ASPR 3.

55 See note 49 in my second chapter for these names.

56 See Hill, *Minor Heroic Poems*, 12, and the notes to *Widsith* 82–7 on pp. 41–2.

Goths (18, 58, 89, 109, 113, and 120), the Continental Angles (8, 35, 44, and 61), the Danes (28, 35, and 58), and so on. Most of the identifiable peoples listed live in central or northern Europe, north of Rome and west of the Holy Land.[57]

Widsith minimizes England's isolation by connecting it to a broader, mostly European world. To a lesser extent, *Deor*'s much briefer catalogue does the same. It names Ravenna, as "Mæringa burg" (19), but the individuals mentioned are clearly Germanic, and the only peoples named are the Goths (23) and the Heodenings (36).[58] Where Widsith named rulers he had known along with their peoples, and then added a number of people names without rulers, Deor offers the tales of individuals: Weland, Beadohild, Ðeodric, and Eormanric. All come from Germanic legends.[59]

These poems create and reinforce a sense of connection with a broader world beyond the British Isles. Poets offer these tales in English catalogue poems, and Widsith claims to have met personally each individual or people he names. In these poems, England is not isolated or attached to the Mediterranean world by a thin thread. Instead, it appears to have a central role in a vibrant European culture, so rich with myths that we now cannot understand some of the allusions in each poem and cannot always tell which were well known to the audience and which may have been concocted by the poet. Quite enough can be identified to guarantee that the poems are not simply fantasies about previously unknown people, however. Though the poet of *Widsith* (or a later reviser) may have invented some names to fill out lines or short sections, most of the names, personal and tribal, remain recognizable to twenty-first-century scholars. These poets display no anxiety about England's place in the world.

While *Widsith* has the highest density of people names of any extant Old English poem, *Beowulf* gives more extended attention to northern Europe than any other work in Old English. Like *Deor* and *Widsith*, *Beowulf* never

---

57 Joyce Hill argues that some of the names are "epic fictions," but that we cannot always know which – and the uncertainty itself makes effective the addition of fictional names to real ones. "*Widsið* and the Tenth Century," *NM* 85 (1984): 305–15.

58 Again, I follow Hill's identifications in *Minor Heroic Poems*.

59 Many would add Mæðhild here, but it is not clear this is a compound, let alone a name. Vladimir Brljak recounts the history of editing this third section of *Deor* and the dispute over whether to read *Mæðhild* as a name, *mæð hild* as two common nouns, or *mæð Hild* as a common noun plus a shortened form of Beadohild: "Unediting *Deor*," *NM* 112.3 (2011): 297–321. He argues that this section does not present a new allusion but continues the Theodoric-Nithhad story.

mentions England.[60] The poem gives almost fifty different epithets for about two dozen different peoples or places a total of almost 250 times.[61] In other words, on average, a people or place name appears every thirteen lines. *Beowulf* is thick with geographical and ethnic information.

The poem works with northern Europe using three of the techniques shown in the previous chapter. Names become familiar with repetition and connections to other peoples and places: of 246 people or place names, fewer than twenty are named a single time.[62] All the others occur at least twice, with Danes or their land named ninety-one times with different epithets, and Geats or Geatland eighty. The Danes become an anchoring name, helping *Beowulf*'s audience relate less familiar people or places to one more familiar, at least in later periods because of the Danish attacks and settlement in England.[63] Moreover, places and peoples in *Beowulf* have histories. Digressions often supply such details: readers learn of four generations of Danish rulers in the opening lines (Scyld, Beowulf the

60 There may be one indirect reference, if "Offa" in 1949 and 1957 refers to the English king; scholars now generally agree, however, that the explicit reference is to the Continental Angle Offa, with any allusion to the Mercian king at best indirect and secondary. See Klaeber 4, especially the commentary on 222–4. John M. Hill writes that "the extended reference to the Anglian Offa has little if anything to do with the Mercian Offa"; "Episodes Such as the Offa of Angeln Passage and the Aesthetics of *Beowulf*," *Philological Review* 34.2 (2008): 36. Other scholars see a possible allusion here, perhaps an indirect evocation of the English Offa; see Nicholas Howe, *Migration and Mythmaking in Anglo-Saxon England* (New Haven, CT: Yale University Press, 1989), 157, n. 23.

61 Counting how many separate people or places are named is difficult: are the North Danes the same as the South Danes, the East Danes, and the West Danes? Should Sweden and the Swedes count as one name or two, one for the place and one for the people? I count 52 separates epithets (with the North Danes separate from the South Danes) for 24 peoples or places (North Danes, South Danes, *Dena*, *Deniga*, etc., are all Danes). *Dena land* and *Dena* both refer to Danes, so I have counted them together: *Dena land* is a place, but literally "the land of the Danes."

62 The count here is complicated by the use of synonyms: "Hrefna Wudu" (2925) and "Hrefnes Holt" (2935) name the same place and both mean "Raven's Wood," but the poet has used two different words for "wood." The term "Hreðlingas" (2960) is only used once, but it is a name for the Geats, a people named seventy-eight other times in the poem with other terms. If I am uncertain whether two names are synonyms or not, I have erred on the side of assuming that they are not; if I am mistaken, there may be as few as eleven peoples or places named a single time in the whole poem.

63 Arguments about the dating of *Beowulf* can literally fill a book and more; I cannot engage with them here. Certainly by the time of the sole surviving copy of *Beowulf*, around the year 1000, the scribes and readers knew Danes not only as people who lived across the sea and might continue to attack, but also as people who had settled alongside the English.

Dane, Healfdene, and Hroðgar, 1–64), and, through the course of the poem, come to know that Hreðel, Hygelac, Heardred, and then Beowulf rule the Geats.[64] The poem shows us Heorot being built (76–82) and foreshadows its end in treachery and fire (82–5). Finally, places hold significance because of who or what lives there. Not even wasteland in *Beowulf* is uninhabited: Grendel's mere is the home of Grendel, his mother, and numerous monsters; the barrow houses a dragon.[65] Place names appear because of the people who live or fight there.

Beowulf never names England because it never needs to do so. England remains at the heart of its audiences' lived experiences. The Danes had great impact on the Anglo-Saxons and their neighbours the Franks, but were scarcely more central on medieval maps than Britain was. They enter the *Orosius* only in the interpolated interviews. They appear in some late antique geographies but play little role there or in histories. Irmeli Valtonen comments that the *Orosius* has the first appearances of the name *Denemearc*, in Ohthere and Wulfstan's narratives only; the term does not appear again until the early tenth century.[66] The Geats prove tricky even to identify; Stephen Harris describes them as a mythological confabulation of *Getæ*, used for Scythians, Thracians, and Goths and borrowed from Greek and Latin literature into European traditions spread by Isidore of Seville, among others.[67] The peoples of *Beowulf* do not threaten the English with marginality; if anything, their lack of connection to Christianity, Rome, or Jerusalem throws England's Christianity and ties to distant places into sharp relief.

Northern Europe could operate in two different ways in early English texts, sometimes simultaneously. Anglo-Saxon texts such as the *Orosius* and *Beowulf* constructed knowledge of Scandinavia that surpassed classical sources and made England a locus of geographical mastery. These same texts also implicitly contrasted English connections to the Mediterranean world and Christianity with Scandinavia's lack of such links. While some accept the importance of key Mediterranean sites and others do not even

---

64 I follow the manuscript reading of "Beowulf" for the name of Scyld's son at 18 and 53, though Klaeber 4 does not; I read the name here as foreshadowing the poem's protagonist, Beowulf the Geat.

65 See chapter 5 for more on waste and water in this poem.

66 Valtonen, *The North*, 349. There are saints' lives and miracle stories that feature Vikings, but few compared with texts set in the Mediterranean world.

67 Harris, *Race and Ethnicity*, 85–6. See also Valtonen, *The North*, 188–9 and 548–55 on the Geats and the Goths.

talk about such distant places, all these writers implicitly give England a central place in the world by giving attention to its nearer neighbours.

Decentring: Place and Transcendence

Northern Europe and England predictably dominate several Anglo-Saxon texts. England even finds its way into texts set elsewhere: prefaces to some of the translations associated with Alfred and his circle put England explicitly in the line of transmission for the texts; runic signatures in Cynewulf's poems remind audiences that these distant events have been related in their own language and their own land; and homilies and *Seasons for Fasting* bring religious lessons home from distant lands.

Yet these geographical and historical strategies remain in constant tension with other work many of these texts do. Bede's *Historia* and its Old English translation tell the story of England as part of a universal church. The Alfredian translation program's cosmological bent emphasizes the small size and brief life of the world and shifts attention to the larger universe and lasting realms.[68] Such cosmology simultaneously and equally diminishes not only *Angelcynn* but also Rome and Jerusalem. Homilies and religious poems ultimately aim to bring audiences from England to salvation. England's importance diminishes in comparison with heaven's – but then so does the importance of any earthly place.

As the geographical place of England was graphically represented by maps, so the place of the earth in the universe was graphically represented by figures called *rotae* ("wheels"). Isidore of Seville produced many of these representing the winds, zones of the earth, seasons, and so on. While Bourdieu declares that different schemes can coexist because they come into practical use at different times and there is no "assembling of these meanings in simultaneity," Isidore and other writers and compilers heap together circular diagrams with very different meanings and sometimes dizzying shifts of viewpoint.[69] Two common Isidorean *rotae* show earth at the centre of the planets and the relationship between microcosm and

---

68 Margaret Bridges notes Augustine's similar strategies, "problematizing the representation of geographical reality through diverting attention away from the map in favour of moralizing allegorizations as well as through his replacement of tribes and nations by communities of believers"; "Of Myths and Maps: The Anglo-Saxon Cosmographer's Europe," in *Writing & Culture*, ed. Engler, 79.

69 Bourdieu, *Outline*, quotation at 123.

macrocosm. Earth may be central, but it occupies the centre of a sphere or disk several times its size.[70] In a huge universe, neither England nor Rome nor Jerusalem seems terribly significant. The Alfredian texts, even while they make Anglo-Saxon England a place of importance, deny the importance of place. As *Angelcynn* claims its place in the tradition of learning, the texts present places that signify symbolically. Real distance from these points is not important so long as the mental distance can be closed and the signification read correctly. Changing from physical to mental geography thus represents a third strategy for translators and authors.

The *Orosius* makes the point historically. While Britain seems minor compared to the four great empires God ordained, just how important are those empires? The text gives us the answer:

Seo ilce burg Babylonia, seo ðe mæst wæs 7 ærest ealra burga, seo is nu læst 7 westaste. Nu seo burg swelc is, þe ær wæs ealra weorca fæstast 7 wunderlecast 7 mærast, gelice 7 heo wære to bisene asteald eallum middangearde, 7 eac swelce heo self sprecende sie to eallum moncynne 7 cweþe: "Nu ic þuss gehroren eam 7 aweg gewiten, hwæt, ge magan on me ongietan 7 oncnawan þæt ge nanuht mid eow nabbað fæstes ne stronges þætte þurhwunigean mæge." (43.33–44.6)

("That same city Babylon, which was the greatest and the first of all cities, it is now the last and most desolate. And now the city that was before the strongest and most wonderful and most famous of all works is just as if it were

---

70 For examples, see Edson, *Mapping*, plates 3.1–3.6 on pp. 41–5, and Naomi Reed Kline, *Maps of Medieval Thought: The Hereford Paradigm* (Woodbridge, UK: Boydell, 2001), figs. 1.2–1.26, and her discussion in chapter 1, "The Cosmological Wheel," 7–43. Woodward, "*Mappaemundi*," gives examples of an Isidorean rota (fig. 18.39, p. 337) and a diagram from Bede's *De natura rerum* that maps out the relations between the cardinal directions, the continents, the elements, the seasons, and the properties of matter (18.38, p. 335). Cambridge, Trinity College O.3.7 and Cambridge, University Library Kk.3.21 show *rotae* rather like Edson's 3.1–3.4; these post-Conquest manuscripts present Boethius's *De consolatione philosophiae* with glosses, and their diagrams illustrate the cosmological metre 3m9. Other microcosm-macrocosm diagrams might relate man to the whole universe, as does the unique Byrhtferth's Diagram in Oxford, St John's College, MS 17, f. 7v: http://digital.library.mcgill.ca/ms-17/folio.php?p=7v&showitem =7r_2ComputusRelated_20ByrhtferthsDiagram. Peter S. Baker and Michael Lapidge's edition of *Byrhtferth's Enchiridion*, EETS ss 177 (Oxford: Oxford University Press, 1995) offers a clear black-and-white graphic of the diagram with all the Latin inscriptions in their appendix A, page 374.

established as an example to all earth, and also as if she herself were speaking to all mankind and said, 'Now I am thus fallen and departed away; look, you may understand and know in me that you have with you no fastness nor strength that can survive.'")

The *Orosius* later explains at some length God's plan for the four empires and how long they lasted (132.24–133.28), but ultimately what matters is not the places but the salvation of God's people. The translator here has altered the meaning of the source text: where Orosius's *History* described Rome as an ongoing empire and the culmination of God's plan, Stephen Harris demonstrates that the Old English translator presents Rome as having fallen like the three previous great empires in the text.[71] Rome might once have been greater than England, but where is its empire now?

Bede similarly concentrates not so much on England as a place, but on the "Historiam gentis Anglorum ecclesiasticam" ("Ecclesiastical history of the English people").[72] The narrative centres on the conversion of the Anglo-Saxons and their adoption of Roman practice to assume their place as God's people.[73] The place of England matters because of its place in a larger scheme of salvation: Bede ends his narrative,

> Hic est inpraesentiarum uniuersae status Brittaniae, anno aduentus Anglorum in Brittaniam circiter ducentesimo octogesimo quinto, dominicae autem incarnationis anno DCCXXXI. In cuius regno perpetuo exultet terra, et congratulante in fide eius Brittania, laetentur insulae multae et confiteantur memoriae sanctitatis eius. (560)

("This is the state of the whole of Britain at the present time, about 285 years after the coming of the English to Britain, in the year of our Lord 731. Let the earth rejoice in His perpetual kingdom and let Britain rejoice in His faith and

---

71 Harris, *Race and Ethnicity*, 93–100; see also Malcolm R. Godden, "The Old English *Orosius* and Its Context: Who Wrote It, for Whom, and Why?" *Quaestio Insularis* 12 (2011): 19–27. For the most explicit passage on the four empires, see pp. 86–7 above.

72 I have not followed Colgrave and Minors here; for my translation and the sense of "Anglorum" in the quotation, see note 6 above.

73 Molyneaux emphasizes the salvific message in Bede's *Historia* and the Old English translation in "The *Old English Bede*." He argues that nation building is not part of the agenda of either work, but I read the two goals as compatible and see a desire for more English unity (though not modern nation building) in both works.

let the multitude of isles be glad and give thanks at the remembrance of His holiness," Colgrave and Mynors, 561)

The verbs in the last sentence are subjunctive, expressing the author's hopes and urgings rather than simple fact. The Old English translation ends even more enthusiastically, not with the hope of rejoicing but with what appears to be its present indicative reality: "in þæs Drihtnes þæm ecean rice gefeoð eal eorþe; 7 efen blissiendre Breotone in his geleafan 7 monig ealond blissiað 7 ondettað gemynde his haligness" ("the whole earth is rejoicing in the eternal kingdom of the Lord; and while Britain shares the joy in his faith, many islands also rejoice and acknowledge the memory of his holiness," 480.17–19).[74] England becomes one of many places united in faith, and the wording of rejoicing in both texts surely calls heaven to mind.[75]

The Old English Prose Psalms, while solidly grounded in the physical setting of the Holy Land, remind readers that God's creation goes beyond earth with five mentions of angels.[76] Psalm 48 concerns hell. The text constructs a cosmology rather than a geography, making the space of earth smaller and of secondary importance. It brings readers to an awareness of the universe as described in the first chapter. Moreover, God's temple and Mount Zion in the Psalms are real historically and geographically, but they are simultaneously figurative. This overlap begins in the source text, but Alfred makes the figurative implications more explicit. Such transformation can be seen in this example. Where the Latin reads:

---

74 Because Old English lacks a separate future tense, it is possible that the present here expresses a future: "the whole earth [will] rejoice in the eternal kingdom ... many islands [will] also rejoice and acknowledge ..." In either case, however, the Latin subjunctive has become the English indicative (subjunctive would be *gefeon*, *blissien*, and *ondetten*).

75 Of the histories, only the *Anglo-Saxon Chronicle* has no overt salvific or providential drive; at least in its first recension, it seems rather to have a dynastic drive, with Alfred as the pinnacle of Anglo-Saxon kingship. See Renée R. Trilling, *The Aesthetics of Nostalgia: Historical Representation in Old English Verse* (Toronto: University of Toronto Press, 2009), 175–213, on the *Chronicle*'s teleology, in verse and in prose.

76 Introduction to 33; 8.6, 33.8, 34.5, and 34.6. All quotations from the Prose Psalms of the Paris Psalter come from *King Alfred's Old English Prose Translation of the First Fifty Psalms*, ed. Patrick P. O'Neill, Medieval Academy Books 104 (Cambridge, MA: Medieval Academy, 2001), http://www.medievalacademy.org/resource/resmgr/ maa_books_online/oneill_0104.htm; their translations are my own. I use O'Neill's parenthetical line numbers to facilitate comparison with Latin psalms.

et statuit super petram pedes meos
stabilivit gressus meos.
et inmisit in os meum canticum novum ...   (39.3–4)

("he set my feet upon a rock, and directed my steps.
And he put a new canticle into my mouth ...," Douay-Rheims)

the Old English Prose Psalm reads:

And he asette mine fet on *swiðe* heanne stan (þæt ys, on swyðe heah setl and
on swyðe fæstne anweald), and he gerihte mine stæpas, and sende on minne
muð niwne sang (þæt is, lofsang urum Gode). (39.3–4)

("And he set my feet on a very high stone [that is, on a very high seat and on a
very strong power], and he steadied my steps, and sent into my mouth a new
song [that is, a praise song for our God].")[77]

The translator interprets the imagery overtly, telling readers the spiritual
signification of the physical landscape. Such imagery is contained throughout the Psalms, ranging from local topography to mentions of Israel and
the temple. Sometimes it is difficult to tell whether the referent is the earthly or the heavenly temple (26.5–6, 47.8); one so evokes the other, however,
that it hardly matters. The physical Holy Land had great importance for
medieval Christians, but they did not have to travel there to experience its
salvific power. Anglo-Saxons could encounter God through translated
texts in their own language, at home in England.

The *Pastoral Care*, like the Psalms, transcends place. It makes direct reference to heaven thirty-nine times and hell seven times.[78] Most of the earthly places named in the *Pastoral Care* also carry more symbolic resonance
than literal. Zion is a real place, but its import is not limited to the geographical. While the nearly thirty passages mentioned before refer to real
geographical places, many of those carry some figurative weight. Another
ten specify real places for an overwhelmingly figurative sense, as in:

---

77 For further examples, see Psalms 10.5 and 18.6.
78 All word searches and counts were performed using the *Corpus* online unless otherwise
    noted.

Ðu ðe wilt godspellian Sion, astig ofer heane munt. Ðæt is ðætte se sceal, se
ðe wile brucan ðara godcundra ðinga & ðara hefonlicra lara, forlætan ða[s]
niðerlican & ðas eorðlecan weorc, forðam he bið gesewen standende on ðam
hrofe godcundra ðinga. (81.12–16)[79]

("You who would preach to Zion, ascend over the high mountain. That is, he
who would enjoy the divine things and the heavenly lore must abandon the
lowly and the earthly works, because he must be seen standing on the roof
of divine things.")

Several are purely figurative: "Ðin nosu is suelc [suel] se torr on Liuano
ðæm munte" ("Your nose is just as the tower on Mount Libanus," 65.23–
4) is quoted to explain that a big nose means "gesceadwisnesse" ("discern-
ment," 65.25; he expands on the same verse at 433.19–29).[80] Even without
the help of the translator's addition, readers would surely not take the
image literally; the Old English text, however, helps readers get past the
recognition that an image has spiritual significance to an understanding of
how it signifies.[81]

In closing the *Pastoral Care*, Gregory uses the image of being lost at sea
as a humility topos; Alfred neatly translates it:

Ðær ic hæbbe getæht hwelc hierde bion sceal. To ðæm ic wæs gened mid
ðinre tælnesse, ðæt ic nu hæbbe manege men gelæd to ðæm stæðe full-
fremednesse on ðæm scipe mines modes, & nu giet hwearfige me self on ðæm
yðum minra scylda. Ac ic ðe bidde ðæt ðu me on ðæm scipgebroce ðisses

---

79 See also 101.24–103.5, 103.11–105.1, 197.11–201.3, 267.9–16, 385.21–4, 397.32–399.31,
    403.29–405.10, 415.13–417.1, and 427.26–429.2.
80 See also 311.7–13 and 367.2–22. Vaguer geographical references are to navigating at sea
    (59.1–7), the gold and stones of the temple scattered in the street (133.8–135.20), and
    the inner city as a retreat from the world (385.4–9). At least two passages quoted from
    Scripture already have literal and figurative meaning so intertwined that it is hard to
    say which dominates: Ezekiel besieges a model of Jerusalem, with a literal meaning for
    the city and a lesson about pride for teachers at 161.2–165.23; Isaiah says to Sidon that
    the sea told it to be embarrassed at 409.31–411.1, and a complicated exegesis follows.
    When Jerusalem is said to be fornicating, the city's inhabitants are literally meant, but
    so are all believers – and fornication means not just sexual sin but worshipping false
    gods, 463.23–465.3. How literally one is to take Satan's "Ic wille wyrcean min setl
    on norðdæle" ("I will build my seat in the northern parts," 111.24) is unclear.
81 Similarly, a metaphor for Christ goes beyond the earthly to the cosmological realm:
    "sio sunne, ðæt is Crist" ("the sun, that is Christ," 285.14).

andweardan lifes sum bred geræce ðinra gebeda, ðæt ic mæge on sittan oð ic to londe cume, & arær me mid ðære honda ðinre geearnunga, forðæmðe me hæfð gehefegad sio byrðen minra agenra scylda. (467.19–27)

("There I have taught how a pastor must be. I was compelled to this task by your reproof, that I have now led many men to the shore of perfection in the ship of my mind, and yet I myself still toss in the waves of my guilt. But I pray you that you offer me the board of your prayers in the shipwreck of this present life, that I may sit on it until I come to land, and lift me with the hands of your merits, because the weight of my own guilt so burdens me.")

External figures internal space, as geography has so often throughout the Old English *Pastoral Care*.

Alfred's two most introspective works emphasize internal geography. Though the *Boethius* is packed with historical and geographical references, those references illustrate metaphorical points. One must not mistake earthly things for the real good, for doing so makes mental space into a prison. The opening of the dialogue emphasizes the narrator's physical setting in a prison, but the prison's location is unclear, as discussed in the previous chapter. Well before the end, the *Boethius* stops referring to the physical setting at all. The location of the exchange has been virtually forgotten – or, rather, transcended.

The mind must be freed not so much from a specific prison or house of exile as from the prison that is earth, so that it may seek its heavenly homeland, as Wisdom repeatedly tells the narrator. Turning inward will lead the narrator outward and upward. As the narrator recalls himself more and more, Wisdom encourages him: "þu eart nu fulneah cumen innon þa ceastre þære soðan gesælðe, þe ðu lange ær ne meahtest aredian" (35.60–1; "you have very nearly come within the city of true felicity, which for a long time before you could not approach," trans. Godden and Irvine, vol. 2, 62). This homeland becomes more clearly linked to heaven when Wisdom sings about flying to it: "ic sceal ærest þin mod gefiðerian, þæt hit mæge hit þe eð up ahebban ær þon hit fleogan onginne on ða heanesse, þæt hit mæge hal and orsorg fleogan to his earde and forlætan ælce þara gedrefednessa þe hit nu þrowað" (36.34–8; "I must first give feathers to your mind, so that it can raise itself more easily before it begins to fly into the heights, so that it may safely and securely fly to its homeland and forsake all the anxieties that it now suffers," trans. Godden and Irvine, vol. 2, 67). Thus the *Boethius*, for all its classical geography, grounds readers in this world only to move them to a higher one – reached by going inside.

At the same time, the *Boethius* offers a more complete cosmology than any of the other Alfredian texts. It situates the earth among the stars, naming constellations (Boötes, 39.59, and Ursa, 39.337) in passing. Frequent references to heaven, hell, angels, and devils reduce the entire earth to a "rondbeah on scilde" (18.18; "a shield boss on a shield," trans. Godden and Irvine, vol. 2, 27) of the cosmos.[82] In the *Boethius*'s most famous metaphor, God is the centre of a wagon wheel; to escape the effects of Fortune, one must move up the spokes to Him (39.155–93). The image of an earth-centred universe that the *rotae* present is here replaced by a very similar but God-centred universe.

Wisdom explains that much of this vast world is uninhabitable, and that fame does not travel widely (18.2–133). If fame neither spreads far nor lasts long, those who can read of the greatness of Rome and the Holy Land, and then set their sights on an even greater destination, are not marginal but privileged. The Anglo-Saxons need not fear their liminality, but neither should they exult in their local power. The shift from physical geography to mental and spiritual ground allows England to be a place of learning too. Even so, some readers and hearers surely recall that they are reading the text in English because they cannot read it in Latin.[83] They do not share the learning of Boethius. Conceptions of Brittania as significant and insignificant remain in constant tension.

The *Soliloquies* takes this strategy even further, providing a purely mental geography which begins with the image of a man building a house from lumber provided by the wood of the Fathers (47.9–12).[84] These works of his predecessors will, Alfred hopes,

---

82 The *Boethius* repeatedly proclaims that God is Creator and Ruler of a great universe whose complex workings, controlled by His love, are described especially in the famous Old English translation of 3m9, OE 33.142–251 and C Metre 20; see also 21.2–46 and CM11; 25.2–8 and CM13.3–17; 34.289–321, 39.132–52, and 39.331–70 and CM29. (Passages without a C Metre equivalent are in prose and substantially the same in both versions.) For this Metre, see Paul E. Szarmach, "*Meter 20*: Context Bereft," *American Notes and Queries* 15.2 (2002): 28–34; and "The *Timaeus* in Old English," in *Lexis and Texts in Early English: Studies Presented to Jane Roberts*, ed. Christian J. Kay and Louise M. Sylvester (Amsterdam and Atlanta, GA: Rodopi, 2001), 255–67.

83 Readers may also recall that their ancestors thought they would never lose Latin, as Alfred said in his preface to the *Pastoral Care* (5.22–3).

84 *King Alfred's Version of St. Augustine's Soliloquies*, ed. Thomas A. Carnicelli (Cambridge, MA: Harvard University Press, 1969); all translations of it are my own. Their books create the walls and ceiling, reminiscent of a passage from the *Boethius* where Wisdom tells Mod that she wants not a physically beautiful library, but his mind (5.28–32).

hure mines modes eagan to þam ongelihte þæt ic mage rihtne weig aredian to
þam ecan hame, and to þam ecan are, and to þare ecan reste þe us gehaten is
þurh þa halgan fæderas. sie swa. (48.1–3)

("open my mind's eyes to the light that I may find the right way to that
eternal home, and to that eternal honour, and to that eternal rest which is
promised us through the holy fathers. Let it be so.")

The narrator's wishes are further detailed in an evocatively domestic image
of using the dwelling he has built:

he hine mote hwilum þar-on gerestan, and huntigan, and fuglian, and fiscian,
and his on gehwilce wisan to þere lænan tilian, ægþær ge on se ge on lande,
oð þone fyrst þe he bocland and æce yrfe þurh his hlafordes miltse geear-
nige. swa gedo se weliga gifola, se ðe egðer wilt ge þissa lænena stoclife ge
þara ecena hama. Se ðe ægþer gescop and ægðeres wilt, forgife me þæt me to
æðrum onhagige; ge her nytwyrde to beonne, ge huru þider to cumane.
(48.6–12)

("He is able to rest himself there sometimes, and hunt, and fowl, and fish, and
in each way tend to the lease, both in the sea and on the land, until that time
when through his lord's mercy he win bookland and eternal inheritance. May
the wealthy Giver make it so, He who wills both in this borrowed dwelling
and the eternal homes. May He who made each and wills each grant that I
may be suitable both to be useful here and indeed to come there.")

The forest is a library metaphorically, and perhaps more literally in wood-
en boards used as book covers. The *Soliloquies'* dialogue is even more internal than the *Boethius*'s. This text lacks any historical context aside from
the fact that Augustine, bishop of Carthage, wrote this book.[85] Geography
and cosmology figure greater truths. The only specific geographical reference outside the preface occurs near the end: the narrator did not see Rome

---

85 "Agustinus, *Cartaina* bisceop, worhte twa bec," 1 and 2 of the *Soliloquies*. This metaphysical and epistemological investigation begins with an extraordinarily long prayer
   (50.10–56.9) that makes frequent reference to God as creator of everything in this world
   and the next. For more on this prayer, see Paul E. Szarmach, "Augustine's *Soliloquia* in
   Old English," in *A Companion to Alfred the Great*, ed. Discenza and Szarmach, 227–55,
   esp. 230–2 and 237–9.

built, but that does not preclude any possibility of knowledge about it (97.5–8). Rome is important here not as the city itself, but for what the narrator can know about it and *how* he can know it.[86] All the physical settings, however concrete or abstract, are likewise images: the sun becomes an image of God (69.16–26); the view from a ship crossing the sea parallels how people learn (61.17–22); and so on.[87] Here *all* the geography and history that matter are mental and spiritual.

Ælfric uses setting similarly in his *Life of St. Swithun*:

Sum þegn wæs on engla lande on æhtum swyðe welig .
se wearð færlice blind . þa ferde he to rome .
wolde his hæle biddan . æt þam halgum apostolum .
He wunode þa on rome and ne wearð gehæled .
feower gear fullice . and befran þa be swyðune
hwylce wundra he worhte syððan he gewende þanon .
he efste þa swyðe and to his earde gewende .
and com to þam halgan were and wearð gehæled þær .
and ham gewende mid halre gesihðe .[88]

("There was a certain thane in England, very rich in possessions,
who became suddenly blind; then journeyed he to Rome,
desiring to pray for his cure from the holy Apostles,
he dwelt at Rome, but was not cured,
for four full years; then he heard of Saint Swithhun,
what miracles he had wrought since he [the thane] had journeyed thence;
then made he much haste, and returned to his own country,
and came to the holy man, and was there healed,
and returned home with perfect sight.")

Here Ælfric overturns the expected hierarchy of place. Most significant events in his homilies and lives happen in the Holy Land or in Rome, and he names those places far more than he does England. Yet this story shows

---

86 Rome, to Augustine the greatest city, the centre of political and religious power, has a history that cannot be fully known even by personal experience.

87 For other generic physical settings, see 77.5–78.2, 78.2–17, 78.17–23, 92.22–93.6, and 93.14–20. The implications always point to the heavenly home, and explicit mentions of angels (82.15–18 and 85.18) underscore that ultimate destination.

88 *Ælfric's Lives of Saints*, vol. 1, 21, "Saint Swithun, Bishop," 193–201. I use Skeat's translation.

a man whose blindness is simultaneously real and symbolic: he cannot see that he need not go far for miraculous healing. He wastes four years in Rome seeking a cure that he does not find. In Ælfric's account, the only wisdom that the man acquires in the seat of Christianity is knowledge of Swithun, in his own land (197–8). The thegn must return to England to be healed. God is omnipresent: seekers find him as much in Winchester as in Rome. Those in England do best to seek God there, not abroad.

Ælfric gives his clearest perspective on geography in his *Catholic Homilies*:

> Nis þeos woruld na ure eþel; ac is ure wræcsið; for ði ne sceole we na besettan urne hiht on ðisum swicelum life; Ac sceolon efstan mid godum geearnungum to urum eðele. þær we to gesceapene wæron. þ[æt] is to heofonanrice; Soðlice hit is awriten; Swa hwa swa wile beon freond þisre worulde; se bið geteald godes feond; (1.10.161–6)

> ("This world is not our homeland, but it is our exile. Therefore we should not set our hopes in this deceptive life, but we must hasten with good earnings to our homeland, where we were created; that is the kingdom of heaven. Truly it is written: whoever wishes to be a friend of this world, he will be reckoned God's enemy.")[89]

England is no more home to the Anglo-Saxons than Rome, Ælfric declares. Their true home is heaven. With such a theology, Anglo-Saxons did not need to worry about their distance from Rome or the Holy Land, or even where they were in England. They only needed to worry about their distance from God.

Old English religious poetry also effectively decentres geography. The greatest drama in *The Dream of the Rood* takes place in the Holy Land: the cross tells its story from lines 28 through 121 of the 156 lines. Its tale covers its own felling, the crucifixion and death of Christ, and its burial and rediscovery. Yet the action the cross narrates might as well have happened in England. Both cross and dreamer identify themselves not as residents of any particular earthly territory, but as subjects of a heavenly king. The cross describes serving a "ricne cyning" ("rich king," ASPR 2, 44), while

---

89 See also *Catholic Homilies* 1.18.73–4: "we ealle syndon cuman on ðysum life. 7 ure eard nis na hér; ac we synd hér swilce weigfærende menn" ("we are all strangers in this life, and our land is not here; but we are all here as wayfarers").

the dreamer's friends have already gone to seek "wuldres cyning" ("the king of glory," 133), whom the dreamer himself aspires to meet. Earthly borders have no meaning when a tree cut down, buried, and rediscovered in the Holy Land can shine "on lyft" ("in the sky," 5), where "Beheoldon þær engel dryhtnes ealle/…/… halige gastas,/men ofer moldan, ond eall þeos mære gesceaft" ("All the angels of God beheld it there … holy spirits, men on earth, and all this splendid creation," 9, 11–12). The Old English poem presumably features an Anglo-Saxon dreamer, but his distance in space and time from the events that the cross recounts hardly matters. Though the dreamer does not witness the crucifixion himself, he hears of it from a participant. He has the same hope of salvation, and the same ultimate destination of heaven, as if he had been physically present at the crucifixion. His concern is not with this world but the "heofonlicne ham" ("heavenly home," 148), "godes rice" ("God's kingdom," 152).

So too *The Wanderer* and *The Seafarer* focus less on earthly surroundings than on an ultimate destination, though the two poems describe recognizably Germanic social structures and northern climates.[90] *The Wanderer*'s main character recalls the pleasures of lord and hall (see especially 41–4), and *The Seafarer*'s thinks briefly of "medodrince" ("mead-drinking," 22) and the joys of the *burh* ("city" or "enclosure," 27–8). *The Wanderer* describes a decidedly northern seascape: "hreosan hrim ond snaw, hagle gemenged" ("frost and snow fall, mixed with hail," 48). The "waþema gebind" ("binding of waves," 57) probably refers to ice in the waters. The frost on ruined walls (76–7) and the mention of wolves (82) also indicate the north. The narrator of *The Seafarer* too suffers from the climate: "Calde geþrungen/wæron mine fet, forste gebunden,/caldum clommum" ("My feet were afflicted by cold, bound with frost, cold fetters," 8–10). He travels the "iscealdne sæ" ("ice-cold sea," 14), and words about ice and cold are repeated (17, 24, 31–3). Yet the poems offer no further geographical specificity. Readers can identify with the narrator from anywhere one might read or understand Old English read aloud, but they are all redirected to the "fæder on heofonum, þær us eal seo fæstnung stondeð" ("the father in heaven, where all security awaits us," *Wanderer* 115), "ecan eadignesse" ("eternal happiness," *Seafarer* 120), "hyht in heofonum" ("joy in heaven," *Seafarer* 122).

---

90 For both *The Wanderer* and *The Seafarer*, see ASPR 3.

Even *Elene* ends with the other world. The poet grounds the narrative in earthly geography, taking its characters and readers on a journey from the Danube to Rome, through Greek lands, and thence to Jerusalem. Cynewulf's runic signature returns us mentally to England, but only in preparation for yet another perspective: the end times. Lines 1277–1321 (ASPR 2) prepare readers for the apocalypse: sinners will end in everlasting fire, but true believers will be purified for their heavenly home.

Rethinking geography is a double-edged sword. On the one hand, England might seem small and marginal compared with Jerusalem or Rome, as we saw in the previous chapter. When one's place already appears marginal, one may find it relatively easy to accept the lack of importance of one's homeland and look forward to another one; thus readers and hearers might experience first the vertigo of realizing that they are near the edge of the world and then the reassuring message that the world has little value anyway, and their place on the edge gives them no less access to God than anyone else has. In this way, Anglo-Saxons could make a virtue of necessity, "the *double negation* which inclines agents ... to refuse what is anyway refused and to love the inevitable."[91]

On the other hand, devaluing one's home in favour of a heavenly home that one has never seen cannot be easy or simple. The same clash between experience and Latinate learning that Anglo-Saxons would feel at finding that their home has no clear place in many texts and stories would be felt in rejecting that home for one unseen. English texts cannot entirely reject the world. The *Pastoral Care* and the *Boethius* urge their audiences to practise their virtues and skills in the here and now. Ælfric's homilies tell listeners and readers to direct themselves towards heaven, but in this life they must have faith, hope, and love as they "efstan mid godum geearnungum to urum eðele" ("hasten with good earnings to our homeland," *Catholic Homilies* 1.10.163–4). The theological virtues must be practised, and the rewards earned, in this world. The lives of saints and biblical stories give models to follow *here*. Anglo-Saxons had to live in this world even while they were told to reject it. They must have found themselves at times torn among celebrating their home, recognizing the importance of more central places, and rejecting all earthly places. Each of these attitudes towards space and place appear in turn in the texts studied in this chapter

---

91 Bourdieu, *Outline*, 77, his emphasis.

and the previous. Authors take different approaches even within the same text because the tensions can never be resolved.

Conclusions

Readers were continually pulled in different directions by the texts examined in this chapter. England *was* marginal to most of the world, as maps and classical histories represented it, and as reflected in some translations from Latin, homilies, saints' lives, and biblical poems. Yet Anglo-Saxons' own dispositions, which Bourdieu would argue "give disproportionate weight to early experiences,"[92] would tell them that their people, be they West Saxons, Mercians, or even transplanted Franks, could not be hanging off the edge of the world, as maps and texts seem to portray them. While works with Latin roots brought Anglo-Saxon readers perhaps sometimes uncomfortably close to a viewpoint centred on Rome or the Holy Land, none of these *solely* marginalizes England. Various texts recentre, if only temporarily, around Brittania. At other times, they take an entirely different perspective, from which all of earth is marginal. Finally, place becomes metaphor, with not just political importance but a spiritual significance available to readers everywhere.

The program as a whole redirects readers from a marginalization of England, though not to replace Jerusalem, Rome, or Francia with Winchester, Anglia, or *Angelcynn*. Realistically, such replacement could not succeed: many Anglo-Saxons constructed these distant places mentally as centres of religion, power, and learning. They remained destinations for pilgrims and ambassadors. Spiritually, replacement would conflict with the emphasis that most of these texts placed on divine gifts and responsibilities. Yet the program also did not encourage readers to accept classical views of the world; England's place may be minor in the universe and in the fullness of time, but in the here and now it matters a great deal.

Despite differences between the worlds of Scripture, late antiquity, and Anglo-Saxon England, homologies appear in both prose and poetic texts. *Angelcynn* can be as central – and as insignificant – as Rome. All it needs are the tools of learning and devoted minds. Translators, homilists, and poets provide the former; the latter, the audience must supply, turning from texts to God himself. Still, these texts provide rich reminders of the

---

92 Bourdieu, *Outline*, 78; see also the previous chapter.

complex, inhabited world that Anglo-Saxons could hope to leave behind in favour of an orderly, inhabited heaven.

The Anglo-Saxons encountered named places and peoples frequently in the world of their texts, but there are other kinds of space than regions and nations. The final two chapters will examine how Anglo-Saxons constructed other kinds of spaces: waste and water, or open spaces; and cities and halls, or closed spaces. We will see that like specific lands and peoples, these more general kinds of spaces could also be constructed as comprehensible and inhabited spaces.

4 Fruitful Wastes in *Beowulf*, *Guthlac A*, and *Andreas*

As the previous two chapters have shown, Anglo-Saxons construct earthly places in literature by connecting them to other places, relating the history of individual places, and giving special attention to the inhabitants. Such points of reference work effectively for relatively well defined places, both those nearby and those far from England: from Ely to India, places have names, are constructed in relation to other knowable places, and are known by their inhabitants and what they have done. The Anglo-Saxons even constructed outer space with reference to who lives there, as seen in chapter 1: the regions with atmosphere and those without had their own inhabitants, from holy men to dragons to demons.

This chapter will explore how wastelands and bodies of water also became understood places through knowledge of their inhabitants and histories. These dangerously open spaces lack stability and a sense of the "proper," in Michèl de Certeau's terminology.[1] Though the term "waste" might initially bring barren places to mind for twenty-first-century readers, we can also think of wastes that once held life, or that still hold people or animals struggling for existence.[2] We probably find it easier to think of

---

1 De Certeau, *Practice of Everyday Life*, 117. Note that while I use de Certeau's notion of the "proper," which marks comprehensible space and excludes two objects occupying the same space at the same time, I do not follow his terminology of "place" and "space" because they are the reverse of the terminology used in the field of human geography; see my Introduction for more details.

2 For an excellent treatment of medieval English landscape and contrasts with North American expectations and terms, see Oliver Rackham, "The Medieval Countryside of England: Botany and Archaeology," in *Inventing Medieval Landscapes: Senses of Place in Western Europe*, ed. John Howe and Michael Wolfe (Gainesville: University Press of Florida, 2002), 13–32.

seas and oceans as places accommodating many kinds of life and many stories. For Anglo-Saxons, waste and water offered perilous, disorderly fullnesses that could threaten more proper places; at the same time, these spaces were not distant or rare but close and common. Sigmund Freud's notion of the uncanny is useful here, starting with his own term for it: what is *unheimlich* (literally, "unhomely" or "unfamiliar") is not simply the opposite of *heimlich* ("homely, familiar"), but combines aspects of the familiar with those that make it unfamiliar.[3] In Freud's view, the uncanny, or *unheimlich*, results from the resurfacing of something repressed, recognizable and unrecognizable at the same time. Wastes and waters seem inimical to human society and the self as places of danger where most cannot live for long, yet they also help create and sustain society. Wastes hold what society cannot, and water promotes life as well as threatening it. The variety and chaos of the cosmos impinge on the world in these places, threatening the more unified hearth that may lie quite close to the waste or the water.[4]

This chapter will first examine the fruitful wastes found in three poems. *Beowulf* depicts two wastelands close to human habitation in Europe, the first of which is also a body of water. *Guthlac A* presents a waste in England itself, and again one associated with water. *Andreas* transports us to the most surprising waste of the three poems: the Mermedonians' citadel, built in marble and stone but described as a waste. Wastelands in the other two poems help us understand how the marvellous city of *Andreas* is *weste*. These spaces are difficult to reach, mysterious lands on the border between civilized space and something else, and yet most of them are not distant. They are also not dead, as we might think of wasteland, but alive with creatures hostile to humanity even as these sites share qualities of human habitation. Those qualities allow them to be redeemed for humanity (at least in part) and permit areas that might otherwise appear frighteningly outside human control to be conceptually bounded and managed.

The chapter will then turn to depictions of water. In the Alfredian translations, water seems to be a dangerous medium through which one must be guided to safe harbour; seas are a means to reach some more important end. Poetry conceives of water more expansively. It is inhabited in *Beowulf* and in *The Whale*, a place of danger but also a place of honour and sustenance. While waste can be redeemed and ordered by human beings, water remains always outside human comprehension and control.

---

3 Freud, "The Uncanny," in *Collected Papers*, ed. Riviere, 4: 368–407.
4 For cosmos and hearth, see Tuan, *Cosmos and Hearth*.

Wasteland

Wasteland in Anglo-Saxon England is not what modern readers, particularly those in North America, tend to imagine when they hear the word "wasteland." It is rarely the kind of arid desert that may come to mind. At the same time, it is not "primordial" or "old-growth" forest, which did not exist in early medieval England, whose land had been managed by inhabitants for centuries before Anglo-Saxons arrived.[5] Oliver Rackham notes that in Domesday Book, recorded in 1086, only about 15 per cent of the land was woodland.[6] Wasteland did exist, but it was not large and barren; wastes were more likely to be areas abandoned just for a time or frontiers between different groups or kingdoms.[7] Fens were more common, but they were also inhabited and sources of wealth.[8] The poets embellished, taking the most threatening aspects of real landscapes that audiences might have known and exaggerating them for literary effect.

Nor were hostile inhabitants in unused land mere literary flights of fancy. The Anglo-Saxons had rituals to clear land of enemies.[9] The metrical charm "For Unfruitful Land" (Cotton Caligula A.vii) asks God and "Erce, eorþan modor" ("Erce, mother of the earth," 51, ASPR 6) to make the land fruitful; along the way, it includes the request "þæt hys yrþ si gefriþod

---

5 See John Howe and Michael Wolfe, eds, *Inventing Medieval Landscapes: Senses of Place in Western Europe* (Gainesville: University Press of Florida, 2002), especially their introduction (1–10) and its references; and in the same volume, Rackham, "Medieval Countryside," 13–32, and Nicholas Howe, "The Landscape of Anglo-Saxon England: Inherited, Invented, Imagined," 91–119.

6 Rackham, "Medieval Countryside," 15. For more details about woodland in Anglo-Saxon England, see Della Hooke, *The Landscape of Anglo-Saxon England* (London: Leicester University Press, 1998), chap. 7, "Woodland Resources," 139–69.

7 See Hooke, *Landscape*, 139.

8 Rackham, "Medieval Countryside," 27–8. Jeffrey Jerome Cohen notes that Felix's *Vita Guthlaci* and the Old English poem *Guthlac A* depict the fen as a hostile landscape and "a *locus certaminis*" ("a place of contest,"137), while William of Malmesbury describes the nearby Thorney as productive and beautiful, though the fens had not yet been drained; "The Solitude of Guthlac," in his *Medieval Identity Machines*, Medieval Cultures 35 (Minneapolis: University of Minnesota Press, 2003), 137–8. Hooke, however, writes: "Some areas, like the empty fenland to the south of Spalding, indeed, appear to have been abandoned" and specifically names Guthlac's retreat, which might have looked quite different by the time of William of Malmesbury, even before the draining; *Landscape*, 171.

9 Thanks to Sarah Hamilton for suggesting that I consider these charms and prayers.

wið ealra feonda gehwæne" ("that this land be protected against all kinds of enemies," 61), including any kind of sorcery or witchcraft.[10] Several prayers in the Durham Collectar explicitly ask God to protect homes, barns, and fields against worms, birds, and even demons.[11] If inhabited spaces are filled with such harmful creatures, how much more dangerous must sites farther from civilization be?

Beowulf, *Guthlac A*, and *Andreas* employ the related words *weste* and *westen* for spaces outside civilization. *Beowulf* applies them to Grendel's mother's abode: "westen warode" ("she inhabited wasteland," 1265); the area around the dragon's barrow is described as "westenne" ("wasteland," 2298).[12] *Guthlac* tells us near the start that certain saints choose to remove themselves from society: "Sume þa wuniað on westennum" ("Some then dwell in wasteland," 81, ASPR 3). It later describes its protagonist's chosen retreat with the same noun (208 and 296). *Andreas* uses the word twice, first in a story that Andrew recounts about how Jesus "þurh wundra feala on þam westenne / cræfta gecyðde" ("through many wonders in that wasteland made his power known," 699–700). The second time, the poet says, "Hornsalu wunedon / weste, winræced" ("The horned halls, the wine-houses, stood empty," *Andreas* 1158–9).[13] All of these examples except the last appear to be what we would consider waste: places where few human beings go and survival can be difficult. The last shows a central human dwelling *made* waste, empty of inhabitants.

Bosworth-Toller offers straightforward definitions that fit our initial impressions of waste:

---

10 ASPR 6, 116–18.

11 Karen Louise Jolly, "Prayers from the Field: Practical Protection and Demonic Defense in Anglo-Saxon England," *Traditio* 61 (2006): 95–147.

12 For *Beowulf*, see Klaeber 4. The translations are my own except as noted. I omit diacritics for ease of reading, but I have kept italics and brackets to indicate editorial differences from the manuscript. One other place is also described as a *westen* and will be discussed later in this chapter: the old man whose son has been hanged inhabits "winsele westne" ("a waste winehall," 2456).

13 I follow here the punctuation of Kenneth R. Brooks, *Andreas and the Fates of the Apostles* (Oxford: Oxford University Press, 1961 and 1998). In the ASPR, the lines read "Hornsalu wunedon, / weste winræced" ("The horned halls stood [empty], empty the wine-houses"). In either case, the adjective and the verb seem to be shared by both nouns; Brooks's punctuation makes it easier to see how. The ASPR may have kept "weste" with "winræced" because of the closeness of the phrase to "winsele westne" ("waste winehall," 2456) in *Beowulf*; see below.

> wéste, adj. I. of open country, waste, uncultivated and uninhabited, desert ...
> II. waste, empty, unused ... III. waste, useless, unproductive IV. of habita-
> tions, waste, deserted, desolate ... V. waste, spoiled ...
>   wésten, wésten[n], wéstern (*in northern dialect*), es, e ; m. f. n. *A desert,
> wilderness* ... (1211)

These senses seem comparable to today's meanings of *waste* (noun) in the
Oxford English Dictionary:

> I. Waste or desert land.
>   1. a. Uninhabited (or sparsely inhabited) and uncultivated country; a wild
> and desolate region, a desert, wilderness. Somewhat rhetorical.
>   b. *transf.* Applied, e.g., to the ocean or other vast expanse of water (often
> waste of waters, watery waste), to land covered with snow, and to empty
> space or untenanted regions of the air.

The connection that this chapter makes between waste and water still
holds in the *OED*'s definition of the word "waste," though the *OED* considers the use for bodies of water a "transferred sense." *Wasteland* is a
more recent coinage, the Old English *westen* having dropped out of use,
but the *OED* gives a definition that by now must seem familiar:

> 1. a. Land in its natural, uncultivated state. Also attrib. ...
>   b. Land (esp. that which is surrounded by developed land) not used or
> unfit for cultivation or building and allowed to run wild ...
>   c. spec. a waterless or treeless region, a desert. (Not distinguishable from
> some examples at sense 1a) ...

The sense of unused or useless land may be accompanied by a sense that
little or nothing lives in the region. That latter point is more modern than
the former.

Wastes in Old English poetry share a handful of characteristics, though
they may differ greatly from each other in other ways. They are hidden or
difficult to reach, even though they are often not far from human communities. Ordinary people do not live there, yet each has its own residents, and heroes (religious or secular) enter these realms and may even
stay. They are liminal spaces, ones on or across a border that will not remain separate from safer, human spaces. Despite their lack of proper inhabitants, they carry traces of humanity, which may also help in the last
element they have in common: they are, or can be made, fruitful. None of

the three poems on which I focus here makes the connection overtly, but wordplay on *westen* (wasteland) and *wæstm* (fruit) may have been available to the poets: Ælfric's sermon on the nativity of John the Baptist declares that he "wunode on westene oþ fullum wæstme" ("he dwelled in the wilderness until his full fruitfulness" or maturity, *Catholic Homilies* 1.25.43).[14]

The wastes of *Beowulf*, *Guthlac*, and *Andreas* are all secret, mysterious, dark, or difficult of access. Though Hrothgar knows the mere's location, he calls it "dygel lond" (1357), which the editors of *Klaeber's Beowulf* gloss as "secret, hidden, mysterious" (364).[15] The route to the mere is short but difficult:

steap stanhliðo,   stige nearwe,
enge anpaðas,   uncuð gelad,
neowle næssas ...   (1409–11)

("steep stony slopes, close path, narrow defiles, unknown route, precipitous headlands ...")

The mere thus lies close to Heorot and yet cannot be easily reached. Fabienne Michelet describes the mere and the hall as "conflicting centres of power," close to each other and like yet unlike.[16] The mere is also described as dark (87, 1360, 1405), except for the unnatural "fyr on flode" ("fire in the water," 1366), and its depths seem to be unknown to civilized people until Beowulf plumbs them. The mere in *Beowulf* is "fen and fæsten" ("fen and stronghold," 104), and other "fen" words later describe it as well.[17] The *DOE* gives the sense for this line as the modern "fen,

---

14 Thanks to Leslie Lockett for suggesting that paranomasia might be operating here
    when I gave part of this chapter as a paper ("Fruitful Wastes in *Beowulf*, *Guthlac A*,
    and *Andreas*," 15th Meeting of the International Society of Anglo-Saxonists, Madison,
    WI, 31 July–6 August 2011). It is difficult to know for certain whether the poems were
    making the same connection that Ælfric did, but the possibility was open to them. *Ælfric's
    Catholic Homilies: Introduction*, ed. Godden; *Ælfric's Catholic Homilies: First Series*,
    ed. Clemoes; *Ælfric's Catholic Homilies: Second Series*, ed. Godden.
15 The *DOE* gives for this occurrence of "digol": "2. out of the way, secluded; remote,
    isolated."
16 Michelet, *Creation, Migration, and Conquest*, 83.
17 "morhopu" (450), "fenhopu" (764), "fenhleoðu" (820), "fenfreoðo" (851), "fenne"
    (1295), "fengelad" (1359). *Guthlac A* never uses "fen" or "mor" or their compounds,

marsh" (*fenn*). The word may also carry connotations from its primary sense: "mud, dirt, mire; filth."

This filthy mere has inhabitants. Grendel is a "mearcstapa" (103; see also 1348): "wanderer in the waste borderland."[18] A "mearc" or boundary sets off what is human or alive from what is not, as we can see from the description of Heardred's death: the poet says "Him þæt to mearce wearð" ("That became for him the boundary," 2384) when Heardred crossed from life to death.[19] As "mearcstapan" (1348), Grendel and his mother straddle the boundary between human and not-human, and they take men across the boundary from life to death. Heide Estes notes that Grendel's mother leaves Æschere's head "to mark the entrance to her home," illustrating literally the figurative division between her people and the Danes.[20] Grendel and his mother cross from their own waste, wild space into what had been ordered, civilized space, bringing chaos and destruction into the Danes' world. That is what makes wastelands so threatening.

Grendel and later his mother come out of the wastes to attack the hall and the men in it. These attacks threaten the whole social fabric of Hrothgar's people, for community life centres upon the hall. They threaten the proper place of Heorot: proper as in property, something that the Danes possess and control; and proper as in propriety.[21] Grendel's incursions threaten the ability of the Danes to hold the hall, and his onslaughts make the place of society and rejoicing into a very improper killing ground. Grendel's first attack kills thirty of Hrothgar's thegns (*Beowulf* 123), a serious blow. Repeated incursions leave the hall vacant at night, and word soon spreads that the Danes are powerless against this threat. Yet Michelet

---

though in his Latin *vita*, Felix repeatedly describes Guthlac's retreat as a fen or swamp, as does an Old English prose life of Guthlac: see *Felix's Life of Saint Guthlac*, ed. and trans. Bertram Colgrave (Cambridge: Cambridge University Press, 1956, repr. 1985). The poet of *Guthlac A* either did not know or chose not to mention that Guthlac lived in a swamp.

18 From the glossary to *Klaeber's Beowulf* on 411.

19 Andy Orchard, *A Critical Companion to Beowulf* (Rochester, NY: Brewer, 2003), 63, notes wordplay on "mær-/mearc-mor" at 103; I see "mearcað morhopu" as repeating the play at 450.

20 Heide Estes, "*Beowulf* and the Sea: An Ecofeminist Reading," in *The Maritime World of the Anglo-Saxons*, ed. Klein, Schipper, and Lewis-Simpson, 209–26.

21 French "propre" means both "proper" (fitting or right) and "owned" or "belonging to"; see de Certeau, *Practice*, xix; for the role of the proper in space, see esp. 117–18. See also Tuan for the importance of naming in establishing proper place, *Space and Place*, 29–30.

notes that invasion itself helps to construct spaces such as Heorot as central places:

> The most rewarding way to think about the centre is to consider it as a place constantly threatened by the outside world, as a place that is in fact always invaded and violated. The notion of invasion is crucial to conceptualize centre and periphery, for before transgression, only undifferentiated space existed ... The spaces *Beowulf* depicts also need transgression to exist.[22]

The irruption of chaos and violence from outside into Heorot clarifies what Heorot should be: a safe hearth for the Danes.

Beowulf ends Grendel's attacks through his own assertion of the proper use of Heorot.[23] He meets Grendel in single, hand-to-hand combat, having eschewed weapons and armour because Grendel rejects them (677–80). Grendel comes "of more under misthleoþum" ("from the marsh under mist-slopes," 710); Beowulf pretends to sleep but keeps watch as befits a warrior, unlike the man whom Grendel kills that night, a "slæpendne rinc" ("sleeping warrior," 741). Beowulf emerges triumphant, and Grendel's arm is displayed as a trophy when its owner runs off to die in the mere. Yet the hall is not fully cleansed, fully safe, fully proper yet. Grendel's mother returns the following night to kill in revenge for her son's death. Beowulf must enter the wasteland himself to save the people from what comes out of it. His actions there protect Heorot and the Danes.[24]

Scholars have long noted that the mere where Grendel and his mother live resembles hell, as presented in the *Visio Sancti Pauli* and Blickling Homily 16. All are watery spaces surrounded by trees and cliffs, with frightening creatures. *Beowulf* and Blickling Homily 16 even share the phrase "harne stan" (*Beowulf* 1415; Blickling Homily 16, 199).[25] Though a

---

22 Michelet, *Creation, Migration, and Conquest*, 94.

23 Michelet remarks that Beowulf himself is an outsider, yet Hrothgar entrusts the hall to him, making it his to defend. She reads Hrothgar as ruling the hall in the day, with Grendel and Beowulf competing to rule at night, 91–7. Once Beowulf has won, he returns control to Hrothgar by leaving peacefully.

24 The poem keeps reminding us, however, that even Beowulf's success only saves Heorot for a time. The true threat comes not from the wasteland, but from within. The hall setting will be examined more in the next chapter.

25 *The Blickling Homilies: Edition and Translation*, ed. and trans. Richard J. Kelly (London: Continuum, 2003).

literal translation of "hoary stone" would not be wrong here, William Cooke points out that the phrase explicitly indicates in Blickling Homily 16 a boundary stone marking the edge of hell.[26] The texts also echo each other with "hrinde bearwes" (*Beowulf* 1363) and "hrimige bearwas" (Blickling 16, 200), both meaning "frost-covered woods." Even if audiences did not know these intertexts, they could not miss the connection to hell. Grendel is a "feond on hell" ("fiend in hell," 101), "helle hæfton" ("hell-captive," 788), "ellorgast" ("alien spirit," 807) and "helle gast" ("hell-spirit," 1274). His mother is also an "ellorgast" ("alien spirit," 1621). Passing the stone and entering the mere is very much like entering another world. Thus, *Beowulf*'s mere shades from the kind of landscape Anglo-Saxons could have encountered often, a marsh or other body of water that might have "wulfhleoþu" ("wolf-slopes," 1358) nearby, into one even more fearful. In addition to details and phrases that connect the mere to hell, the poet tells us that the water teems with monsters of various descriptions. The mere is a "fifelcynnes eard" ("dwelling-place of a race of sea-monsters," 104) and "ælwihta eard" ("dwelling-place of a race of foreign creatures," 1500).[27] One might find a "sinnigne secg" ("a sinful man," 1379) there, but not a good man. The mere lies outside human society, and its inhabitants actively threaten that society.[28]

The mere in *Beowulf* is not only hellish but also uncanny, simultaneously monstrous and yet familiar. Grendel and his mother's home is a recognizable habitation for people, described in the same terms used for dwellings of the Danes and Geats. Grendel's mother brings Beowulf "to hofe sinum" ("to her house," 1507) just as Hrothgar departed "to hofe sinum" ("to his house," 1236) to sleep. Grendel's mother's home is a "recede" ("house, hall," 1572) with "wealle" ("walls," 1573), all terms used

---

26 William Cooke, "Two Notes on Beowulf (with Glances at *Vafþruðnismál*, Blickling Homily 16, and *Andreas*, Lines 839–846)," *Medium Ævum* 72 (2003): 297–301. On the *harne stan* as signalling danger and the setting for heroic action, see Lori Ann Garner, *Structuring Spaces: Oral Poetics and Architecture in Early Medieval England* (Notre Dame, IN: University of Notre Dame Press, 2011), 52–4 and 60.

27 See also 1425–7, 1498, and 1510–12.

28 Paul Langeslag makes the same point in "Monstrous Landscape in Beowulf," *English Studies* 96.2 (2015): 119–38, but he argues that the landscape derives from both theological and folk traditions. The former connects watery places to hell, sin, and the giants; the latter connects them to darkness and danger, and that very danger generally placed marshlands outside the centre of society, leaving them to more marginal inhabitants.

for Heorot.[29] The abode contains at least one bed (upon which Grendel lies dead, 1585–6) much as Heorot contains beds (676, 1240). "fyrleoht" ("firelight," 1516) illuminates the place, as it would all contemporary halls. Grendel's attacks on Heorot may proceed from jealousy or a simple dislike of noisy neighbours.[30] Grendel's mother seeks vengeance. Grendel and his mother frighten precisely because they are human (at least in part) and yet do things that we would like to deny that humans do.[31] In that passage, the referent of a given masculine pronoun is not always clear. Thus, the underwater hall where Grendel and his mother reside both resembles familiar human spaces and inverts them.

Water itself is unstable: as Kelley Wickham-Crowley reminds us, water holds no boundaries, and the boundaries between land and water constantly change.[32] Water is a dangerous space that can never be fully defined and made into place. The womb-like space of the mere is particularly dangerous, even uncanny. The infant Beowulf once emerged from a watery feminine space; now Beowulf must struggle in a second such space to survive and re-emerge. Here, instead of nurturing him, a woman poses a serious threat, even though we were told in the hall that her strength is much

---

29 Heorot as *reced* (and compounds thereof): 310, 326, 412, 704, 714, 720, 724, 728, 770, 993, 1237, 1799; its *weal(l)*, 326, 785. The poet also terms the Grendelkin's home "hrof-sele" ("roofed hall," 1515); that specific term is not used for Heorot, but it is called a *sele* at 81, 323, 411, 713, 826, 919, 1016, 1640 (and several compounds add occurrences of –*sele* for Heorot), and the poem refers to its *hrof* 403, 836 (by emendation), 926, 999, and 1030. However, Estes, "*Beowulf* and the Sea," understands the cave as a natural and not a built space (225).

30 Surely some of us have at least a trace of sympathy for the introvert who shuts down the neighbour's loud party.

31 Indeed, the differences are small enough that we can confuse Grendel and Beowulf in their fight: see Orchard (and his references), *Pride and Prodigies*, 31–3; and *Critical Companion*, 192 and 197–201. Jennifer Neville seems to overlook these similarities when she writes, "What Grendel is not defines what the human is or should be," in *Representations of the Natural World in Old English Poetry* (Cambridge: Cambridge University Press, 1999), 38. She gives a more complicated view later, when she speaks of Grendel and his mother as outsiders who live in nature and with monsters, 133–7.

32 Kelley M. Wickham-Crowley, "Living on the *Ecg*: The Mutable Boundaries of Land and Water in Anglo-Saxon Contexts," in *A Place to Believe in: Locating Medieval Landscapes*, ed. Clare A. Lees and Gillian R. Overing (University Park: Pennsylvania State University Press, 2006), 85–100. For a brief introduction to lentic (slow-moving or still) bodies of water in Anglo-Saxon England with further references, see Mattias Jacobsson, *Wells, Meres, and Pools: Hydronymic Terms in the Anglo-Saxon Landscape*, Acta Universitatis Upsaliensis, Studia Anglistica Upsaliensia 98 (Uppsala: Reklam & Katalogtryck AB, 1997), 177–81.

less than that of Grendel, whom Beowulf dispatched more easily: "Wæs se gryre læssa / efne swa micle swa bið mægþa cræft, / wiggryre wifes be wæpnedmen" ("The horror was less by just as much as the strength of a maiden, the war-terror of a woman, is less than fighting men's," 1282–4).[33] Where the hall was a proper space for two warriors to meet, the mere is no place for a warrior. Renée Trilling argues persuasively that where Beowulf wore no armour and used no weapons against Grendel in the Danes' hall, here he must arm himself heavily to assert his masculinity against a female foe.[34] Grendel never got the upper hand in his fight with Beowulf in Heorot, but in the maternal mere, Beowulf falls under the attack of Grendel's mother (1544), and only his armour keeps her knife from penetrating his body (1545–9). The sword he carries fails him (1523–5), and he must use an "ealdsweord eotenisc" ("ancient giants' sword," 1558) to kill her. The maternal cave is nearly Beowulf's grave. Only through his heroic efforts, and intervention by "halig God" ("holy God," 1553), does it become the grave for Grendel and his mother instead.[35] Heide Estes notes that Beowulf's re-emergence from the bloody, feminine waters marks a rebirth for him: he leaves feminine space for a masculine economy where he now occupies a different place.[36] The text gives no indication that the space of the mere will have any further use after Beowulf's cleansing and departure; the waters remain dangerous to human life.

In a similar vein, though the dragon's barrow lies near enough Beowulf's hall that men can reach it easily on foot, the dragon has lain undisturbed in his barrow for three hundred years before the action of the poem (2278). Notably, someone who is not a hero can enter: a frightened man steals a

---

33 Paul Acker also notes the disjunction between the actual fight and the narrator's commentary on Grendel's mother's strength, "Horror and the Maternal in *Beowulf*," *PMLA* 121.3 (2006): 705.

34 Renée Rebecca Trilling, "Beyond Abjection: The Problem with Grendel's Mother Again," *Parergon* 24.1 (2007): 1–20.

35 Beowulf takes Grendel's head as a trophy but leaves the body in the mere. For Grendel's mother as abject, see Acker, "Horror and the Maternal"; for her as *chora* instead, see Trilling, "Beyond Abjection." Linda Marshall approaches the mere somewhat differently in "Grendelsmere as *Vagina Dentata*: Grendel's Mother and the Fear of Women's Power," in *The Image of the Outsider II in Literature, Media, and Society: Proceedings of the 2008 Conference, Society for the Interdisciplinary Study of Social Imagery*, ed. Will Wright and Stephen Kaplan (Pueblo: Society for the Interdisciplinary Study of Social Imagery, Colorado State University, 2008), 90–2, though the short space does not allow Marshall to develop the topic much.

36 Estes, "*Beowulf* and the Sea," 220.

cup (2280–93). The narrator even remarks on the success of the theft, crediting God's intervention: "Swa mæg unfæge eaðe gedigan / wean and wræcsið, se ðe waldendes / hyldo gehealdeþ" ("So may the unfated easily pass safely through woes and exile-journey, he who holds the protection of the Creator," 2291–3). Though he survives his adventure, the thief's penetration of the barrow results in disaster, awakening the dragon, who goes on a rampage. The thief must then guide ("wisian," 2409) Beowulf and his companions, implying that the barrow is difficult to find. *Beowulf*'s wastelands never lie far from human habitation, yet they remain mysterious and difficult to reach. This time, Beowulf does not go in after his enemy. The dragon comes out to him for a fight that will kill them both.

Mortally wounded, Beowulf cannot enter the dragon's barrow, but Wiglaf, the only man brave enough to join him in the battle, plunges into the barrow after the dragon's death to carry out treasures for Beowulf to admire in his last moments. He later takes other men in to do the same (3120–31). The dragon's barrow, like Grendel and his mother's mere, is "on þ(*am*) westenne" ("in the wasteland," *Beowulf* 2298). It is called a *beorg*, a "barrow" (sense 2 in the *DOE*), twelve times.[37] *Beorgas*, like *mearclondas*, are transitional places, often serving as boundary markers, as evident in Anglo-Saxon charters and place names.[38] The dragon's barrow, like Grendel's mere, straddles worlds. The dragon covets treasure and takes revenge as a warrior would, yet unlike a warrior, he keeps treasure from circulation and offers no possibility of settlement. This barrow has associations with death: it saw the end of an entire people, "æþelan cynnes" ("a noble race," 2234), and Beowulf and the dragon meet their deaths just outside. The dragon's residence, like the mere, is marked by a "harne stan" (2553 and 2744), leaving no doubt about the liminal nature of the place.[39] The dragon too lives in a human structure: the poet calls it "eorðreced" ("earth building" 2719) and "ærnes" (*DOE*, "ærn": "specifically: house" 2225).[40] The building has "wealle" ("walls," 2307), "stanbogan" ("stone arches," 2545, 2718), and "stapulum" ("posts" or "pillars," 2718). It is so

---

37 2213, 2241, 2299, 2304, 2322, 2524, 2529, 2546, 2559, 2580, 2755, and 2842.

38 More than a third of the occurrences of the word *beorg* in the *Corpus*, according to the *DOE*, are in this sense: "ca. 650 occ. (ca. 275 in boundary markers and place names)."

39 On the *harne stan* here see Garner, *Structuring Spaces*, 53–4 and 60.

40 The quotation is from the *DOE*, which notes MS damage here: "MS reading almost illegible, most editors read æ:n:". Michelet also notes the constructed nature of the dragon's lair and the resemblances between it, the cave in the mere, and kings' halls, *Creation, Migration, and Conquest*, 88–91.

impressive that it is also called "enta geweorc" ("giants' work," 2717).[41] The dragon seems very far from human in some ways, but it does not differ from some humans in its motives (greed and revenge) and its dwelling. In the three poems, the site of dragon's barrow comes closest to what most of us would consider a true wasteland: it has a much narrower range of inhabitants – namely, one dragon – but it has supported that life for centuries.

This barrow in some ways echoes the womb-like space of the mere. Both are dark, enclosed places with a single exit, but inverting the work of a proper womb, they end rather than begin life. Both mere and barrow birth monsters, bringing forth creatures that wreak havoc on more civilized spaces. From each a hero comes forth as well, but only after that hero has gone in: Beowulf from the mere, Wiglaf from the barrow. Real wombs are living tissue, but mere and barrow combine built with natural environments. The cavern in the mere contains weapons, allowing Beowulf to kill Grendel's mother and emerge from the space victorious. Both are filled with treasures, yet no human being lingers in either.

The cave and the barrow present themselves as spaces that echo the womb – and as potential graves. Freud finds fear of being buried alive an effect of a repressed desire to return to the pleasure of the womb.[42] Though being buried alive does not appear as an overt anxiety in Old English literature, fear of caves and barrows certainly does, as a justified fear.[43] Beowulf nearly dies in the underwater cave, and the Danes abandon him when blood rising to the surface of the mere makes them think that he has died (1591–1602). Beowulf's next encounter with a cave or barrow is with a *stanbeorh* or "stone barrow" (2213). The root *beorg-* or *beorh-* recurs several times over the last third of *Beowulf* as Beowulf heads inexorably towards his own burial, killed by the "beorges hyrde" ("guardian of the barrow," 2304). Though as noted above, Beowulf does not actually enter

---

41 See also Garner, *Structuring Spaces*, 61–2.

42 Freud, "The Uncanny," 397.

43 See, however, *The Wife's Lament*, where the narrator's "bearwe" ("barrow," 27) is also an "eorðscræfe" ("earth cave" or "earth grave," 28) under an "actreo" ("oak tree," 28); "actreo" and "eorðscrafu" reappear at 36, ASPR 3. The poem carries overtones of being buried alive not literally but metaphorically: the woman is no longer among living people but isolated from society. See also Garner, *Structuring Spaces*, 61–4 and 169–74, on the association of underground places with death; and 168–76 on the locations in *The Wife's Lament*.

the dragon's barrow himself, he is soon cremated and memorialized by his own *beorh* nearby (3097; see also 3143 and 3163).

Beowulf turns hostile, threatening spaces partly into places, but they are never entirely tamed. The mere and the barrow are not fully redeemed and made useful to people. Each is purged of harmful inhabitants, but each seems to be abandoned once its inhabitants have died. Beowulf takes Grendel's head and the sword hilt from the underwater cavern and leaves. Wiglaf carries out treasures from the barrow, and then returns one last time with companions to bring more for Beowulf's pyre. These spaces become known to and through heroes. They remain liminal, no longer wholly unknown space but never fully proper place. *Beowulf* makes some reference to the Christian God, but the pagan people in it lack the divine help they need to redeem space. Guthlac and Andrew, by contrast, can with God's help remake hostile spaces into fruitful places.

Guthlac A presents the saint as far removed from human dwellings, though unsurprisingly it gives us no real sense of measurable distance. Instead, the poem uses the rare word *anad*, "solitude, wilderness" (*DOE*; *Guthlac A* 333, 356), to emphasize its hero's remove from society.[44] *Guthlac A* depicts its saint settling in a "dygle stow" ("secret place," 215); indeed,

Wæs seo londes stow

bimiþen fore monnum,   oþþæt meotud onwrah
beorg on bearwe,   þa se bytla cwom
se þær haligne   ham arærde   (146–9)

("The place of this land was concealed from men until the creator revealed the barrow in the grove; when the builder came, he who raised a holy home there")

The space Guthlac chooses to inhabit has a barrow, a liminal space connected with boundaries and with death. This wilderness has been hidden even more effectively than Grendel's mere: no human has previously found it, and Guthlac does so only with the help of God.[45]

---

44 Neither *Beowulf* nor *Andreas* use this root, though Beowulf goes alone into the mere and against the dragon, and Andrew leaves his companions to enter the citadel of the Mermedonians alone.

45 See Cohen, "The Solitude of Guthlac," for the literary heritage of Guthlac's swamp in contrast with William of Malmesbury's depiction, also before the fens were drained, 137–8; and above, note 8.

Yet Guthlac soon finds that his new space already has occupants, demons who resent his disruption of their home.[46] Guthlac's chosen home is a place of contradiction: a wilderness that is also a *locus amoenus* ("pleasant spot"), as Catherine Clarke has shown, a hermitage frequented by visitors (mostly unwelcome).[47] Unusually, this westen is "grene" (232), a word associated nearly as much with being "verdant, flourishing" as with the colour green.[48] Despite the greenness, at the start, the poet tells only of Guthlac and the hostile creatures who dwell there, demons described as formidable adversaries: "Oft þær broga cwom / egeslic ond uncuð, eald-feonda nið, / searocræftum swiþ" ("Often terror came there, horrible and strange, hatred of old enemies, mighty with clever treachery," *Guthlac A* 140–2).[49] Guthlac meets there "hwearfum wræcmæcgas" ("a troop of exiles," 262–3), "wærlogan" ("oath-breakers," 298, 623). Only after the demons are gone do we hear of more pleasant companions, birds who visit

---

46 *Guthlac A* offers a good example of a wasteland in an eremetic saint's life but by no means the only one. Readers may also consult other versions of Guthlac's life, including the Latin one by Felix; multiple lives of Cuthbert; miracle stories from Bede's *Historia ecclesiastica*; and many more sources. For detailed treatment of angels and demons in Anglo-Saxon England with more attention to Latin sources, see Helen Foxhall Forbes, *Heaven and Earth in Anglo-Saxon England: Theology and Society in an Age of Faith* (Farnham, Surrey: Ashgate, 2013), esp. chap. 2, "Creator of All Things, Visible and Invisible," 63–127. Jennifer Neville comments, "When the demons arrive, neither the poet nor Guthlac expresses any surprise. They appear to assume that this lonely spot in the natural world, like any other isolated from human settlement, will naturally contain devils"; *Representations*, 127.

47 Catherine A.M. Clarke traces the notion of secluded areas as both pleasant places and retreat for demons back to Bede and the prose *Cuthbert* in *Literary Landscapes*, 28; she treats *Guthlac* at 45–60. Unlike Clarke, Cohen considers the place a *locus amoenus* solely after its cleansing, "The Solitude of Guthlac," 138–9. The positive descriptions of the *grene* land and Guthlac's enjoyment before he defeats the demons support Clarke's reading. Rackham calls attention to the fact that even though Guthlac seeks solitude, he cannot find a place without human history: "There was no primeval wilderness in Anglo-Saxon England ... Even Saint Guthlac, trying to get away from human distractions in the depths of the Fens, found himself living on a prehistoric tomb"; "Medieval Countryside," 15.

48 Definition B from the *DOE*. For other uses of "grene" for fertile land, see *Genesis* (several times); *Andreas* 776; *Phoenix* (several times, ASPR 3), and Riddles 12, 15, 21, 66 (ASPR 3).

49 Alfred K. Siewers connects the spirits at the barrow, especially in Felix's version, with Celtic inhabitants being Othered by Mercians, "Landscapes of Conversion: Guthlac's Mound and Grendel's Mere as Expressions of Anglo-Saxon Nation-Building," *Viator* 34 (2003): 9–11.

Guthlac (*Guthlac A* 735–8). John Howe's description of the *locus horribilis* ("horrible spot") is equally apt here: this is a dangerous space sought by a saint for isolation, and Guthlac eventually converts it to a more paradisiacal space with divine aid.[50]

Demonic habitation was real to Anglo-Saxons. The Durham Collectar contains both prayers original to the manuscript and others added later, in Latin but glossed in Old English, to bless homes, barns, and fields.[51] They invoke divine and angelic aid against worms and birds that might damage or eat crops and against demons and demonic temptation. Guthlac enacts a struggle in poetry that Anglo-Saxon rituals show in more quotidian life, among those who were not saints or heroes. Almost any landscape not currently in use by humans could be waste inhabited by creatures hostile to them and their works. Guthlac showed audiences an extreme possibility for such infestation, but he also demonstrated that faith could conquer hostile forces and make waste into useful human place.

Christopher Jones calls our attention to the poet's construction of Guthlac in *Guthlac A* as "bytla," builder (148, 733).[52] Jones contrasts Guthlac's *hus* ("house") with the *hus* of hell.[53] The demons occupy the space as a temporary home, and while they do not have human structures, they react in very human ways to Guthlac. He builds a home for himself (148–9) and erects a cross (179–80). The demons complain that he has broken their barrows (209). In their minds, *he* is the enemy, the fiend, the "earme ondsacan" ("wretched adversary," 210).[54] Such language usually describes the devils, not the saints: later in *Guthlac*, the demons are called

---

50 John Howe, "Creating Symbolic Landscapes: Medieval Development of Sacred Space," in *Inventing Medieval Landscapes*, 208–23.

51 See Jolly, "Prayers from the Field."

52 Christopher A. Jones, "Envisioning the *cenobium* in *Guthlac A*," *Mediaeval Studies* 57 (1995): 259–91. Jones also calls attention to the words *getimbrian* (275) and *bold* and *botl* (275–6), suggesting a play on the words wherein "Guthlac the builder becomes himself the 'building' of faith or fortress of *ellen* ('virtue' or 'valor')" (277).

53 Ibid., 274.

54 When I read the demons' rejection of Guthlac's home and particularly the cross he erects, I cannot help but think of the restrictions imposed by some US homeowners' associations, which have the power to fine or evict residents or to force removal of unapproved changes to their property or religious symbols deemed too large or in the wrong place. For examples, see the covenants at http://crystalforestestates.com/uploads/governingDocuments/26.pdf and http://lakewoodcovehoa.org/GuidelinesReligiousItems.pdf. Presumably the *Guthlac* poet did not have American HOAs in mind, but HOAs make explicit the human hope that the neighbours will not build anything they judge excessive.

"earme aglæcan" ("wretched opponents," 575), using the same adjective they used for Guthlac.[55] The demons react as a people whose territory has been disturbed. Guthlac does not enter an uninhabited space but a home for fiends.

This land is also "mearclond" (174). Again we find a hero on the border, and again it seems to be a border between life and death, for, going further than Beowulf and Wiglaf, Guthlac not only enters but also inhabits a *beorg*.[56] Jane Roberts remarks that the author insistently uses this word associated with burials and never any of the other "large conventional vocabulary for mound- and cave-dwellings (e.g. moldern, eorðscræf, eorðsele)."[57] Guthlac is alone and yet not alone. He says, "Ic me anum her eaðe getimbre / hus ond hleonað" ("Alone here, I easily build for myself a house and shelter," 250–1) and the poet uses the rare "anad" for "solitude, wilderness" (333, 356; *DOE* definition).[58] Yet he has for company an angel (172–3) and "feonda mengu" ("a host of fiends," 201). Angered by his disruption of their temporary rest in the place (205–25), perhaps as Grendel was angered by the loud joys of Heorot, the demons begin a campaign to exorcise Guthlac. The demons occupy a liminal space from which they can take Guthlac elsewhere. They snatch him and reveal to him monks at a minster wasting their time (412–20).[59]

When the sight fails to drive Guthlac to despair, to the demons' surprise, they then take him

                 æt heldore
þær firenfulra   fæge gæstas

---

55 They are also repeatedly called *earme gæstas* ("wretched spirits," 297, 339, 405, 519, 686). See Cohen, "The Solitude of Guthlac," for a reading of Guthlac as a colonizer displacing the Celtic Other through the figure of the demons.

56 102, 140, 148, 192, 209, 232, 262, 329, 383, 429, 439, 733. Laurence K. Shook was perhaps first to note that due to its setting, *beorg/beorh* in *Guthlac A* must mean barrow and not simply hill or mountain, though translators often use the latter; "The Burial Mound in *Guthlac A*," *Modern Philology* 58.1 (1960): 1–10.

57 The poet follows Felix's use of *tumulus*, but that does not fully explain his word choice, Jane Roberts continues in her edition, *The Guthlac Poems of the Exeter Book* (Oxford: Clarendon Press, 1979), 132, note to line 140.

58 The *DOE* records three occurrences, all in poetry; two of those are in *Guthlac*.

59 On this scene, see Robin Norris, "The Augustinian Theory of Use and Enjoyment in *Guthlac A* and *B*," *NM* 104 (2003): 166–8. The disjunction between the horror the demons expect from Guthlac and the sympathy he shows for the monks may have a comic effect.

æfter swyltcwale   secan onginnað
ingong ærest   in þæt atule hus,
niþer under næssas   neole grundas.   (559–63)

("to the door of hell, where the doomed spirits of the sinful after death begin
first to seek entrance into that horrible house, below, under the headlands,
the deepest abysses.")

This literal hell echoes *Beowulf*'s figurative hell, the mere, which was also
set among "næssas" (*Beowulf* 1411). Even the heroic Guthlac is affected
by the sight of torments: they begin "in sefan swencan" ("to oppress him
in his mind," 570) with threats of "þone grimman gryre" ("the terrible
horror," 571). Yet this terrible place seems somehow still familiar; it may
be an "atule hus" ("horrible house," 562), but it is a *house*, the same word
employed for the dwelling that Guthlac built (251). God then sends
Bartholomew from on high to help Guthlac: Guthlac's place is indeed liminal, opening as readily onto heaven as hell.

Guthlac A, like *Beowulf*, creates an uncanny space, though not with the
vividness of the longer poem. *Guthlac*'s ongoing juxtaposition of home
and grave remind audiences of the physical and metaphysical closeness of
these two places, and readers must be impressed that even the saint feels
the horror of hell. Audiences surely knew from the outset that Guthlac
would triumph and that death would lead him to heaven; his fate is more
certain than Beowulf's from the outset, before audiences see him in the
wasteland that he will eventually tame.

The association of *westen* with mystery or difficult access, with borderland, and with death is so strong that a place not even Anglo-Saxons would
not normally conceive as wasteland attracts that terminology. The city of
the cannibals in *Andreas* must have seemed fantastic to Anglo-Saxons. It is
a *ceaster* or *burh*, a fortified city with walls, gates, and streets; "tigelfagan
trafu, torras" ("buildings decorated with multicoloured tiles, towers," 842);
"hornsalu" ("horn-roofed halls," 1158); and even "marmanstan" ("marble," 1498).[60] The stunning architecture appears to be "eald enta geweorc"
("the old work of giants," 1495). Yet the poet dubs this marvellous city
mearcland ("borderland") from the start of the poem in a line which connects borderland with violence and enmity: "Eal wæs þæt mearcland

---

60 *Ceaster*, 41, 207, 281, 719, 829, 929, 939, 1058, 1174, 1677; *ceaster* compounds at 1125,
1237, 1646; *burhwealle*, 833; *burggeatum*, 840; *stræte*, 985.

morðre bewunden, / feondes facne" ("That whole borderland was wound around with murder, the treachery of the fiend," 19–20).[61] The architectural wonders stand in tension with Mermedonia's designation as wasteland. The inhuman behaviour of its residents renders the beautiful city of marble and stone a very real waste and a liminal space under the influence of hell: "Oft hira mod onwod / under dimscuan deofles larum" ("Often their minds passed into darkness by the teaching of the devil," 140–1). Less the physical setting than the moral one make the space a wasteland.

The poet plays with paradox: the site of cannibalism is explicitly called a waste until Andrew ends the eating of people, paradoxically making "weste" of the halls where feasts once featured humans as food (*Andreas* 1159). That collocation might be less startling if it were not borrowed from *Beowulf*. The sole occurrence of *westen* in *Beowulf* not treated earlier in this chapter is the "winsele westne" ("waste winehall," 2456) of the father whose son has been hanged.[62] *Beowulf* makes it immediately clear why the wine-hall is waste: the man has lost his son in such a way that he can never take revenge nor receive any settlement for the loss. *Andreas* makes the hall waste when the deaths and cannibalism stop. The sympathy in *Beowulf* goes to the bereft father; *Andreas* seems shockingly to direct sympathy towards the Mermedonians rather than their victims at this moment in the poem, though elsewhere it has sympathy enough for the prisoners. If that were the only portion of the poem to use the language of wasteland for Mermedonia, then the poet could be borrowing a half-line carelessly from *Beowulf* (albeit with a change to the second element of the "wine-hall" compound). The borrowing far exceeds a single word, however; a whole complex of vocabulary sets Mermedonia in the context of wasteland, ruling out a careless borrowing.

Like other wastes in this chapter, the land of the Mermedonians seems mysterious and difficult to reach. Matthew the Apostle has already found it, but presumably not easily, for Andrew must "secan digol land" ("seek hidden land," 698) to rescue Matthew from the cannibals there. The poet also says that the place lies "on ælmyrcna eðelrice" (432), which J.R. Hall convincingly argues should be rendered "into the native realm of the

---

61 Brooks, *Andreas*, Commentary 62, writes "*morðor* is not necessarily 'murder,' but rather 'violence' or 'deadly sin'" and offers comparisons to *Andreas* 1170 and 1313 and *Daniel* 451 (ASPR 2). I have kept the Modern English reflex for its powerful connotations, which I find present in the Old English as well.

62 Thanks to Matt Hussey for pointing out this connection to me. For details of the likely influence of *Beowulf* on *Andreas*, see Brooks, *Andreas*, esp. xxiii–xxvi in the Introduction.

wholly dark," a reference to moral darkness.[63] Mermedonia lies far from Andrew's initial location in Achaia, and the saint must travel a long way, the poem recounts (see especially 190–1, 420–4). God tells Andrew that Matthew has only three days left to live (185); Andrew initially refuses to undertake the rescue mission, offering as his first excuse that he cannot travel so far so quickly (190–2). After he agrees, Andrew unknowingly hires the Lord's boat to make the journey. They sail for a full day from Achaia at great speed (505), but even so they remain too far from Mermedonia. Angels fly Andrew to the city while he sleeps so that he arrives in time (820–8). Clearly, Mermedonia lies far from Achaia and presumably from Anglo-Saxons, though the poem never gives a firm location for Mermedonia, even in relation to other places in the poem.[64]

Like *Beowulf* and *Guthlac A*, *Andreas* features *beorgas*. *Beorg* can, of course, mean "mountain" as well as "barrow." Among the top senses in the *DOE* for *beorg* are:

1. mountain, hill (freq. in Or and PPs); mountain range (in Or)
   1.b.   *heah / steap beorg* 'high / steep mountain'
2. barrow, tumulus, burial mound (both Saxon and pre-Saxon burial mounds; freq. in charters)
3. in boundary markers and place names where it is not always possible to distinguish between senses 1 and 2

As the *Dictionary* notes, these senses may be difficult to separate. Frequent references to death give *Andreas*'s repeated *beorgas* (840, 1306, 1587) a dual meaning. The advanced architecture houses the spiritually dead, and

---

63 See Brooks's commentary on these lines, *Andreas*, 76–7, and J.R. Hall, "Two Dark Old English Compounds: *ælmyrcan* (*Andreas* 432a) and *guðmyrce* (*Exodus* 59a)," *Journal of English Linguistics* 20 (1987): 41. Both reject earlier interpretations of the word as referring to Ethiopians or dark skin colour. I follow Brooks here in not capitalizing "ælmyrcna" as the ASPR does.

64 For the location of Mermedonia, see Brooks, *Andreas*, Introduction, xxvii–xxx; and Garner, *Structuring Spaces*, 105. Charles Wright argues persuasively that the terms "igland" (*Andreas* 15) and "ealand" (*Andreas* 28) follow biblical usage of *insula* for lands that are not islands but are distant and unbelieving, often in context of punishment or conversion: "'Insulae gentium': Biblical Influence on Old English Poetic Vocabulary," in *Magister Regis: Studies in Honor of Robert Earl Kaske*, ed. Arthur Groos et al. (New York: Fordham University Press, 1986): 19–21. Andrew Scheil argues that the distance Andrew must cover draws on romance tradition, which requires the hero to go to faraway sites. At the same time, because *Andreas* is specifically a Christian romance, God pervades all of space; see "Space and Place," esp. 201–5.

the whole city briefly becomes a necropolis when God floods it and the cannibals all die. Moreover, the first mention of the *beorgas* in *Andreas* carries with it another significant term. These lines illustrate sense 1b in the *DOE*: "And 840: beorgas steape, hleoðu hlifodon, ymbe harne stan …" ("High mountains, cliffs towered around a boundary stone," 840–1). A similar *harne stan* marks borders in three of the four wastes that are major settings in *Beowulf* and *Andreas*. The vocabulary of borderlands and even the underworld characterizes the citadel of the Mermedonians while the poet plays on the dual senses of *beorg* as mountain and grave.

The wastelands in *Beowulf* and *Guthlac A* threaten chaos and terror. They mark the borders between human and inhuman, life and death, a *harne stan* sometimes signalling the entrance. Yet wastes are not simply uninhabited; they would be less threatening if they did not host monsters, dragons, and beings that may or may not be human.[65] Mermedonia proves in some ways the opposite of the mere, the barrow, and Guthlac's hermitage: at the outset, it appears to support human life exclusively. The island is repeatedly described as rocky or stony. The cannibals have not been cultivating the land, for they have a very restricted diet:

> Næs þær hlafes wist
> werum on þam wonge,   ne wæteres drync
> to bruconne,   ah hie blod ond fel,
> fira flæschoman,   feorrancumenra,
> ðegon geond þa þeode.   (21–5)

("Nor was there sustenance of bread for men on that plain, nor drink of water to enjoy, but among the people they consumed blood and flesh, the bodies of men, travellers.")

The people's practices kept the land a wasteland: uncultivated, stony ground. Yet life thrives in the city, despite their distasteful eating habits, until Andrew arrives.

Where the other two poems presented wasteland outside of civilization, retaining only some of the trappings of human work, *Andreas* presents a city that visually appears a pinnacle of human civilization but is morally a waste. The poet uses the roots *-burg-* and *-ceaster-* repeatedly to designate

---

65 For the humanity of Grendel and his mother, or lack thereof, see Trilling, "Beyond Abjection," 6–7.

the place and its inhabitants, and he describes its rich architecture in some detail, as noted above; where the other poems presented largely non-human spaces, Mermedonia seems only to support humans. The poem mentions no other life until Andrew allows himself to be taken by the cannibals and grievously wounded (1395–7). His self-sacrifice changes the nature of the city. Trees only appear when they grow and bloom from Andrew's blood: "Geseh he geblowene bearwas standan / blædum gehrodene, swa he ær his blod aget" ("He saw groves standing, blooming, adorned with leaves, as he had earlier poured forth his blood," 1448–9). The wastelands in *Beowulf* and *Guthlac* were uncanny because of their echoes of human habitation where full humans did not reside; *Andreas* offers an excessively human space, one that rejects all other life and even drains the life from visitors. Therein lies its horror: the same people embrace architectural wonders and routinely violate the deep-seated taboo against cannibalism. While they live in a city Anglo-Saxons might envy, the Mermedonians reflect the worst that humanity can offer. Mermedonia is both beautiful and chilling, and only divine intervention can make the space into a place appropriate for Saints Andrew and Matthew.

Fruitful Wastes

Just as none of the wastes in these three poems are truly dead, all experience some degree of redemption resulting from the actions of heroes. Where before they held life but were destructive to human life, at the end of the poem each area becomes more fruitful. Human actions redeem waste spaces and convert them, to lesser or greater extents, into fruitful places.

All these wastelands begin as home to *feondas*, enemies who are sometimes literal fiends in our modern sense of the word.[66] They are improper,

---

66 Grendel is a "feond on helle" (101) and "feond" (or a compound) at 143, 164, 279, 294, 439, 636, 698, 725, 748, 962, 970, 984, 1273, 1276; he and his mother are both dubbed "feondum" at 1669. Related words are also used for him: "wergan gastes" ("evil spirit" or "guest," 133), "ellorgast" ("alien spirit/guest," 807), "helle gast" ("hell spirit/guest," 1274), and son of "dyrne gasta" ("secret spirit/guest," 1357). Grendel and his mother are "ellorgæstas" (1349), and she is described individually as "ellorgast" (1621) also. The dragon is a "feond" at 2706 (interestingly, from the dragon's point of view, so is the man who steals his cup, 2289). The same word appears repeatedly in *Guthlac A*: 136, 152, 186, 201, 265, 326, 421, 436, 442, 566, 691, 748, 803. It designates the Mermedonians in *Andreas* at 20, 49, 1196, and 1294, as do "wærlogan" ("warlocks," 71 and 109) and "wælwulfas" ("slaughter-wolves," 149).

even unsettling, because they combine recognizably human features with inhuman or anti-human ones. These connections paradoxically may also ease the reversal from wasteland to fruitful land in each of the poems. The mere in *Beowulf*, unlike the hell of the *Visio Sancti Pauli* and Blickling Homily 16, can be tamed and reclaimed for human use. Beowulf's victories cleanse the waters:

> wæron yðgebland   eal gefælsod,
> eacne eardas,   þa se ellorgast
> oflet lifdagas   ond þas lænan gesceaft.   (1620–2)

("the surging waters were all purified, the vast regions, when that alien spirit left the days of life and this mortal creation.")

Though the troop went out to the mere on "enge anpaðas, un*cuð* gelad" ("narrow defiles, unknown route," 1410, emphasis added), their return is on "*cuþe* stræte" ("a known road," 1634, emphasis added). The dragon's treasure is converted from the hoard of a solitary creature to the communal commemoration of a hero's life and death. As Jennifer Neville argues, even in death Beowulf serves his people, his barrow retaking the landscape from the dragon's mound. Beowulf's barrow stands as a "beacon" ("becn," 3160) for sailors (Neville 138).[67] Neither the cavern in the mere nor the barrow chamber itself are fully reclaimed by or for people. The land around them, however, has some use and ceases to be hostile to human life.

Guthlac A makes Guthlac's victory over his enemies visible as a conversion to a beautiful landscape now populated not by fiends but by animals that greet Guthlac happily (in a scene oddly prefiguring Disney movies):

>   Hine bletsadon
> monge mægwlitas,   meaglum reordum,
> treofugla tuddor,   tacnum cyðdon
> eadges eftcyme.   Oft he him æte heold,

---

67 Siewers views Beowulf's barrow as simply a "cenotaph," space marked off from human use, "Landscapes of Conversion," 38n157. Beowulf's stated desire for the place to be visible to sailors (2802–8, qtd. in Neville, *Representations*, 138) and the poet's insistence that the barrow and treasure are still there ("þær hit nu gen lifað," "where it now still remains," 3167) suggest that that barrow serves not just as a memorial but also as an aid to navigation, imagined as a site that many have seen even in the poet's own time.

þonne hy him hungrige   ymb hond flugon,
grædum gifre   geoce gefeogon.   (733–8; see also 742–8)

("Many species blessed him with earnest voices, the offspring of tree-birds
made known by signs the return of the blessed one; often he held food for
them when, hungry, they flew around his hand, greedily voracious, rejoicing
in the aid.")

Guthlac's return also pleases "wildeorum" ("wild animals," 741). Though
the place was already described as green and pleasant, now the poem adds
a note of renewal.[68] Guthlac's home has been purified.[69]

Andreas not only offers us the most unusual wasteland of the three poems but also redeems it most spectacularly. Andrew must come to Mermedonia and sacrifice himself to convert this place of horror into one whose
people are worthy of their architecture. The saint's blood fertilizes barren
land: budding groves spring up in his wake (1446–9). Andrew calls water
from the columns of the city (1498–1521) for a physical cleansing that
precedes and prefigures the spiritual one. The Mermedonians drown, then
revive in answer to Andrew's prayer and formally receive baptism as they
had been symbolically baptized by the swell of waters through their city.
The poem ends with the Mermedonians' words of praise for their newly
adopted God, the rocky wasteland of the cannibals transformed into a
Christian city of stone, marble, and now verdant trees.

Wastelands are, after all, merely lands not being used (or properly used)
by humans at a particular time – though they can be terrifying, as no doubt
were real wastes inhabited by wolves or boars or other threats Anglo-
Saxons encountered in life. These literary wastes bear within themselves
the seeds of fertility and redemption. Heroes and saints can clear hostile

---

68 Smolt wæs se sigewong ond sele niwe ...
   Stod se grena wong   in godes wære;
   hæfde se heorde,   se þe of heofonum cwom,
   feondas afyrde. (742, 746–8)
   ("Pleasant was the victory plain, and the dwelling new ... The lush plain stood in God's
   protection, the guardian possessed it, he who came from heaven, expelled the demons.")
69 Jones, "Envisioning": "The accompanying transfiguration of the *beorg* is no abrupt
   turn; rather it signifies the culmination of a process that began with Guthlac's first
   conversion to the wilderness and 'profession' there" (285).

life and water those seeds into growth, transforming waste into land useful to civilized human beings. Wastelands encompass contradictions: deserts that are not deserted, wildernesses that turn fruitful at the hands of holy men. Anglo-Saxons thus defined wastes more expansively than most of us do now. Wasteland often lies not far from human habitation and is never entirely unlike it, but poetry offers means to comprehend and delimit its threats imaginatively. These spaces border on the home places of halls and societies, and heroes must exert control over them in order to keep proper human space safe. Wastes also illustrate the broader trend in Anglo-Saxon thinking to conceive space not as empty, waiting to be filled and ordered, but as God's creation, always occupied and potentially fruitful, no matter how desolate it may at first appear. Such spaces may be Other, but not permanently so; God is in wastes as He is everywhere, and He allows saints to make some of these spaces into fruitful places.

Water

Water and wastelands sometimes overlap, most notably in the mere of *Beowulf*, where a lake dominates the waste. Rivers, streams, lakes, and ponds appear in charters in both Latin and Old English.[70] The sea or ocean appears far more rarely, and then often in set phrases concerning God, not boundaries. Rivers and lakes could be proper spaces, bounded and relatively safe. Not so the sea. The experience of many Anglo-Saxons would include interaction with the sea, most obviously because England has

---

70 Some of the most common roots for water in Anglo-Saxon charters are *stream* (Old English, "stream"), in sixty-three charters in *The Electronic Sawyer*; *flum-* (Latin *flumen, fluminis*, "river"), in sixty-two; *aqua-* (Latin *aqua, aquae* "water"), in thirty-five; *riu-* (Latin *rivus, rivi*, "brook"), in thirty; *pol-* (Old English *pol*, "pool"), in twenty-two; and *palu-* (Latin *palus, paludis*, "swamp") and *fons-* or *font-* (Latin *fons, fontis*, "spring" or "font"), each in nineteen. Many other words for bodies of water occur a handful of times or fewer. Sometimes these water words establish property boundaries, but often they establish the rights to water within a set of boundaries. Two dozen charters have variations on this formula: "cum omnibus ad se rite pertinentibus, campis, pascuis, pratis, siluis diriuatisque cursibus aquarum" ("with all things that rightly pertain [to the property], plains, pastures, meadows, woods, and channeled watercourses"). *The Electronic Sawyer: Online Catalogue of Anglo-Saxon Charters*, by a project team led by Simon Keynes, 2014, is available at http://www.esawyer.org.uk/about/index.html; it is an updated, searchable version of P.H. Sawyer, *Anglo-Saxon Charters: An Annotated List and Bibliography* (London: Royal Historical Society, 1968).

thousands of miles of coastline.[71] Today, one cannot be more than seventy miles from the coast while in England.[72] Many Anglo-Saxons must have been familiar with the sea, and yet writers of Old English frequently portrayed open water as dangerous. Though important to Anglo-Saxon life, open waters lacked propriety. The sea could be traversed in a boat, giving access to a wider world and allowing trade that provides food and wealth, as we see in everything from saints' lives to heroic poetry to histories. Yet the sea could never be ordered or comprehended by people. Open water is simply too big and too full of life.[73]

The sense of sea as improper appears in Alfredian texts' imagery of boats and anchors, where open water represents exile, something to be crossed and then left behind, with the help of God. Jennifer Neville writes, "The figure of the dangerous sea journey exemplifies the use of the natural world in Old English poetry: the natural world, largely stripped of particularity and imagery, instils a physical insecurity that represents not the effect of the environment but the more profound insecurity of the human individual."[74]

---

71 How many thousands of miles of coastline can be difficult to calculate; that depends on how closely one follows each bend in the coastline and how high the water is at the time of measurement. See the British Cartographic Society on "How Long Is the UK Coastline?" at http://www.cartography.org.uk/default.asp?contentID=749. They conclude, "The length of coastline of England only is about 5581 miles (8982 kms), and of mainland England plus the Isle of Wight, Lundy and the Scilly Isles is 6261 miles (10,077 kms)." For more details, see Benoit Mandelbrot, "How Long Is the Coast of Britain? Statistical Self-Similarity and Fractional Dimension," *Science* 156.3775 (5 May 1967): 636–8, DOI: 10.1126/science.156.3775.636. On the other hand, Allen J. Frantzen writes, "Most Anglo-Saxons lived inland and away from water"; "*Be mihtigum mannum*: Power, Penance, and Food in Late Anglo-Saxon England," in *The Maritime World of the Anglo-Saxons*, ed. Klein, Schipper, and Lewis-Simpson. 157–85. *The Maritime World* contains a wide range of approaches to Anglo-Saxon experiences of the sea.

   I am using the term "sea" here in the modern sense, for open water; in Old English, as Jacobsson notes, the term meant not only "sea" or "ocean" but also freshwater lake or a landlocked body of salt water; *Wells, Meres, and Pools*, 182–90.

72 Brady Haran, "The Farm Furthest from the Sea," *BBC News Online*, 23 July 2003, http://news.bbc.co.uk/2/hi/uk_news/england/derbyshire/3090539.stm.

73 Howe notes that "there was no primeval wilderness in the Anglo-Saxon landscape, no place so dramatically and starkly beyond the mark of human habitation and use that it could serve as the setting for *The Wanderer*," so only open water would do; "Landscape," 104. See also the notes at start of the "Wasteland" section of this chapter.

74 *Representations*, 112.

I would modify Neville's statement, saying instead that sea travels in poetry convey both "the effect of the environment" and "the more profound insecurity of the human individual." Open water is real, and Anglo-Saxons travelled on it; its appearances in literature are not mere abstractions but build upon the lived experiences of some Anglo-Saxons and the secondhand or literary experiences of others. Waters frequently seem almost devoid of human life, but they have their own ecology, in reality and in poetry. Birds in *The Wanderer* and *The Seafarer* accentuate the solitude of the narrators, though at least they pose no threat.[75] That solitude itself is notable, for no Anglo-Saxon would sail out to sea alone in a boat.[76] Creatures that live *in* the water are more dangerous, from Ælfric's *Colloquy* to *Beowulf* to *The Whale*. Where wastelands may be redeemed for human habitation and use, as shown above, the sea remains alien, not a place for humanity. Only God makes them fruitful, and waters can never fully become proper places, subject to human control.

Open water emerges in the translations associated with Alfred the Great and his court as an image of something to be endured and crossed, but not a place where one can ever be at home.[77] These metaphorics of water have roots in the work of Gregory the Great and particularly his *Regula pastoralis*. The Old English *Pastoral Care* represents Gregory's nautical imagery faithfully in several passages and develops it further in a few. Sin is compared with shipwreck near the end of the work and in its epilogue.[78] An inexperienced pilot may fare well on a calm sea, but a rough one requires an accomplished pilot (OE 59.1–3, Latin 1.9.30–2). Later the image becomes more elaborate: a ship's pilot must stay awake to anticipate and avoid sins where possible, passing over them when they cannot be avoided; one who falls asleep will be lost (OE 431.28–433.8; Latin 3.32.34–44). A small leak can sink a ship as surely as a rough sea (OE 437.14–17). The translator has added the image in a place where the source text refers to drops of rain and floods, but not ships (3.33.10–12). Ships tend to go with the current and need anchors or active rowing to oppose the flow; thus

---

75 In *The Wanderer* 41–8, the narrator dreams that he embraces his lord but then wakes to find only birds around him. Birds' songs have replaced men's laughter at *The Seafarer* 19–22, and they endure storms as he does at 23–6. Both poems are in ASPR 3.

76 See Howe, "Landscape," 104–5; and Wickham-Crowley, "Living on the *Ecg*," 103.

77 For detailed discussion of these images in Alfred's translations, see Miranda Wilcox, "Alfred's Epistemological Metaphors: *egan modes* and *scip modes*," *ASE* 35 (2006): 179–217.

78 Compare the OE at 403.11–14 with the Latin 3.28.5–6, and 467.20–5 with 4.89–91.

people tend not to do good works but let them slip away (OE 445.10–16; Latin 3.34.79–85). In each invocation of ships, Gregory and Alfred characterize water as a hostile medium that can turn deadly very quickly. All these passages except the reference to the shipwreck specifically name the sea (*sæ* in Old English, *mare* in Latin). The authors and their audiences fear open water rather than lakes or rivers.

Gregory also gives an extended image of a ship on rough seas in the preface to his *Dialogues*, which Wærferth renders:

> geseoh nu, Petrus, þæt me is gelicost þam, þe on lefan scipe byð, þæt byð geswenced mid þam yþum mycclan sæs: swa ic eom nu onstyred mid þam gedrefednyssum þissere worulde, 7 ic eom gecnyssed mid þam stormum þære strangan hreohnesse in þam scipe mines modes. 7 þonne ic gemune mines þæs ærran lifes, þe ic on mynstre ær on wunode, þonne asworette ic 7 geomrige gelice þam, þe on lefan scipe neah lande gelætað, 7 hit þonne se þoden 7 se storm on sæ adrifeð swa feorr, swa he æt nyhstan nænig land geseon ne mæg.[79]

> ("See now, Peter, that for me it is most like when one is in a frail ship that is tossed in the waves of a great sea: thus I am now troubled with turmoil of this world, and I am buffeted with the storms of this heavy roughness in the ship of my mind. And when I recall my earlier life, before, when I lived in the monastery, then I sigh and lament like one allowed near land on a frail ship, and then the whirlwind and the storm at sea drives him so far that he cannot see any land nearby.")

Wærferth follows the Latin fairly closely here with one significant addition: where the Latin simply invokes the "navi mentis" ("ship of the mind," 33–45), Wærferth twice adds the adjective *lef*, defined by Bosworth-Toller as "weak, injured, infirm" (627).[80] This adjective appears fewer than ten times in the *Corpus*, and all the other occurrences modify a person or

---

79 Cotton 5.13–30; the Hatton lines are similar but not identical because a reviser changed much of the wording, with recourse to the original Latin. See *Bischof Wærferths von Worcester*. For more on the Hatton revision, see David Yerkes, *Two Versions of Wærferth's Translation of Gregory's Dialogues: An Old English Thesaurus* (Toronto: Universty of Toronto Press, 1979).

80 For the Latin text, see Gregory the Great, *Dialogues*, ed. Adalbert de Vogüé and trans. (into French) Paul Antin, Sources Chrétiennes vols. 251, 260, 265 (Paris: Les Éditions du Cerf, 1980).

a body part. The use of an adjective that normally refers to human beings reminds us that the ship is figural.

Nautical images also appear in the *Boethius* and the *Soliloquies*. The first two times the Old English *Boethius* refers to a ship, it follows the Latin in comparing people who allow worldly goods to rule their lives with sailors who let the wind carry them where it wishes and in comparing God to a rudder or pilot.[81] The third image presents God as a pilot trying to anticipate bad weather (41.97–102). The Latin text lacks anything comparable, and Godden and Irvine note in their commentary that it creates a theological problem by suggesting that God lacks certitude regarding the future (vol. 2, 491). The translator finds nautical imagery so compelling that theological logic appears to be sacrificed to metaphor here. Finally, in the *Soliloquies*, Alfred compares the process of the eye bringing things to the mind for internal consideration with a man who sails the sea but leaves the boat to cross dry land more easily (OE 61.17–22), elaborating an image from the Latin.[82] Both the eye and the ship here are merely means to a more important end; that more important work happens on dry land, that is, in the inner mind ("ingeþance," 61.14).

These texts consistently present the sea as a dangerous place that a person must cross, usually with God's help and certainly with a ship, but the sea is not home. Home is the dry land for which the narrators long, the land where a ship is no longer needed but a hindrance. The imagery is consistent across these translations: the sea is life. Human beings must cross the sea, or live their lives, in control of their ships, or their earthly bodies and behaviours. When they reach dry land – that is, heaven – they will be home and will no longer need their ships.[83] The authors' consistent use of sea imagery reveals a shared understanding that the sea is dangerous, a place to be used but not inhabited by human beings.

---

81 The first instance is in the *Boethius* B-text 7.57–9, from the Latin in 2p1.18; the second comes from Latin 3p12.14, developed more in the Old English at 35.74–6. The C-text corresponds closely to the B-text unless otherwise noted.

82 For the Latin, see Augustine, *Soliloquies and Immortality of the Soul*, ed. and trans. Gerard Wilson (Warminster, UK: Aris & Phillips, 1990), 1.9, p. 36.

83 The question of the resurrected body comes to mind; if ships are not needed on dry land, how will the soul ultimately live in heaven? Anglo-Saxons believed in a resurrected body, a belief that appears in a prayer that the petitioner may "æriste lichamlice arise to þam ecan life" ("arise in bodily resurrection to eternal life," lines 88–9); from "Forms of Confession and Absolution," in Henry Logeman, "Anglo-Saxonica Minora," *Anglia* 11 (1889): 112–15; see also the poetic *Creed* 55–7 (ASPR 6). The phrase "carnis resurrectionem," found in the Apostles' Creed, also occurs hundreds of times in patristic writings. This resurrected body will apparently not suffer the same vagaries as the earthly body.

Poets adopted imagery similar to that which we find in Alfredian translations to convey the Christian idea that life is an exile. *The Wanderer* and *The Seafarer* add elements not seen in the prose texts. Water is still feared and land still desired, but animals appear in the otherwise desolate seascapes of these two poems. The animals' presence underscores the idea that the sea is not a proper home for a human narrator.[84]

Both poems emphasize the isolation of a man at sea. As *The Seafarer* says,

> Forþon nis þæs modwlonc   mon ofer eorþan,
> ne his gifena þæs god,   ne in geoguþe to þæs hwæt,
> ne in his dædum to þæs deor,   ne him his dryhten to þæs hold,
> þæt he a his sæfore   sorge næbbe,
> to hwon hine dryhten   gedon wille.   (39–43)

("For there is no man on earth so courageous in heart, nor so generous in gifts, nor so bold in his youth, nor so fierce in his deeds, nor to whom his lord is so gracious, that he never has anxieties about his seafaring, about how the lord will use him.")

Sea journeys produce anxiety for everyone, regardless of courage, generosity, strength, or favour. Nothing on this earth can take the fear from going to sea. The echo of "dryhten" at 41 and 43 may contrast an earthly lord with the heavenly one; most translators render the poem into Modern English this way, and some editors even distinguish the two by using a capital D for the second "dryhten" but not the first.[85] Yet we might also take the two *dryhtnas* as the same, as I have done above. In this reading, an

---

84 For the mind as ship, see Antonina Harbus, "The Maritime Imagination and the Paradoxical Mind in Old English Poetry," *ASE* 39 (2010): 21–42. Harbus argues that at times the sea represents the mind, in its energy and expansiveness, and birds represent the travelling mind or soul (see esp. 34–6 and her notes to previous work). I agree that the sea and birds represent these qualities of the mind, for poetic images can have multiple and even contradictory meanings, but I focus here on the literal level.

85 See, for instance, Kevin Crossley-Holland, *The Anglo-Saxon World: An Anthology*, Oxford World Classics (Oxford: Oxford University Press, 1982), 54, who contrasts the "gracious lord" at 41 with "the Lord" at 43 (lines unnumbered in translation). Elaine Treharne leaves the first "dryhten" without an initial capital but capitalizes the second and translates "lord" and "Lord" respectively, in *Old and Middle English: An Anthology*, 3rd ed. (Malden, MA: Blackwell, 2010), 62–3. The ASPR and Muir's *Exeter Book* do not use capitals for either word. For the latter, see *The Exeter Anthology of Old English Poetry: An Edition of Exeter Dean and Chapter MS 3501*, ed. Bernard J. Muir, 2 vols. (Exeter: University of Exeter Press, 2000); *The Seafarer* is at 229–33.

earthly lord, no matter how gracious, sends the seaman into danger.[86] Only the next life and God offer security.

The narrators in the two poems express some fear, but their sense of isolation is more acute. Both poems begin with a narrator apart from other people: the first verse of *The Wanderer* names the "anhaga," the "solitary one," with the prefix *an-* meaning "one, single"; the word recurs at line 40. The opening of *The Seafarer* also sets the narrator apart, if not quite as strongly: "Mæg ic be me sylfum soðgied wrecan" ("I can perform a true song about my self," 1). Both narrators use the word "wræclast," from *wræc,* "misery" or "exile," and *last,* "step" or "path": *The Wanderer* tells us the *anhaga* must "wadan wæclastas" ("traverse exile-paths," 5) and that "Warað hine wræclast, nales wunden gold" ("The exile-track, not twisted gold, holds him," 32). Similarly, *The Seafarer* recalls "hu ic earmcearig iscealdne sæ / winter wunade wræccan lastum" ("how I, anxious and wretched, spent the winter on an ice-cold sea, on paths of exile," 14–15) and invokes *wræclastas* again later in the poem (57). In both poems, the sea reveals the nature of life on earth: Christians believe it to be an exile, a time that must be spent away from one's true home, heaven. Again, the image works because of a shared understanding among poets and audiences that the sea is not a place for human habitation or enjoyment, but at best a place to be endured in the hopes of something better.[87]

The two poems differ in how they represent that something better. For the narrator of *The Wanderer,* something better seems at times to be a hall with kin and a generous lord: he has lost this life and sought it again (23–44). Then he recounts how everything dies and falls as his former life did. Only at the very end does the poem make an explicit appeal to heaven as the true home that can never be lost: "Wel bið þam þe him are seceð, / frofre to fæder on heofonum, þær us eal seo fæstnung stondeð" ("It is well

---

86 In the more typical reading, where the earthly lord contrasts with the divine, no matter how faithful the speaker may be, he remains anxious about God's plans for him in this world. Full safety can only be found in the next.

87 Neither poem fully represents the reality of Anglo-Saxon seafaring; both present isolated narrators at a time when ships, though small, would have had several crew members in close quarters. See, for instance, Anton Englert and Waldemar Ossowski, "Sailing in Wulfstan's Wake: The 2004 Trial Voyage Hedeby-Gdansk with the Skuldelev 1 reconstruction, *Ottar,*" in *Wulfstan's Voyage: The Baltic Sea Region in the Early Viking Age as Seen from Shipboard,* ed. Anton Englert and Athena Trakadas, Maritime Culture of the North 2 (Roskilde: Viking Ship Museum), 257–70. The poet may use realistic details about weather to strike a chord with his audience, but the literary representation does not match real life in every particular.

for he who seeks grace, comfort from the Father in heaven, where for us all permanence abides," 114–15).[88] *The Seafarer*'s narrator, like *The Wanderer*'s, thinks of what is happening on land without him. He has no harp, ring-giver, wife, or worldly joy (44–7). He misses the life of the land specifically: "Bearwas blostmum nimað, byrig fægriað, / wongas wlitigiað, woruld onetteð" ("The groves take blossom, the city becomes fair, the plains become beautiful, the world hastens," 48–9). Yet in *The Seafarer*, the joys of heaven emerge much earlier than in *The Wanderer*. "me hatran sind / dryhtnes dreamas þonne þis deade lif" ("I am more fervent for the joys of the Lord than this dead life," 64–5); this narrator rejects "eorð-welan" ("earthly riches," 67) and embraces worthy deeds as protection against the devil (75–6), looking forward to living with the angels in perpetual joy (78–80).

Each narrator longs for the land while at sea, but each also acknowledges that the joys of land fail. Nearly twenty lines before the poem reaches its religious conclusion, *The Wanderer* already questions,

Hwær cwom mearg? Hwær cwom mago?   Hwær cwom maþþumgyfa?
Hwær cwom symbla gesetu?   Hwær sindon seledreamas?   (92–3)

("Where has the horse gone? Where has the kinsman gone? Where have the treasure-gifts gone? Where have the seats of feasts gone? Where are the hall-joys?")

The hypermetric lines force a reader to slow down here, the repeated "Hwær" building up to the repeated "Eala!" in the next three half-lines, mourning the things that are lost. Just before the poem's turn to God, it concludes

Her bið feoh læne,   her bið freond læne,
her bið mon læne,   her bið mæg læne,
eal þis eorþan gesteal   idel weorþeð!   (*The Wanderer* 108–10)

---

88 So much of the poem focuses on loss and so little on consolation that some scholars have argued that any Christian consolation is a later addition to the poem. That interpretation has largely fallen out of currency, but debate remains about how the poem accommodates Christian as well as heroic values. For a recent reading with good references for various positions, see Manish Sharma, "Heroic Subject and Cultural Substance in *The Wanderer*," *Neophilologus* 96.4 (2012): 611–29.

("Here is wealth transitory, here is friend transitory, here is man transitory, here is kin transitory, all this earth's structure will become empty!")

The Seafarer too notes the passing of all things: "næron nu cyningas ne caseras / ne goldgiefan swylce iu wæron" ("nor are now kings, nor caesars, nor gold-givers as they were before," 82–3). The uncertainty and inconstancy of water illustrates the uncertainty and inconstancy of all life in the world. Hall-joys and groves contrast with the desolation of the open sea, but the poems reveal in turn that the attraction of halls and woods are also desolation compared with the never-failing beauty of heaven. The oxymoron "deade lif" ("dead life") at *The Seafarer* 65 reveals the truth of the world, and life "on londe" ("on land," 66) is as uncertain as life on the sea. As we saw in the previous chapter, some authors use attention to place and space to redirect minds to heaven. They do not ignore earthly spaces but use real details from them to move audiences more effectively.

Thus, though the ultimate goal of *The Wanderer* and *The Seafarer* lies beyond the seas, their details about the sea remain telling. The sea is cold in both, a realistic detail: the English Channel, the Irish Sea, and the North Sea all have temperatures that even in the summer can quickly lead to hypothermia, and the winter would bring greater risk.[89] *The Wanderer* speaks of the "hrimcealde sæ" ("frost-cold sea," 4) and "waþema gebind" ("the binding of waves," 24): icy waters contrast with the remembered warmth of the hall. *The Seafarer* mentions the "iscealdne sæ" ("ice-cold sea," 14) and gives more detail about how the boat feels: "Calde geþrungen / wæron mine fet, forste gebunden, / caldum clommum" ("My feet were oppressed by cold, bound by frost in cold fetters," 8–10). He even suffers hail (17).

Though inhospitable to humans, the sea supports other kinds of life. *The Wanderer* and *The Seafarer* present characters isolated from human beings but visited by birds. *The Wanderer*'s narrator awakens from dreams or memories of his lord to see "brimfuglas" ("seabirds," 47). The birds do not relieve but emphasize his isolation; they belong in this harsh environment more than he does. *The Seafarer* presents a more complex

---

89 A variety of weather websites offer average temperatures and temperature ranges for each of these bodies of water. See also the Channel Swimming Association's website for cautions about temperature: http://www.channelswimmingassociation.com/swim-advice/channel-water-temperatures/. Temperatures may have been somewhat different in Anglo-Saxon times and may well have varied through the period, but the waters around England have never been congenial to human life.

picture. The narrator says, "Hwilum ylfete song/dyde ic me to gomene, ganetes hleoþor/ond huilpan sweg fore hleahtor wera" ("Sometimes I made the song of the swan an entertainment for myself, the sound of the waterfowl and the song of the curlew in place of men's laughter," 19–21).[90] He also describes "mæw singende" ("a gull singing," 22). We cannot know for certain whether to take the narrator's mention of turning bird-song into entertainment at face value or as sarcasm. Either way, having birdsong as one's entertainment seems sad rather than comforting. Yet the poem goes further:

> Forþon nu min hyge hweorfeð   ofer hreþerlocan,
> min modsefa   mid mereflode
> ofer hwæles eþel   hweorfeð wide,
> eorþan sceatas,   cymeð eft to me
> gifre ond grædig,   gielleð anfloga,
> hweteð on hwælweg   hreþer unwearnum
> ofer holma gelagu.
>
> (*The Seafarer* 58–64)

("Therefore now my thought turns over my breast, my mind ranges widely with the waters over the whale's homeland, the corners of the earth, and comes again to me, avid and greedy, the lone flyer calls, excites the heart without hindrance on the whale-way, over the ocean's surface.")

Here the soul takes on qualities of the birds: like them, the mind can range widely over earth and sea.[91] It is "gifre and grædig," longing avidly for something beyond itself that the rest of the poem reveals as the heavenly homeland ("ham," 117) that fulfils the soul's desire "in þa ecan eadignesse" ("in the eternal happiness," 120).

Metaphors must work at a literal level to function effectively at any other level; "faster than a speeding bullet" conveys celerity where "faster than a patch of moss" would not. The birds at sea help flesh out the scene at the literal level as well as contributing to the metaphorics of these

---

90 I follow Margaret Goldsmith's identification of the birds in "*The Seafarer* and the Birds," *Review of English Studies* ns 5, no. 19 (July 1954): 225–35. Other scholars identify some of the birds differently, but the species of bird covered by each Old English term does not affect my argument.

91 For further readings of bird as mind and for references, see Harbus, "The Maritime Imagination," particularly 36–7.

poems.[92] Seafarers truly would see avian life while they were out on the waters, especially when they were close to coasts. The birds signify more than physical reality and indeed have a dual symbolic valence: they represent the movement and aspiration of human souls, particularly in *The Seafarer*, but they also represent desires always frustrated here on earth. The narrator of *The Wanderer* wishes to embrace his dead lord and kin, but he only finds birds who immediately fly away from him. The narrator in *The Seafarer* compares his mind or soul to birds and their flight, but he cannot be satisfied on earth. Aspirations for wholeness and intimacy reflect the true nature of souls, made for ultimate union with God in heaven but unable to experience it on earth.

Birds live around and even on the waters, but they do not fully live in them. The creatures that inhabit the seas or oceans frequently endanger humans in Old English literature. Of these animals, fish are mentioned the most, and they seem to be the least harmful to Anglo-Saxons, as we might expect. More frighteningly, *Beowulf* places monsters in the waters. Whales appear in Ælfric's *Colloquy* and the poem *The Whale*. They represent danger to people, both at literal and metaphorical levels.

We have already seen that Grendel and his mother live under the waters in *Beowulf*, though they live in an air-filled cave, not in the waters themselves. The creatures that live in the waters are little better. Beowulf and his companions see "wyrmcynnes fela, / sellice sædracan" ("many reptiles, wondrous sea-serpents," 1425–6), "nicras" ("water-monsters," 1427), "wyrmas ond wildeor" ("snakes and wild beasts," 1430). A Geat manages to kill one with an arrow, a "gryrelicne gist" ("gruesome guest," 1441), and only Beowulf's mail-shirt protects him from the creatures' sharp teeth (1510–12). These threatening sea creatures are unusual in that they occur in a body of water that seems to be bounded by land, not the open sea.[93] *Beowulf* also reveals the dangers of the open sea when the protagonist retells the story of his competition with Breca: "wit on garsecg ut / aldrum neðdon" ("we two ventured our lives out at sea," 537–8). They swim with swords: "wit unc wið hronfixas / werian þohton" ("we two thought to protect both of us against the horn-fish," 540–1). *Klaeber's Beowulf* and

---

92 Howe makes a similar point about imagined landscapes as metaphor in "Landscape," 104–5.

93 *Beowulf*'s description of the mere combines elements that refer to it as inland with some that refer to it as open water; see Richard Butts, "The Analogical Mere: Landscape and Terror in *Beowulf*," *English Studies* 68 (1987): 113–21, esp. 116–17.

Bosworth-Toller interpret "hronfixas" as "whales"; the element "hron" ("horn") may indicate specifically the narwhal.[94] Whatever kind of whale Beowulf means, he clearly sees them as a threat to life. Even the "mere-fixa" ("sea-fish," 549) attack. These are not the kind of fish most of us would wish to swim among; one is a "fah feondscaða" ("hostile enemy harmer," 554), an alliterating phrase in which every morpheme expresses hostility or enmity. That same one is an "aglæcan" ("awesome opponent," 556, *DOE*, "āg-læca"). There are also "laðgeteonan" ("hateful harmers," 559), "nicoras nigene" (575, "nine water-monsters") who cannot pierce Beowulf's mail shirt but drag him down to the bottom (553). They wish to feast on him (562–4), but he kills them (574–5). Creatures that inhabit bodies of water in *Beowulf* repeatedly prove hostile to human life. Heide Estes argues that only Beowulf himself can live in the sea: his long swim and his victory over the sea-creatures in the competition with Breca show a superhuman ability unavailable to others in the poem. Aside from Beowulf, human beings cannot live in or on water.[95]

Ælfric's *Colloquy* offers a more balanced presentation of sea life, but still presents open water as dangerous. The fisherman figure says that he works on the river ("in amne"/"on ea," 91), and he lists a number of things he catches there (101–2), until the master asks him why he does not fish in the sea ("ad mare"/ "to sæ," 104).[96] The speaker objects that he does fish in the sea at times and again lists his catches (106–8).[97] The fisherman names dolphins; dolphins and some of the fish, such as sturgeon, can become quite large and potentially dangerous, but he does not mention any threat from them.[98] The fisherman specifies, however, that he does not

---

94 Klaeber 4, 400; Bosworth-Toller, 556. For whales in Anglo-Saxon England more generally, see the four essays in the section "From the Sea: Whales" in *The Maritime World*, 275–354.

95 Estes, "*Beowulf* and the Sea," 217.

96 *Ælfric's Colloquy*, ed. G.N. Garmonsway, Methuen Old English Library, 2nd ed. (London: Methuen, 1947, repr. 1965). The original Latin and later Old English version are very close; my translations cover both.

97 Most of the Old English names for fish appear only rarely in the *Corpus*, and sometimes the words are rare in Latin too, making it difficult now to define some of the words.

98 *The Thesaurus of Old English Online* lists "delfin," "hran," and "mereswin" for the Modern English "dolphin." See Flora Edmonds, Christian Kay, Jane Roberts, and Irené Wotherspoon, *The Thesaurus of Old English Online*, University of Glasgow, http:// oldenglishthesaurus.arts.gla.ac.uk/; it is based on the print version: Jane Roberts and Christian Kay, with Lynne Grundy, eds, *The Thesaurus of Old English* (Amsterdam and Atlanta, GA: Rodopi, 2000). "Delfin" does not appear in the *DOE*. It appears

catch whales because they are too dangerous ("periculosa"/"plyhtlic," 112), then adds that it is safer for him to fish in the rivers. Asked "Why so?" he answers, "Because I would prefer to catch fish that I may kill than fish which could with one blow sink or kill not only me but also my companions" (116–18). His questioner adds, "And yet many catch whales, and escape danger, and thereby acquire great reward," to which the speaker replies, "You speak the truth, but I do not dare because of my cowardice of mind" (119–22). Though the dialogue requires the pupil playing the fisherman to admit that he is a coward not to hunt whales, neither speaker disputes the notion that whales are dangerous.

The whale in this dialogue may have a moral meaning, as it does more explicitly in *The Whale*.[99] This Old English poem likens the whale to the

---

seventeen times in the *Corpus*, yet fifteen or sixteen of those are as a Latin word. See the *DMLBS*, vol. 3, 604, "delphin, -inus" for the sense and usage of the Latin word. Of the eleven times the Latin word *delfin-* is glossed in the *Corpus* with a different word in Old English, eight give the Old English equivalent as "mereswin," one as "hron" (usually used for whale [*ballena*] or mussel [*musculus*] rather than dolphin), and one as "seoles" (where I suspect the gloss has been misplaced, because a Latin word on the previous line is glossed "mereswin": "*luligines, i* mereswin./ *delfini, i simones vel* seolas," glosses to Isidore's *De natura rerum* via the *Corpus*). One case is ambiguous: the *Old English Corpus* uses italics to indicate that both occurrences of *delfin* at Ælfric's *Grammar* 56.17 are Latin, but the latter appears to me to be an anglicization of the Latin term: "*huius delfinis* ys swa ðeah gecweden *delfin*": "'of the dolphin' [Latin] is thus said 'dolphin.'" A search for *mereswin* turns up seventeen occurrences, of which most are simply glosses. The remaining mentions are in the OE *Bede*, Ælfric's *Colloquy*, a charter, and *Bald's Leechbook*. Apart from the Colloquy, the texts do not extend the discussion of the dolphin beyond the mere mention of the animal (or, in the case of the *Leechbook*, the mention of its skin). I could not identify a single occurrence of *hran/hron* as referring specifically to dolphins; they could all refer to whales, and some very clearly do, glossing *ballena* a dozen times or referring to ivory.

Sturgeon can be deadly; see, for instance, Elisha Fieldstadt, "Leaping Sturgeon Kills 5-Year-Old Florida Girl Boating with Family," *NBC News*, 5 July 2015, http://www. nbcnews.com/news/us-news/leaping-sturgeon-kills-5-year-old-florida-girl-n386791; not only was the girl killed, but her mother and brother were also injured. Four other people had been previously injured by sturgeon in 2015. The death was unusual, but several injuries, sometimes major, are caused by leaping sturgeon each year.

99 Haruko Momma rejects a moral interpretation of the whale in Ælfric's *Colloquy* and contrasts this whale with that of *The Whale*; see her "Ælfric's Fisherman and the *Hronrad*: A Colloquy on the Occupation," in *The Maritime World*, 303–21. For more on *The Whale* and the *Physiologus* tradition from which it comes, see Carolin Esser-Miles, "'King of the Children of Pride': Symbolism, Physicality, and the Old English Whale," 275–301 in the same volume.

devil: it deceives men to destroy them. The whale is "frecne ond ferðgrim, fareðlacendum" ("dangerous and fierce-hearted to sailors," 5, ASPR 3). Sailors see the whale in the ocean and think it an island, mooring to it and even starting a fire on it before they rest. Then the whale suddenly plunges, drowning them all. The poem compares the whale with "scinna" and "deofla" ("devils," 31 and 32) who lure men into sin and hell. The whale has another trick: its breath smells good so that it can lure in unwary fish and eat them. The moral level is explicit here: the whale, like a devil, lulls men into complacency, making them think themselves safe when they are in mortal danger. The whale can also make itself seem pleasant and then devour. The poem compares the whale with demons in hell or returning to hell three times (45, 68, 78): the ocean is like hell, not a place where men belong. Fish are at best innocents, prey for the whale as men are; far worse is the whale. God appears only at the end of the poem, "dryhtna dryhtne" ("lord of lords," 83) and "wuldorcyning" ("glory-king," 84), the one to whom readers must turn when they turn away from "deoflum" ("devils," 83).

I suggest that the whale in Ælfric's *Colloquy* also takes on aspects of the devil. A good Christian cannot simply shy away from him but must fight – hence the criticism of the fisherman's "cowardice." Anglo-Saxons caught whales in reality, but they must have been dangerous prey, and they appear to have begun whaling only late in the period; Mark Gardiner, John Stewart, and Greg Priestley-Bell argue that the Anglo-Saxons did little whale hunting based on the scarcity of whale-bone finds.[100] The poets manipulate audience expectations to reveal a deeper reality: the well-known dangers of the water and whale show us the more subtle dangers of life and the devil. One cannot simply avoid these dangers, but must engage them consciously.

Unlike wastelands, water in Old English literature never turns from chaotic space to a place that humans can order and inhabit. Though Anglo-Saxons seek to understand and thus to some extent to control space and wasteland, water eludes them. The ocean's resemblance to hell in *The Whale* should not come as a surprise; both are spaces where humans cannot live, and what lives there is hostile to people. Men can live on the water on boats, but to do so makes clear to them that they have no control and

---

100 The authors think the two whales they investigate specifically were possibly hunted, but more likely stranded: "Anglo-Saxon Whale Exploitation: Some Evidence from Dengemarsh, Lydd, Kent," *Medieval Archaeology* 42 (1998): 96–101. See also note 49 on p. 119, above.

must rely on God, as in *The Wanderer* and *The Seafarer*. The ocean may be endured or crossed on the way to a more proper space: literally, land; allegorically, the heavenly homeland.

Conclusions

Wastes and waters reveal the limits of human place making. Wastes seem to defy humanity, and they may escape human organization for a time, but saints such as Guthlac and Andrew can retake wastes and remake them into fruitful places that produce life and even Christian converts. Heroes may reshape wastes with partial success: Beowulf can cleanse the mere and end the dragon's terror, but the cave at the bottom of the mere and the dragon's barrow seem to be abandoned quickly again, never used by humans (unless Beowulf's barrow is indeed an aid to navigation, and even then it is used from a distance). Water shows the absolute limits. It cannot be comprehended and remade by people; water and the things that live in it remain hostile to humans. God is there but not always easy to find: he appears only at the end of *The Whale* and the start and end of *The Wanderer*, seeming elusive through the bulk of both poems. Only *The Seafarer* finds him through most of the journey.

We will turn now from the spaces in nature that resist humanity to the proper places built only by people: cities and halls. Here we find space most obviously made into place and inhabited by humans. Yet these places too are fraught with danger, and their inhabitants require the divine presence here as much as anywhere else.

5 Halls and Cities as Locuses of Civilization and Sin

As previous chapters have shown, Anglo-Saxon space is always full and inhabited, and Anglo-Saxons look for points of familiarity to convert distant or unfamiliar space into comprehensible place. Some spaces prove relatively amenable: the space beyond the earth, though it cannot be reached in this lifetime, can be described, schematized, and understood. Many points of contact can be made with the peoples of the Mediterranean and beyond, despite their differences, while northern Europe has closer ties to England. Other spaces prove resistant: wastelands and enclosed waters may be made into coherent place and even redeemed from hostile creatures, but only by the right heroes. Open water lacks propriety and can never be defined well enough to be constructed as place. People cannot make their lives there, only traverse waterways.

Halls and cities would seem to be exemplary human spaces. They are not only mentally but physically constructed by people, built from earth and wood and stone.[1] Their main inhabitants are people. They can contain

---

1 For cities as environments planned and built by people, see Roger Keil, "City," in *Dictionary of Human Geography*, ed. Gregory et al., 86. My usage of the term "cities" is American: D.M. Pallister writes, "'Town' is used throughout these volumes to mean 'that sort of place which, however it was governed and however small its population, fulfilled the functions which are normally implied by the modern use of the word "town" in British English, "city" in American English, *ville* in French, *Stadt* in German, and *città* in Italian,'" in "Introduction" to *The Cambridge Urban History of Britain*, vol. 1, *600–1540*, ed. D.M. Pallister (Cambridge: Cambridge University Press, 2000), 3, footnote 1, quoting Susan Reynolds, *Kingdoms and Communities in Western Europe*, 2nd ed. (Oxford: Clarendon Press, 1997), 157. My usage is consonant with the Latin *civitas* and Old English *ceaster*, as demonstrated later in this chapter, so I have not adopted "town," though most historians of medieval England prefer the latter term for settlements.

both order and plenitude, to use Yi-Fu Tuan's terminology.[2] Sometimes such spaces represent the pinnacle of civilization. Living mostly in rural locations or (less often) in small settlements, Anglo-Saxons built halls and aspired to the ideal of cities, their desires for such places evident in the glittering settings of *Beowulf*, the Old English *Genesis*, and *Andreas*. Yet paradoxically, Anglo-Saxons feared that human order would prove insufficient for human plenitude: halls and cities become hubs for disorder, sin, and decay, as shown by these poems and others such as *The Ruin*. Anglo-Saxon writers impose a sense of place on communal and urban spaces, but their literature reveals the nature of place as always in process.[3] They simultaneously desire and fear such places, which ultimately escape human control despite their very human origins.

This chapter will explore first the hall, a familiar structure in the Anglo-Saxon landscape early in the period and one that must still have had resonance around the year 1000, when most extant Old English poetry was copied. The hall did not bring together everyone in a community, but it hosted those who held the most power in society and in literature: the elite, the warriors. The hall was a real, central place and a symbol visible to all on the landscape. Bede's *Historia ecclesiastica* and its Old English translation use the hall in a metaphor, assuming audience familiarity with the location described. *Beowulf* creates a marvellous hall in Heorot, going well beyond the familiar to imagine a site that must have seemed fantastic. Yet Bede, *Beowulf*, and *The Ruin* make it clear that the hall is ephemeral and hint at something better to come.

The city is a greater marvel than the hall, even a hall such as Heorot. The Anglo-Saxon landscape did not feature cities to match either classical Mediterranean landscapes or modern European ones, but the Anglo-Saxons adapted Latin terminology and used their own to describe as "cities" what we might term settlements or small towns. Desire for cities appears in Anglo-Saxon poetry from *Genesis* to *Andreas*. However, like halls, cities are temporary; furthermore, they are linked to sin. Anglo-Saxons aspire to build great halls and cities while they fear that the frailties of human (and occasionally even angelic) nature debase these sites. Only visions of heaven or literature can offer perfect halls or cities, places that went far beyond

---

2 *Cosmos and Hearth.*
3 See Allan Pred's seminal "Place as Historically Contingent Process: Structuration and the Time-Geography of Becoming Places," *Annals of the Association of American Geographers* 74 (1984): 279–97.

what most Anglo-Saxons could witness in this life. Tensions remain in the desire for both order and plenitude, accompanied by the fear that plenitude may undermine or even defeat order, as Tuan has argued that people cannot ever fully reconcile these two principles.

Hall as Hearth

For many Anglo-Saxons, the hall must have been among the greatest achievements of the community. In the hall, space has been organized and built by humans into an intimate place. In Tuan's terminology, an Anglo-Saxon hall would be more hearth than cosmos.[4] John Hines notes that halls would be central not only to the elite who used them but to everyone: "The text of *Beowulf* rarely looks down from or outside its own elevated social context. Even there, though, the *londbūend* – 'ordinary inhabitants' who would have occupied the thousands of hides granted to Beowulf by Hygelac, and to Eofor and Wulf by that same king after they slew Ongentheow – cannot be completely excluded."[5]

Halls would be places of power and security, central to some settlements, symbols on the landscape even for those who never entered them.[6] Many, however, did enter them: the warrior class, and presumably servants and slaves who ministered to them. A large hall such as that found at Lejre, Denmark, could hold not only a single gathering space, but other spaces inside and sometimes outside, including porches, storage, and cellar space.[7] Anglo-Saxon halls found so far have not been as large as the one at

---

4 See also Bachelard on the house as safe space, *The Poetics of Space*, 3–73.

5 John Hines, "Foreword," to John D. Niles, Tom Christensen, and Marijane Osborn, *Beowulf and Lejre* (Tempe: Arizona Center for Medieval and Renaissance Studies, 2007), ix.

6 Large, centrally located halls begin in the seventh century; see Helena Hamerow, "Anglo-Saxon Timber Buildings and Their Social Context," in *The Oxford Handbook of Anglo-Saxon Archaeology*, ed. Helena Hamerow, David A. Hinton, and Sally Crawford (Oxford: Oxford University Press, 2011), 128–55, esp. 136–44; and in the same volume, Katharina Ulmschneider, "Settlement Hierarchy," 159. Mark Gardiner suggests that by the late period, even large individual farmsteads would have their own halls; *Oxford Handbook*, "Late Saxon Settlements," ibid., 199.

7 The hall at Lejre was exceptionally large, an estimated forty-eight metres long and eleven and a half metres wide at the midpoint, narrowing to eight metres at the gabled ends; it seems to have been subdivided into multiple rooms, one of which had a cellar. The hall also had contemporary outbuildings. See Niles, Christensen, and Osborn, *Beowulf and Lejre*, esp. 42–8 and 103–8.

Lejre and contained only a single room.[8] The largely homogeneous main space of such a hall could welcome guests as well as locals: emissaries from other rulers, missionaries, travellers. The Anglo-Saxon hearth thus admitted members of the wider cosmos. At the same time, the hall as bulwark against the dangers of the world appears in a central image in Bede's *Historia ecclesiastica*, and the horror of Grendel's attacks on Heorot reveals how frightening bloodshed can be in what should be a safe place. However, halls themselves may encompass dangerous plenitudes. *Beowulf* offers multiple stories of halls, all of which ultimately fall to foes. Anglo-Saxons desire and embrace halls, yet they recognize that these places too fail to protect their inhabitants in the end and will eventually themselves fall. They are subject to threats from without and within.

Anglo-Saxon halls varied in archaeology and in literature. As Rosemary Cramp describes, both *heall* and *bur* could be used of individual buildings in a settlement.[9] The *DOE* connects *bur* more with a private chamber, for business, guests, or high-ranking people (usually women); its use as a translation of "camera, cubiculum, spatula (*for* spartula) +tabernaculum, thalamus, +triclinium (2x *with* sedes)" suggests that a *bur* is distinct from a hall and may be a smaller building in a complex that has a hall.[10] A *heall* may be in its own enclosure or in a larger enclosure with other buildings; enclosures may have indicated high status from the sixth century on.[11] Halls were rectangular constructions of timber, "usually with opposed central doors, often with a subdivision at one end, and sometimes with annexes on their narrow end walls."[12] These annexes could be anterooms or entry halls through which one might enter. Cramp describes two

---

8 See Hamerow, "Anglo-Saxon Timber Buildings," esp. 136–44.

9 Rosemary Cramp, "The Hall in *Beowulf* and in Archaeology," in *Heroic Poetry in the Anglo-Saxon Period: Studies in Honor of Jess B. Bessinger*, ed. Helen Damico and John Leyerle, Studies in Medieval Culture 32 (Kalamazoo: Medieval Institute Publications, Western Michigan University, 1993), 331–46, esp. 334–8.

10 *DOE*, "būr[1]." The plus indicates "Latin equivalents … which are significantly more frequent than the others"; *DOE*, "Entry Format." See also Cramp, "The Hall," 236, for the idea that Heorot has *buras* around it.

11 Cramp connects enclosures with status in "The Hall," 336. Andrew Reynolds argues that enclosure increased even in middle- and lower-status settlements with the growth of laws in the Anglo-Saxon kingdom, making people legally responsible for the areas around their buildings; see "Boundaries and Settlements in later Sixth to Eleventh-Century England," *Anglo-Saxon Studies in Archaeology and History* 12 (2003): 98–136. Those laws offered protection for such buildings, or at least penalties for those who violated their enclosure.

12 Cramp, "The Hall," 337.

different kinds of sites: one with large halls and smaller buildings around them; and another with smaller buildings throughout, where the largest of the small buildings are comparable to the smaller buildings on the sites with the large halls.[13] Two distinct types of hall construction also emerge: half-timbered halls and halls built of planks.[14] Andrew Reynolds distinguishes between posthole construction and construction on foundations.[15] Halls might be adorned with horn gables; while wood examples do not survive, stone equivalents have been found on English churches, suggesting a similar form in wood.[16]

Though a variety of settlements and building types could be found in Anglo-Saxon England, authors seem to have taken for granted that audiences would be familiar with some form of hall. One of the most famous halls in Anglo-Saxon literature appears in the extended metaphor offered by one of King Edwin's advisers in Bede's *Historia ecclesiastica*:

> "Talis" inquiens "mihi uidetur, rex, uita hominum praesens in terris, ad conparationem eius quod nobis incertum est temporis, quale cum te residente ad caenam cum ducibus ac ministris tuis tempore brumali, accenso quidem foco in medio et calido effecto cenaculo, furentibus autem foris per omnia turbinibus hiemalium pluuiarum uel niuium, adueniens unus passerum domum citissime peruolauerit; qui cum per unum ostium ingrediens mox per aliud exierit, ipso quidem tempore quo intus est hiemis tempestate non tangitur, sed tamen paruissimo spatio serenitatis ad momentum excurso, mox de hieme in hiemem regrediens tuis oculis elabitur." (Bede, *Historia*, 2.13)[17]

("This is how the present life of man on earth, King, appears to me in comparison with that time which is unknown to us. You are sitting feasting with your ealdormen and thegns in winter time; the fire is burning on the hearth in the middle of the hall and all inside is warm, while outside the wintry storms of rain and snow are raging; and a sparrow flies swiftly through the hall. It enters in at one door and quickly flies out through the other. For the few moments it is inside, the storm and wintry tempest cannot touch it, but after the

---

13 Ibid., 337.

14 Ibid., 338.

15 Reynolds, "Boundaries and Settlements," 101, and see his citations.

16 Cramp, "The Hall," 339. See also Lori Ann Garner, *Structuring Spaces: Oral Poetics and Architecture in Early Medieval England* (Notre Dame, IN: University of Notre Dame Press, 2011), esp. 32–42.

17 *Bede's Ecclesiastical History*, ed. Colgrave and Mynors.

briefest moment of calm, it flits from your sight, out of the wintry storm and into it again," trans. Colgrave and Mynors, 183–5)

The counsellor uses the image of the hall to figure protection from the elements, warmth, and certainty. The later Old English *Bede* follows the speech closely in the vernacular (134.24–136.5), suggesting that the image remains powerful and effective for late-ninth- or early-tenth-century audiences.[18] The hall is the site of security par excellence, a haven in a dangerous, even hostile world.

The text that presents the hall as locus of desire most emphatically is *Beowulf*, which offers multiple, conflicting models. The desired hall is a place of safety, joy, and art – an exemplary human achievement. Yet the poem offers the desired hall only to turn it into the feared hall: a place of destruction whose very accomplishments attract violence and death. Three kinds of threats menace the hall: threats from outsiders, threats from within, and threats from time. Those menaces seem all the more horrible for the beauty of the hall at the outset of the poem.

Beowulf begins with an accounting of Danish accomplishments. First we hear of Scyld Scefing, a mysterious foundling who grows up to lead the Danes to victory over neighbouring peoples ("ymbsittendra," 9). His son Beowulf builds on his father's legacy, becoming "leof leodcyning longe þrage / folcum gefræge" ("dear people-king, famed to the folk for a long time," 54–5).[19] His son in turn is "heah Healfdene" ("high Healfdene" 57), who is both "gamol ond guðreouw" ("old and fierce in battle," 58) and fathers Hrothgar. The line of great kings culminates in Hrothgar, who is also "heresped gyfen" ("given battle-victory," 64).

            Him on mod bearn
þæt healreced   hatan wolde,
medoærn micel   men gewyrcean

---

18 *Old English Version of Bede's Ecclesiastical History*, ed. Miller. For the translator or translators' freedom with the text, see Sharon M. Rowley, *The Old English Version of Bede's Historia Ecclesiastica*, CSASE 16 (Cambridge: 2011).

19 Most editions dub Scyld's son "Beow," avoiding confusion with the eponymous hero of the poem, but the manuscript has "Beowulf" for every occurrence of the son's name. I have kept the name as it is in the manuscript because I read the usages as foreshadowing its main hero. For gaps and limits in the genealogy, see Helen T. Bennett, "The Postmodern Hall in *Beowulf*: Endings Embedded in Beginnings," *Heroic Age* 12 (May 2009): http://www.heroicage.org/issues/12/ba.php, esp. §2 and 3.

> þon[ne] yldo bearn   æfre gefrunon,
> ond þær on innan   eall gedælan
> geongum ond ealdum   swylc him God sealde ...   (68–72)

>   ("It came to his mind
> that he wanted to command a hall-building,
> a greater mead-hall,[20] that men should build,
> than ever the sons of men had heard of,
> and there within to share everything,
> with young and old, that God gave him ...")

Hrothgar plans Heorot as the achievement that will crown his own and his family's success, a superlative place where he can share his treasures, binding the whole community together. The poet emphasizes this as a human achievement ("men gewyrcean," 69) that will in turn beget stories among the peoples ("yldo bearn," 70). Heorot emerges in *Beowulf* from an account of Hrothgar's lineage. It is bound to family and to something close to dynasty. Heorot exemplifies Tuan's hearth, a product of human planning and building where people gather together.

The poem constructs Heorot as as exceptional achievement: it is "healærna mæst" ("greatest of hall-buildings," 78). Beowulf and his men first see the place "geatolic ond goldfah ... / ... foremærost foldbuendum / receda under roderum" ("magnificent and gold-adorned ... to earth-dwellers, the most honoured of buildings under the heavens," 308, 309–10). The gold here stands out as something unlikely on a real building, though archaeological and literary evidence show that Anglo-Saxons at least occasionally used lead for roofs.[21] Audiences aware of lead roofs could imagine gold adornments or even a gilded roof on an exemplary literary hall. Beowulf calls it "reced selesta" ("best of buildings," 412). As Lori Ann Garner observes, the poet emphasizes Heorot's height (116, 713, 919) and its placement on an elevated site (285).[22] Surviving Anglo-Saxon churches and

---

20 My translation, while typical, requires construing "micel" as if it were comparative rather than simply the positive that it normally is; see Klaeber 4, 118–19, notes to 69f. John D. Niles translates instead "a great big mead-hall, one that the children of men have heard of ever since" in his chapter "*Beowulf* and Lejre," in *Beowulf and Lejre*, 223.
21 Cramp, "The Hall," 339–40.
22 Garner, *Structuring Spaces*, 43–4.

other depictions in visual and verbal arts reveal that Anglo-Saxons valued height in buildings and their locations, Garner demonstrates.[23]

The poem calls attention to its functions as well as its aesthetics. Heorot is a "goldsele gumena" ("gold-hall of men," 715) and a "beahsele beorhta" ("bright ring-hall," 1177): as Hrothgar planned, Heorot is a place for the distribution of treasure. The hall offers hospitality as a "gestsele" ("guest-hall," 994), uniting the safe space of the hearth with an openness to more cosmopolitan elements in the form of travellers. The poetic compounds "beer-hall" ("beorsele ," 482, 492), "mead-hall" ("medoheal," 484, 638), and "wine-hall" ("winærn," 654; "winreced," 714 and 993; and "winsele," 695 and 771) all remind the audience of a central social activity of the hall, the circulation of the cup, itself dubbed a "hall-cup" ("seleful," 619). Sharing the cup reinforces unity, while the order in which warriors are served reinforces hierarchy.[24] The poem shows Heorot both as a great work of art and as a place that serves its community, even holding the community together. The hall is so central to community life that the term "selerædende" ("hall-counsellors," 51) functions as a synonym for "men" (50) or "hæleð" ("men" or "warriors," 52).[25]

Indeed, Heorot continues to hold the community together despite the fact that by the time Beowulf arrives, the Danes have been abandoning the hall every night for a dozen years (147). Heorot showcases the first kind of threat to the hall: from outside. Grendel's visits cause Heorot to receive not only the positive appellations above, but also more negative ones: it becomes a "guðsele" (443), a "battle-hall" in which men die. Grendel first appears as "se ellengæst" (86), a *hapax legomenon* for which the *DOE* has, under "ellen-gǣst": "powerful spirit, bold spirit; emendation to *ellorgæst* 'alien spirit' has been suggested (cf. Beo 1617 where *ellengæst* is altered to *ellorgæst* in MS); second element has also been interpreted as a form of *gyst*[1] 'visitor, guest,' or word-play on both senses."

Grendel is thus a formidable spirit and a formidable guest in the "heal-le" (89), a place of hospitality that he inverts into a place of death. The very sound of hospitality (OE *dream*, "joy," 88) and specifically the song and

---

23 Ibid., 37–8.
24 See Michael J. Enright, *Lady with a Mead Cup: Ritual, Prophecy and Lordship in the European Warband from La Tène to the Viking Age* (Dublin: Four Courts Press, 1996).
25 Hrothgar uses "selerædende" the same way in 1346, in apposition to "londbuend" (1345). This chapter will later show that "burhsittend" or "city-dweller" similarly comes to mean "person" in *Genesis* and other poems.

harp of the singer (89–90) enrage "se grimma gæst" ("the grim guest" or "the grim spirit," 102). This uninvited guest recapitulates the ancient enmity of his ancestor, Cain (107), who slew his brother Abel in *Genesis* and its scriptural source before he and his kin become founders of cities (as will be shown later in this chapter). Grendel, however, founds nothing. He only destroys, leaving thirty thegns dead after that first attack (123). Soon, the survivors abandon the hall at night until Beowulf comes. Heorot paradoxically remains the heart of the community even when they leave it at dark; it is first named "Heort" (78), a spelling that brings to mind the Old English "heorte" or "heart."[26] Its name connects even more directly with the "heorot" or stag, an animal perhaps linked with Germanic royalty: one of the finds at Sutton Hoo, Mound 1, is a whetstone topped with a stag figure that seems to have been a ceremonial object for someone of high rank.[27] Heorot signfies community, power, and royalty; attacks on the hall damage the community and the king, weakening their power.

So great is the hall's importance that the Danes do not even wait for Grendel's death to reoccupy it; buoyed by the arrival of Beowulf and his men, they return to sleep in Heorot, and one of them is killed before Beowulf begins his fight (720–45). After Beowulf has torn off Grendel's arm and presumably killed their enemy, the Danes again sleep in the hall and again lose one of their number when Grendel's mother visits (1251–78). Andy Orchard writes of the repetition of this motif, "Nor do the Danes ever learn," criticizing their "empty celebration" and sleep, which he links to death.[28] "Sleep is indeed a natural expectation after the feast," Harry E. Kavros notes, but the theme that makes sense at a literal level also signifies spiritual sleep or death; he sees it as a structuring motif in *Beowulf*.[29] Yet we need not read the repetition as mere criticism of a moral failing. The Danes use the hall as they might reasonably expect to use it: as a safe place to gather and to sleep. That the hall is *not* safe demonstrates that even a central Germanic structure – a structure both literally built in

---

26 *Heorte* for "heart" is usually spelled with a final "e," but several psalm glosses and one gloss in *Liber scintillarum* clearly show the spelling "heort" glossing the Latin "cor"; see the *Old English Corpus*.

27 See Klaeber 4, 119–20, commentary to line 78. Thanks to Katherine O'Brien O'Keeffe for her assistance on this point.

28 Orchard, *Critical Companion*, 239; see also 199 and 254, n. 55.

29 Harry E. Kavros, "*Swefan æfter symble*: The Feast-Sleep Theme in *Beowulf*," *Neophilologus* 65 (1981): 122.

the centre of settlements and metaphorically associated with the heart of the community – cannot be fully secure.

Halls and Falls

Threats from outside do not ultimately destroy Heorot; Beowulf defeats the external enemies of the hall so that the Danes may live there safely again. What will finally bring down Heorot, the poem hints strongly, are threats from within. No sooner has Heorot been named (78) and Hrothgar begun to distribute treasure there (80–1) than the poet tells us its how it will end:

> Sele hlifade
> heah ond horngeap;   heaðowylma bad,
> laðan liges –   ne wæs hit lenge þa gen
> þæt se *ecg*hete   aþumsweoran
> æfter wælniðe   wæcnan scolde.   (*Beowulf* 81–5)

("The hall rose tall, high and horn-gabled; it awaited battle-welling, loathsome flames – nor was it long then yet that the sword-hate of son- and father-in-law after slaughter-enmity would awake.")

The seeds of Heorot's destruction are already present at its birth. It will fall not to strangers but to relations: though not all agree on the form, sense, and derivation of "aþumswerian" or "aþumsweoran," most scholars take it to be a compound of "son-in-law" and "father-in-law."[30] Alliance by marriage will be ruptured, and that breach will destroy Heorot. In his description to Hygelac and his court, Beowulf himself gives greater detail about Freawaru and the fate that awaits her (2020–68). She has been promised to Ingeld (2024–5), but the old enmities between Ingeld's people, the Heathobards, and the Danes cannot be easily forgotten. Beowulf predicts that an old warrior, seeing a Dane carrying the sword of a dead Heathobard, will incite the dead man's son to violence, and a chain of retribution will ensue (2041–68). The two passages together imply that the violence will spread beyond Ingeld's hall to Heorot.

The poet foreshadows an even closer betrayal within Heorot. Other passages hint that Hrothulf, Hrothgar's nephew, will betray Hrothgar's

---

30 See the *DOE*, "aþum-swerian," and the commentary to Klaeber 4, 120, line 84b.

sons. The first time Hrothulf appears, the poem links his name with Hrothgar's: "Hroðgar ond Hroþulf" (1017), both "blædagande" ("possessors of fame," 1013). This sentence casts a positive light on both men, enjoying the mead bench, "swiðhicgende" ("strong-minded," 1016). Yet the next sentence casts a shadow over the bright image:

Heorot innan wæs
freondum afylled;   nalles facenstafas
Þeod-Scyldingas   þenden fremedon.   (1017–19)

("Heorot within was filled with friends; not at all then did the Danes work deceit-deeds.")

By telling what had not yet happened at this time, the poem strongly implies that later, Danes *would* work deceitful deeds. Later medieval sources treat Hrothulf, a more popular character than Hrothgar in the extant literature; he succeeded Hrothgar and at least exiled, and possibly killed, Hrothgar's sons in Norse literature.[31] Even without knowledge of intertexts, audiences were likely to see foreshadowing here. When Wealhtheow next brings the cup around the hall, half a dozen hypermetric lines contain references to "suhtergefæderan" ("uncle and nephew," 1164) being still at peace – as is Unferth, despite his kin-killing (1165–8).[32] Wealhtheow then publicly insists on Hrothulf's loyalty in the speech that follows: she says that she *knows* Hrothulf ("Ic … can," 1180), that he will honour their sons if Hrothgar predeceases them, and that he will do well by their sons if he recalls all they have done for him (1180–7). She thus attempts to bind

---

31 See Orchard, *Critical Companion*, 245–7. Saxo Grammaticus specifically says that Hrothulf (whom he calls Rolvo) killed Hrethric (Røricus). See also Orchard's notes on other scholars' treatments of Hrothulf. Others argue that we should not import ideas from outside sources to our reading of *Beowulf*. For instance, Michael D.C. Drout argues that Wealhtheow supports Hrothulf's claim to the throne in *Beowulf*, over her own sons' chances, in an attempt to keep alive a system of blood inheritance in which women have an important role: "Blood and Deeds: The Inheritance Systems in *Beowulf*," *Studies in Philology* 104.2 (2007): 199–226. *Beowulf* is so allusive at so many points, however, that it is hard to imagine audiences *not* importing ideas from other poems and legends.

32 Both "suhtergefæderan" and "aþumswerian" appear to be dvandva compounds (see *DOE* for the status of "aþum-swerian" and Klaeber 4, 120, note to 84b), a single word made from two equally important words that would normally be joined by an "and." They are rare in English, and their structure may make them stand out and recall each other.

Hrothulf by praise that encourages him to act nobly, as she construes noble action, and by public words that Danes and Geats witness together.
Gillian Overing concludes that "Wealhtheow … affirms ambiguity and
escapes definition." She could be doing any of the following (or more),
Overing argues, but we cannot determine which: giving confident direc-
tives, using language effectively but within a masculine economy; "afraid
for herself and her children"; aware of the potential for violence within
language; or wielding real power herself through public speech.[33] *Beowulf*
portrays this moment in the hall as one of peace and celebration, but it also
points to a future in which family ties will rupture, and division among kin
will destroy Heorot. Beowulf has ensured Heorot's safety against outside
forces for a time, but he cannot secure it forever, nor against internal dis-
sension. Wealhtheow too seems to be powerless to prevent disaster in the
longer term.[34] The poem never directly shows battle between father-in-law
and son-in-law, or struggles between uncle and nephews, or the confla-
gration that will destroy the hall. The web of allusions, however, clearly
indicates that kin will battle kin, destroying Heorot. The *scop*'s story of
Hildeburh also helps to foreshadow Heorot's end: Hildeburh's brother's
visit to her home ends with her brother, husband, and son dead, and her
remaining kin take Hildeburh back home, bereft (1063–1124).

Helen Bennett reminds us that *Beowulf* also calls "halls" the places
inhabited by Grendel and his mother and by the dragon, introducing ambiguity into the terminology.[35] She argues that the mere where Grendel
and his mother live "is all the things that Heorot is not: dark, watery,
below ground, surrounded by monsters, and not 'constructed.'"[36] This
hall is not an obviously human construction as Heorot is, yet it is not
merely natural either. We do not know who built it or when. It is lit by
firelight ("fyrleoht," 1516).[37] As noted in the previous chapter, several

---

33 Gillian Overing, *Language, Sign, and Gender in Beowulf* (Carbondale: Southern Illinois
University Press, 1990), 100; see 88–101 for more detailed discussion and bibliography
including a variety of positions on Wealhtheow and her speech.

34 Orchard, *Critical Companion*, argues that Wealhtheow's speech shows weakness and
is not even answered by Beowulf or Hrothgar, 219–22. However, she achieves her
short-term goal: Beowulf returns home as a hero but not as heir to the Danish throne
after Wealhtheow urges her husband to remember his kin rather than the man he
verbally adopted, 1175–80.

35 Bennett, "The Postmodern Hall," §13–14.

36 Ibid., §13.

37 Garner sees the fire here as more pervasive and threatening than I do, pointing to "fyr
on flode" ("fire on water," 1366) as highlighting "Heorot's greatest threat"; *Structuring*

words and characteristics associated with Heorot are used for this home. Garner observes that Beowulf says he took the sword from a *wage* (1662), a word for wall, but one that can also be used for high waves (walls of water) and so has more associations with nature than the word *weall* does.[38] The floor ("flet," 1540 and 1568) is also described as "earth" ("eorðan," 1532) when Beowulf throws his useless sword onto it; earth floors would be the norm for Anglo-Saxon halls, but the term also suggests that a nature/construction dichotomy cannot be maintained here.[39] Under the mere, Beowulf enters a "niðsele" ("hatred-hall," 1513), a "hrofsele" ("roofed hall," 1515); there, he becomes a "selegyst," ("hall-guest," 1545), a term tinged with irony given its context: "Ofsæt þa þone selegyst, ond hyre seax geteah / brad [ond] brunecg; wolde hire bearn wrecan / angan eaferan" ("Then she beset that hall-guest, and drew her knife, broad and bright-eged; she wanted to avenge her son, her only offspring," 1545–7).[40] Hosts ordinarily protect guests, and guests respect hosts, but this underwater hall does not follow the social norms expected on land. This irony reiterates that of the poem's earlier description of Grendel as "guest" (86 and 102). The underwater hall also holds many treasures (1613), but unlike the riches of Heorot, this wealth has been removed from circulation. Beowulf takes only the hilt of the now-melted sword that he used to kill Grendel's mother and behead Grendel; he does not claim these other riches for himself or the Danes. The hall and its contents remain, for the most part, excluded from human society, though the Danes could not successfully exclude its inhabitants while they were alive.[41]

The dragon's barrow is also a perverted hall. The poet calls it a "dryhtsele dyrnne" ("hidden noble hall," 2320). Klaeber glosses the noun "*splendid*

Spaces, 52. I view the fire more as paradoxical because underwater, and ominous less because it would destroy Heorot than because it goes against what audiences know about water and fire.

38 Ibid., 55. See also my previous chapter, esp. pp. 148–9.

39 Anglo-Saxons, like speakers of Modern English, could also use "floor" in an extended sense for the ground, as the *DOE* notes ("flett"), but nearly all instances of *flet* in the *Corpus* seem to involve a floor in a building, sometimes in a "heall" or "sele."

40 I have followed the relatively neutral translation of "ofsæt" here as "beset" in Klaeber 4's glossary, 420. Some render it as "sit on," which would not affect my argument: whether she beset or sat upon Beowulf, she is hardly the model host, nor is he an ideal guest.

41 Beowulf takes no trophy of Grendel's mother. For her exclusion, see Renée Rebecca Trilling, "Beyond Abjection: The Problem with Grendel's Mother Again," *Parergon* 24.1 (2007): 1–20.

hall (orig. *retainers' hall*)," and the *DOE* follows his lead (see "dryht-sele");
the term suggests the hall's connection to social order.[42] It was not originally
built as a dragon's hall but by people, probably the same people whose last
survivor gives a speech at 2247–66 before he too dies. Yet the sense of noble
and social purposes may be undermined when the poet next calls it "eorðsele" ("earth hall," 2410), a term Beowulf himself echoes (2515). "Earth
hall" contrasts with the term "hringsele," "ring-hall" or hall for giving treasures to the warriors, invoked for this same structure at 2840 and 3053.[43]
Moreover, Garner shows that the poem associates *eorð-* compounds such as
eorðsele and *eorðreced* with death.[44] This barrow/hall projects a sense of
menace before Beowulf even encounters the dragon.

The barrow combines features of human construction with those of
natural origin in the passage where Wiglaf looks in:

> Ða se æðeling giong,
> þæt he bi wealle   wishycgende
> gesæt on sesse;   seah on enta geweorc,
> hu ða stanbogan   stapulum fæste
> ece eorðreced   innan healde.   (2715–19)

("Then the young hero sat on a seat by the wall, wise in thought; he saw into
the giants' work, how the stone arches held the eternal earth-hall fast within
by pillars.")

The barrow is both constructed and natural, an earthwork supported by
stone architecture and built not by ordinary humans but by giants. Garner
finds an ambivalence towards stone in Anglo-Saxon literature, particularly
in the vernacular: while often used for churches after Christianity has been
established, stone construction remains foreign, associated with other cultures, including Romans and giants.[45] Like Grendel and his mother's home
in the mere, this barrow holds a treasure. Also like the mere, the barrow is
associated with death: the last survivor of a people consigned a hoard to it
(2236–70). This treasure too will not be returned to circulation despite

---

42 Klaeber 4 retains this definition, 366, from Klaeber's previous edition, and the *DOE*
     has a very similar one: "noble hall, splendid hall; originally: the retainers' hall."
43 It is also called a "biorsele" ("beer hall," 2635).
44 Garner, *Structuring Spaces*, 57–64.
45 *Structuring Spaces*, 32–7 and 54.

Beowulf's wishes: it moves from the barrow to the pyre to be burned with Beowulf's body.

All the halls in the poem are connected with death and destruction from the time they are introduced. Heorot and Beowulf's hall are built by men and later destroyed. Bennett notes that the mere-hall and the barrow remain standing within the poem.[46] The two halls cut off from society are the sites of their inhabitants' deaths: Grendel made it back to the mere before dying, for Beowulf finds his body there, and Grendel's mother dies in their own hall. The dragon dies not in the barrow but within sight of it. Halls do not offer lasting safety. Yet people continue to build them: Hrothgar surely knew the story of Hildeburh and her kin before he ordered Heorot built. While no hall will survive forever, halls are sites of desire and celebration while they last. The *scop* who sings of the destruction of Finnsburg does so in a joyous setting: "Þær wæs sang ond sweg samod ætgædere" ("There were song and clamour both together," 1063). The transient nature of the hall makes its moments of joy all the more worth celebrating: Heorot will not last, but *now* it stands triumphant, cleansed of its foe of many years. Its denizens can celebrate their own contrast with Finn, Hengest, and the others; they can indulge in the sadness of a tragic song while they themselves are between tragedies.[47]

Cities

Historians and archaeologists do not refer to early medieval "cities" in England but to "settlements" or "towns."[48] Twenty-first-century human

---

46 Bennett, "The Postmodern Hall," §15.

47 Bennett, "The Postmodern Hall," §12, notes that Beowulf's own hall is only mentioned at its destruction, never shown in use. Could it be the same hall where Beowulf addressed Hygelac and Hygd? Halls were at least sometimes rebuilt, on the same site or nearby; see Niles, Christensen, and Osborn, *Beowulf and Lejre*. Della Hooke, speaking more generally of rectangular houses, estimates their typical lifespan at only fifteen to twenty years, at least early in the Anglo-Saxon period; *Landscape*, 110. It is difficult to know whether audiences would take Beowulf's hall to be the same as Hygelac's or a different one.

48 See, for instance, chapters in *Medieval Landscapes*, ed. Mark Gardiner and Stephen Rippon, Landscape History after Hoskins 2 (Bollington, Macclesfield: Windgather Press, 2007). For lack of agreement on the definition of a medieval town, see Oliver Creighton, "Town Defences and the Making of Urban Landscapes," in *Medieval Landscapes*, 44, and his references. In *The Dictionary of Human Geography*'s entry for "town," Ron Johnston writes that there are "no generally accepted criteria on which to distinguish such a settlement" (764). The same is true for "city" and "village."

geographers generally use the word "city" for something bigger than a town, often with a specific relationship to a larger geographical and political entity; they "are usually trading centres and marketplaces," distinguished from surrounding areas reliant upon agriculture.[49] Scholars do not agree on whether there was continuity between Romano-British towns or *civitates* and Anglo-Saxon ones, or how urbanized Anglo-Saxon England was at various times.[50]

Regardless of how scholars in the twentieth and twenty-first century interpret different settlements, the early English used *burh* and *ceaster*, and less often *urbs* and *civitas*, both for their own largest urban spaces and for much grander urban ones such as Rome. The *DOE* begins with the sense of "fortification" for both *burh* and *ceaster*, but they become commonly used for larger communities before the year 1000.[51]

Though an Anglo-Saxon *ceaster* would surely be less impressive than a Roman or a modern one, Anglo-Saxons' usage of *civitas* and *ceaster* for their own urban areas shows that they distinguished between urban and

---

49 Keil, "City," 85.

50 For the view that most major Roman towns had at least some continuous settlement into and through the Anglo-Saxon period, see Martin Henig, "The Fate of Late Roman Towns," in *The Oxford Handbook of Anglo-Saxon Archaeology*, 515–33, and his references (which include differing views). For an opposed position, see in the same volume R.A. Hall, "*Burhs* and Boroughs: Defended Places, Trade, and Towns. Plans, Defences, and Civic Features," 600–21, which starts from the premise that Roman settlements in Britain were largely abandoned for a century or two before people began settling in them again; and D.M. Pallister, "The Origins of British Towns," in *The Cambridge Urban History of Britain*, vol. 1, 17–24, esp. 21–4. For differences between Roman and early English towns, see ibid., esp. 19–21. Though Pallister argues that the evidence supports the abandonment of Roman towns for a time after Roman withdrawal, he notes that key early medieval towns in Britain were built on Roman sites that had not been settlements by earlier Celts; ibid., esp. 24. Hooke writes that parts of western and south-western England show evidence of continuous settlement, but much of the rest does not (*Landscape*, 106–13); and that while Roman ruins may have persisted, they generally did not experience continuous urban habitation but went largely uninhabited before being reoccupied with changed street plans; *Landscape*, 199–203.

51 Because *burh* and *ceaster* are used for fortifications and even the enclosures for manors or small settlements, attention must be paid to the context of occurrences. I do not claim that all *burgas* or *ceastra* are cities, even to Anglo-Saxons. However, Martin Henig writes that evidence suggests "blurring of distinctions between forts and towns by the later fifth century"; "The Fate of Late Roman Towns," 528. See also Hall, "*Burhs* and Boroughs," on Anglo-Saxon terminology, esp. 600–4. The Anglo-Saxons did not make the kind of neat distinctions in terminology that we might wish they made.

rural at the same time as they identified their own urban areas with cities elsewhere. Indeed, the use of the native terms *burh* and *ceaster* for large settlements outside of England and within hints at an Anglo-Saxon desire for cities. Early medieval Rome existed on a scale only imagined in Anglo-Saxon England, where London, Canterbury, and other English settlements would not be called "cities" by modern scholars. For the early English, however, the same Latin and Old English words could describe them both. Latin writers used the term *civitas* for the larger settlements in England, *civitas* having become a common noun for "city" in post-classical Latin:

civitas [CL], city, major town (esp. episcopal see). b (w. *emendatio*) burhbote. c (w. *Dei* or *Christi*) the Church. d (w. *superna* or sim.) Heaven. e (w. *diaboli*) company of the damned.[52]

London (*Lundoni-*/*Lunduni-*) is called a *civitas* repeatedly by writers such as Bede, Goscelin of St Bertin, and William of Poitiers.[53]

More notably, London is called an *urbs* by Bede and also by Osbern of Canterbury, in his *Vita sancti Dunstani*. Canterbury is *urbs* or *civitas Doruuernensis* to Bede. Alcuin calls his beloved York *urbs* a dozen times in his poem on York alone, and he also refers to other "urbes" in Northumbria.[54] *The DMLBS* gives the following senses for *urbs*:

urbs [CL]
    1 city, large town; b (~s ~ium, w. ref. to Rome).
    2 (spec.) the city of Rome.
    3 the city of heaven.
    4 district, region. (Fasc. 17, Syr–Z, 3563)

---

52 *DMLBS*, fasc. 2, C, 350. In classical Latin, *civitas* generally meant (1) "citizenship" or (2) "the citizens united in a community," according to *Lewis and Short*; of this sense, they write: (2) "B. Meton., = urbs, *a city* (rare and mostly post-Aug.; not in Cic. or Cæs.)."

53 For Bede, see *Bede's Ecclesiastical History*, ed. and trans. Colgrave and Mynors. Other writers were found using the *Patrologia Latina Database: The Full Text Database* (Ann Arbor, MI: ProQuest, 1996) and *Library of Latin Texts* (Turnhout, Belgium: Brepols: 2002–).

54 Alcuin, *York*, also dubs Bamburgh a city: "Bebbamque ... urbem," 305. He mentions multiple *urbes* in Northumbria (74, 113–14, 219, 514). He uses the word *urbs* for Rome as well (135, 206, and 1458). Alcuin, *The Bishops, Kings, and Saints of York*, ed. Peter Godman (Oxford: Clarendon Press, 1982).

Throughout the period, Anglo-Saxons used the same words in Old English and Latin for their cities that they used for much grander ones. Bede had no personal experience of Rome or larger Frankish cities, but Alcuin did. For some authors, labels such as *civitas*, *urbs*, *ceaster*, or *burh* may have voiced aspirations; others may simply have accepted Anglo-Saxon settlements as comparable to greater urban spaces that they had never seen.

Anglo-Saxon authors also had English words for "city."[55] *Burh* can be used for fastnesses, towns, and cities of widely varying size. Simon Draper demonstrates connections in the earlier part of the Anglo-Saxon era between the root *burh* and enclosure, whether by ditch or fence.[56] Lori Ann Garner notes that *burh* originally meant "'fortified enclosure' or 'fortified dwelling.'"[57] By the tenth century, due to semantic shift, the root had come to indicate "settlement" or "town" as well as enclosure.[58] The main points of the *DOE*'s entry for *burh* are:

> *burh*: Noun, f., cl. 5; occas. n. (Li), occas. m. (ChronE)
> ca. 2100 occ.
> A. fortified enclosure, fortification
> A.1. stronghold, fortress, citadel
> A.1.b. of Hell; *feonda burh* "the stronghold of fiends"
> A.2. fortified dwelling, estate, manor (cf. *burhbryce*)
> B. Town
> B.1. fortified town; generally, town or city; *open burh* "unwalled city"
> B.4.a. for Jerusalem …

---

55 *Fæsten*, *tun*, and *wic* are not treated here because they usually signify smaller enclosures. *Fæsten* refers to fortresses and enclosures, although it occasionally extends to towns; the *DOE* finds *fæsten* glossing or translating Latin "arx, claustrum, clausula, clustellum, municipium, obsidio (3x *with* civitas), obsidium, oppidum." *Tun* generally translates *villa*, *vicus*, or *hortulus*, referring to individual estates rather than settlements of many houses with people who are not all related. In non-translated texts, it sometimes applies to larger settlements in England, but not generally outside. *Wic* apparently derived from Latin *vicus*, again, referring more to individual dwellings than large groups of them: see the *OED*, "wick," n. 2. *Fæsten*, *tun*, and *wic* are not used for cities such as Rome, Jerusalem, or even Winchester.

56 Simon Draper, "The Significance of Old English *Burh* in Anglo-Saxon England," *Anglo-Saxon Studies in Archaeology and History* 15 (2008): 240–53.

57 *Structuring Spaces*, 7.

58 Draper, "*Burh*," 247. See also Brian K. Roberts, "The Village: Contexts, Chronology and Causes," *Medieval Landscapes*, 73–88, fig. 24, at 85: he dates English *burhs*, both the more and the less planned, starting from the reign of Alfred and extending to about 1000.

B.4.b. for the Heavenly Jerusalem, the City of God …
B.7.a. glossing *civitas* in transferred sense: the town, i.e., people of the town
Lat. equiv. in MS: arx, castellum, +civitas,[59] municipium, oppidum, patria, praedium, territorium, urbs; forus (*with* prorostra) = *motstow on byrig*; suburbanus = *se þe sitt butan þære byrig*

Burh designates the great cities of Rome and Jerusalem roughly a hundred times each in the extant *Corpus*. The compound *Romebur-* (or *Romebyr-*) occurs 179 times; Rome set a standard for the ideal city. Indeed, Rome was so much the paradigmatic city that the second sense under *urbs* in the *DMLBS* is "(spec.) the city of Rome" (vol. 17, 3563). Some late antique and early medieval authors writing in Latin used *ab urbe condita*, "from the founding of the city," as the standard of dating, not naming Rome because it is so pre-eminently *the* city that it need not be named.[60] Other cities frequently called *burgas* include Sodom and Gomorrah, Carthage, Babylon, and Bethlehem. Yet many places in England also qualify as *burgas*, though they never had the scale of Rome or Jerusalem. The word appears regularly in charters of the tenth and eleventh centuries, often in the phrase *binnan burh 7 butan* ("inside the *burh* and outside") and variants on it.[61] The element also appears in many place names, from Æscburhg in Sawyer 553 to Wynburhe in Sawyer 786.

---

59 The + means Latin equivalents found significantly more than others; see note 10 above. *Burh* renders *urbs* in glosses on at least a dozen different texts in the *Old English Corpus*.

60 The *ab urbe condita* formula was used hundreds of times by historians until Bede established *anno ab incarnatione Domini* ("year from the incarnation of the Lord"), or *anno Domini*, as the dating standard in the Christian world for times after the birth of Christ; for Bede's dating as "his main contribution to historical writing," see Colgrave and Mynors, "Historical Introduction," in *Bede's Ecclesiastical History*, xviii–xix. Paulus Orosius is particularly notable for beginning almost every chapter of his work with the "urbe condita" formula, *Orose: Histoires (contre les Païens)*, ed. and trans. Marie-Pierre Arnaud-Lindet, 2nd ed., 3 vols. (Paris: Belles Lettres, 2003). See also p. 66 above for the phrase in Orosius's work and its translation "Ær ðæm ðe Romeburh getimbred wære" or "Æfter þæm þe Romeburg getimbred wæs." Bede himself uses *ab urbe condita* for years before Christ in his *Historia eccelesiastica* and then counts years from the birth of Christ.

61 See *The Electronic Sawyer*, a revised, searchable database edited by Simon Keynes et al. based upon Peter Sawyer's 1968 *Anglo-Saxon Charters: An Annotated List and Bibliography* (London: Royal Historical Society, 1968), at http://www.esawyer.org.uk/about/index.html. Some of the charters included are forgeries, but they use wording from genuine charters to create an air of authenticity. The word *burh* and the phrase *binnan burh and butan* appear in genuine charters and later (though still usually Anglo-Saxon) forgeries.

Ceaster also means encampment, town, or city, particularly a walled city; the *DOE*'s entry for the word, again excerpted, includes:

> Noun, f., cl. 2, rarely m.
>> ca. 950 occ.
>> 1. fortification, fortified settlement
>> 1.a. glossing *castra* "encampment"
>> 1.b. glossing *arx* "citadel, stronghold"
>> 2. more generally: city, town, especially a walled town
>> 2.c. *Godes / dryhtenes ceaster* "the city of God"
>> 2.d. referring to heaven
>> 2.e. referring to hell

Rome is occasionally called a *ceaster*, and the word is applied to Jerusalem more than twenty times. Sawyer 904 offers "*urbe* Wentana" as a synonym for "Winta*ceastre*," showing a clear equation of *urbs* and *ceaster*. *Ceaster* appears twice as a free morpheme in the charters in Sawyer, in S333, where "Dornwara ceaster" appears as two words (though the scribe or editor could perhaps equally well have chosen "Dornwaraceaster"); and S1276, where "Hrofes cestre" is two words instead of the more usual "Hrofescester." Scores of place names in Anglo-Saxon England incorporate "ceastr/cestr" as an element, and indeed, one of the later Anglo-Saxon cities now bears the simple name Chester from its Anglo-Saxon name *Legaceaster*, though the Roman name was *Deva*.[62]

The Anglo-Saxon sense of "city" differed greatly from modern views of what makes a city as evident in their terminology in both Latin and Old English. We cannot know now to what extent most Anglo-Saxons realized their *urbes* and *civitates*, their *burgas* and *ceastra*, were much smaller and less complex than Rome and other distant places for which they used the same terms; we can only know that they used the same language for their own urban spaces and for great foreign ones. Some Anglo-Saxons visited Rome, Jerusalem, and Frankish cities and must have noticed differences, and they presumably shared this knowledge. Bede, with his detailed descriptions of sites in the Holy Land, and Alcuin, with his personal experience of the Continent, must have been among those aware of distinctions.

---

62 Also spelled *Legceaster*, *Liegecester*, *Ligeceaster*, and *Legerceaster*; see Bosworth-Toller, the *Old English Corpus*, and the indexes to the volumes of the ASCCE.

What did these spaces have in common that allowed authors to use the same terms for all of them? For Bede and Alcuin, perhaps the most notable commonalities are that these places are religious and political centres. Jerusalem was the focus of Christ's ministry, death, and resurrection; Rome became the hub of the Church founded after those events. Both were also crucial seats of secular power: Jerusalem was a key site from which the Romans controlled the surrounding area, and they destroyed the temple there to quell unrest. Rome was the heart of an empire that conquered parts of Britain, and even after that empire had largely dissolved, it remained a hub of trade and diplomacy, as evident in the busy marketplace that inspires the future Gregory the Great to convert the English and in the *Anglo-Saxon Chronicle*'s tales of travels and legations to and from Rome. London and York became important episcopal seats, and Bede and Alcuin call them cities. Other sites have monasteries or important churches. Bede's *Historia ecclesiastica* and Alcuin's poem on York emphasize ecclesiastical history and the political history interwoven with it, particulary acts of conversion and saintly rulers. Works in Old English present cities as centres of religious and political power, even when that religious power is not Christian, as in *Andreas*. Extant works do not emphasize the role of trade, but commerce may have played a part too in perceptions of which settlements qualified as cities and which did not.

In Latin and Old English, Anglo-Saxons classify their largest urban areas together with the greater cities of Europe and the Middle East. This usage may also be at least partly aspirational. York and London certainly did not rival Aachen or Rome, but Anglo-Saxons knew that their coming as a people to England was relatively recent; Nicholas Howe has shown how this knowledge pervades particular texts.[63] In Bede's lifetime, missionaries went to the Continent because Anglo-Saxon clerics, aware of their roots there, felt it important to convert those whom they saw as relations. Their cities, then, must also be newer than the cities of the Roman empire. Anglo-Saxons certainly had a sense that cities were not eternal but had origins and were built over time.

Desire for Cities

Genesis and its manuscript, Junius 11, offer valuable insights into Anglo-Saxon conceptions of cities because they present the origins of cities, and

---

63 *Migration and Mythmaking in Anglo-Saxon England.*

repeated images, in words and illustrations, of *burgas*, *ceastra*, and the occasional *fæsten*. Junius 11 links cities to the key concepts of kinship and protection. Its poems and illustrations show cities as desirable achievements even as they are dangerous places, morally and physically. Poems elsewhere in the corpus also place high value on cities: *Andreas* presents the marvellous Mermedonia, while *The Ruin* commemorates a city that once flourished in England itself but now stands desolate. These poems reveal a complex desire for cities.

Genesis A's usage of words for city is consistent within the poem and with other texts as discussed above; the poem presents urbanity as a significant concern. The manuscript's illustrations of fortifications and cities often mesh with the verbal pictures that the poem paints, though scholars have suggested that the images draw upon Continental forebears as well as on the poem itself. Catherine Karkov argues that the drawings "are active translations of [the text] and can be understood as forming a narrative distinct from that of the text."[64] The manuscript thus gives two views, not fully independent of each other but not fully dependent either. Both poem and image point to the origins of cities and make them appealing, even as they also present danger.

Starting with line 1056, the words *burh* and *ceaster*, and *fæsten* in the sense of man-made enclosure, begin to appear in *Genesis*, densely at first as true settlement begins. Cain and his offspring build the first city:

Se æresta wæs   Enos haten,
frumbearn Caines.   Siððan [fæsten][65] ongon
mid þam cneomagum   *ceastre* timbran;
þæt wæs under wolcnum   *weallfæstenna*
ærest ealra   þara þe æðelingas,
sweordberende,   settan heton.
Þanon his eaforan   ærest wocan,
bearn from bryde,   on þam *burhstede*.   (ASPR 1, 1055–63, emphasis added)

---

64 Catherine E. Karkov, *Text and Picture in Anglo-Saxon England*, 36.

65 Krapp supplies *fæsten* in the ASPR to remedy defective metre and alliteration. Murray McGillivray supplies "fæder" ("father") here in his edition in the *Online Corpus of Old English Poetry* at http://www.oepoetry.ca/. A. N. Doane supplies nothing in *Genesis A: A New Edition* (Madison: University of Wisconsin Press, 1978) but leaves the line "siððan ongon," commenting that more than one word is missing. Because it is unclear whether the word was ever written in the line, I do not base any arguments on the possibility that "fæsten" occurs in this passage. Certainly readers of the extant copy would not have read "fæsten" here.

("The first-born son of Cain was called Enoch. He began to build a town, a *city*, with his kin; that was the first *walled town* under the skies of those which nobles, sword-bearers, commanded to be made. From there his descendants first arose, child from wife, in that *fortified town*.")[66]

The poem suggests that the first city was built to organize and protect the kin-group. In his commentary on the passage, A.N. Doane notes the word *sweordberende*, emphasizing that this is a lineage of bloodshed. The participle contrasts with Seth as *sædberend* ("seed-bearer," 1145).[67] The biblical book of Genesis says that Cain established a *civitatem* (4:17), a city, but it does not reiterate terms for "city" as the Old English poem does.[68] In the manuscript, opposite the page that tells the story from the Mark of Cain through the establishment of the city, is a full-page, three-register illustration of Cain's story.[69] The top shows Cain separated from God by a line that goes from the ground they stand on into the frame above them. The middle register shows Cain holding a spear and gesturing towards a tower over a tall arch.[70] The bottom register depicts Cain and his wife with a child inside an elaborate architectural frame that represents a city. Though the poem does not at this moment indicate that Cain himself builds a city, Genesis clearly does: "cognovit autem Cain uxorem suam quae concepit et peperit Enoch et aedificavit civitatem" ("And Cain knew his wife, and she conceived, and brought forth Henoch: and he built a city," Genesis 4:17). The illustration seems to follow the biblical text more closely than the poem does, and the lavish depiction emphasizes the accomplishment more than the brief phrase in Scripture. This place has walls with crenellations at the top and towers with windows. The centre of the structure has a door. On either side, tall arches vanish into the margins of the page. Cain and his family are under a domed roof. Thus, the first third of the page depicts the separation from God that the sin has caused, but the other two-thirds of the illustration are dominated by buildings and kin. The illustrated Old English *Hexateuch* shows Cain similarly building a structure for his wife and Enoch

---

66 "Fortified town" for *burhstede* is sense 1 in the *DOE*.

67 Doane, *Genesis A*, 249, commentary to 1055–60.

68 All biblical quotations come from the Vulgate; all translations are from the Douay-Rheims.

69 See http://image.ox.ac.uk/show?collection=bodleian&manuscript=msjunius11; this illustration is on page 51 of the manuscript.

70 Karkov notes that the ground under Cain here is "barren"; *Text and Picture*, 81.

(centre register of British Library Cotton MS Claudius B.IV, fol. 9r, appearing on the cover of this book).[71] Cities seem desirable as places of protection for one's family and significant human achievements; Karkov notes that "neither the text nor the illustrations of Cain's descendants down to his slayer Lamech portray them as obvious outcasts."[72] The poem and its illustrations place more emphasis on cities than the scriptural source text does.

From this point forward the poem associates cities with offspring or kin. The word *mægburh*, defined by Bosworth-Toller, "Kindred, family, relatives, tribe" (654), combining morphemes for "kin" (*mæg*) and "city" (*burh*), now begins to occur. A strong lineage establishes cities:

> Us gewritu secgað
> þæt her eahtahund   iecte siððan
> mægðum and mæcgum   mægburg sine
> Adam on eorðan;   ealra hæfde
> nigenhund wintra
> and þrittig eac ...   (*Genesis* 1121–6)

("Scripture tells us that there afterwards he increased his kindred, women and men on earth, for 800 years; Adam had 930 winters on earth [at his death].")

A similar passage a few lines later mentions Seth's kin, his *mægburh*, as it relates how many years he lived (1130–3). Cities provide a place to establish and protect one's kin. Indeed, eight of the nineteen occurrences of the compound *mægburg* in the *Corpus* occur in *Genesis*, with another three in *Exodus*, leaving only five for all the rest of the poetic corpus, plus two in laws and one in a glossary. The *Genesis A* poet seems to have made an unusually strong link between the two, but a connection that can be found elsewhere in Old English.

Foreign cities in the poem *Genesis* are dangerously attractive, even to Abraham, one of its heroes:

> Abraham maðelode,   geseah Egypta
> hornsele hwite   and hea byrig
> beorhte blican ...   (1820–2)

---

71 The full page, and the whole manuscript, can be seen at http://www.bl.uk/manuscripts/Viewer.aspx?ref=cotton_ms_claudius_b_iv_fs001r.
72 Karkov, *Text and Picture*, 82.

("Abraham spoke; he saw the shining horn halls and the high cities of Egypt gleam brightly ...")

Cities display human artistry, and this one is particularly beautiful. The biblical Genesis has neither words for city nor description of Egypt here; the poet makes Egypt seem far more desirable than the first book of the Bible does. In the Junius manuscript at this point, an illustration of Egypt portrays it as a city of walls and towers looming over a rough landscape sketched with red and brown strokes. Straight lines mark the boundaries of the city, though it seems to have landscape within, drawn in the same colours and the same quick lines. The roofs have tiles, some scallop-shaped and others diamond-shaped, and the front wall is decorated. Windows and arches appear in the same red, green, and brown as the walls. Abraham, Sarah, and four other figures stand outside, protected by Abraham's spear; five figures, including two women, look out from the protective walls of the city. Both poem and illustration make Egypt's cities enticing, strongholds that do not fully separate people from the world but contain it in orderly and aesthetically pleasing form.

At the same time, Abraham treats the urban stronghold and its people as a threat. He fears that Sarah's beauty will lead men to attack him to win her, so he tells her to pretend to be his sister rather than his wife (1824–43). Word of her beauty indeed spreads and reaches the Pharoah, who takes Sarah for himself until God punishes him (1847–72). Pharoah returns Sarah to Abraham, but they must leave Egypt. Abraham then builds his own cities, a good portion of the treasure of the king of Egypt now in his possession to make amends for taking his wife.[73] Once in the area of *Bethlem*, Abraham and his retinue

Ongunnon him þa bytlian   and heora burh ræran,
and sele settan,   salo niwian.
Weras on wonge   wibed setton ...   (1880–2)

("began then to build for themselves and raise their own city, and create their halls, create a palace. The men made an altar on the plain ...")

---

73 Abraham also leaves the city of Haran; Doane suggests that this departure may be influenced by allegorical readings of the Christian leaving behind the body for the church in his edition of *Genesis A*, 288, notes to 167–8.

The hall, that central feature of Anglo-Saxon settlements discussed earlier in this chapter, takes pride of place in the new *burh*. The altar, or *wibed* (1882), also becomes a central feature of the new settlement. The *tabernaculum* or *altar* is biblical, drawn from Genesis 13:3–4, but the Scriptures do not use any words for settlement or city here. The Anglo-Saxon version of Abraham shows more interest in emulating Egypt's cities than the Hebrew or Latin one. That interest affects the illustrations, too; the top register of the full-page illustration on page 87 of the manuscript shows Abraham not before a simple altar but between two elaborate buildings. The poet and the illustrator stress Abraham's building activities as much as the altar. The lower left-hand part of the illustration shows Abraham with his hands out towards God without any buildings, but the other two parts seem to connect worship to structures. As Bede and Alcuin used urban terminology for sees, so too Abraham's centre of worship is more than an altar: the altar occupies the heart of a city. Worship is tied to elaborate urban structures.

Even Sodom first appears as a desirable city in *Genesis*, though its beauty does not indicate worship of God. Out of the thirty-seven occurrences of *burh*, *ceaster*, and their compounds in the poem, seventeen refer to Sodom – far more than to any other single place.[74] Scripture calls Sodom an *urbs* or a *civitas* sixteen times in two chapters, and the poet seems to have taken his cue from there, but he elaborates on the city's wealth and beauty.[75] Its land promises fertility (1921–4), and Sodom itself is not just a *burh* but a *hord-burh*, a treasure city (2007), and a *goldburg*, a gold city (2551), with high walls (2404).[76] We share the angels' first sight of the place: "Gesawon ofer since salo hlifian / reced ofer readum golde" ("They saw halls towering over treasure, palaces over red gold," 2405–6). The city is characterized by buildings and treasures, products of human civilization. Those treasures prove *too* alluring; even before the divine condemnation of Sodom and Gomorrah for sin, the riches attract a group of foreign kings to attack the city. The attackers seize Lot and others, along with treasure, and Abraham must gather allies to free the captives. The countryside may yield great

---

74 Sodom is a *burg*, *burh*, *or byrig* at 1928, 1975, 2013, 2404, 2408, 2560, 2564, and 2585; other compounds used are *burhgeate*, 2428; *burhwarena*, 2493; *goldburgum*, 2551; *hordburh*, 2007; *leodbyrig*, 2503. It is a *ceaster* at 2009, 2427, 2509, and 2548. Some of these occurrences also refer to Gomorrah.

75 *Civitas*: 18:24 and 26; 19:1, 4, 14, 15, 17, 20, 25, and 29; *urbs*: 18:28; 19:12, 21, 22, 25, and 29.

76 In his commentary to *Genesis A* 2403b–6a, Doane notes that both Jewish tradition and Christian commentary stressed the wealth of Sodom, 309.

crops, but it is in cities that the fruits of human labour come to ripeness – in halls, palaces, and gold. Yet what one city can produce, another can take. Cities are a blessing and a curse, as *Genesis* and its illustrations show.

Ambivalence towards cities is not limited to *Genesis* and the Junius manuscript. Another city associated with sin and death appears in *Andreas*, in the Exeter Book. Mermedonia, as the previous chapter showed, is paradoxically both waste and city. The poem repeatedly insists on its status as a city, calling it "mæran byrig" ("famous city," ASPR 2, 40, 287) and using the morpheme -*bur*- (city) in another thirty references to it or its residents. The poem also calls it a *ceaster* thirteen times and a *fæsten* four times. Its architecture includes familiar Anglo-Saxon landmarks such as "Hornsalu" ("horned halls," 1158) and "winræced" ("wine-houses," 1159). At the same time, it contains grander elements that would be known to some Anglo-Saxons from Roman ruins and Continental sites: a bronze column (1062), pillars described as the work of giants ("stapulas … / eald enta geweorc," 1494–5), and marble (1498). Mermedonia is a city of fantasy, with rich buildings on an impressive scale. Much of the architectural description concentrates on the prison where Matthew and then Andrew are incarcerated, calling on a host of details associating the place with captivity, torment, and death, as Garner has shown in her excellent study.[77] The external beauty conceals the torment within the prison, and the place would have remained a horror had not God and a saint intervened.

The Ruin brings Anglo-Saxon readers to a wasteland much closer to home. It appears to describe a particular fallen Roman city, perhaps Bath.[78] The fragmentary poem reveals the same longing for cities that *Genesis* and *Andreas* demonstrate, and Ann Thompson Lee classifies it not as an elegy

---

77 Garner, *Structuring Spaces*, 69–83 and 91–111.

78 The text of *The Ruin* is in ASPR 3. The poem's combination of architectural marvels and natural hot springs running through the city make Bath a likely candidate; see R.F. Leslie, ed., *Three Old English Elegies: The Wife's Lament, The Husband's Message, The Ruin*, Old and Middle English Texts (Manchester: Manchester University Press, 1961, repr. 1966), 22–8; and Karl P. Wentersdorf, "Observations on *The Ruin*," *Medium Aevum* 46.2 (1977): 171–2. For the idea that any actual location is "at best peripheral to our understanding of" the poem, see Ann Thompson Lee, "*The Ruin*: Bath or Babylon? A Non-Archaeological Investigation," *NM* 74 (1973): 443–4. Nicholas Howe usefully notes that while the exact location is not necessarily relevant, the fact that it is a specific location matters: these ruins "are contingent on circumstances of time and place" (97), not a generic ruined Roman site, "The Landscape of Anglo-Saxon England: Inherited, Invented, Imagined," in *Inventing Medieval Landscapes: Senses of Place in Western Europe*, ed. John Howe and Michael Wolfe (Gainesville: University Press of Florida, 2002), 91–112, esp. 95–8. See also Garner, *Structuring Spaces*, 155–62.

(as many scholars do) but as an *encomium urbis* ("encomium of the city").[79] The ruins are clearly not a single building but a settlement. R.F. Leslie remarks that the poem uses the word *burh* or a compound of it five times, meaning at least a fortified town and here, he argues, a city.[80] The narrator admires the architecture of the lost city, the men who built and maintained it, and the warriors it once held. The opening verse declares, "Wrætlic is þes wealstan" ("Magnificent is the wall-stone," 1). The place contains multiple *torras*, towers, though they are now ruined (3). The words "orþonc ærsceaft" appear in one of the damaged lines, meaning "cunning ancient work"; though we do not know to exactly what part of the ruins these words refer, they clearly add to the sense of the city as an architectural gem (16). The poem continues, "hwætred in hringas, hygerof bebond / weallwalan wirum wundrum togædre" (19–20); Mitchell and Robinson read here "one strong in intelligence (*hygerof*) bound the wall-braces together marvellously with wires."[81] This urban site seems to have been dense in buildings:

Beorht wæron burgræced,   burnsele monige,
heah horngestreon,   heresweg micel,
meodoheall monig   [mon]dreama full,[82]
oþþæt þæt onwende   wyrd seo swiþe.   (21–4)

("Bright were the city buildings, many the bath-halls, high the treasure-gables,[83] great the army-sound, many a meadhall full of human pleasures, until powerful fate changed that.")

---

79 Lee, "*The Ruin.*"
80 Leslie, *Three Old English Elegies*, 67, commentary to line 2.
81 Bruce Mitchell and Fred C. Robinson, *A Guide to Old English*, 8th ed. (Malden, MA: Wiley Blackwell, 2012), 262, note to lines 18–20. Leslie reads *weallwalan* as "foundations of walls" by analogy to *wyrtwalan* for Latin *radices*; *Three Old English Elegies*, 72, note to line 20. Nicholas Howe notes that the description of wire and rust stains from rebar would make clear to original audiences that these builders worked very differently from Anglo-Saxons; "Landscape," 96.
82 "Mon" in "mondreama" is represented in the manuscript by the rune ᛗ rather than being spelled out.
83 Wentersdorf argues that "horngestreon" refers to Roman gilded roofs; "Observations," 173. I have translated the word in a way that preserves the potential ambiguity between literal gold and metaphorical value in the gables. Leslie takes the "streon" element to indicate "profusion" and translates "a profusion of lofty gables"; *Three Old English Elegies*, 72, note to line 22.

The poet singles out for description its gables, arches, and red roof tiles (30).[84] This site has the magnificence of the Egyptian cities of *Genesis* or of Mermedonia while containing the familiar Anglo-Saxon mead hall. Though the city has now fallen, it remains a wonder: the verb of the poem's first line is not in past tense but in present (see above). By contrast, the brightness of the city's structures in 21–4 takes a past-tense verb.[85] Renée Trilling argues, "As the piece stands, its final image is not one of destruction, decay, or ruin, but rather of the very full lives of the people who once inhabited this spot; it ends not in nostalgia but in redemption."[86] Even empty, this city suggests life and remains a marvel.

Past and present wonder are connected to the builders and inhabitants, the people who filled the city. The second line refers to "enta geweorc" ("work of giants"); this phrase and "enta ærgeweorc" ("ancient work of giants") occur seven times in Old English poetry, earning a sub-entry in the *DOE* under "ent": "a. referring to stonework, roads, buildings, artifacts, etc. of ancient manufacture: *enta geweorc / ærgeweorc* 'work / ancient work of giants.'" Such edifices at first seem too grand to have been built by humans. A few lines later, *The Ruin* offers the *hapax legomenon* "waldend wyrhtan" (7). Whether taken as the single word that Muir's edition prints or the two words in the ASPR, the compound or phrase links "lord" or "master" with "worker" or "craftsman."[87] Fred C. Robinson argues that "waldendwyrhtan" does not mean "master builder" (as R.F. Leslie would have it), but "the king's builder, royal artisan," and thus the buildings are not merely "representative" but "specifically royal dwellings": "the very best of the vanished civilization."[88] The combination of morphemes has precedent: they appear closely linked in the phrases "wyrhta and waldend" or "waldend ond wyrhta," which appears seven times in the *Corpus*.

---

84 Wentersdorf also sees a hall invoked in the "hof" of 29b. See Garner, *Structuring Spaces*, 156–60, on the positive valence of red in Anglo-Saxon architecture.

85 See Renée R. Trilling, "Ruins in the Realm of Thoughts: Reading as Constellation in Anglo-Saxon Poetry," *JEGP* 108 (2009): 141–67, esp. 158–66, on the tension between past and present and how the poem keeps the two in suspension.

86 Trilling, *Aesthetics of Nostalgia*, 55.

87 Muir notes Siper's emendation to "waldend [and] wryhtan" in his edition, *The Exeter Anthology of Old English Poetry: An Edition of Exeter Dean and Chapter MS 3501*, 2 vols. (Exeter: University of Exeter Press, 2000), Commentary, vol. 2, 700. Leslie argues that the word is a compound similar in construction to "*agendfrea, winedryhten* and *freawine*"; *Three Old English Elegies*, 68, note to line 7.

88 Robinson, "Notes and Emendations to Old English Poetic Texts," *NM* 67 (1966): 363; see Leslie's *Three Old English Elegies*, glossary, 85, for "master builder."

Those seven usages all refer to God. Whether we take the word as "master builder" or "royal artisan," the Old English compound seems to align the creators of the city with God. Like giants, they are greater than normal human beings.

When the poet begins to imagine people in the city, however, they are a little closer to ordinary:

> ... iu beorn monig
> glædmod ond goldbeorht   geloma gefrætwed,
> wlonc and wingal   wighyrstum scan   (32–4)

("long ago, many a man glad in heart and bright in gold, often adorned, bold and light with wine, shone in war-adornments")

These men are heroes, but not giants or gods themselves. They drank in the halls and used the baths and populated the city.[89] Leslie Lockett further argues that for readers familiar with the hydraulic model of mental activity, the welling of hot water from the springs conveys an image of surging negative emotions evoked by the devastation of the grand site.[90] The ruins are not unimaginably different from Anglo-Saxon structures; their functions are familiar enough to spark sadness and longing in an Anglo-Saxon viewing them – or reading the poem.

A desire for cities, for spaces planned and constructed by humans, rich in architecture and people, appears in *Genesis* and its illustrations, *Andreas*, and *The Ruin*. Anglo-Saxon England did not hold such living cities, however; the greatest were located in distant lands or in the past. Their marvellous work is sometimes ascribed to giants, but though magnificent cities seem to be superhuman achievements, they do not last. Order and plenitude coexist in human spaces only temporarily, in a tension that ultimately snaps.

Cities, Sin, and Death

Even while they paint cities as desirable conjunctions of art and human joys, Anglo-Saxon poets connect them to fall and death, as *The Ruin* most

---

89 See also Garner, *Structuring Spaces*, 155–62, on the heroic life in the poem.
90 Leslie Lockett, *Anglo-Saxon Psychologies in the Vernacular and Latin Traditions* (Toronto: University of Toronto Press, 2011), 66–7.

obviously illustrates. The narrator piles up verbs of destruction: "scearde scurbeorge scorene, gedrorene, / ældo undereotone" ("gashed storm-protection cut, lacerated, eaten away by age," 5–6). Both alliteration and internal rhyme bind together the words telling how the buildings have been fragmented; similar soundplay occurs in the even terser half-line "steap geap gedreas" ("the high, curved [wall] collapses," 11).[91] Fifteen different verbs are used a total of twenty times in this roughly forty-nine-line fragment to describe the city or its buildings as fallen, ruined, destroyed.[92] Even as the poet admires the edifices, he reminds the reader that they are ruined. The first word, "wrætlic" ("wondrous"), establishes the wonder of the site, but that same line ends with the verb "gebræcon" ("broke," 1): for speaker and audience, the beauty of the place is immediately connected to its brokenness. The people there have died: the "waldendwyrhtan" mentioned above appear in these mournful lines:

> Eorðgrap hafað
> waldend wyrhtan   forweorone, geleorene,
> heardgripe hrusan,   oþ hund cnea
> werþeoda gewitan.   (6–9)

("Earth-grip holds the master craftsmen, decayed, lost in the hard clutch of the ground, until a hundred generations of people departed.")

The warriors too are dead: "Crungon walo wide cwoman woldagas, / swylt eall fornom secgrofra wera" ("The slaughtered fell all around, pestilence days came, death took hosts of men," 25–6). These people may have fallen due to sin, depending on how one reads line 27, "wurdon hyra wigsteal westenstaþolas" ("their *wigsteal* became waste sites"). *Wigsteal* can mean "defensive position" (Bosworth-Toller, 1222), and most editors have taken the word in this sense, but *wig* or *wih* can also mean "idol" (Bosworth-Toller, 1219 and 1222), resulting in a reading "their places of idols became

---

91 See also Trilling, *The Aesthetics of Nostalgia*, 52–6, on aural effects in *The Ruin*.
92 *berofen* 4, *gebræcon* 1, *gebrocen* 32, *brosnað* 2, *brosnade* 28, *burston* 2, *gecrong* 31, *crungon* 25 and 28, *dreorgiað* 29, *gedreas* 11, *gedrorene* 5, *fornom* 26, *forweorone* 7, *gegrunden* 14, *gehrorene* 3, *geleorene* 7, *sceaded* 30, *scorene* 5, *undereotone* 6. Forty-nine lines is overstating the case slightly given that some lines are incomplete, one with a mere two letters decipherable.

waste sites."[93] The same root "wig" is invoked in 34 with "wighyrstum scan" ("shone in war-adornments"), so the martial meaning is probably uppermost. The ambiguity of the word, however, also allows for the connection to idolatry. In either case, "wyrd seo swiþe" ("fortune the strong," 24) fells great places. Plenitude is not infinite. The people in cities fall, often due to sin, and the cities themselves crumble. Wonder may remain in *The Ruin*, but inhabitants cannot.

Similarly, while *Genesis*, its illustrations, and *Andreas* celebrate cities through verbal portraits and manuscript illuminations, they connect them to fallenness, in sin and in death. As noted above, the kin of Cain build the first city (*Genesis* 1055–63). The associations that the word *mægburg* forges between kin and city must have had some positive resonance for Anglo-Saxons, for whom kin held great importance. At the same time, that it is *Cain*'s kin, not Seth's, who build the first city associates urbanity with sin and death. Though Karkov notes that after his exile, Cain does not obviously appear as an outcast, the visual settings for Seth and his kin are more elaborate and have more of the trappings of power because Cain and his kin are cursed, while Seth and his are blessed.[94] Both kins have cities, but Cain's are lesser.[95]

The human drive to build better places leads to the Tower of Babel, described as a "ceastre" ("city," 1674), "stænnene weall" ("stone wall," 1676), and "beorna burhfæsten" ("fortified city of men," 1680).[96] Here the poet's language follows the biblical Genesis, which calls the project "civitatem" ("city," 11:4) and "turrem" ("tower," 11:4; repeated at 11:5). This citadel unites "cræft" ("art" or "craftsmanship," 1674) and "larum" ("learning," 1671), inherently good things – but "ofer monna gemet"

---

93 Muir notes the difference of opinions; *Exeter Anthology*, 703, note to 27. For "idol," see Leslie, *Three Old English Elegies*, 73, note to line 27; and Mitchell and Robinson, *Guide*, 263, note to 27. Mitchell and Robinson also note two possible readings for the following line: "Betend crungon / hergas to hrusan" (28–9); "betend" could mean "The tenders (i.e., repairmen), the armies fell to the earth" or "The tenders, the idols, fell to the earth," 263, note to 28–9. If the latter is the case, the poem underscores the sinfulness of the inhabitants.

94 Karkov also notes that the OE *Hexateuch* features similar architectural settings for the genealogical sequence, though less elaborate; *Text and Picture*, 82–3.

95 Karkov goes further, finding kin a central structuring idea for the poem: "The *Genesis* poem can be divided into four sections, each dealing with the creation of a people or dynasty by God, Adam, Noah and Abraham respectively"; *Text and Picture*, 143.

96 "Fortified city" for *burhfæsten* comes directly from the *DOE*; the word is a *hapax legomenon*.

("exceeding the measure of men," 1677). The kin become estranged and disperse, now as foreign *mægburgas*, when God changes their language and disrupts their ties:

> wæs oðere   æghwilc worden
> mægburh fremde   siððan metod tobræd
> þurh his mihta sped   monna spræce.
> Toforan þa   on feower wegas
> æðelinga bearn   ungeþeode
> on landsocne. (1694–9)

("each became to the other a foreign people, after the Creator divided men's speech through the power of his might. The offspring of nobles went then in all four directions, divided in a search for land")

Seth's kin will grow, the poem reassures (1702–3). The Tower of Babel marks a serious setback for humanity, one that will limit the size and magnificence of future cities, but it does not stop people from building cities.[97]

Sodom offers the example of a city that appears externally to be ideal, situated in fertile lands and rich in architecture and treasure. Yet it proves fatally corrupt. Even before *Genesis* tells us of the city's glory, the poem says, "Wæron Sodomisc cynn synnum þriste, / dædum gedwolene; drugon heora selfra / ecne unræd" ("The people of Sodom were shameless in sin, perverted in their deeds; they perpetrated endless bad counsel for themselves," 1935–7).[98] Lot avoids the "facen and fyrene" ("sin and crime,"

---

97 Scholars disagree about whether the manuscript provides one or two separate illustrations for the Tower of Babel episode. Bernard Muir argues that p. 81 illustrates Heber; *A Digital Facsimile of Oxford, Bodleian Library, MS. Junius 11*, ed. Bernard J. Muir, software by Nick Kennedy, CD-ROM (Oxford: Bodleian Library, 2004). Catherine E. Karkov and Thomas H. Ohlgren identify the illustration as the tower in, respectively, *Text and Picture*, 95–6, and *Anglo-Saxon Textual Illustration: Photographs of Sixteen Manuscripts with Descriptions and Index* (Kalamazoo: Medieval Institute Publications, Western Michigan University, 1992), 97–8. The illustration on 82 is generally agreed to be the tower and the dispersal of the people.

98 The last phrase might also be translated "work[ed] endless folly," as Charles Kennedy renders it in *The Cædmon Poems, Translated into English Prose by Charles W. Kennedy, With an Introduction and Facsimiles of the Illustrations in the Junius MS* (London: G. Routledge; New York: E.P. Dutton, 1916), https://archive.org/details/cu31924013340207. Doane notes on 293, in his commentary to *Genesis A* 1931a–44, that Bede writes that the fertility of the land highlights the perversity of its inhabitants in his *In Genesim*.

1941) there, but ultimately they will cost him his home and his wife. First, Abraham and his allies have to recover Lot, his family, and his possessions from the foreign kings who have taken them. Then, more famously, he and his family must flee the city's destruction, leaving all their possessions behind, and he loses his wife (2535–67). Sigor, where Lot initially flees, is also a *burh* (2519, 2528, 2539), a *ceaster* (2520), and a *fæsten* (2530 and 2536) that has not been implicated in the sin of Sodom, but it is still too close to be secure. Lot does not dare stay there long but leaves the city together with his family to seek a more distant place (2595). Cities may be desirable, but they are not safe.

The plenitude of Sodom corrupts. It is too rich; it offers too many possibilities. The poem calls its people's sins "ecne unræd," "endless bad counsel" (1937), figuring the city's plenitude negatively. Lot and his family must leave after the townspeople demand that he give them his angelic visitors for sexual exploitation. He offers his two virgin daughters in place of his guests (2466–75), but his fellow citizens refuse. Even though the angels warn Lot's family so that they may escape the destruction, the family is touched by sin. Lot's wife looks back, contrary to orders, and becomes a pillar of salt (2562–5). Lot's daughters decide to have children with their own father, who in his own culpable drunkenness does not realize that he is committing incest (2600–9). Thus, even the surviving members of the family do not escape the depravity of Sodom, but fall victim to its plenitude.

The decisive destruction of Sodom and the sinful behaviour of its survivors does not resolve the tension between desire for cities and fear of their sinfulness. Cities remain a crowning achievement of humanity. As *Genesis* nears its end, the word *burhsittend*, city-dweller, comes simply to mean "people": all the *burhsittende* will call Abraham and Sarah's son Isaac (2327–9), that the Lord has made Abraham flourish is known to "burhsittendum" (2815–16), and Abraham settles in a place that *burhsittende* call Beersheba (2837–9). No comparable term appears in the scriptural source text, but the Old English word can also be found four times in *Daniel* and once each in several other poems.[99] In the Old English

---

99 *Burhsittende* appears at *Daniel* 298, 659, 723, and 729 (ASPR 1); *Andreas* 1201 (ASPR 2); *Judith* 159 (ASPR 4); *Elene* 276 (ASPR 2); *Christ* 337 (ASPR 3); *Azarias* 19 (ASPR 3); and Riddle 25, line 3 (ASPR 3). *Burhwara* or *burgwara*, with over 180 occurrences in the *Corpus*, is likewise sometimes used to indicate people in general rather than city-dwellers or residents of a specific city.

Genesis, civilizations and cities require each other. Similarly, Mermedonia in *Andreas*, paradoxically at once wasteland and city, remains an object of desire. Once it has been cleansed of its sin and its inhabitants baptized, the city literally flourishes, new groves blooming from Andrew's blood (1448–9). Cities present unprecedented opportunities for sin in Old English poetry, but the poems also represent the hope that new cities can be founded and old cities redeemed to make them proper dwelling places for good people.

Halls and Cities in Eternity

Mixtures of accomplishment and failure, human halls and cities will not last forever. Two spaces described as these structures will endure, however: heaven and hell. George Lakoff and Mark Johnson show in *Metaphors We Live By* that human thought is structured around metaphors, and some of the most basic structuring metaphors are spatial.[100] They discuss how land areas or territories are themselves metaphors that in reality lack concrete divisions between inside and outside. Cities resemble territories in this way. Some have physical borders such as walls, or the water boundaries that mark some of the edges of England. Many have more abstract boundaries: cities without walls may have bounds set at an arbitrary line, and the line between England and Wales is an abstract one and has not always been in the same place. Even what seem like clear-cut boundaries may not be. Towns with walls may have outbuildings beyond those walls. Oliver Creighton explains how towns had layers and zones rather than simple walls: "Frequently, the medieval traveller would know he or she had reached the urban limits not because of formal walls and gates, but because of movable bars, chains, or turnstiles that marked toll-collection points, often well in advance of the walls."[101] Whether bordering waters are considered inside a city or country, outside, or some of both is arbitrary. Halls have walls to delineate inside and outside, making them seemingly more concrete, but early medieval halls also had entryways and sometimes annexes. At the same time, whether borders are physical or conceptual, solid or porous, people experience them as real. Halls and cities were part of the Anglo-Saxon mental landscape even if we would not

---

100 Lakoff and Johnson, *Metaphors We Live By* (Chicago: University of Chicago Press, 1980).
101 Creighton, "Town Defences," 48.

now describe any Anglo-Saxon settlements as "cities." People had clear concepts of them though the boundaries of these constructions were not always firm. Halls and cities in turn become metaphors for what one cannot see: heaven and hell are figured by Anglo-Saxon writers and translators as cities and halls.

Heaven is *the* originary space: pre-existing, everlasting, and yet not quite unchanging, for *Genesis* recounts the rebellion and banishment of one group of angels. Heaven appears as a hall in Latin hymns and their Old English glosses, and in two homilies.[102] For instance, Inge B. Milfull's hymn 74, "Ymnus ad nocturnam" ("Hymn at Night") includes: "Agamus ergo gratias / nostrae salutis vindici, / nostrum quod corpus vexerit / sublimem ad caeli gloriam" ("Let us therefore give thanks to the champion of our salvation, because he brought our body to the sublime glory of heaven," 74.21–4).[103] The end of the line has been glossed in Latin "regiam" ("hall"), while other manuscripts add "regiam" to "gloriam" or replace "gloriam" with "regiam."[104] These readings would give us "the sublime glory [and] hall of heaven" or "the sublime hall of heaven." The interlinear Old English gloss elaborates a little on the hall: "uton dón eornostlice þancas ure hæle wrecendum urne þæt he lichoma upawæh healicne to heofones wuldre cynelicre healle" ("Let us therefore solemnly give thanks to the avenger of our salvation that he carried our body up to the sublime, royal glory hall"). Alcuin too calls heaven a hall, "Dei patris ... aulam" ("the hall ... of God the Father," *Versus de patribus regibus et sanctis Euboricensis ecclesiae* 14).[105] Heaven is also called a hall

---

102 I found no use of "heal-" for hell, and no use of "sæl-" or "sele-" (when used for hall) for hell or heaven. *Botl/bold* appears only rarely for heaven, and its sense may be broader than "hall"; the first definition in the *DOE* for the word is "dwelling, home; house, building."

103 Inge B. Milfull, ed., *The Hymns of the Anglo-Saxon Church: A Study and Edition of the Durham Hymnal*, CSASE 17 (Cambridge: Cambridge University Press, 1996); the translations here are my own.

104 Milfull, *Hymns*, pages 299–301; see also the apparatus and notes to hymn 74.

105 See Godman's edition for this poem. The first sense for *aula* in the *DMLBS* is "hall, (large) room, esp. dining room." The word can also be used for "2 church building"; "3 royal (or papal) residence, palace, court"; "5 hall, manor-house, manor"; and other senses, vol. 1, 161–2. The *DMLBS* notes that the usage has been influenced by Old English *heall*. Whether Alcuin envisions God's "aula" here as a large room in a building, a church, a palace, or a free-standing hall is not entirely clear, nor does it need to be; the word could bring any or all these meanings to mind for audiences.

by Ælfric (*Catholic Homilies* 1.3.129) and the author of the Old English *Life of Machutus* (16v.1).[106]

Sometimes authors are more allusive; in his translation of Gregory the Great's *Dialogues*, Wærferth writes that we must not doubt that Christ is in heaven, Paul is in heaven, and "we witon gif þis eorðlice hus ures lichaman byþ tolysed, þæt we habbað mid Gode þa ecan getimbru in heofonum" ("we know that if this earthly house of our body be dissolved, we will have with God the eternal timbers in heaven," 296.3–4), timbers surely suggesting a hall by metonymy. The Latin here reads, "Scimus quoniam si terrestris domus nostra huius habitationis dissoluatur, quod aedificationem habemus ex Deo, domum non manufactam, sed aeternam in caelis" ("For we know, if our earthly house of this habitation be dissolved, that we have a building of God, a house not made with hands, eternal in heaven," *Dialogi* 4.26.17–19, quoting 2 Corinthians 5:1; Douay-Rheims translation given). Gregory's original building could be in wood or stone; his emphasis is on the eternal and heavenly ("aeternam," "in caelis") versus the terrestrial and manmade ("terrestris," "manufactam"). That opposition remains in Wærferth's translation, but complicated by his specification of building materials. As Garner establishes, Old English poetry associates wood with the heroic and with Anglo-Saxon modes of building, even as poets recognize its vulnerability to fire and decay over time.[107] Wærferth's "ecan getimbru in heofonum" ("eternal timbers in heaven") seem oxymoronic, but he emphasizes familiar, native construction, not mentioning the more enduring stone.

Heaven is figured as a city or a series of cities more often than as a hall, appearing thus more than twenty-five times in the *Old English Corpus*.[108] Anglo-Saxons had much precedent to follow, so their usage is unsurprising: the Bible itself presents a new Jerusalem as future or heavenly city or both. Sometimes, as in the Psalms, the current Jerusalem may be conflated with an idealized future Jerusalem. The city of God appears prominently in the books of Isaiah, Ezekiel, and Revelation. Perhaps Augustine's most famous work is *De civitate Dei* (*The City of God*), which opposes worldly

---

106 *The Old English Life of Machutus*, ed. David Yerkes, Toronto Old English Series 9 (Toronto: University of Toronto Press, 1984).

107 *Structuring Spaces*, especially chap. 2, "From Structure to Meaning in Old English Verse," 21–64.

108 A *Corpus* search was performed for "heof-" and either "ceas-," "burg-," or "burh-," and then those that did not describe heaven as a city or as having city-dwellers were eliminated.

cities to the City of God.[109] Anglo-Saxons generally use the city of God to express not an earthly territory, even in the future, but heaven itself. Such references appear across a range of genres: glosses on Aldhelm and hymns, the poem *Guthlac*, the Old English *Bede* and *Dialogues* (and an Old English preface original to the translation of the latter), and homilies and saints' lives. For instance, *Guthlac* presents heaven as a collection of cities ruled by God, in the angel's address near the beginning, where he describes what will happen to the good:

He him ece lean

healdeð on heofonum,   þær se hyhsta

ealra cyninga cyning   ceastrum wealdeð.   (15–17)

("He will have eternal reward in the heavens, where the highest king of all kings rules the cities.")

"Cities" is probably plural here because "heaven" is also plural, perhaps expressing the expansiveness of heaven. Alternatively, the poet may be adapting John 14:2, "In domo Patris mei mansiones multae sunt" ("In my Father's house there are many mansions"). Other Old English texts also speak of *heofon* as a *burh* or *ceaster* or its inhabitants as "ceastergewara," "city-dwellers." Heaven and hell are likened to cities far more often than the number of occurrences a simple proximity search of the *Corpus* would indicate. In *Guthlac*, for instance, the reference to Jerusalem at 813 surely indicates heaven, as does "þa halgan burg" ("the holy city") in the previous line, but a *Corpus* search does not find this description because

---

109 *De civitate Dei* seems to have been known by a number of Anglo-Saxon authors throughout the period. One set of excerpts and three full copies (one with Lanfranc's notes on the text) are still extant, in manuscripts ranging in date from the second half of the ninth century to around the year 1100; see Helmut Gneuss and Michael Lapidge, *Anglo-Saxon Manuscripts: A Bibliographical Handlist of Manuscripts and Manuscript Fragments Written or Owned in England Up to 1100* (Toronto: University of Toronto Press, 2014). In *The Anglo-Saxon Library* (Oxford: Oxford University Press, 2006), Michael Lapidge writes that *De civitate* appears in a booklist of the late eleventh or early twelfth century, possibly from Peterborough (145); and was cited by Aldhelm (179), Bede (197–8), Lantfred (240), Ælfric (252), and Byrhtferth (125 and 267–8). Christine Rauer identifies *De civitate* as a certain source for multiple passages in *Liber monstrorum*, "The Sources of *Liber monstrorum* (Cameron L.N.100)," *Fontes*, 2003.

"heaven" is not named as such nearby. Anglo-Saxon literature depicts heaven as a city in rich and allusive ways.

Hell is also figured as a hall or city, though less often.[110] In *Judith*, hell is a "wyrmsele" ("worm-hall," 119).[111] Hell is figured repeatedly as a city in *The Descent into Hell*, which describes the power of the city whose walls Christ will destroy (34–6, ASPR 3) and refers to its "burggeatum" ("city gates," 38) and its "burgwara" ("city-dwellers," 56 and 134). Ælfric speaks of heaven as the city of Jerusalem and hell as Babylon: "Seo gode burh hierusalem hæfð gode ceastergewaran. and seo yfele babilonia hæfð yfele ceastergewaran" ("The good Jerusalem has good city-dwellers, and the evil Babylon has evil city-dwellers," *Catholic Homilies* 2.4.247–8).

Manuscript illustrations also suggest that other spaces may be cities or like cities. The poem *Genesis* itself figures neither heaven nor hell explicitly as a *burh* or a *ceaster*, but the illustrations depict them as walled sites with multiple buildings just as the manuscript depicts Egypt with its cities. In the very scene of his fall, Lucifer creates his own palace or perhaps *burh*, a collection of tightly packed buildings with arches, windows, columns, and roofs (Junius 11, p. 3). When the rebel angels fall, pieces of this citadel fall into hell with them. Further representations of hell also depict it as at least a fortification and perhaps a city.[112] Heaven is no Romantic rural paradise, either; some illustrations similarly show God's kingdom as a walled area with a suggestion of buildings at the back (Junius 11, 11). These illustrations of heaven and hell imagine them much as the artist depicted the first city, built by Cain, on the lower register of page 51 as a walled area with multiple towers. The poem presents heaven and hell as kingdoms, though the latter is an inversion and a perversion of the former, and the artist portrays both as *burgas*. The biblical Genesis supplies none of these details of heaven or hell; the fall of the angels does not even appear in the book, nor does hell.

---

110 Numbers are again not very helpful because *Corpus* searches require explicit invocation of both hell and city within 120 characters. I found only five occurrences in the *Corpus* of *hell* within 120 characters of *ceas-*, *burg-*, or *burh-*, but a search of *The Descent into Hell* for words dealing with "city" alone immediately turned up additional instances where the word applied to hell.

111 For the text, see ASPR 4. See also Garner, *Structuring Spaces*, 89.

112 See Junius 11, 16. Barbara Raw argues that the fortification derives from Continental sources, "The Probable Derivation of Most of the Illustrations in Junius 11 from an Illustrated Old Saxon Genesis," *ASE* 5 (1976): 133–48, ill. at 147.

Heaven and hell are not eternal and unchangeable in the way that God is, for heaven has seen the loss of angels, and hell was created. Yet these changes are complete by the time of the Anglo-Saxons: more inhabitants will be added to each, but otherwise these spaces have become permanent. Heaven is "ungeendode rice" ("unending kingdom") in multiple works.[113] The epithet *ece*, "perpetual" or "eternal," sometimes applies directly to heaven: it is "ece rice" in several. Heaven is the place of "eternal joys" ("ece dreamas"), "eternal rest" ("ece reste"), very often "eternal life" ("ece lif"), and "eternal reward" ("ece lean" and "ece mede"). The idea of heaven as specifically a city of eternal joys appears in the poem *Christ*: after Christ's sixth leap, to heaven (ASPR 3, 736–8), "Þa wearð burg-warum / eadgum ece gefea æþelinges plega" ("Then to the blessed city-dwellers [in heaven] came eternal joy, the play of princes," 742–3). Similarly, hell has become a place of "eternal fire" ("ece fyr") where people suffer eternally ("ece wite," "ecelice ðrowiað," etc.).

When authors turn to the afterlife, they imagine it in terms of earthly spaces: heaven and hell are conceived as cities or halls, but ones that, unlike earth's, are everlasting.[114] It is difficult to tell whether authors and audiences think of earth's cities and halls as flawed reflections of the perfect ones in heaven, believing that heaven (and hell) came first; or as ways of understanding a heaven and a hell that exceed the imaginations of humans on earth. Given that Anglo-Saxons could hold more than one model of a place or relations between places in their minds, it would be too reductive to declare that either earthly or otherworldly cities and halls take precedence. Either model might predominate at some moments, with the other taking the fore at other times. Earthly halls and cities are intimately connected to those in heaven – and hell.

Conclusions

Like all other forms of Anglo-Saxon space, the city and the hall are simultaneously organized and comprehensible, and yet admitting of disorder

---

113 These phrases were found with the help of the *Old English Corpus*. I have not given individual citations due to the number of different texts involved and the fact that many of these phrases recur with minor variation in different texts.

114 These are not the only ways in which heaven and hell are conceived like earth. For the earthly paradise and some connections to heaven, see Kabir, *Paradise, Death and Doomsday*.

and heterogeneity. Halls appear in literature as exemplary places of human accomplishment and human sin. Bede's hall is only a brief respite from the world outside, and its ephemerality contrasts with the certainty and permanence of heaven. *Beowulf* describes Heorot in loving detail and mentions Beowulf's hall, but both halls end in flames. Threats from inside and outside can destroy the hall. Similarly, Anglo-Saxons admired cities, often using the same terminology for the historic metropolises of Rome and Jerusalem as for their own, far more modest London and York. *Genesis* and *Andreas* present cities as beautiful places, high points of human achievement. Yet these same poems show intimate connections between cities and sin, and *The Ruin* shows that great cities cannot last. Large groups of people succumb to their fallen natures: they try to reach God and are dispersed, or give in to avarice and lust, or degenerate into cannibalism. Cities are not humanly perfectible. God can send his saints to redeem Mermedonia, but no earthly city will stand forever or remain free of crime. Only heaven is eternal and free of sin. Thus, the traditional Anglo-Saxon hall and the city that Anglo-Saxons can only aspire to build both fall short; reflection redirects the audiences of these texts to the heavens, the starting point for this study. We have come full circle, and it is time to close.

Conclusions

While Anglo-Saxons lived on a small island, they were hardly insular in their interests. A number of texts from different genres in Latin and Old English reveal Anglo-Saxon writers actively engaged in transforming space, an abstract and extensive concept, into place, areas and locations that can be named and given boundaries. While both space and place are always in process, never permanent, place has more definition. Anglo-Saxon texts transform most space into populated, orderly place. Anglo-Saxon places and spaces are always inhabited: no area is entirely free of life, whether water, land, air, or space; residents include demons, holy men who would in the natural course of events have died some time before, and the occasional dragon. God's order prevails in heaven and in hell and in all spaces in between: outer space, inner space, waste, and water, as well as the land here on earth.

Human control of space has its limits in Anglo-Saxon texts. Some spaces are unreadable to living people: heaven and hell are only rarely visited before death, and ordinary human beings cannot live in wastes or waters for long. Yet people try again and again to control space and place. The most obvious mechanism of human control over space and place is building: boundaries define where human beings may live. They distinguish inside and outside. A hall provides a central focus for a society, a hearth where people can gather and feel safe, and a site to which even those who never go inside can point as a place of power and protection. A city is an even greater achievement, combining the plenitude of the cosmos with some of the familiarity, boundedness, and order of the hearth. Halls and cities do not offer perfect protection, of course: they all fall in time, brought down from without or from within, prone to sin and death as all things mortal are. Human control of space does not end with those areas that may be physically controlled, however.

Anglo-Saxons sought to understand places they could not control politically and thereby to achieve a different sort of mastery: when they could not rule a place, they could still connect with it and archive it, putting it into their own memories and texts to attain a different sort of power over it. Some of the early English knew that they lived on the edge of the world as defined by classical and contemporary authorities, yet their own lived experiences privileged that marginal space, making it a central place. English writers often translated and adapted texts to make not only the texts but also the places in them more knowable, connecting sites to other places, particularly such well-known ones as Rome and Jerusalem. They studied the histories of even distant lands, expanding their mental and literary archives. Most of all, they desired to know the inhabitants: animals held some interest, but Anglo-Saxon writers and audiences preferred knowledge of human or human-like beings. They wanted to know how distant peoples looked, how they lived, how they related to one another and to strangers. Writers and audiences identified both similarities and differences, even when the people in question lived in a very distant land and looked or acted very differently from Anglo-Saxons.

We run two risks when we look back at the past. One is to make it as much like our own era as we can; in this, we are sometimes like Anglo-Saxons wanting to know about the human beings living far distant from them. We may want to stress that they knew the earth was round, that some knew that planets and stars were different kinds of celestial objects, that they had rich connections with Rome and the Holy Land as well as with their northern neighbours. We may want to find modernity in their recognition that halls, cities, and empires alike rise and fall, never lasting. We should recognize the similarities, but we must also recognize the differences. Those celestial objects existed for Anglo-Saxons in a fixed hierarchy that included heaven, a physical place occupying the same kind of space as planets. Their relations with other places, while productive, happened very differently than our own easy travel between one continent and another. They explained the endings of human foundations as the results of sin where we name many other causes.

Yet another risk lies in constructing the past as irretrievably other, insisting that we are never like the Anglo-Saxons, who thought the sun and planets and stars revolved around the earth and that beyond the atmosphere, space was filled with light, not darkness. The presence of demons, dragons, and holy men in space may amuse us or disgust us rather than prompting us to ask what these three kinds of being have in common and why writers located them beyond earth itself: because they could not conceive of space truly empty of life, so it must be filled with beings named in biblical and patristic texts and in Germanic and Christian mythology. We must recognize that we differ significantly from Anglo-Saxons in what we require of explanations and what we consider fact and fiction. Where twenty-first-century scientists desire testable hypotheses and theories supported by experiments, observations, and calculations, Anglo-Saxon scholars relied primarily on authoritative texts, even as they transformed them with their own perspectives, approaches influenced by lived experiences both personal and shared. Those differences do not mean that Anglo-Saxons did not have explanations or recognize distinctions between fact and fiction; they mean that we must work to understand how their explanations and distinctions function.

This study has sought to make its way between Scylla and Charybdis, recognizing similarity and difference to build a coherent account of Anglo-Saxon concepts of place and space. As the Anglo-Saxons liked to do, we can find many points of connection with these people distant in time. Their great interest in places for their inhabitants finds echoes in our own times, when human geography is an important field within geography, and oceanography and astronomy often seek knowledge of life in places where the Anglo-Saxons confidently placed non-human creations. We deny the existence of some creatures the Anglo-Saxons would accept, most of us banning demons and dragons from any existence outside the imagination. At the same time, we know many creatures that the Anglo-Saxons could not: species found outside Europe, the Mediterranean, and northern Africa; and a plenitude of microscopic creatures whose existence they never suspected. While we may differ in the details of the creation stories we accept, like the Anglo-Saxons, we constantly seek patterns and rules. Though we may not posit God's love as the force keeping all the elements in place, we acknowledge that everything from subatomic particles to heavenly bodies follow what we call the laws of physics. We seek the origins of the universe and of life. We no longer fear monsters as in *Beowulf*, demons as in *Guthlac*, or cannibals as in *Andreas*. Yet we attach fears as well as desires to places and the people who live in them, and we even use some of the same language: places that some people find threatening may be constructed as "wastelands," whether urban or rural. In finding only one group of people unworthy to live (see chapter 2), *Wonders of the East* looks quite tame next to what people say about the Other on the Internet.

The oceans are still well known to be hostile to human life, as sailors and vacationers continue to learn at their peril. Most of us enjoy the hearth but sometimes long to leave it, and we embrace plenitude but sometimes fear disorder.

I have been highly selective in my choice of texts and topics in order to illuminate some of the major features of Anglo-Saxon thinking about space and place without taking up undue space myself. Indeed, concentrating on texts is a choice: excellent work has already been done on Anglo-Saxon maps and diagrams of the world and the cosmos, but much more remains to be done. Work on England's depiction of specific places continues to flourish in areas from art history to numismatics, while ecocriticism provides new tools to examine how the early English conceived and interacted with their environments. Archaeological work reveals more and more about how Anglo-Saxons farmed, fished, built buildings and settlements, related to the ruins of previous peoples, and connected with the world around them.

We can never set aside our own lived experiences of place any more than the Anglo-Saxons could. We can, however, shift our perspectives as the early English did each time they encountered a different civilization textually, aurally, or visually. We can use a range of strategies to realize our own situatedness and comprehend that of others. The Anglo-Saxons conceived of space and place as inhabited plenitudes, rich with variety and often full of light, and always having system and order, even if the human mind could not always understand them. This study has revealed some of the plenitude, order, variety, and illumination found in Anglo-Saxon literature. Yet like space itself, the fullness of this literature cannot be fully mapped and known. It holds much yet for us to discover.

Bibliography

Primary Sources

Alcuin. *Alcuin: The Bishops, Kings, and Saints of York*. Ed. Peter Godman.
  Oxford: Clarendon Press, 1982.
Alfred the Great. *King Alfred's Old English Prose Translation of the First Fifty
  Psalms*. Ed. Patrick P. O'Neill. Cambridge, MA: Medieval Academy of
  America, 2001. http://www.medievalacademy.org/resource/resmgr/maa_
  books_online/oneill_0104.htm.
– *King Alfred's Old English Version of Boethius De Consolatione Philosophiae*.
  Ed. Walter John Sedgefield. Oxford: Clarendon Press. 1899.
– *King Alfred's Version of St. Augustine's Soliloquies*. Ed. Thomas A. Carnicelli.
  Cambridge, MA: Harvard University Press, 1969.
– *King Alfred's West-Saxon Version of Gregory's Pastoral Care*. Ed. Henry
  Sweet. EETS os 45, 50. London: N. Trübner and Co., 1871; repr. as 1 vol.,
  Oxford: Oxford University Press, 1996.
– *Liber Psalmorum: The West-Saxon Psalms, being the prose portion, or the 'first
  fifty,' of the so-called Paris Psalter, edited from the manuscript, with an intro-
  duction and an appendix*. Ed. James Wilson Bright and Robert Lee Ramsay.
  Boston and London: D.C. Heath and Co., 1907.
– *The Old English Boethius: An Edition of the Old English Versions of Boethius's
  De consolatione philosophiae*. Ed. Malcolm Godden and Susan Irvine with
  a chapter on the Metres by Mark Griffith and contributions by Rohini
  Jayatilaka. 2 vols. Oxford: Oxford University Press, 2009.
– *The Old English Boethius with Verse Prologues and Epilogues Associated with
  King Alfred*. Ed. and trans. Susan Irvine and Malcolm R. Godden. Dumbarton
  Oaks Medieval Library 19. Cambridge, MA: Harvard University Press, 2012.

Das altenglische Martyrologium. Ed. G. Kotzor. Phil.-Hist Klasse, Neue Forschung 88. Munich: Bayerische Akademie der Wissenschaften, 1981.

Andreas and the Fates of the Apostles. Ed. Kenneth R. Brooks. Oxford: Oxford University Press, 1961 and 1998.

The Anglo-Saxon Chronicle: A Collaborative Edition. Ed. David Dumville and Simon Keynes. Cambridge: Brewer, 1983–.

– *MS A*. Ed. Janet M. Bately, ASCCE 3. Cambridge: Brewer, 1986.

– *MS B*. Ed. Simon Taylor, ASCCE 4. Cambridge: Brewer, 1983.

– *MS C*. Ed. Katherine O'Brien O'Keeffe, ASCCE 5. Cambridge: Brewer, 2001.

– *MS D*. Ed. G.P. Cubbin, ASCCE 6. Cambridge: Brewer, 1996.

– *MS E*. Ed. Susan Irvine, ASCCE 7. Cambridge: Brewer, 2004.

– *MS F*. Ed. Peter Baker, ASCCE 8. Cambridge: Brewer, 2000.

"Anglo-Saxonica Minora." Ed. Henry Logeman. *Anglia* 11 (1889): 97–120.

The Anglo-Saxon Poetic Records. 6 vols. Ed. George Philip Krapp and Elliott Van Kirk Dobbie. New York: Columbia University Press, 1931–42.

Augustine of Hippo. *Soliloquies and Immortality of the Soul*. Ed. and trans. Gerard Wilson. Warminster, UK: Aris & Phillips, 1990.

Ælfric. *The Anglo-Saxon Version of the Hexameron of St. Basil, or, Be Godes Six Daga Weorcum, and the Anglo-Saxon Remains of St. Basil's Admonitio ad filium spiritualem*. Ed. Henry W. Norman. 2nd ed. London: John Russell Smith, 1849. https://books.google.com/books?id=lnAEAQAAIAAJ&dq=anglo-saxon%20version%20of%20the%20hexameron&pg=PA9#v=onepage&q=anglo-saxon%20version%20of%20the%20hexameron&f=false.

– *Ælfric's Catholic Homilies: Introduction, Commentary and Glossary*. Ed. Malcolm Godden. EETS ss 18. Oxford: Oxford University Press, 2000.

– *Ælfric's Catholic Homilies: The First Series*. Ed. Peter Clemoes. EETS ss 17. Oxford: Oxford University Press, 1997.

– *Ælfric's Catholic Homilies: The Second Series, Text*. Ed. Malcolm Godden. EETS ss 5. Oxford: Oxford University Press, 1979.

– *Ælfric's Colloquy*. Ed. G.N. Garmonsway. Methuen Old English Library. 2nd ed. London: Methuen, 1947; repr. 1965.

– *Aelfric's De temporibus anni*. Ed. Heinrich Henel. EETS 213. London: Oxford University Press, 1942.

– *Ælfric's De temporibus anni*. Ed. with trans. Martin Blake. Anglo-Saxon Texts 26. Rochester, NY: Brewer, 2009.

– *Ælfric's Lives of Saints*. Ed. Walter W. Skeat. EETS os 76, 82, 94, 114. London: Trübner, 1881–1900.

– "Ælfric's Version of *Alcuini interrogationes Sigeuulfi in Genesin*. Ed. George Edwin MacLean. *Anglia* 7 (1884): 1–59.

– *Exameron Anglice or The Old English Hexameron*. Ed. S.J. Crawford.
  Bibliothek der angelsachsischen Prosa 10. 1921. Repr. Darmstadt:
  Wissenschaftliche Buchgesellschaft, 1968.
– *Homilies of Ælfric: A Supplementary Collection*. Ed. John C. Pope. 2 vols.
  EETS 259–60. London: Oxford University Press, 1967–8.
Bede. *Bedae Venerabilis Opera*. Pars I: *Opera didascalica*. Ed. Charles W. Jones.
  CCSL 123A. Turnholt: Brepols, 1975.
– *Bedae Venerabilis Opera*. Pars VI: *Opera Didascalica 2*. Ed. Charles W. Jones,
  CCSL 123B. Turnhout: Brepols, 1977.
– *Bede: On the Nature of Things and on Times*. Trans. and ed. Calvin B. Kendall
  and Faith Wallis. Liverpool: Liverpool University Press, 2010.
– *Bede: The Reckoning of Time*. Ed. and trans. Faith Wallis. Translated Texts
  for Historians 29. Liverpool: Liverpool University Press, 1999.
– *Bede's Ecclesiastical History of the English People*. Ed. and trans. Bertram
  Colgrave and R.A.B. Mynors. Oxford: Clarendon Press, 1969.
Biblia sacra iuxta vulgatam versionem. Ed. Robert Weber. 3rd ed. Stuttgart:
  Deutsche Bibelgesellschaft, 1983.
The Blickling Homilies: Edition and Translation. Ed. and trans. Richard J. Kelly.
  London: Continuum, 2003.
Boethius. *De consolatione philosophiae, Opuscula theologica*. Ed. Claudio
  Moreschini. 2nd ed. Munich: K.G. Saur, 2005.
Byrhtferth. *Byrhtferth's Enchiridion*. Ed. and trans. Peter S. Baker and Michael
  Lapidge. EETS ss 15. Oxford: Oxford University Press, 1995.
The Challoner Revision of the Douay-Rheims Bible. Rev. Richard Challoner.
  Baltimore, MD: John Murphy, 1899. http://www.intratext.com/IXT/
  ENG0011/_INDEX.HTM.
Christ and Satan: A Critical Edition. Ed. Robert Emmett Finnegan. Waterloo,
  ON: Wilfrid Laurier University Press, 1977.
Crossley-Holland, Kevin, ed. and trans. *The Anglo-Saxon World: An Anthology*.
  Oxford World Classics. Oxford: Oxford University Press, 1982.
English Medieval Lapidaries. Ed. Joan Evans and Mary S. Serjeantson. EETS
  os 190. London: Oxford University Press, 1960.
*The Exeter Anthology of Old English Poetry: An Edition of Exeter Dean and
  Chapter MS 3501*. Ed. Bernard J. Muir. 2 vols. Exeter: University of Exeter
  Press, 2000.
Felix. *Felix's Life of Saint Guthlac*. Ed. and trans. Bertram Colgrave. Cambridge:
  Cambridge University Press, 1956; repr. 1985.
Genesis. Ed. Murray McGillivray. *Online Corpus of Old English Poetry* at http://
  www.oepoetry.ca/.

Genesis A: A New Edition. Ed. A.N. Doane. Madison: University of Wisconsin Press, 1978.

The Guthlac Poems of the Exeter Book. Ed. Jane Roberts. Oxford: Clarendon Press, 1979.

The Hymns of the Anglo-Saxon Church: A Study and Edition of the "Durham Hymnal." Ed. Inge B. Milfull. CSASE 17. Cambridge: Cambridge University Press, 1996.

Kennedy, Charles, trans. *The Cædmon Poems, Translated into English Prose by Charles W. Kennedy, with an Introduction and Facsimiles of the Illustrations in the Junius MS.* London: G. Routledge; New York: E.P. Dutton, 1916. https://archive.org/details/cu31924013340207.

Klaeber's Beowulf and the Fight at Finnsburg. Ed. R.D. Fulk, Robert E. Bjork, and John D. Niles. 4th ed. Toronto: University of Toronto Press, 2008.

Leechdoms, Wortcunning and Starcraft of Early England. Ed. T.O. Cockayne, Rolls Series 35, vol. 2. London: Longman, Green, Longman, Roberts, and Green, 1865. https://books.google.com/books?id=iP9AAQAAMAAJ&pg=PA339#v=onepage&q=moon&f=false.

Library of Latin Texts. Turnhout, Belgium: Brepols: 2002–.

Milfull, Inge B. *The Hymns of the Anglo-Saxon Church: A Study and Edition of the "Durham Hymnal."* CSASE 17. Cambridge: Cambridge University Press, 1996.

Muir, Bernard J., ed. *A Digital Facsimile of Oxford, Bodleian Library, MS. Junius 11.* Software by Nick Kennedy. CD-ROM. Oxford: Bodleian Library, 2004.

Old English Glossed Psalters: Psalms 1–50. Ed. Phillip Pulsiano. Toronto Old English Series 11. Toronto: University of Toronto Press, 2001.

The Old English Herbarium and Medicina de quadrupedibus. Ed. Hubert Jan de Vriend. EETS os 286. London: Oxford University Press, 1984.

The Old English Life of Machutus. Ed. David Yerkes. Toronto Old English Series 9. Toronto: University of Toronto Press, 1984.

Old English Minor Heroic Poems. Ed. Joyce Hill. Durham and Fife: Universities of Durham and St Andrews, 1983.

The Old English Orosius. Ed. Janet M. Bately. EETS ss 6. London: Oxford University Press, 1980.

The Old English Version of Bede's Ecclesiastical History of the English People. Ed. Thomas Miller. EETS 95, 96, 110, 111. London: 1890–8; repr. Millwood, NY: Kraus Reprint, 1978.

Orosius, Paulus. *Orose: Histoires (contre les Païens).* Ed. and trans. Marie-Pierre Arnaud-Lindet. 2nd ed. 3 vols. Paris: Belles Lettres, 2003.

Patrologia Latina Database: The Full Text Database. Ann Arbor, MI: ProQuest, 1996.

Three Old English Elegies: The Wife's Lament, The Husband's Message, The Ruin. Ed. R.F. Leslie. Old and Middle English Texts. Manchester: Manchester University Press, 1961; repr. 1966.

Treharne, Elaine. *Old and Middle English: An Anthology*. 3rd ed. Malden, MA: Blackwell, 2010.

Wærferth. *Bischof Wærferths von Worcester Übersetzung der Dialoge Gregors des Grossen*. Ed. H. Hecht. Leipzig, 1900–7; repr. Darmstadt: Wissenschaftliche Buchgesellschaft, 1965.

Wulfstan. *Wulfstan*. Ed. Arthur Napier. Sammlung englischer Denkmäler 4. Berlin: Weidmannsche, 1883.

Secondary Sources

Acker, Paul. "Horror and the Maternal in *Beowulf*." *PMLA* 121.3 (2006): 702–16.

Astill, Grenville. "General Survey 600–1300." In *The Cambridge Urban History of Britain*, ed. D.M. Pallister, 27–49.

Atherton, Mark. "The Sources of Ælfric's *De temporibus anni* (Cameron C.B.1.9.4)." 1996. *Fontes*.

Bachelard, Gaston. *The Poetics of Space*. Trans. Maria Jolas, foreword by Étienne Gilson. Boston: Beacon Press, 1964.

Bately, Janet M. "Alfred as Author and Translator." In *A Companion to Alfred the Great*, ed. N.G. Discenza and P.E. Szarmach, 113–42.

– "The Compilation of the *Anglo-Saxon Chronicle* 60 BC to AD 890: Vocabulary as Evidence." *PBA* 64 (1978): 93–129. Rpt. in *British Academy Papers on Anglo-Saxon England*, ed. E.G. Stanley, 261–97. Oxford: Oxford University Press, 1990.

– "The Compilation of the *Anglo-Saxon Chronicle* Once More." *Leeds Studies in Engl.*, ns 16 (1985): 7–26. Also in a separate volume, entitled *Sources and Relations: Studies in Honour of J.E. Cross*. Ed. Marie Collins, Jocelyn Price, and Andrew Hamer. Leeds: University of Leeds School of English, 1985.

– "Did King Alfred Actually Translate Anything? The Integrity of the Alfredian Canon Revisited." *Medium Ævum* 78 (2009): 189–215.

Bately, Janet, and Anton Englert, eds. *Ohthere's Voyages: A Late 9th-Century Account of Voyages along the Coasts of Norway and Denmark and Its Cultural Context*. Maritime Culture of the North 1. Roskilde: Viking Ship Museum, 2007.

Bennett, Helen T. "The Postmodern Hall in *Beowulf*: Endings Embedded in Beginnings." *Heroic Age* 12 (May 2009): http://www.heroicage.org/issues/12/ba.php.

Blum, Pamela Z. "The Cryptic Creation Cycle in Ms. Junius xi." *Gesta* 15.1/2 (1976): 211–26.

Bourdieu, Pierre. *Language and Symbolic Power*. Ed. John B. Thomson and trans. Gino Raymond and Matthew Adamson. Cambridge, MA: Harvard University Press, 1991.

– *Outline of a Theory of Practice*. Trans. Richard Nice. Cambridge: Cambridge University Press, 1977.

– *Practical Reason: On the Theory of Action*. Stanford, CA: Stanford University Press, 1998.

– *The Rules of Art: Genesis and Structure of the Literary Field*. Trans. Susan Emanuel. Stanford: Stanford University Press, 1996.

Bridges, Margaret. "Of Myths and Maps: The Anglo-Saxon Cosmographer's Europe." In *Writing & Culture*, ed. Balz Engler, 69–84. Swiss Papers in English Language and Literature 6. Tübingen: G. Narr, 1992.

Brljak, Vladimir. "Unediting *Deor*." *NM* 112.3 (2011): 297–321.

Bosworth, Joseph. *An Anglo-Saxon Dictionary Based on the Manuscript Collections of the Late Joseph Bosworth*. Comp. Sean Christ and Ondřej Tichý. Faculty of Arts, Charles University in Prague. Ed. and enlarged by T. Northcote Toller. Oxford: Oxford University Press, 1898. http://bosworth.ff.cuni.cz/.

Brincken, Anna-Dorothee von den. "Europa in der Kartographie des Mittelalters." *Archiv für Kulturgeschichte* 55 (1973): 289–304.

British Cartographic Society. "How Long Is the UK Coastline?" http://www .cartography.org.uk/default.asp?contentID=749.

Butts, Richard. "The Analogical Mere: Landscape and Terror in *Beowulf*." *English Studies* 68 (1987): 113–21.

Catterall, Caren. *Gardening by the Moon*. Guerneville, CA: Divine Inspiration Publications, 2000–14. http://www.gardeningbytheMoon.com/.

de Certeau, Michel. *The Practice of Everyday Life*. Trans. Steven Rendall. Berkeley: University of California Press, 1984.

Clarke, Catherine A.M. *Literary Landscapes and the Idea of England, 700–1400*. Woodbridge, UK: Brewer, 2006.

Clemoes, Peter. *The Chronology of Ælfric's Works*. 1959. Repr. Old English Newsletter Subsidia 5. Binghamton, NY: CEMERS, 1980

Cohen, Jeffrey Jerome. "The Solitude of Guthlac." In his *Medieval Identity Machines*, 116–53. Medieval Cultures 35. Minneapolis: University of Minnesota Press, 2003.

Cooke, William. "Two Notes on Beowulf (with Glances at *Vafþrúðnismál*, Blickling Homily 16, and *Andreas*, Lines 839–846)." *Medium Ævum* 72 (2003): 297–301.

Cramp, Rosemary. "The Hall in *Beowulf* and in Archaeology." In *Heroic Poetry in the Anglo-Saxon Period: Studies in Honour of Jess B. Bessinger*, ed. Helen

Damico and John Leyerle, 331–46. Studies in Medieval Culture 32. Kalamazoo: Medieval Institute Publications, Western Michigan University, 1993.

Creighton, Oliver. "Town Defences and the Making of Urban Landscapes." In *Medieval Landscapes*, ed. M. Gardiner and S. Rippon, 43–56.

Cresswell, Tim. *Geographic Thought: A Critical Introduction*. Malden, MA: Wiley-Blackwell, 2013.

– *Place: A Short Introduction*. Short Introductions to Geography. Malden, MA: Blackwell Publishing, 2004.

Davis, Kathleen. "National Writing in the Ninth Century: A Reminder for Postcolonial Thinking about the Nation." *Journal of Medieval and Early Modern Studies* 28.3 (1998): 611–37.

– "The Performance of Translation Theory in King Alfred's National Literary Program." In *Manuscript, Narrative, Lexicon: Essays on Literary and Cultural Transmission in Honour of Whitney F. Bolton*, ed. Robert Boenig and Kathleen Davis, 149–70. Lewisburg, PA: Bucknell University Press, 2000.

The Dictionary of Medieval Latin from British Sources. Ed. R.E. Latham, D.R. Howlett, and R.K. Ashdowne. 17 vols. Oxford: Oxford University Press for the British Academy, 1975–2013.

The Dictionary of Old English: A to G online. Ed. Angus Cameron, Ashley Crandell Amos, and Antonette diPaolo Healey. Toronto: Dictionary of Old English Project, 2007–.

The Dictionary of Old English Corpus on the World Wide Web. Ed. Antonette diPaolo Healey with John Price Wilkin and Xin Xiang. Toronto: Dictionary of Old English Project, 2009.

Discenza, Nicole Guenther. "Alfred the Great and the Anonymous Prose Proem to the *Boethius*." *JEGP* 107 (2008): 57–76.

– "Alfred's Verse Preface to the *Pastoral Care* and the Chain of Authority." *Neophilologus* 85 (2001): 625–33. Rpt. in *Classical and Medieval Literature Criticism* 79 (2006): 79–84.

– *The King's English: Strategies of Translation in the Old English Boethius*. Albany: State University of New York Press, 2005.

– "The Old English *Bede* and the Construction of Anglo-Saxon Authority." *ASE* 31 (2002): 69–80.

– "Sources of King Alfred's Old English Version of Boethius's *De consolatione* (Cameron C.B.9.3)." 2001. *Fontes*.

– "The Unauthorized Biographies of Anicius Manlius Severinus Boethius." *The Alfredian Boethius Project*. 9 December 2003. http://www.english.ox .ac.uk/boethius/Symposium2003.html.

Discenza, Nicole Guenther, and Paul E. Szarmach, eds. *A Companion to Alfred the Great*. Brill Companions to the Christian Tradition 58. Leiden: Brill, 2015.

Draper, Simon. "The Significance of Old English *Burh* in Anglo-Saxon England." *Anglo-Saxon Studies in Archaeology and History* 15 (2008): 240–53.

Drout, Michael D.C. "Blood and Deeds: The Inheritance Systems in *Beowulf*." *Studies in Philology* 104.2 (2007): 199–226.

Eastwood, Bruce, and Gerd Graßhoff. *Planetary Diagrams for Roman Astronomy in Medieval Europe, CA. 800–1500*. Transactions of the American Philosophical Society vol. 94, pt. 3. Philadelphia: American Philosophical Society, 2004.

Edson, Evelyn. *Mapping Time and Space: How Medieval Mapmakers Viewed Their World*. British Library Studies in Map History 1. London: The British Library, 1997.

The Electronic Sawyer: Online Catalogue of Anglo-Saxon Charters. Ed. Simon Keynes et al. 2014. http://www.esawyer.org.uk/about/index.html. Based upon P.H. Sawyer, *Anglo-Saxon Charters: An Annotated List and Bibliography*. London: Royal Historical Society, 1968.

Englert, Anton, and Waldemar Ossowski. "Sailing in Wulfstan's Wake: The 2004 Trial Voyage Hedeby-Gdansk with the Skuldelev 1 reconstruction, *Ottar*." In *Wulfstan's Voyage*, ed. A. Englert and A. Trakadas, 257–70.

Englert, Anton, and Athena Trakadas, eds. *Wulfstan's Voyage: The Baltic Sea Region in the Early Viking Age as Seen from Shipboard*. Maritime Culture of the North 2. Roskilde: Viking Ship Museum, 2009.

Enright, Michael J. *Lady with a Mead Cup: Ritual, Prophecy and Lordship in the European Warband from La Tène to the Viking Age*. Portland: Four Courts Press, 1996.

Esser-Miles, Carolin. "'King of the Children of Pride:' Symbolism, Physicality, and the Old English Whale." In *The Maritime World of the Anglo-Saxons*, ed. S.S. Klein, W. Schipper, and S. Lewis-Simpson, 275–301.

Estes, Heide. "*Beowulf* and the Sea: An Ecofeminist Reading." In *The Maritime World of the Anglo-Saxons*, ed. S.S. Klein, W. Schipper, and S. Lewis-Simpson, 209–26.

Farr, Carol. *The Book of Kells: Its Function and Audiences*. London: British Library, 1997.

Fontes Anglo-Saxonici: World Wide Web Register. http://fontes.english.ox.ac.uk/; also available on CD-ROM: version 1.1. Oxford: Fontes Anglo-Saxonici Project, 2002.

Foot, Sarah. "The Making of *Angelcynn*: English Identity before the Norman Conquest." *TRHS* 6th ser. 6 (1996): 25–49.

Foxhall Forbes, Helen. *Heaven and Earth in Anglo-Saxon England: Theology and Society in an Age of Faith*. Farnham, Surrey: Ashgate, 2013.

Foys, Martin. "The Virtual Reality of the Anglo-Saxon *Mappamundi*." *Literature Compass* 1 (2004): 1–17.

– *Virtually Anglo-Saxon: Old Media, New Media, and Early Medieval Studies in the Late Age of Print*. Gainesville: University Press of Florida, 2007.

Frantzen, Allen J. "*Be mihtigum mannum*: Power, Penance, and Food in Late Anglo-Saxon England. In *The Maritime World of the Anglo-Saxons*, ed. S.S. Klein, W. Schipper, and S. Lewis-Simpson, 157–85.

Freud, Sigmund. "The Uncanny." Trans. Alix Strachey. In *Collected Papers*, ed. Joan Riviere, vol. 4: 368–407. London: Hogarth, 1950.

Gardiner, Mark. "Late Saxon Settlements." In *The Oxford Handbook of Anglo-Saxon Archaeology*, ed. H. Hamerow, D.A. Hinton, and S. Crawford, 198–217.

Gardiner, Mark, and Stephen Rippon, eds. *Medieval Landscapes*. Landscape History after Hoskins 2. Bollington, Macclesfield: Windgather Press, 2007.

Gardiner, Mark, John Stewart, and Greg Priestley-Bell. "Anglo-Saxon Whale Exploitation: Some Evidence from Dengemarsh, Lydd, Kent." *Medieval Archaeology* 42 (1998): 96–101.

Garner, Lori Ann. *Structuring Spaces: Oral Poetics and Architecture in Early Medieval England*. Notre Dame, IN: University of Notre Dame Press, 2011.

Gneuss, Helmut, and Michael Lapidge. *Anglo-Saxon Manuscripts: A Bibliographical Handlist of Manuscripts and Manuscript Fragments Written or Owned in England Up to 1100*. Toronto: University of Toronto Press, 2014.

Godden, Malcolm R. "The Anglo-Saxons and the Goths: Rewriting the Sack of Rome." *ASE* 31 (2002): 47–68.

– "Did King Alfred Write Anything?" *Medium Ævum* 76.1 (2007): 1–23.

– "The Old English *Orosius* and Its Context: Who Wrote It, for Whom, and Why?" *Quaestio Insularis* 12 (2011): 1–30.

– "The Old English *Orosius* and Its Sources," *Anglia* 129 (2011): 297–320.

– "The Sources of King Alfred's Old English Version of Augustine's *Soliloquies* (Cameron C.B.9.4)." 2001. *Fontes*.

– "Wærferth and King Alfred: The Fate of the Old English *Dialogues*." In *Alfred the Wise: Studies in Honour of Janet Bately on the Occasion of Her Sixty-fifth Birthday*, ed. Jane Roberts and Janet L. Nelson with Malcolm Godden, 35–51. Cambridge: Brewer, 1997.

Goldsmith, Margaret. "*The Seafarer* and the Birds." *Review of English Studies*, ns 5, no. 19 (July 1954): 225–35.

Gorst, E.K.C. "Latin Sources of the Old English *Phoenix*." *N&Q*, ns 53 (2006): 136–42.

Gregory, Derek. "Imaginative Geography." In *The Dictionary of Human Geography*, ed. D. Gregory et al., 369–71.

– "Space." In *The Dictionary of Human Geography*. Ed. Gregory et al., 707–10.

Gregory, Derek, Ron Johnston, and Geraldine Pratt, eds. *The Dictionary of Human Geography*. 5th ed. Malden, MA, and Oxford: Blackwell, 2009.

Gretsch, Mechthild. *The Intellectual Foundations of the English Benedictine Reform*. CSASE 25. Cambridge: Cambridge University Press, 1999.

Guillory, John. *Cultural Capital: The Problem of Literary Canon Formation*. Chicago: University of Chicago Press, 1993.

Hall, J.R. "Two Dark Old English Compounds: *ælmyrcan* (*Andreas* 432a) and *guðmyrce* (*Exodus* 59a)." *Journal of English Linguistics* 20 (1987): 38–47.

Hall, R.A. "*Burhs* and Boroughs: Defended Places, Trade, and Towns. Plans, Defences, and Civic Features." In *The Oxford Handbook of Anglo-Saxon Archaeology*, ed. H. Hamerow, D.A. Hinton, and S. Crawford, 600–21.

Hamerow, Helena. "Anglo-Saxon Timber Buildings and Their Social Context." In *The Oxford Handbook of Anglo-Saxon Archaeology*, ed. H. Hamerow, D.A. Hinton, and S. Crawford, 128–55.

Hamerow, Helena, David A. Hinton, and Sally Crawford, eds. *The Oxford Handbook of Anglo-Saxon Archaeology*. Oxford: Oxford University Press, 2011.

Haran, Brady. "The Farm Furthest from the Sea." *BBC News Online*, 23 July 2003. http://news.bbc.co.uk/2/hi/uk_news/england/derbyshire/3090539.stm.

Harbus, Antonina. "The Maritime Imagination and the Paradoxical Mind in Old English Poetry." *ASE* 39 (2010): 21–42.

Harley, J.B., and David Woodward, eds. *The History of Cartography*, vol. 1: *Cartography in Prehistoric, Ancient, and Medieval Europe and the Mediterranean*. Chicago: University of Chicago Press, 1987. http://www.press.uchicago.edu/books/HOC/HOC_V1/Volume1.html.

Harris, Stephen. *Race and Ethnicity in Anglo-Saxon Literature*. Studies in Medieval History and Culture. New York: Routledge, 2003.

Hart, J. "The Sources of The Old English Bede, History of the English Church and People (Cameron C.B.9.6)." *Fontes*.

Harvey, P.D.A. *Medieval Maps*. Toronto: University of Toronto Press, 1991.

Heffernan, Thomas J. "'The sun shall be turned to darkness and the moon to blood': How Sin and Redemption Affect Heavenly Space in an Old English Transfiguration Homily." In *Place, Space, and Landscape in Medieval Narrative*, ed. Laura L. Howes, 63–78. Tennessee Studies in Literature 43. Knoxville: University of Tennessee Press, 2007.

Henderson, George. "Place." In *The Dictionary of Human Geography*, ed. D. Gregory et al., 539–41.

Henig, Martin. "The Fate of Late Roman Towns." In *The Oxford Handbook of Anglo-Saxon Archaeology*, ed. H. Hamerow, D.A. Hinton, and S. Crawford, 515–33.

Higham, N.J. "Changing Spaces: Towns and Their Hinterlands in the North West, AD 900–1500." In *Medieval Landscapes*, ed. M. Gardiner and S. Rippon, 57–70.

Hill, John M. "Episodes Such as the Offa of Angeln Passage and the Aesthetics of *Beowulf*." *Philological Review* 34.2 (2008): 29–49.

Hill, Joyce. *Bede and the Benedictine Reform*. Jarrow Lecture 1998. Jarrow: 1999.

– "*Widsið* and the Tenth Century." *NM* 85 (1984): 305–15.

Hines, John. "Foreword." To J.D. Niles, T. Christensen, and M. Osborn, *Beowulf and Lejre*, vii–xi.

Hooke, Della. *The Landscape of Anglo-Saxon England*. London: Leicester University Press, 1998.

Howe, John. "Creating Symbolic Landscapes: Medieval Development of Sacred Space." In *Inventing Medieval Landscapes*, ed. J. Howe and M. Wolfe, 208–23.

Howe, John, and Michael Wolfe. "Introduction." In their *Inventing Medieval Landscapes: Senses of Place in Western Europe*, 1–10.

Howe, John, and Michael Wolfe, eds. *Inventing Medieval Landscapes: Senses of Place in Western Europe*. Gainesville: University Press of Florida, 2002.

Howe, Nicholas. "The Landscape of Anglo-Saxon England: Inherited, Invented, Imagined." In *Inventing Medieval Landscapes*, ed. J. Howe and M. Wolfe, 91–119.

– *Migration and Mythmaking in Anglo-Saxon England*. New Haven and London: Yale University Press, 1989.

– "Rome: Capital of Anglo-Saxon England." *Journal of Medieval and Early Modern Studies* 34 (2004): 147–72.

– *Writing the Map of Anglo-Saxon England: Essays in Cultural Geography*. New Haven: Yale University Press, 2008.

Hurley, Mary Kate. "Alfredian Temporalities: Time and Translation in the Old English *Orosius*." *JEGP* 112.4 (2013): 405–32.

Insa Sales, Salvador. "The Treatment of Some Spanish Matters in the Old English *Orosius*." *SELIM* 9 (1999): 173–9.

Irvine, Susan. "The Anglo-Saxon Chronicle." In *A Companion to Alfred the Great*, ed. N.G. Discenza and P. Szarmach, 344–67.

– "The Sources of The Anglo-Saxon Chronicle MS E (Cameron C.B.17.9)." *Fontes*.

Jacobsson, Mattias. *Wells, Meres, and Pools: Hydronymic Terms in the Anglo-Saxon Landscape*. Acta Universitatis Upsaliensis, Studia Anglistica Upsaliensia 98. Uppsala: Reklam & Katalogtryck AB, 1997.

Jayatilaka, Rohini. "The Sources of Orosius, *History against the Pagans* (Cameron C.B.9.2)." *Fontes*.

Johnson, David F. "Alfredian Apocrypha." In *A Companion to Alfred the Great*, ed. N.G. Discenza and P. Szarmach, 368–95.

– "Divine Justice in Gregory the Great's *Dialogues*." In *Early Medieval Studies in Memory of Patrick Wormald*, ed. Stephen David Baxter et al., 115–28. Studies in Early Medieval Britain. Farnham, Eng.: Ashgate, 2009.

Johnston, Ron. "Town." In *The Dictionary of Human Geography*, ed. D. Gregory et al., 764.

Jolly, Karen Louise. "Prayers from the Field: Practical Protection and Demonic Defense in Anglo-Saxon England." *Traditio* 61 (2006): 95–147.

Jones, Christopher A. "Envisioning the *cenobium* in *Guthlac A*." *Medieval Studies* 57 (1995): 259–91.

Kabir, Ananya Jahanara. *Paradise, Death and Doomsday in Anglo-Saxon Literature*. CSASE 32. Cambridge: Cambridge University Press, 2001.

Karkov, Catherine E. *Text and Picture in Anglo-Saxon England: Narrative Strategies in the Junius 11 Manuscript*. CSASE 31. Cambridge: Cambridge University Press, 2001.

Kavros, Harry E. "*Swefan æfter symble*: The Feast-Sleep Theme in *Beowulf*." *Neophilologus* 65 (1981): 120–8.

Keil, Roger. "City." In *The Dictionary of Human Geography*, ed. D. Gregory et al., 85–6.

Kendall, Calvin B. "Bede and Islam." In *Bede and the Future*, ed. Peter Darby and Faith Wallis, 93–114. Studies in Medieval Britain and Ireland. Farnham, Surrey: Ashgate, 2014.

Ker, N.R. *Catalogue of Manuscripts Containing Anglo-Saxon*. Oxford: Clarendon Press, rpt. with supplement, 1990.

Klein, Stacy S., William Schipper, and Shannon Lewis-Simpson. *The Maritime World of the Anglo-Saxons*. Medieval and Renaissance Texts and Studies 448. Essays in Anglo-Saxon Studies 5. Tempe: Arizona Center for Medieval and Renaissance Studies, 2014.

Kline, Naomi Reed. *Maps of Medieval Thought: The Hereford Paradigm*. Woodbridge, UK: Boydell, 2001.

Lakoff, George, and Mark Johnson. *Metaphors We Live By*. Chicago: University of Chicago Press, 1980.

Langeslag, Paul. "Monstrous Landscape in *Beowulf*." *English Studies* 96.2 (2015): 119–38.

Lapidge, Michael. *The Anglo-Saxon Library*. Oxford: Oxford University Press, 2006.

Lavezzo, Kathy. *Angels on the Edge of the World: Geography, Literature, and English Community, 1000–1534*. Ithaca, NY: Cornell University Press, 2006.

Lee, Ann Thompson. "*The Ruin*: Bath or Babylon? A Non-Archaeological Investigation." *NM* 74 (1973): 443–55.

Le Goff, Jacques. "The Marvelous in the Medieval West." In *The Medieval Imagination*, trans. Arthur Goldhammer, 27–44. Chicago: University of Chicago Press, 1988.

Lewis, Charlton T., and Charles Short, *A Latin Dictionary*. Oxford: Clarendon Press, 1879. http://www.perseus.tufts.edu/hopper/resolveform?redirect=true& lang=Latin.

Lockett, Leslie. *Anglo-Saxon Psychologies in the Vernacular and Latin Traditions*. Toronto: University of Toronto Press, 2011.

Love, Rosalind. "Latin Commentaries on Boethius's *Consolation of Philosophy*." In *A Companion to Alfred the Great*, ed. N.G. Discenza and P. Szarmach, 82–110.

Lozovsky, Natalia. *"The Earth Is Our Book": Geographical Knowledge in the Latin West ca. 400–1000*. Ann Arbor: University of Michigan Press, 2000.

Mandelbrot, Benoit. "How Long Is the Coast of Britain? Statistical Self-Similarity and Fractional Dimension." *Science* 156.3775 (5 May 1967): 636–8. DOI: 10.1126/science.156.3775.636.

Marshall, Linda. "Grendelsmere as *Vagina Dentata*: Grendel's Mother and the Fear of Women's Power." In *The Image of the Outsider II in Literature, Media, and Society: Proceedings of the 2008 Conference, Society for the Interdisciplinary Study of Social Imagery*, ed. Will Wright and Stephen Kaplan, 90–2. Pueblo: Society for the Interdisciplinary Study of Social Imagery, Colorado State University, 2008.

Mason, David. *Chester AD 400–1066: From Roman Fortress to English Town*. Stroud, Gloucestershire: Tempus, 2007.

Michelet, Fabienne. *Creation, Migration, and Conquest: Imaginary Geography and Sense of Space in Old English Literature*. Oxford: Oxford University Press, 2006.

Mitchell, Bruce, and Fred C. Robinson. *A Guide to Old English*. 8th ed. Malden, MA: Wiley Blackwell, 2012.

Mittman, Asa Simon. *Maps and Monsters in Medieval England*. New York: Routledge, 2006.

Molinari, Alessandra. "Alcuni calchi dell'epos biblico anglosassone Genesis A." In *Il plurilinguismo in area germanica nel Medioevo. Atti del XXX convegno dell'Associazione Italiana di Filologia germanica, Bari, 4–6 giugno 2003*, ed. Lucia Sinisi, 129–90. Palomar athenaeum 49. Bari: Palomar, 2005.

Molyneaux, George. "The *Old English Bede*: English Ideology or Christian Instruction?" *English Historical Review* 124 (2009): 1289–1323.

Momma, Haruko. "Ælfric's Fisherman and the *Hronrad*: A Colloquy on the Occupation." In *The Maritime World of the Anglo-Saxons*, ed. S.S. Klein, W. Schipper, and S. Lewis-Simpson, 303–21.

Naismith, Rory. "Islamic Coins from Early Medieval England." *Numismatic Chronicle* 165 (2005): 193–222.

Naylor, John. *An Archaeology of Trade in Middle Saxon England*. BAR British Series 376. Oxford: Archaeopress, 2004.

Neville, Jennifer. *Representations of the Natural World in Old English Poetry*. Cambridge: Cambridge University Press, 1999.

Niles, John D., Tom Christensen, and Marijane Osborn. *Beowulf and Lejre*. Tempe: ACMRS, Arizona Center for Medieval and Renaissance Studies, 2007.

Norris, Robin. "The Augustinian Theory of Use and Enjoyment in *Guthlac A* and *B*." *NM* 104 (2003): 159–78.

Núñez, Rafael E. "Conceptual Metaphor and the Embodied Mind: What Makes Mathematics Possible?" In *Metaphor and Analogy in the Sciences*, ed. Fernand Hallyn, 125–45. Origins: Studies in the Sources of Scientific Creativity 1. London: Kluwer Academic, 2000.

Ó Carragáin, Éamonn. *The City of Rome and the World of Bede*. Jarrow Lecture 1994. Jarrow: St Paul's Church, 1994.

Ohlgren, Thomas H. *Anglo-Saxon Textual Illustration: Photographs of Sixteen Manuscripts with Descriptions and Index*. Kalamazoo: Medieval Institute Publications, Western Michigan University, 1992.

Orchard, Andy. *A Critical Companion to Beowulf*. Rochester, NY: Brewer, 2003.

– *Pride and Prodigies: Studies in the Monsters of the Beowulf-Manuscript*. Cambridge: Brewer, 1995.

Overing, Gillian. *Language, Sign, and Gender in Beowulf*. Carbondale: Southern Illinois University Press, 1990.

The Oxford English Dictionary. Oxford: Oxford University Press, 2015. www.oed.com.

Pallister, D.M. "Introduction." In *The Cambridge Urban History of Britain*, ed. D.M. Pallister, 3–15.

– "The Origins of British Towns." In *The Cambridge Urban History of Britain*, vol. 1, ed. D.M. Pallister, 17–24.

Pallister, D.M., ed. *The Cambridge Urban History of Britain*, vol. 1, *600–1540*. Cambridge: Cambridge University Press, 2000.

Pelteret, David A.E. "Eleventh-Century Anglo-Saxon Long-Haul Travelers: Jerusalem, Constantinople, and Beyond." In *The Maritime World of the Anglo-Saxons*, ed. S.S. Klein, W. Schipper, and S. Lewis-Simpson, 75–129.

Pred, Allan. "Place as Historically Contingent Process: Structuration and the Time-Geography of Becoming Places." *Annals of the Association of American Geographers* 74 (1984): 279–97.

Rackham, Oliver. "The Medieval Countryside of England: Botany and Archaeology." In *Inventing Medieval Landscapes*, ed. J. Howe and M. Wolfe, 13–32.

Rauer, Christine. "The Sources of *Liber monstrorum* (Cameron L.N.100)." *Fontes*, 2003.

Raw, Barbara. "The Probable Derivation of Most of the Illustrations in Junius 11 from an Illustrated Old Saxon Genesis." *ASE* 5 (1976): 133–48.

Reynolds, Andrew. "Boundaries and Settlements in Later Sixth to Eleventh-Century England." *Anglo-Saxon Studies in Archaeology and History* 12 (2003): 98–136.

Reynolds, Susan. *Kingdoms and Communities in Western Europe.* 2nd ed. Oxford: Clarendon Press, 1997.

Roberts, Brian K. "The Village: Contexts, Chronology and Causes." In *Medieval Landscapes*, ed. M. Gardiner and S. Rippon, 73–88.

Robinson, Fred C. "Notes and Emendations to Old English Poetic Texts." *NM* 67 (1966): 356–64.

Rowley, Sharon M. *The Old English Version of Bede's "Historia ecclesiastica."* Anglo-Saxon Studies 16. Woodbridge, UK, and Rochester, NY: Boydell and Brewer, 2011.

Roy, Gopa. "The Anglo-Saxons and the Shape of the World." In *Essays on Anglo-Saxon and Related Themes in Memory of Lynne Grundy*, ed. Jane Roberts and Janet Nelson, 455–81. London: King's College London, Centre for Late Antique and Medieval Studies, 2000.

Russell, Jeffrey Burton. *Inventing the Flat Earth: Columbus and Modern Historians.* Foreword by David Noble. New York: Praeger, 1991.

Scarfe Beckett, Katherine. *Anglo-Saxon Perceptions of the Islamic World.* CSASE 33. Cambridge: Cambridge University Press, 2003.

Scheil, Andrew. "Space and Place." In *A Handbook of Anglo-Saxon Studies*, ed. Jacqueline Stodnick and Renée R. Trilling, 197–213. Malden, MA: Blackwell, 2012.

Sharma, Manish. "Heroic Subject and Cultural Substance in *The Wanderer*." *Neophilologus* 96.4 (2012): 611–29.

Shook, Laurence K. "The Burial Mound in *Guthlac A*." *Modern Philology* 58.1 (1960): 1–10.

Siewers, Alfred K. "Landscapes of Conversion: Guthlac's Mound and Grendel's Mere as Expressions of Anglo-Saxon Nation-Building." *Viator* 34 (2003): 1–39.

Simek, Rudolf. "Wulfstan's Account in the Context of Early Medieval Travel Literature." *Wulfstan's Voyage*, ed. A. Englert and A. Trakadas, 37–42.

Slater, Terry R. "The Landscape of Medieval Towns: Anglo-European Comparisons." In *Medieval Landscapes*. Ed. M. Gardiner and S. Rippon, 11–26.

Smyth, Marina. *Understanding the Universe in Seventh-Century Ireland.* Studies in Celtic History 15. Woodbridge, UK: Boydell, 1996.

Stephenson, Rebecca. *The Politics of Language: Byrhtferth, Ælfric, and the Multilingual Identity of the Benedictine Reform.* Toronto Anglo-Saxon Series. Toronto: University of Toronto Press, 2015.

Stodnick, Jacqueline. "Writing Home: Place and Narrative in Anglo-Saxon England." PhD dissertation, University of Notre Dame, 2002.

Szarmach, Paul E. "Augustine's *Soliloquia* in Old English." In *A Companion to Alfred the Great*, ed. N.G. Discenza and P. Szarmach, 227–55.

– "*Meter 20*: Context Bereft." *American Notes and Queries* 15.2 (2002): 28–34.

– "The *Timaeus* in Old English." In *Lexis and Texts in Early English: Studies Presented to Jane Roberts*, ed. Christian J. Kay and Louise M. Sylvester, 255–67. Amsterdam and Atlanta, GA: Rodopi, 2001.

The Thesaurus of Old English Online. Ed. Flora Edmonds, Christian Kay, Jane Roberts, and Irené Wotherspoon. University of Glasgow, 2005. http://oldenglishthesaurus.arts.gla.ac.uk/. Online version of Jane Roberts and Christian Kay with Lynne Grundy, eds, *The Thesaurus of Old English*. Amsterdam and Atlanta, GA: Rodopi, 2000.

Toller, T. Northcote. *An Anglo-Saxon Dictionary Based on the Manuscript Collections of the Late Joseph Bosworth: Supplement.* Oxford: Oxford University Press, 1921. http://bosworth.ff.cuni.cz/.

Trilling, Renée Rebecca. *The Aesthetics of Nostalgia: Historical Representation in Old English Verse.* Toronto: University of Toronto Press, 2009.

– "Beyond Abjection: The Problem with Grendel's Mother Again." *Parergon* 24.1 (2007): 1–20.

– "Ruins in the Realm of Thoughts: Reading as Constellation in Anglo-Saxon Poetry." *JEGP* 108 (2009): 141–67.

Tuan, Yi-Fu. *Cosmos and Hearth: A Cosmopolite's Viewpoint.* Minneapolis: University of Minnesota Press, 1996.

– *Space and Place: The Perspective of Experience.* Minneapolis: University of Minnesota Press, 1977.

Ulmschneider, Katharina. "Settlement Hierarchy." In *The Oxford Handbook of Anglo-Saxon Archaeology*, ed. H. Hamerow, D.A. Hinton, and S. Crawford, 156–71.

Urbańczyk, Przemysław. "On the Reliability of Wulfstan's Report." In *Wulfstan's Voyage*, ed. S. Englert and S. Trakadas, 43–7.

Valtonen, Irmeli. *The North in the Old English Orosius: A Geographical Narrative in Context.* Mémoires de la Société Néophilologique de Helsinki 73. Helsinki: Société Néophilologique, 2008.

Wallis, Faith. *The Calendar and the Cloister: Oxford, St John's College MS17.* 2007. McGill University Library. Digital Collections Program. http://digital.library.mcgill.ca/ms-17.

Wentersdorf, Karl P. "Observations on *The Ruin*." *Medium Aevum* 46.2 (1977): 171–80.

Westrem, Scott. *The Hereford Map: A Transcription and Translation of the Legends with Commentary*. Terrarum Orbis 1. Turnhout: Brepols, 2001.

Wickham-Crowley, Kelley M. "Living on the *Ecg*: The Mutable Boundaries of Land and Water in Anglo-Saxon Contexts." In *A Place to Believe in: Locating Medieval Landscapes*, ed. Clare A. Lees and Gillian R. Overing, 85–100. University Park: Pennsylvania State University Press, 2006.

Wilcox, Miranda. "Alfred's Epistemological Metaphors: *egan modes* and *scip modes*." *ASE* 35 (2006): 179–217.

Woodward, David. "Medieval *Mappaemundi*." In *The History of Cartography*, vol. 1, ed. J.B. Harley and D. Woodward, 286–370.

Wright, Charles. "'Insulae gentium': Biblical Influence on Old English Poetic Vocabulary." In *Magister Regis: Studies in Honour of Robert Earl Kaske*, ed. Arthur Groos et al., 9–21. New York: Fordham University Press, 1986.

Yerkes, David. *Two Versions of Wærferth's Translation of Gregory's Dialogues: An Old English Thesaurus*. Toronto: University of Toronto Press, 1979.

Index

Toronto Anglo-Saxon Series

General Editor:
ANDY ORCHARD

Editorial Board
ROBERTA FRANK
THOMAS N. HALL
ANTONETTE DIPAOLO HEALEY
MICHAEL LAPIDGE
KATHERINE O'BRIEN O'KEEFFE

1 *Preaching the Converted: The Style and Rhetoric of the Vercelli Book Homilies*, Samantha Zacher
2 *Say What I Am Called: The Old English Riddles of the Exeter Book and the Anglo-Latin Riddle Tradition*, Dieter Bitterli
3 *The Aesthetics of Nostalgia: Historical Representation in Anglo-Saxon Verse*, Renée Trilling
4 *New Readings in the Vercelli Book*, edited by Samantha Zacher and Andy Orchard
5 *Authors, Audiences, and Old English Verse*, Thomas A. Bredehoft
6 *On Aesthetics in* Beowulf *and Other Old English Poems*, edited by John M. Hill
7 *Old English Metre: An Introduction*, Jun Terasawa
8 *Anglo-Saxon Psychologies in the Vernacular and Latin Traditions*, Leslie Lockett
9 *The Body Legal in Barbarian Law*, Lisi Oliver
10 *Old English Literature and the Old Testament*, edited by Michael Fox and Manish Sharma
11 *Stealing Obedience: Narratives of Agency and Identity in Later Anglo-Saxon England*, Katherine O'Brien O'Keeffe
12 *Traditional Subjectivities: The Old English Poetics of Mentality*, Britt Mize
13 *Land and Book: Literature and Land Tenure in Anglo-Saxon England*, Scott T. Smith
14 *Writing Women Saints in Anglo-Saxon England*, edited by Paul E. Szarmach
15 *Anglo-Saxon Manuscripts: A Bibliographical Handlist of Manuscripts and Manuscript Fragments Written or Owned in England up to 1100*, Helmut Gneuss and Michael Lapidge